CLINICAL TRIALS IN INFANT NUTRITION
METHODOLOGY, STATISTICS, AND ETHICAL ISSUES

The 40th Nestlé Nutrition Workshop, Clinical Trials in Infant Nutrition, was held in Washington, DC, USA, September 9–12, 1996.

Workshop participants (*left to right, from front to back*): Karl Zwiauer, Kai Voepel, George D. Ferry, Ferdinand Haschke, Jean Rey, Philippe Steenhout, Mauro Fisberg, Frank Pohlandt, Cecil T. Vella, Michael Radke, Daniel Brasseur, Frank Iber, Ralph E. Kauffman, Peter Aggett, Betsy Lozoff, Jay Perman, Alan Lucas, Jesse Berlin, Stephen Walter, Henry S. Sacks, Alex Roche, Roger Whitehead, Ricardo Uauy-Dagach, Jean-Pierre Cezard, Robert Hamburger, Cindy Brown, Linda Hsieh, Hildegard Przyrembel, Cesar Velasco Rodas, Madeleine Sumpaico, Jose Saavedra, Ali Debbabi, Umaporn Suthutvoravut, Ana Culcer, Christine Secretin, Larissa Chtchepliaguina, Robyn Wimberly, Jean-Marc Aeschlimann, John Kerner, Roger Clemens, Chouraqui, Pierre Guesry, Marie-Christine Secretin, Larissa Chtchepliaguina, Robyn Wimberly, Jean-Marc Aeschlimann, John Kerner, Roger Clemens, Wei Ping Wang, Lajos Hanzel, Véronique Millet, Bianca-Maria Exl, Eileen Madden, Abdesselam N'Bou, Tzee-Chung Wu, Christina Zehaluk, Ernie Strapazon, Marie-José Mozin, Elena Trofimenko, Dominique Turck, Frank Falkner, Nick Melachouris, Staffan Polberger, William Klish, Bernard Salle, Maciej Kaczmarski, Elisabeth Becher, Ronald Kleinman, Michael Lentze, L.D. Van Egroo, Gayle Crozier, Walter Glinsmann, Marcel Baumgartner

Nestlé Nutrition Workshop Series
Volume 40

CLINICAL TRIALS IN INFANT NUTRITION

METHODOLOGY, STATISTICS, AND ETHICAL ISSUES

Editors

Jay A. Perman
Virginia Commonwealth University
Medical College of Virginia
Department of Pediatrics
Richmond, Virginia, USA

Jean Rey
Hôpital des Enfants Malades
Département de Pédiatrie
Paris, France

NESTLÉ NUTRITION SERVICES

Nestlé

LIPPINCOTT-RAVEN ■ PHILADELPHIA

Acquisition Editor: Beth Barry
Developmental Editor: Ellen DiFrancesco
Manufacturing Manager: Dennis Teston
Production Manager: Lawrence Bernstein
Production Editorr: Lawrence Bernstein
Indexer: Dorothy Jahoda
Compositor: Maryland Composition
Printer: Quebecor-Kingsport

Nestec Ltd., 55 Avenue Nestlé,
CH-1800 Vevey, Switzerland
Lippincott-Raven Publishers,
227 East Washington Square,
Philadelphia, Pennsylvania 19106

Printed in the United States of America

Library of Congress Cataloging-in-Publication Data

Clinical trials in infant nutrition : methodology, statistics, and
    ethical issues / editors, Jay A. Perman, Jean Rey ; Nestlé
Nutrition Services.
        p.   cm.—(Nestlé Nutrition workshop series ; v. 40)
    Proceedings of the 40th Nestlé Nutrition Workshop, held in
Washington, D.C., USA, Sept. 9–12, 1996.
    Includes bibliographical references and index.
    ISBN 0-7817-1564-4
    1. Infants—Nutrition—Congresses.   2. Clinical trials—
Methodology—Congresses.   I. Perman, Jay A.   II. Rey, Jean.
III. Nestlé Nutrition Services.   IV. Nestlé Nutrition Workshop (40th
: 1996 : Washington, D.C.)   V. Series.
    [DNLM: 1. Infant Nutrition—congresses.   2. Clinical trials—
congresses.
W1 NE228 v.40 1997 / WS 120 C641 1997]
RJ216.C64   1997
174'.28—dc21
DNLM/DLC
for Library of Congress

Preface

The theme of this Workshop is different from that of the previous Nestlé Nutrition Workshops. It does not assess state-of-the-art knowledge in a particular area of nutrition, as in earlier workshops, beginning with maternal nutrition during pregnancy in 1981. Nor does this Workshop deal with a major problem of nutritional pathology in the infant, as was the case, for example, when diabetes or diarrhea were recently Workshop topics.

The original subject of this 40th Nestlé Nutrition Workshop is its examination of the methodological, statistical, and ethical problems of conducting clinical trials in pediatric nutrition. The topics covered included: the legislative framework of the industrialized countries in which trials are conducted; moral obligations in developing countries, in particular where ethics committees have not yet been established; the regulations that the industry must observe in formulating product claims so as not to mislead the consumer and not to discourage breastfeeding; and, finally, the need to adhere to the fundamental ethical principle that is the primacy of protecting the best interest of individual infants and of children at large.

Randomized trials, meta-analyses, multicenter studies—all of these strategies have their advantages and disadvantages, which have been emphasized and discussed at length during this Workshop. It will surprise no one that participants easily accepted randomized controlled trials as the ideal method for the evaluation of nutritional factors that might influence the growth and development of low-birth-weight, full-term, healthy or ill infants.

Incomplete studies and incomplete subjects within the sample are related problems that deserve consideration. The selection of outcome variables is a crucial factor, since it determines the length and complexity of a study. As such, the choice of variables plays a decisive role in the percentage of studies abandoned in mid-course. The longer the study, the more essential is the cooperation of all those involved, in particular, that of the parents or caregivers. Despite their power, crossover studies may also be difficult to complete. They have the disadvantage of obliging participants to submit to two treatments instead of just one. This reduces compliance and increases attrition in the sample. However, there is nothing to prevent those who are less compliant from constituting a subset within a population—quite the contrary. Ignoring those who leave the study, especially those studies designed to evaluate the effects of nutrition on psychomotor development and intellectual performance, would thus be a major potential bias. On the other hand, analyzing the drop-out as a result reflects, to some extent, the acceptability of a treatment and is one way of evaluating its clinical usefulness.

Multicenter clinical trials offer, for their part, a certain number of advantages, in particular that of obtaining broader patient representation and enhancing the validity of results. However, such studies are generally very time-consuming and demand considerable effort in order to maintain the interest of participating investigators until their conclusion. Problems likely to arise during the study must therefore be anticipated, which presupposes the involvement of all investigators in the protocol planning. However, just as it seems to be essential to involve all investigators in the intellectual process, it is necessary to use specially prepared staff at each site to gather results and perform all practical tasks. When this is not the case, the undertaking is often doomed to failure. One further challenge in multicenter clinical trials is that the standardized protocols may limit the imagination and research questions of individual investigators.

Meta-analyses also pose challenges and these were emphasized during this Workshop. The objective of this statistical approach is to synthesize the results of numerous randomized controlled trials to highlight benefits or drawbacks that trials carried out on smaller numbers of individuals are unable to detect. The basic problem is obviously that of selecting studies that can reasonably be grouped together, since the decision as to whether or not to include a study in the meta-analysis should take only its methodology, and not its results, into account. The major criticism levied against meta-analyses is the difficulty of analyzing all of the studies, including those that have not been published, since negative results have a smaller chance of being published than positive results. Unpublished results could, indeed, contradict those that have been published. This highlights the importance, in the interests of validity, of using tests making it possible to calculate the number of unpublished studies liable to refute evidence drawn from published studies. It is also important, as has been said, to take into consideration in the analysis the fact that some studies conducted among small numbers of individuals evince huge differences—if not for this, they would be insignificant—while others, conducted among large numbers of individuals, show only minimal, if significant, differences.

Various scientific journals have recommended that, whenever justified, appropriate indicators of uncertainties, such as the confidence interval (CI), be used. Despite this, an analysis of publications shows that CIs are used only in exceptional cases, demonstrating that the Vancouver recommendations have little impact on nutritional research at the present time. This observation, which came to the fore during the Workshop, confirmed our belief that it was necessary to clarify the significance of the various tests and to try to demystify the concept of a ''significant'' value. Statistical significance is often expressed as important, in contrast to an ''insignificant'' result, which is generally considered to be unimportant. A high percentage of ''negative'' results is said to be only due to inadequate sample size. However, studies conducted among large numbers of individuals often produce results that are declared to be statistically significant, although differences are so slight that they are meaningless in practical terms.

There are countless biases that we must all be aware of and, if possible, avoid. If we look at data in written publications alone, we can readily see that there is an inverse correlation between sample size and the magnitude of the effects observed;

this is easily explained by the fact that studies conducted among small numbers of individuals must evince huge differences to be significant. Of more interest to Workshop participants, however, and also more serious, is that the decision to submit an article for publication and that of the journal to accept or reject it are linked to the research results; significant results are favored at each stage. Authors apparently play an even more important role than publishers in this form of bias. These publication biases are liable to distort the interpretation of meta-analyses and, more generally, may misconstrue strategies for preventing and treating illness. Thus, profound reflection is necessary in order to try to remedy this source of bias. The idea of a register in which all clinical trials in progress would be recorded prospectively, whether or not they were subsequently published, is one way of achieving this. The prospective registration of studies would enable everyone to know that the study has been conducted, or should have been conducted, and this is the only means of avoiding any selection bias in the register itself.

All of these considerations are not peculiar to the field of clinical trials in pediatric nutrition, but should be borne in mind by those with an interest in it. This is all the more important given that the regulations imposed upon scientists are ever more strict and it will be increasingly necessary to demonstrate the "efficacy" (benefit) and "safety" (risk) of advances in pediatric nutrition. Safety has, to date, commanded less attention than efficacy. As a matter of fact, many participants emphasized that larger numbers of subjects were necessary to verify safety than to test efficacy, as trials conducted on very large samples are necessary to evince an incidence difference for a relatively rare event. This is illustrated perfectly in the discussion concerning the long-term consequences of infant nutrition on neurodevelopment. Indeed, only intervention studies, planned to allow long-term monitoring and having sufficient numbers to evince any undesirable effects, bring satisfactory results. Intervention studies that evaluate long-term effects and the absence of harmful effects must, therefore, be the foundation of public health policy.

It is also helpful to recall that each study raises new questions that modify the way subsequent studies are conceived. This point was illustrated remarkably well by the analysis of environmental factors on mental and motor development in infants. The situation is always more complex than one thinks at first; the approach of most researchers is, more often than not, naïve and simplistic in this respect. Environmental factors can be very different in developing countries than they are in industrialized countries, and the association between a nutritional disorder and poorer development is not necessarily causal. Both outcomes could be the separate results of underdevelopment, poverty, low-level parental education, and unfavorable environment. It is therefore the environment in which the infant lives that must be considered, with attempts to identify those factors that put the infant at risk and those that are most likely to be altered by intervention.

All of this cannot be carried out arbitrarily, without observing a whole series of fundamental principles. These were first stipulated in 1964 in the Declaration of Helsinki and reinforced subsequently on numerous occasions. Today these principles are accepted almost universally. The basic principles that should guide us do not differ between Europe and North America, even if they have force of law in some countries and exist only as recommendations or guidelines in others; this is the result of cultural differences that go far beyond the field of ethics, but which leave its foundations unshaken. In our opinion, it is interesting to recall these principles and to analyze the way in which they influence our practice, especially in developing countries. In fact, the same rules apply throughout the world and every action should be taken to seek the opinion of a properly constituted local ethics committee. It is important that investigators working in developing countries are aware of particular sensitivities in these countries, and are convinced that every infant taking part in the study, including in the control group, will benefit at some level from participation. No long-term collaboration is possible if relationships of trust are not built, not only with those taking part in the study, but with former subjects, so as to obtain their consent ''with hindsight.''

Establishing a relationship of trust, including between industry and Nutrition Committees, is at the heart of this discussion on clinical trials in infant nutrition. Industry must understand the reasoning of pediatricians and nutritionists, but it must also assert its point of view when it does not go against basic principles. One of the difficulties in this respect is knowing just how far industry can go in the messages it conveys. It was therefore worthwhile recalling existing legislation relating to functional and health claims in the United States, Canada and Europe, as well as the principles of the Codex Alimentarius, which apply worldwide. The idea that claims should be authorized, provided that they are not false or misleading, must be the main idea behind all legislation. But, just as the burden of proof should be incumbent on industry and not on government, so industry must be allowed sufficient freedom. To the extent that the benefits claimed are scientifically proven, it would indeed be detrimental to the entire community, and in particular to infant health, if industry were unable to make justifiable claims. The purpose of regulations is not to hinder progress, but to protect consumers and to be of benefit to the population.

The goal of this Workshop is to give future investigators a better understanding of the methods that are the most appropriate to clinical trials in pediatric nutrition. We hope that this monograph will serve the pediatric community, which is so keenly interested in infant nutrition, as well as established and aspiring clinical investigators, biostatisticians, members of ethics committees, and regulatory bodies.

JAY A. PERMAN, M.D.   JEAN REY, M.D.

Foreword

The topic of the 40th Nestlé Nutrition Workshop focused on methodological aspects of clinical research. It deviated from the previous 39 workshops that covered selected topics in the field of clinical pediatrics, pediatric nutrition, and nutrition education. Clinical trials need to be done before medical food, formulas for special target groups, and infant formulas and cereals are newly introduced or substantially revised.

International and national bodies such as the American Academy of Pediatrics or the Committee of the Ministers of the Council of Europe have published principles on the ethics of medical research, which include guidelines for clinical trials. Food companies that produce dietetic products for infants are now challenged to follow these guidelines.

Besides ethical aspects, other aspects of good clinical practice during research need to be observed. No clinical trial without adequate experimental design should be proposed. "Bad science" *per se* is unethical because infants are unnecessarily exposed to potential risks.

This workshop summarized ethical standards for clinical trials in developing and industrialized countries and focused on adequate experimental design. Our primary goal must be to demonstrate that new or renovated infant food is safe and adequate for the target population. Health claims in the infant food area without convincing clinical support from clinical trials are no longer acceptable. Companies are requested to prove health claims and authorities to monitor their adequacy.

PROFESSOR F. HASCHKE, M.D.
Vice-President
Nestec Ltd., Vevey, Switzerland

Contents

Contributors

Speakers

Peter J. Aggett
Institute of Food Research
Norwich Research Park
Colney Lane
Norwich NR4 7UA
England

Jesse A. Berlin
Center for Clinical Epidemiology and
    Biostatistics
University of Pennsylvania
School of Medicine
Room 815 Blockley Hall
423 Guardian Drive
Philadelphia, Pennsylvania 19104
U.S.A.

Margaret C. Cheney
Chief Nutrition and Evaluation Division
Food Directorate, Health Protection
    Branch
Banting Building 2203A,
Tunney's Pasture
Ottawa, Ontario K1A OL2
Canada

George D. Ferry
Gastroenterology and Nutrition #3-3391
Texas Children's Hosptial
6621 Fannin
Houston, Texas 77030
U.S.A.

Frank L. Iber
Loyola University
Edward Hines Jr. VA Hospital
Gastroenterology—Room 1289
5th and Roosevelt
Hines, Illinois 60141
U.S.A.

Ralph E. Kauffman
Office of Medical Research
Children's Mercy Hospital
University of Missouri
2401 Gillham Road
Kansas City, Missouri 64108
U.S.A.

Betsy Lozoff
The Center for Human Growth and
    Development
University of Michigan
300 North Ingalls
Ann Arbor, Michigan 48109
U.S.A.

Alan Lucas
MRC Childhood Nutrition Research
    Centre
Institute of Child Health
30 Guilford Street
London WC1N 1EH
England

Jay A. Perman
Jessie Ball DuPont Professor and
    Chairman
Department of Pediatrics
Medical College of Virginia
Virginia Commonwealth University
Box #980646
Richmond, Virginia 23298
U.S.A.

Jean Rey
Hôpital des Enfants Malades
Département de Pédiatrie
149, rue de Sèvres
75743 Paris Cédex 15
France

Alex F. Roche
Department of Community Health
Wright State University
1005 Xenia Avenue
Yellow Springs, Ohio 45387
U.S.A.

Henry S. Sacks
The Mount Sinai Medical Center
Clinical Trials Unit, Box 1042
One Gustave L. Levy Place
New York, New York 10029
U.S.A.

Ricardo Uauy-Dagach
Institute of Nutrition Food Technology
INTA
University of Chile
Casilla 138-11
Santiago
Chile

John N. Udall, Jr.
Department of Pediatrics
Gastroenterology and Nutrition Division
Louisiana State University Medical
Center
1542 Tulane Ave., T8-1
New Orleans, Louisiana 70178
U.S.A.

Stephen D. Walter
Department of Clinical Epidemiology and
Biostatistics
McMaster University
1200 Main Street West
Hamilton, Ontario L8N 325
Canada

Roger G. Whitehead
MRC Dunn Nutrition Center
Downhams Lane
Milton Road
Cambridge CB4 1XJ
England

Elizabeth A. Yetley
Center for Food Safety and Applied
Nutrition
U.S. Food and Drug Administration
200 C Streets, SW
Washington, D.C. 20204
U.S.A.

Session Chairmen

Robert Hamburger / *USA*
M. A. van't Hof / *The Netherlands*
Jay Perman / *USA*
Hildegard Przyrembel / *Germany*

Invited Attendees

Lillian Beard / *USA*
Elisabeth Becher / *Switzerland*
Daniel Brasseur / *Belgium*
Mavilda Brito / *Portugal*
Jean-Pierre Cezard / *France*
Jean-Pierre Chouraqui / *France*
Larissa Chtchepliaguina / *Russia*
Petronella Clarke / *UK*
Ana Culcer / *Romania*
Ali Debbabi / *Tunisia*
Frank Falkner / *USA*
Mauro Fisberg / *Brazil*
Cuberto Garza / *USA*
Walter Glinsmann / *USA*
Maciej Kaczmarski / *Poland*
John Kerner / *USA*
Ronald Kleinman / *USA*
William Klish / *USA*
Michael J. Lentze / *Germany*
Meng Mao / *China*
Véronique Millet / *France*
Abdesselam N'Bou / *Morocco*
Frank Pohlandt / *Germany*
Staffan Polberger / *Sweden*
Michael Radke / *Germany*
Cesar Velasco Rodas / *Mexico*
Jose Saavedra / *USA*
Bernard Salle / *France*
Ricardo Sorensen / *USA*
Madeleine Sumpaico / *Philippines*
Umaporn Suthutvoravut / *Thailand*
Reginald Tsang / *USA*
Dominique Turck / *France*
Cecil T. Vella / *Malta*

Wei Ping Wang / *China*
Tzee-Chung Wu / *Taiwan*
Karl Zwiauer / *Austria*

Nestlé Representatives

Jean-Marc Aeschlimann / *Switzerland*
Steve Allen / *USA*
Marcel Baumgartner / *Switzerland*
Cindy Brown / *USA*
Roger Clemens / *USA*
Gayle Crozier / *Switzerland*
Lennart Dillner / *Switzerland*
Biana-Maria Exl / *Germany*
Melanie Fairchild / *USA*
Roger H. Gould / *Canada*
Pierre Guesry / *Switzerland*
Lajos Hanzel / *Hungary*
Ferdinand Haschke / *Switzerland*
Linda Hsieh / *USA*
Laurie MacDonald / *USA*
Eileen Madden / *USA*
Nick Melachouris / *Switzerland*
Marie-José Mozin / *Belgium*
Vipapan Panitantum / *Thailand*
Ulrich Preysch / *Switzerland*
Carol Savage / *USA*
Marie-Christine Secretin / *Switzerland*
Philippe Steenhout / *Switzerland*
Ernie Strapazon / *USA*
Elena Trofimenko / *Russia*
L.D. Van Egroo / *France*
Kai Voepel / *USA*
Joe Weller / *USA*
Robyn Wimberly / *USA*

Nestlé Nutrition Workshop Series

CLINICAL TRIALS IN INFANT NUTRITION
METHODOLOGY, STATISTICS, AND ETHICAL ISSUES

Clinical Trials in Infant Nutrition, edited by
Jay A. Perman and Jean Rey, Nestlé Nutrition
Workshop Series, Vol. 40, Nestec Ltd.,
Vevey/Lippincott-Raven Publishers,
Philadelphia © 1998.

Guidelines for the Ethical Study of Drugs in Infants and Children and the FDA Regulations

Ralph E. Kauffman

Children's Mercy Hospital, University of Missouri, Kansas City, Missouri, USA

There has been increasing acceptance of children as appropriate subjects of research over the past three decades. This arises from recognition that children differ from mature individuals in many critical respects. It is the process of growth and development that distinguishes children from adults. In addition to size, children differ from adults in many respects, including body proportions, susceptibility (or lack of it) to certain diseases, responses to treatments, vulnerability to certain drug toxicities, nutritional requirements, and their dependent status in society. It is precisely because children differ from adults in many important characteristics that they must share in the research process in order to benefit from advances in diagnosis and treatment unique to their needs. In other words, research in adults cannot necessarily be applied directly to children.

Because of the uniquely dependent status of children in society, special protections must be provided when they participate in research. It is the nature of and basis for these special protections that are discussed in this chapter. In addition, the current status of the Food and Drug Administration (FDA) regulations pertaining to labeling of drugs for children is presented.

HISTORICAL CONTEXT

The evolution of codified guidelines and regulations for the ethical conduct of research in humans, including children, is a relatively recent phenomenon. Before World War II, research in humans of all ages, including children, was conducted with little or no public scrutiny. During the 18th, 19th, and early 20th centuries, much of the research involving child subjects was directed toward preventing or treating infectious diseases, which represented the primary causes of childhood mortality. Nutritional experiments to elucidate the causes of rickets and scurvy also were conducted.

In 1914, Hess and Fish described experiments at the Hebrew Orphan Asylum in which orange juice was withheld from institutionalized infants until they developed the characteristic signs of scurvy (1). Hess and Unger also conducted studies of rickets using similar methods to induce vitamin D deprivation (2). Some of the children apparently did not fully recover from the effects of these experiments. Children were selected as research subjects in most studies primarily on the basis of their availability and convenience, with little or no thought of their personal rights or exposure to undue risk. As a result, child research subjects typically were from impoverished backgrounds or were institutionalized in hospitals or orphanages (3). Although sporadic criticism of such human research practices appeared, and several attempts were made to legislate against use of children in research during the early 1900s (3), formal regulation of human research did not occur until after World War II.

Abuse, exploitation, and murder of prisoners in the name of human experimentation carried out by the Nazis during World War II was revealed during the Nuremburg trials from 1946 to 1949. Revulsion at the atrocities perpetrated on prisoners and residents of concentration camps led to the Nuremburg Code (4), a code of ethics for human experimentation intended to prevent the repetition of such atrocities. However, the Nuremburg Code did not specifically address research in children and received little general attention before the late 1960s.

In 1964, the World Medical Association published the Declaration of Helsinki, in which the need for special protections for individuals with limited capacity to consent to participate as research subjects was recognized (5).

A 1966 paper published in the *New England Journal of Medicine* by Dr. Henry Beecher, entitled "Ethics and clinical research" (6), proved to be a major catalyst for development of guidelines for ethical conduct of human research. Dr. Beecher criticized 22 clinical studies published in prestigious American medical journals for violating basic ethical principles. Two of the 22 studies involved institutionalized children. One of the targets of Beecher's criticism was a study performed at Willowbrook State School, in which 51 mentally retarded children were fed infectious fecal extracts to study the natural course of viral hepatitis. The other involved performing vesicourethrography requiring extensive x-ray exposure in 26 healthy infants to study ureteral reflux in infants with normal urinary bladders. The outcry and debate precipitated by Beecher's article culminated in establishment of the National Commission for the Protection of Human Subjects of Biomedical and Behavioral Research in 1974. In 1977, the National Commission released a report on research involving children (7) and, in 1978, published the *Belmont Report,* which outlined ethical principles for protection of human subjects of research (8). United States federal regulations reflecting the content of the *Belmont Report* and addressing protection of human subjects, including children, followed shortly thereafter (9). Additional regulations providing further protection for children were published in 1983 (10). In 1991, a common rule consolidating all federal regulations on human research—including those pertaining specifically to children—was issued (11). These regulations provide current guidance for conduct of federally sponsored human research in the United States.

Between 1974 and 1977, the American Academy of Pediatrics (AAP) Committee on Drugs, under contract with the FDA, also developed guidelines for the ethical study of drugs in infants and children. These guidelines were initially published in 1977 (12) and were recently revised and republished in 1995 (13). The AAP guidelines are consistent with the federal regulations and, together, the two documents provide the current guidelines for ethical conduct of research involving pediatric subjects. The following discussion is based primarily on the current AAP guidelines and summarizes the ethical considerations of conducting clinical research in infants and children.

ETHICAL CONSIDERATIONS

Ethical guidelines for the protection of all human subjects are based on three fundamental premises articulated in the *Belmont Report:*

- Respect for the rights of the individual;
- The obligation to protect the individual from undue risk;
- Fairness in distribution of the burdens and benefits of research.

The basic rights of children as research subjects are no different from those of adults. However, because of their cognitive immaturity and dependent status in society, children are more vulnerable to violation of their rights than adults. Special measures must be taken to protect their personal rights and ensure that they are not exploited or placed at undue risk when they participate as research subjects. Several specific areas of particular importance to children deserve further discussion.

INFORMED CONSENT

The principle of respect for the individual's rights requires that a person should not participate as a research subject without freely consenting to do so with an informed understanding of the nature of the study and the possible benefits and risks of such participation. However, children have limited ability—which varies with level of maturity—to understand the implications and relative risks of participating in research or to make independent decisions regarding their participation. Because of their limited capacity to make independent decisions, children also are not recognized under federal or state laws as autonomous individuals. Therefore, consent or permission for their participation in research must be given by a surrogate consentor—usually a parent—who presumably is competent to understand the implications of the child's participation. It is assumed when surrogate permission is accepted that the surrogate consentor is acting only in the best interests of the child and is not influenced by factors that may not be in the child's best interest. Unfortunately, this assumption is not always true.

As children mature and develop greater ability for abstract thinking, their capacity to participate in the consent process increases. To the extent of their ability, children should be allowed to give their "assent" or consent in addition to the adult surrogate. The U.S. federal regulations and AAP guidelines generally agree that consent of children more than 13 years old and assent of children of more than 7 and less than 13 years should be obtained unless there is an overriding reason why this should not be done. The AAP guidelines state that "Assent may be waived in therapeutic research studies in which, in the opinions of the parents, investigators, and the IRB [investigational review board], the child's participation in an investigational treatment may be of such benefit that the child's welfare would be significantly jeopardized by failing to provide assent" (13).

RISK/BENEFIT

The obligation to protect the individual from undue risk requires that risk of participation in research be carefully evaluated and minimized. Any decision to participate as a research subject must weigh the known or potential risks against the benefits. Benefits should be construed broadly to include benefits to the population at large as well as benefit to the individual participant. Likewise, risks should be evaluated in the broadest sense and may include inconvenience, pain, fear, discomfort, and separation anxiety for the child as well as physical or psychological risks arising directly from the experimental procedure. Because of their particular vulnerability and inability to give consent independently, extra precautions must be taken to ensure that children are not subjected to undue or unfair risk. In marginal situations, investigators and investigational review boards should err on the side of avoiding risk to the subject.

The federal regulations and AAP guidelines divide risk/benefit into four categories:

1. *Research not involving greater than minimal risk.* Minimal risk is defined as the degree of risk a child would encounter during usual life activities and routine medical care. In general, children may participate in studies involving minimal risk if the study promises benefit to the larger society of children, to a specific group of children, and/or to the individual child. Under certain circumstances, participants in such studies could include normal children.

2. *Research involving more than minimal risk but offering the prospect of direct benefit to the individual subject.* Children may participate in studies entailing more than minimal risk with the prospect of direct benefit to the child if: (a) the risk is justified by the anticipated benefit; (b) the risk/benefit ratio is at least as favorable as that from available alternative nonexperimental approaches; and (c) the child's assent/consent is solicited as well as that of the surrogate consentor.

3. *Research involving more than minimal risk and no prospect of direct benefit to the individual but likely to yield important generalizable knowledge about the subject's disorder or condition.* Children may be considered for this category study if: (a) the risk represents a minor increase over minimal risk; (b) the intervention presents the subject with experiences commensurate with those encountered in their actual or expected medical, dental, psychological, social, or educational life experiences; (c) the study is likely to yield important generalizable

information; and (d) the child is provided the opportunity to give assent/consent to participate.

4. *Research not otherwise approvable that presents an opportunity to understand, prevent, or alleviate a serious problem affecting the health or welfare of children.* This category is difficult to define and would rarely be invoked. It requires that the investigational review board determines that the research presents an opportunity to further the understanding, prevention, or alleviation of a serious problem affecting the health or welfare of children and that the Secretary of Health and Human Services (HHS), after consultation with a panel of experts in pertinent disciplines, concurs and finds that the research will be conducted in accordance with sound ethical and scientific principles.

SELECTION OF SUBJECTS

Fairness in distribution of the burdens and benefits of research requires that no individual be excluded from participation or preferentially included primarily because he or she belongs to a particular socioeconomic, gender, or ethnic group within the larger society unless the selection is a necessary part of the study (for example, study of cystic fibrosis in whites or sickle cell anemia in African Americans). Subjects enrolled in a study should represent, so far as possible, a cross-section of the population from which they are recruited. There should be an equitable distribution of risks, inconveniences, and benefits throughout societal groups.

COMPENSATION AND REWARD FOR PARTICIPATION

Assent and consent to be a research subject is to be given freely and without coercion. Therefore, it is imperative that rewards or compensation for participation be commensurate with the subject's contribution and not of such an extent or nature as to be unduly coercive. At the same time, reimbursement for direct expenses, time, and inconvenience associated with participation may be appropriate. Compensation for contributing to a research endeavor also may be appropriate, although it is important to avoid incentives that are sufficient in themselves to induce parents or guardians to give permission for a dependent child to participate in a study or be subject to painful or invasive procedures. If the child is to receive something of value for participating, it is best to not discuss the reward before the decision to participate, so it is not a consideration in the decision. In general, compensation should not go beyond a token gesture of appreciation for participation and should not remove the element of free choice from the decision on whether or not to participate.

USE OF PLACEBO CONTROLS

Experimental designs that employ placebo controls are frequently desirable to demonstrate efficacy of a new treatment or to identify adverse effects specifically caused by an experimental treatment. However, use of placebo controls in studies involving children must be carefully examined to ensure that doing so will not expose children to undue risk, pain, or discomfort. This is essential because children are typically incapable of fully understanding the implications of participation in such a study and cannot provide independent, competent consent to participate. The American Academy of Pediatrics has recognized five conditions under which placebos may be ethically used in pediatric studies (13):

1. There is no generally accepted therapy of the condition, and the agent under study is the first one that may modify the course of the disease process;
2. The commonly used treatment for the condition is of questionable efficacy;
3. The commonly used treatment carries with it a high frequency of undesirable side effects, and the risks may be significantly greater than the benefits;
4. The placebo is used to identify the incidence and severity of undesirable side effects produced by adding a new treatment to an established regimen;
5. The disease process is characterized by frequent, spontaneous exacerbations and remissions, and the efficacy of the accepted treatment has not been demonstrated.

ESPECIALLY VULNERABLE POPULATIONS

Certain pediatric subpopulations are potentially more vulnerable to coercion or exploitation and require particular attention to protection of their individual rights. These special groups of children must be protected from disproportionate participation in research while at the same time their access is ensured to research studies from which they may receive direct benefit.

Institutionalized and Handicapped Children

Children may be institutionalized for various reasons including severe physical or mental handicap, orphaning, or incarceration for criminal offense. Such children are particularly vulnerable to exploitation because they typically have less freedom of choice in all aspects of their daily life. In addition, surrogate consent presents a special problem in these populations because a parent is often not available, and the legal guardian may not always be acting exclusively in the child's interest. In general, institutionalized children should not be included in studies unless they benefit directly from participation or unless the subject of the research pertains to their special circumstance of being institutionalized. Likewise, such children should not be excluded from research that may provide an important direct benefit not otherwise available to them.

Children with Permanently Debilitating or Lethal Diseases

Children with life-threatening or progressive chronic illness are particularly dependent and vulnerable. Their condition in and of itself may instill a degree of anxiety and desperation in the parents to induce agreement for the child to participate in investigations that entail considerable risk, morbidity, and suffering. This sense of desperation also may be shared by the responsible physicians and investigators. In some instances, potentially effective drugs can only be studied in these populations. Furthermore, investigational treatments may represent the standard of care or the only available treatment for some chronically progressive or potentially fatal diseases. This imposes a heavy responsibility on the investigator and the investigational review board to assure that benefit and risk are thoroughly evaluated and that the parent(s) and child, when appropriate, fully understand the implications and are emotionally capable of making a reasoned decision before agreeing to the child's participation in a research protocol.

Other Especially Vulnerable Populations

The AAP guidelines (13) address ethical issues when dealing with several other vulnerable populations. These include patients requiring emergency care, the dying patient, and the newly dead patient. The reader is referred to the Academy publication for a full discussion.

FDA REGULATION OF DRUG LABELING FOR CHILDREN

Although guidelines for the ethical inclusion of children in research have been available for the past 20 years, there is still a reluctance to include children in clinical trials. Ethical constraints are a frequently cited reason for not studying new medicines in children. There is a sense that children ''should not be experimented on.'' However, not including children in research that potentially benefits not only the individual but the larger peer group deprives children of the benefits and protections of research enjoyed by the adult population. For example, 70% to 80% of prescription medications currently available in the United States have not been studied in children sufficiently to meet FDA requirements for including pediatric indications in the official labeling. Because of this, children often receive drugs that have not been adequately studied to establish appropriate doses or toxicities that may be unique to children. This common practice may expose individual children to greater risk than would be entailed if they were receiving the medication as part of a rigorously controlled clinical trial. Such practice is difficult to defend ethically.

The 1962 Kefauver–Harris amendments to the U.S. Food, Drug, and Cosmetic Act (14) provide that, in addition to being safe, a new drug must be shown by substantial evidence to have the effect it is purported to have under the conditions of use prescribed, recommended, or suggested in its proposed labeling before it may be legally introduced into interstate commerce. Substantial evidence is defined as

> evidence consisting of adequate and well-controlled investigations by experts qualified
> by scientific training and experience to evaluate the effectiveness of the drug involved,

on the basis of which it could fairly and responsibly be concluded by such experts that
the drug will have the effect it purports or is represented to have. . . .

Regulatory interpretation of the statutory efficacy requirements by the FDA typically
has required at least two prospective, blinded, placebo-controlled clinical trials that
include sufficient numbers of patients to establish efficacy with acceptable statistical
probability. Data generated by such trials are submitted in the New Drug Application
(NDA) and become the basis for approval and labeling of the drug for general use.
The approved labeling for a drug may contain only those indications and dosage
recommendations supported by data submitted in the NDA and approved by the
FDA. If the patient population included in the submitted studies excludes certain
patient subpopulations (for example, infants and children), the labeling cannot contain indications for use or dosage recommendations for those excluded subpopulations.

During the past 30 years, the majority of drugs have been approved in the United
States on the sole basis of studies in adult subjects. At the same time, there has been
acknowledgment that data derived from adult studies cannot always be extrapolated
to infants and children. Unfortunately, this recognition has resulted in exclusionary
language pertaining to children in the labeling of most drugs rather than the conduct
of studies in children to support child-appropriate information in the labeling. This
has created the current situation in which physicians must choose between prescribing a great many drugs for children *off label* or deny the child access to those
medications. It clearly is in the best interests of children to have drugs studied in
and labeled for children, so they enjoy the same protections under the Food and
Drug Laws as adults.

During the past 4 years, the FDA has taken several important steps to address
the gap in drug labeling for children. In 1991, a *pediatric studies page* was introduced
into the NDA review process for new drugs and for drugs that already have approved
indications if they are being evaluated for new indications or dose formulations.
The pediatric studies page requires the FDA and sponsoring company at the time
of NDA submission to identify whether pediatric studies are being conducted or
planned and, if not, to explain why. Almost 3 years ago, new regulations were
promulgated to facilitate labeling of drugs for children (15). Under the new rule,
manufacturers must reexamine existing information to determine whether the pediatric labeling of their marketed products can be modified on the basis of existing data,
and, if so, they have 2 years to submit an application for supplemental labeling. In
addition, the FDA has the authority to request specific pediatric use information if
it deems it necessary. Pediatric labeling may be approved, in part, on the basis of
adult efficacy studies for some new drugs for which the pediatric diseases and
indications are substantially the same as for adults. In such cases, pediatric studies
may be limited to safety, metabolic, pharmacokinetic, and dosing studies. A special
pediatric subcommittee of the Medical Policy Coordinating Committee of the
Center for Drug Evaluation and Research has been formed within the FDA, with
representatives from each division. This group is to track the implementation of

the new regulations and to facilitate the inclusion of pediatric testing in the drug development process.

It is too early to determine the impact of these initiatives by the FDA, but they are intended to increase the number of new drugs approved for use in children. Clinical trials in children are feasible and essential for safe and effective use of medications in children. The time is long past when drugs with therapeutic potential in children should be marketed with labeling restricted to adults.

SUMMARY

Because of the uniquely dependent status of children, special protections must be provided when they participate in research. The evolution of codified guidelines and regulations for the ethical conduct of research in humans, including children, is a relatively recent phenomenon. The Nuremburg code of ethics for human research was published following World War II in the aftermath of the Nuremburg war crimes trials. In 1964, the Declaration of Helsinki addressed the need for special protection for individuals with limited capacity to consent. Between 1977 and 1983, the report of the National Commission for the Protection of Human Subjects of Biomedical Research, U.S. federal regulations governing human research, and the AAP guidelines for the ethical study of drugs in children were published. Revised AAP guidelines were republished in 1995. Ethical guidelines for the protection of human subjects are based on three fundamental premises: (a) respect for the rights of the individual; (b) the obligation to protect the individual from undue risk; and (c) fairness in distribution of the burdens and benefits of research. The application of these principles to special ethical considerations for children is discussed. Recent regulatory changes by the U.S. FDA to facilitate more studies of drugs in children are presented.

REFERENCES

1. Hess AF, Fish M. Infantile scurvy: the blood, the blood vessels, and the diet. *Am J Dis Child* 1914; 8:386–405
2. Hess AF, Unger LJ. Dietaries of infants in relation to the development of rickets. *Proc Soc Exp Biol Med* 1919–1920;17:220–221.
3. Lederer SE, Grodin MA. Historical Overview: pediatric experimentation. In: Grodin MA, Glantz LH, eds. *Children as research subjects: science, ethics and law.* New York: Oxford University Press, 1994:3–25.
4. United States Adjutant General's Department. *Trials of war criminals before Nuremburg Military Tribunals under Control Council Law No. 10 (October 1946 to April 1949).* Washington, DC: US Government Printing Office, 1947:2:181–183.
5. World Medical Association. Declaration of Helsinki (1964): the changing mores of biomedical research. *Ann Intern Med* 1965(suppl);7:74–75.
6. Beecher HK. Ethics and clinical research. *N Engl J Med* 1966;274:1354–1360.
7. The National Commission for the Protection of Human Subjects of Biomedical and Behavioral Research. *Report and recommendations: research involving children.* Washington, DC: HEW Publication (OS) 77-004, 1977
8. National Commission for the Protection of Human Subjects of Biomedical and Behavioral Research.

The Belmont Report: Ethical principles and guidelines for the protection of human subjects of research. Washington, DC: HEW Publication (OS) 78-0014, 1978.

9. *Fed Register* 1978;43(9):2084–2109.
10. *Fed Register* 1983;48(46):9814–9820.
11. *Fed Register* 1991;56(117):28003–28032.
12. American Academy of Pediatrics Committee on Drugs. Guidelines for the ethical conduct of studies to evaluate drugs in pediatric populations. *Pediatrics* 1977;60:91–101.
13. American Academy of Pediatrics Committee on Drugs. Guidelines for the ethical conduct of studies to evaluate drugs in pediatric populations. *Pediatrics* 1995;95:286–294.
14. US Department of Health and Human Services, Public Health Service, Food and Drug Administration. *Requirements of laws and regulations enforced by the US Food and Drug Administration.* Washington, DC: US Government Printing Office; 1984:40–41.
15. Specific requirements on content and format of labeling for human prescription drugs: revision of pediatric use subsection in the labeling (21 CFR 201). *Fed Register* 1994;59:64240–64250.

DISCUSSION

Dr. Perman: You touched on the issue of compensation. How does one affix compensation? When is it compensation, and when is it bribery?

Dr. Kauffman: I think it varies with the situation and with the particular subject. This is why it is so important to be aware of the issue and to consider it, knowing that in a particular situation, there is more than one answer. For me, the bottom line is that any compensation should be noncoercive. What is coercive? There might be coercion where a fee is offered in the case of a child who comes from a very impoverished background, though the same fee might not be coercive for a middle-class family. So, there is more than one answer to this. I also think that a reward potentially becomes coercive when the possibility of the reward is discussed before the consent decision, and when the reward is of a nature or quantity to clearly be coercive to most children who might participate in a given study.

Dr. Perman: In a type of study that all of us have been involved in--that is, studies of infant formulas—formula is generally provided as part of the study. For impoverished families, that may make a big difference. Is that appropriate, or is that coercive?

Dr. Kauffman: Again, I don't think there is a single answer to that. If you have an impoverished parent with a new infant who has an available source of food or formula, from a WIC (Women, Infants, Children) program, for example, they will have formula either way, so getting a specific formula through a study doesn't change that. It may be coercive, however, if that parent has no other source of formula available, and this is the only way they can feed their baby.

Dr. Iber: You mentioned that the reward system should be discussed only after the acceptance of the study, but all of the IRBs I have dealt with require a highly legalistically written document that is offered to the parents to go over and that always includes details of the compensation. How can you achieve this particular aim within the guidelines of a written informal consent that does at least require that compensation be specifically outlined.

Dr. Kauffman: We have differentiated fair compensation from reward. I think you can argue that it is ethical to compensate a family and/or a child for the out-of-pocket cost, inconvenience, and time that they contribute to participation in the study that they would not otherwise do—in other words, transportation cost, food away from home, a minimal compensation for the time they put into the experimental interventions, and so forth. I think that can be ethically defended because that is compensation to individuals for a contribution that they are making not only to their own welfare but also for the benefit of others. A reward can be considered as being over and above that type of compensation. The compensation clearly has to be detailed in a consent form because the parent and/or the child needs to understand what is available to them if they participate in the study. I think most consent forms would include that type of compensation. The reward could vary from, for example, certificates to children after participation in the study commending them for their contribution to a reward of several hundred dollars when they complete all aspects of the study. I think rewards that have tangible value in excess of compensation should be presented as a possibility after the formal consent decision is made.

Dr. Klish: You hit upon two issues that I think deserve a bit more discussion. One is the concept of minimal risk, because if you subject control populations to any kind of change to their normal routine, you are perhaps introducing some risk. So, this is something we have discussed a lot in many different protocols that contained control populations. The other has to do with the age of consent and assent, because there are regional differences in those ages. What are your thoughts on those two issues?

Dr. Kauffman: First of all, the minimal risk issue. Again, one has to use judgment in each case. The risk depends on the environment in which the children live. For some children, life is full of horrible risks every day, including tremendous violence. I don't think we considered that as an acceptable normal everyday risk, but we talked about such things as 4-year-olds falling off a piece of playground equipment and skinning their knees—that is a part of their daily risk environment; and school-age children crossing the street or riding their bicycle down the street. Is that an acceptable daily risk? And how does that compare to a venipuncture for drawing blood for sampling during a study? So, one has to look at the environment in which a particular child lives and then decide if this is a reasonable acceptable risk. We have used this guide in considering the ethics of doing vaccine studies in normal children. An acceptable risk, in the United States at least, and in most other developed countries, is that children will have the risk of being vaccinated against certain infectious diseases during their childhood. How do you alter that risk if you expose them to an experimental vaccine? We have accepted that there is either a minimal or a slightly greater than minimal risk in doing such vaccine studies in normal children.

As to the age of consent, in using the term consent in the guidelines, we distinguished between independent consent or permission, which in most places would be the age of majority, and nonindependent consent of the older child. For example, the recommendation is that for the 14-year-old who is not emancipated from parental care, you would be required not only to get informed permission from the parent but also to ask the child to give consent as well; both are necessary to enroll that child in the study. The age is very arbitrary. We know that some children at the age of 10 are much more mature than others at the age of 14 or 15, but you have to have some guidelines, and we assume that the majority of children have the ability to make these kinds of abstract decisions at these approximate ages.

Dr. Guesry: I would like to start with a suggestion. Your first example of an unethical study was done with food, not with a drug, and all your guidelines could equally well be applied to special foods such as infant formulas or to drugs. So, I would suggest that you remove the word drugs from your title. Also, you put all of the burden of decision making on the ethics committees, but my feeling is that not all ethics committees are born equal, and more guidelines would be useful. It might help to have a more detailed breakdown of the four categories of clinical trial.

Dr. Kauffman: A more detailed breakdown would probably be desirable for an individual IRB or an individual organization. However, we were reluctant to write more detailed guidelines, and I suspect that the individuals who wrote the federal regulations were reluctant also, because they did not want to write guidelines that were so restrictive that they would become obsolete or not be applicable to certain situations now or in the future. So, these are an attempt to categorize risk and benefit in very broad categories within which you can develop more specific rules within your own organization or for your specific study.

Dr. Perman: Dr Guesry, what have you observed that makes you think there ought to be more detail with regard to categorization?

Dr. Guesry: One of the arguments that the medical community in general uses is to stress the benefit that other children or other people would get from a given study, while in fact, the children or perhaps the premature babies who are the object of the study often barely benefit from it. To me, this is the real issue; I think the decision may vary from one ethics committee to another, and it is not always completely impartial. I am sure that one study would be passed in one university and not in another.

Dr. Kauffman: You are right. That was shown a number of years ago in a survey in which representative protocols were distributed to some 20 IRBs around the United States, and there were approximately 20 different decisions on them! But I would argue that ethical considerations should not be on the basis of hard and fast rules. I think the purpose is to raise the issues and to point out the principles that need to be followed. With respect to your example of the premature infant as a subject in a study that could benefit other infants in the future, but not necessarily that infant at that moment, I think that falls into the category of minimal risk. In addition, it may be considered ethical because it would benefit either that child in the future or other children in the future. The test is, is this either minimal or only slightly greater than minimal risk? If there is a possibility that you might produce a nutritional problem that could result in irreversible damage to a premature infant, that constitutes greater than minimal risk, and it would be difficult to defend it ethically. If you can argue legitimately and credibly that your protocol would produce only slightly greater than minimal risk, then I think that under these guidelines, you could justify including a premature infant who may not benefit directly from being in the protocol.

Dr. Hamburger: I want to take the opposite side to Dr. Guesry. Dr. Haschke mentioned in his opening statement that the United States is a leader in defining ethical research, but I wonder whether in that leadership role, we haven't made so many rules and regulations, and made it so complex, that this is one of the reasons we see 20 different responses to the same protocol; in fact, we may have begun to handicap really innovative clinical research.

Dr. Kauffman: I am not sure I would agree with that totally, though it is an excellent debate point. I agree that there was a backlash in the 1960s to what occurred during the previous 30 to 40 years to the extent that people may have overreacted a little bit. My experience in interacting with IRBs over the years has been that implementation of the guidelines is frequently the problem rather than the guidelines themselves. There is a lack of information and understanding about the ethical principles that are being applied and about the guidelines themselves. I see our IRB every month getting bogged down in trivia that it shouldn't be arguing about, and I think that is a bigger problem than the guidelines themselves. The HHS has tried to address this over the years by holding workshops around the country to help IRBs become more informed and do their job better, but it is a constant struggle.

Dr. Haschke: The rules we have discussed should also be followed by infant-food-producing companies. For example, specialty formulas for premature infants or formulas for very sick babies should be subject to the same rules as drugs. We should also follow strict rules for infant formulas. But how about cereals? If an infant food company produces an infant cereal that does not fall within the guidelines, say one with a low protein content, should there be different rules?

Dr. Kauffman: From an ethical point of view, I think, in general, it would be wise to follow these guidelines. For example, if you are developing a food product to give to a small subpopulation of children with, say, an inherited metabolic disorder, you will probably study it in that population rather than in the normal child population. In that situation, introducing a formula that has a putative beneficial effect for that inherited metabolic disorder would be ethically justifiable because the child or the population of children may benefit from that formula. On the other hand, if you are testing a cereal product that may cause a major alteration in vitamin content, or salt content, or some other content in the general population of children, then I think there needs to be an assessment of how much this intervention may alter the daily risk for that child that is incurred just from living in his or her usual environment. This is a difficult issue when one is altering the content of major nutrients. It has to be approached very carefully. One way is to have the protocol and the risks assessed by a totally independent body that has no interest in the product and looks at it purely from the child's advocacy point of view.

Dr. Uauy: In assessing the risk/benefit analysis, of course benefit becomes as crucial as risk, because if benefit is small, then the ratio is infinite. Experimental design then becomes crucial to assess potential benefit. Is the IRB the place to examine benefit and experimental design, or should that precede the ethical review? Many studies that have questionable ethics are also inadequately designed to answer the question. So, shouldn't an independent assessment of benefit precede any IRB consideration? At the present time, this is often left to the speculation of the investigator. Which is the best body to examine benefit?

Dr. Kauffman: This is a very important issue, and I see the IRB becoming embroiled in debate with investigators. Investigators will say that it is not the role of the IRB to judge the scientific value of the study. It should simply look at the risk/benefit equation and protect the rights of the patient without worrying about whether the study is scientifically valid or whether the design is good or not. The IRB will say that a poorly designed study that is not going to yield interpretable results can never be ethical because you should never subject a child to participation in a study, even with minimal risk, if the study has no scientific value. I believe the IRB must consider scientific validity and experimental design in assessing the risk/benefit issue because, as stated in the AAP guidelines, poor science is never ethical. I think the two issues go hand in hand. You can't make one judgment without the other.

Dr. Glinsmann: My point was exactly the same. You cannot consider the IRB's function without taking into account the study design. Normally in these cases, I believe that what you are doing is testing some gold standard against a new intervention. You can make an IRB much more comfortable if you set very clear criteria for termination of the study and for looking at the potential adverse events as they occur during the course of the study. So, there is a safety factor, and there are clear rules for termination.

Dr. Saavedra: When we look at the benefits of a study, the risk for a patient, or the relative value of a compensation, what we are really looking at is the relative value of each one of those items within the environment of the patient. From that point of view, it would make relatively little sense to be very specific about guidelines. In other words, if a particular IRB is made responsible for examining the relative value of compensation or the relative risk within a particular population, taking into account the geography, socioeconomic status, and the ethical standards of that population, it makes for a much better informed decision. In that sense, it may not be bad that for the same study, 20 IRBs came up with 20 different decisions, if they truly took into consideration the immediate environment of the population in which that study was to be made. So, I don't think different decisions necessarily make for a bad judgment, and I think that defining the balance between what is a generalizable guideline and what is the specific benefit and relative value of the risks that need to be taken is particularly important.

Dr. Kauffman: I want to add that in United States, we have an ethnically and culturally diverse population, particularly in the major metropolitan areas, and these decisions also have to be very culturally sensitive, because what is important or coercive or negative for one culture may not be so for another, or what might be quite positive for one cultural group may not be for another cultural group.

Dr. Lucas: We have been making some very important general comments, but there is one rather specific one that I want to clarify, and this is the question of where it is reasonable for assent to be waived in a child. Are you saying that a 6-year-old child, for instance, who refuses to be part of a research project, could have that decision overridden by the parents, the IRB, and the investigators if they felt that the study could be of benefit to the child in a way that the child could not perceive? If that is the case, could you give some examples of why that might be legitimate?

Dr. Kauffman: This is a difficult question. The intent of this waiver is to address a situation such as the following: a 6-year-old child has a life-threatening malignancy, say acute lymphocytic leukemia in the third relapse, when the usual chemotherapy protocols are no longer effective. The only hope is some investigational protocol. The child says ''I don't want to participate in this, I don't want the blood tests, I don't want the bone marrow done, I don't want the central catheter, I don't want these drugs because they make me sick.'' The parents, the physician, the investigator, and the IRB concur that this investigational protocol offers a reasonable hope, that the risk/benefit ratio is reasonable, and that it is in the child's best interests to proceed, although the child is too immature to understand that at this point. The other situation is the 10-year-old who, for whatever reason, is mentally incapacitated and cannot comprehend anything even to the level of concurring or not concurring with participation. In that situation, it is appropriate to waive the requirement for assent. So, those are two examples of specific situations that represent what was intended by this waiver.

Dr. Rey: First, I will give an example of differences between states in the United States in the appreciation of the risk of a study. It is a classical one—a study by Selma E. Snyderman and Emmet Holt at the beginning of the 1950s on amino acid requirements. You remember that they deprived young infants of one essential amino acid for a few days, and, in a review paper of their work (1), they said that they were obliged to move from New York to Texas to continue their research. I think this is a good example of the differences.

I would like to comment on Dr. Haschke's question about cereals. We have mainly discussed ethical rules for research, and research tries to increase knowledge. If we don't try to increase our knowledge, we should be more careful with the children or the infants than if we expect a direct or indirect benefit for the child or for science. So, I believe that the same rules apply more strictly if you intend to compare two different types of cereal in normal children than if you wish to study a disease treatment. You should be more careful with cereals than with the treatment of malignant diseases.

I agree with Dr. Guesry that, perhaps, you should delete drugs from the title of your paper. But I am interested in drugs because they represent a particular trial model. If we don't try new drugs in normal children, we will never obtain a license to use them in sick children, and the peculiarity of drugs is that they are sometimes toxic. In infant nutrition, we also have problems with toxicity. A good example is the maximum level of pesticides in infant formulas, about which there is debate in Europe. The Germans are for no more than 10 ppm, but other countries in the European Union have a different opinion. We also have a debate in Brussels about the level of lecithins that we can add to infant formula, and you know that, in rats, high levels of soybean lecithin have produced some behavior disturbances. I am not at all convinced of the reality of this, but I would be happy if you could explain to us, with your expertise in pharmacology, what is the main target that we should be aware of when we are studying drugs in infants: is it the central nervous system, the hormone receptors, the reproductive capacity?

Dr. Kauffman: In the infant particularly, the central nervous system is very important because it is rapidly developing at that age. From the eliminatory organ point of view, obviously the liver and the kidney are very important. But we know from past tragic experience that there can be surprises, and any assumption we make about a particular target organ may not be correct. How could people know in the 1950s that giving tetracycline to young children would cause permanent dental dysplasia, for example? Who would have thought of looking at the teeth and the bones and the thyroid when you give tetracycline? So, we always have to be on the alert that there may be nasty surprises. The bottom line is to look at the places where, at that particular stage of development, the most rapid and dramatic changes are known to be taking place.

REFERENCE

1. Holt LE, Snyderman SE. The amino acid requirements of children. In: Nyhan WL, ed. *Amino acid metabolism and genetic variation.* New York: McGraw-Hill, 1967:381–390.

Clinical Trials in Infant Nutrition, edited by
Jay A. Perman and Jean Rey, Nestlé Nutrition
Workshop Series, Vol. 40, Nestec Ltd.,
Vevey/Lippincott-Raven Publishers,
Philadelphia © 1998.

Specific European Union Aspects on Ethics of Clinical Trials

Peter J. Aggett

Institute of Food Research, Norwich Research Park, Norwich, United Kingdom

All member states of the European Union subscribe to codes of biomedical ethics, including psychological and socioeconomic aspects of such research, and consider it essential for all experimental protocols involving human subjects to be reviewed by independent ethics committees. However, although there is agreement in principle, this cannot yet be represented as a single European perspective on the implementation and policing of ethical review processes (1).

The development of ethical review of experimentation and the acceptance that research needs to be performed on children has followed much the same path in Europe as in North America. Perhaps both started with the traditional professional attitude expressed by Thomas Percival in 1803, when he commented that

> It is for the public good, and in the special degree advantageous to the poor (who, being the most numerous class of society, are the greatest beneficiaries of the healing art) that new remedies and new methods of chirurgical treatment should be devised. But in the accomplishment of the salutary purpose, the gentlemen of the faculty should be scrupulously and conscientiously governed by sound reason, just analogy, or well authenticated facts. And no such trials should be instituted without previous consultation of the physicians or surgeons according to the nature of the case. (A.G.M. Campbell, *personal communication*)

This paternalistic, if not patronizing, attitude to the consent of participants persisted until the mid-1960s, when it was challenged by the publication in the United States of Beecher's review, "Ethics and clinical research" (2), and, in the United Kingdom, the book *Human Guinea Pigs* by Pappworth (3).

The degree of professional ambivalence that existed 30 years ago in Britain is exemplified by the minutes of a meeting of the British Paediatric Association's Academic Board on 7 December 1968; the Chairman presented a paper on the ethics of research investigations in children: " . . . it was obvious that members could not reach complete agreement on a subject which involved individual ethical practise and it was decided to file the paper and take no further action" (A.G.M. Campbell, *personal communication*).

The position of those wishing to conduct studies in children had at that time been compromised, particularly with respect to research of no immediate benefit to the subject, by a report of the Medical Research Council (MRC) in 1963 that stated that "In the strict view of the law, parents and guardians of minors cannot give consent on their behalf to any procedures which are of no particular benefit to them and which may cause some risk of harm" (4). This position was essentially endorsed in 1975 by the Department of Health and Social Security, which advised that "the fact that consent has been given by the parent or guardian and that the risk involved is considered negligible will not be sufficient to bring such clinical research investigation within the law as it stands" (5).

The terms "therapeutic" and "nontherapeutic" research came into usage more recently. "Therapeutic research" has been used by the MRC to cover research not only on the treatment of disease but also on its prevention (for example, by vaccination) and on diagnostic procedures; it offers direct and possibly immediate benefit to the participant, whereas with "nontherapeutic research," such benefit is either long delayed or unlikely (4); this type of research would embrace observational work on normal physiology and maturational processes (6), even though such studies could be just as relevant to understanding the prevention and pathogenesis of disease.

The view of the British MRC was based on a strict interpretation of the law and was reiterated by the amended Helsinki Declaration of 1975 (7), which stated that nontherapeutic research can be conducted only on a volunteer basis and that consent on behalf of minors cannot be given by parents or guardians for procedures that are of no benefit to them and might carry risk of harm. Because the guidelines for many national ethics committees focused on the interests and the protection of the individuals participating in studies, it is understandable that they, too, were cautious about allowing nontherapeutic research involving infants and children.

In 1980, the British Paediatric Association published guidelines to aid "ethics committees considering research involving children" (8). These included four basic premises: (a) research is important for the benefit of all children; it should be supported and encouraged, and it should be conducted in an ethical manner; (b) research should never be done on children if the same investigation can be done on adults; (c) research that involves a child and is of no benefit (nontherapeutic research) is not necessarily either unethical or illegal; (d) the degree of benefit resulting from research should be assessed in relation to the risk of disturbance, discomfort, or pain (the "risk/benefit ratio"). Points c and d asserted the position of all those who wished to advance the discipline of child health in the context of a developing human being rather than being constrained by the perspective of practitioners in adult medicine.

The Council for International Organizations of Medical Sciences/World Health Organization published guidelines in 1982 that were intended to encourage and facilitate the setting up of national policies and processes for independent prospective ethical review (1). European countries provided their own guidelines for the conduct of clinical trials, for example, Ireland in 1986, Germany in 1987, and Italy in 1991;

Denmark created a National Ethical Council in 1987, and The Netherlands are establishing a Central Committee on Medical Experimentation to replace an interim committee set up in 1982. In Finland in 1985, the National Board of Health not surprisingly endorsed the Declaration of Helsinki (1). The United Kingdom has produced a variety of guidelines advising on the structure and conduct of local research ethics committees; this system is self-regulatory. In contrast, France in 1988 enacted Loi No. 88-1138 relating to the protection of persons participating in biomedical research (9). This legislation, named the ''Loi Huriet'' after its sponsor Claude Huriet, set up a Consultative Committee Responsible for the Protection of Persons Participating in Biomedical Research (CCPPBR), whose opinion on studies should be sought. Similarly to the laws of much of the rest of Europe, this law concentrated initially on therapeutic research, but it was made less restrictive in 1990. As well as inspiring, in part, the Convention on the Rights of Children (1990), the Loi Huriet also highlighted the need within the European Union for an agreed framework for ethical review of biomedical research. In February 1990, the Committee of Ministers of the Council of Europe agreed on Recommendation No. R (90) 3, which provided 16 principles on the ethics of medical research (10). These addressed the need for a sound science base; respect for the individual; informed consent; care in the conduct of studies involving children, the mentally ill, pregnant and nursing women, and prisoners; guidelines for emergency situations when the participant is unable to give prior consent; an appreciation of the benefit relative to the risk involved; confidentiality; safety of the research; and ethics review procedures.

To achieve uniformity, the EU Council of Ministers recommended that governments of member states either adopt legislation in conformity with the Recommendation or take measures to ensure its implementation and ensure that its provisions are brought to the knowledge of all relevant persons. These principles will have a considerable impact on research in human beings and on trials in pediatric nutrition, and they have been considered specifically in this context by the French Pediatric Association Committee on Nutrition (9) and, by implication, in the recent United Kingdom guidelines on the ''Nutritional Assessment of Infant Formulas,'' compiled by the Committee on Medical Aspects of Food and Nutrition Policy (COMA) (11). I briefly review the principles in the EU Recommendation and draw on these reports to comment on its implications.

EU PRINCIPLE 1

- Any medical research must be carried out within the framework of a plan and in accordance with the following principles.

A nutritional trial should not necessarily go ahead because it involves no danger or disadvantage for the children involved. If the information to be gained is not novel, or if the scientific basis is unsound, then such a trial would not be justified (see also Principle 11). In short, bad science is unethical (12). The Loi Huriet states that ''no biomedical research may be carried out in humans if it is not based on the latest state of scientific knowledge and on adequate preclinical experiments.'' For studies in infants, the latter could involve animal models, adults, and older consenting children.

The COMA Working Group suggested that all research should be preceded by a critical systematic review (13) of all relevant existing information as a basis to improve innovation and research and that such a review should subsequently be made publicly available, ideally published (11). This entails aspects of the principles of ''evidence-based medicine,'' and, from the point of view of nontherapeutic research in the nutrition of infants and children, the pooling of data from several published studies should improve the quality of such research and the formulation of research questions and might obviate the need for any further study and avoid unnecessary replication. These considerations alerted the COMA panel to the need for a data base of, and information from, abandoned, incomplete, and unpublished studies.

EU PRINCIPLE 2

- In medical research the interests and well-being of the person undergoing medical research must always prevail over the interests of science and society.
- The risks incurred by a person undergoing medical research must be kept to a minimum. The risks should not be disproportionate to the benefits for that person or the importance of the aims pursued by the research.

This principle presents no challenge to nutritional research involving innovative ingredients and interventions, but it might present difficulties in the clinical evaluation of modifications to infant formulas and feeding products that fall within current guidelines on composition. However, a ''new'' formula would not always be acceptable simply because its compositional profile fell within national or European specifications. The COMA report, for example, considered that, even within the statutory compositional guidelines for infant formulas, it is possible that variations could be responsible for nutrient interactions that would influence the absorption and metabolism of interacting nutrients. These interactions in a complex material could not be predicted with certainty; examples include interactions between essential trace elements such as iron, zinc, and copper both with each other and with calcium. Similarly we are not as yet necessarily confident that we have the appropriate balance of levels of protein and energy in formulas within the permitted range. Industrial production processes might have a similar effect on nutritional quality by creating reaction products that limit the utilization of nutrients (11).

A principle of ''substantial equivalence'' has been developed to assist in safety and nutritional evaluations of new products in proposing that traditional foods, accepted as safe in use, can be used as a basis for the safety assessment and acceptance of novel foods, but the COMA panel held that ''further development of this concept would be needed before it could be applied to a complex food matrix such as infant formulas, where the interactions within the food are not fully predictable and the food is the sole source of nutrition.'' Similarly, the French Pediatric Association Committee on Nutrition emphasized that clinical trials are needed for both nutritional and safety evaluations of new products (9).

It is debatable whether or not adding approved ''substances for nutritional purposes'' (for example, nucleotides, taurine, long-chain fatty acids) or a technological modification actually constitutes a ''novel food'' in the context of European regulations. It is probable that in the context of the COMA report they probably would be regarded as ''novel''; even so, there is usually a scientific rationale for such modifications, and this would merit formal evaluation. The COMA noted that ''it has been suggested that infant formulas should be assessed as pharmaceuticals with a registered specification of the product and of the processes used in its manufacture.'' Here again, the vulnerability of infants and their dependence on particular foodstuffs makes it reasonable that there should be some regulation of the composition of such products. This also justifies the view that new emulative products should at least have acceptability and tolerability trials and that, on this basis, the absence of any novel biological and medical knowledge from such trials would not necessarily make them ''unethical.'' These studies should be, nonetheless, appropriately designed and conducted to establish equivalence with comparable products (14,15). Marketing initiatives under the guise of ''acceptability studies'' in infants should be no more acceptable or ethical than similar studies would be in the assessment of pharmaceutical products (see also EU Principle 11).

In France, acceptability studies are not necessarily legally required, but the French Committee on Nutrition accepted that even if these ''clinical trials'' were neither absolutely essential for the advancement of knowledge nor mandatory, they would enable some justification of the product and the continuing improvement of products.

The next three principles can be considered together.

EU PRINCIPLE 3

- No medical research may be carried out without the informed, free, express, and specific consent of the person undergoing it. Such consent may be freely withdrawn at any phase of the research, and the person undergoing the research should be informed, before being included in it, of his right to withdraw his consent.
- The person who is to undergo medical research should be given information on the purpose of the research and of the methodology of the experimentation. He should also be informed of the foreseeable risks and inconveniences to him of the proposed research. The information should be sufficiently clear and suitably adapted to enable consent to be given or refused in full knowledge of the relevant facts.
- The provisions of this principle should apply also to a legal representative and to a legally incapacitated person having the capacity of understanding, in the situations described in principles 4 and 5.

EU PRINCIPLE 4

- A legally incapacitated person may undergo medical research only where authorized by Principle 5 and if his legal representative, or an authority or an individual
authorized or designated under his national law, consents. If the legally incapacitated person is capable of understanding, his consent is also required, and no
research may be undertaken if he does not give his consent.

EU PRINCIPLE 5

- A legally incapacitated person may not undergo medical research unless it is
expected to produce a direct and significant benefit to his health.
- However, by way of exception, national law may authorize research involving a
legally incapacitated person that is not of direct benefit to his health when that
person offers no objection, provided that the research is to the benefit of persons
in the same category and that the same scientific results cannot be obtained by
research on persons who do not belong to this category.

The child's caregivers and relevant health professionals should be told about the
study's design, and sometimes it might be advantageous to involve parents and other
professional carers in pilot studies, study design, and study procedures (16–18).
This would also reduce any perceived risk or discomfort arising from disruption of
family life or separation of the child from its family. Involving health professionals
improves the chances of recruiting participants from sectors of the community that
so often include those who would benefit most from nutritional studies in babies
and infants and ensure so far as is possible that the participants represent the population for which the product is intended.

The "selection" and recruitment of participants in nutrition studies in children
need to be considered in the light of the particular question in mind. If the study
has a demanding protocol, for example a metabolic balance, then recruitment should
probably take place among children of appropriately educated and motivated parents.

To minimize selection bias in clinical trials, infants should be randomly and
blindly allocated to study groups, and it is reasonable to feel that the ideal outcomes
in the assessment of products should be those of healthy breast-fed babies. However,
it is not practically or ethically acceptable to study groups of infants randomly
assigned to or denied breast-feeding. It is debatable whether it is ethically acceptable
to involve in a study breast-fed babies who might not derive any benefit from the
study. This is really the epitome of nontherapeutic research, but to my knowledge
no ethics committee has raised this issue. Nonetheless, data from breast-fed infants
(particularly term infants) are needed as a standard for the evaluation of modifications
in formulas and for further information about infant development, and so the inclusion of breast-fed babies in studies could be optimally exploited by ensuring that
such studies contribute to a reference data base on outcomes in healthy breast-fed
infants. This is consonant with the sentiment in the Loi Huriet that "studies without

direct benefit for the individual are permitted [in children] if they present no serious predictable risk to their health, if they are of value for people of the same age with the same disease or handicap, and if they cannot be carried out in any other way'' (9).

How much the investigator can properly rely on the consent of the parent or guardian is uncertain in United Kingdom law; the position in France seems to be more explicit and reliable. Consent depends on the information given to the parents, the understanding of the parents or guardians, and, in the ethical context, the voluntary nature of any decision taken. In some instances, the French Pediatric Association felt that it would be important to protect children from the susceptibility of their parents to coercion by virtue of a dependent relationship with the investigator or someone else with a vested interest in the study or from inducement by expenses and the prospect of free food or diapers or both (9). Often such parents, if poorly educated, would not be able to participate reliably in a study and would be unreliable recruits.

The design of readable and understandable consent and information sheets is not easy. Some ethics committees evaluate the reading age required to understand information and consent forms. It seems best to aim for a required reading age of 16, but many initial drafts of forms require a higher degree of literacy, so it is not surprising that 80% of adult patients think that consent forms are to protect the investigators rather than to inform participants (19).

Another means of capitalizing on infant feeding trials has been proposed, in that information derived from such studies could be used further by establishing a means by which the original records, with protection of the participants' confidentiality (EU Principle 9), could be preserved in anonymized data archives that could subsequently be made publicly available for analysis (13). In the long term, this would allow the possible pooling of data from a number of trials, for example, for the study of long-term effects of early infant nutrition or the detection of adverse effects that would not necessarily be discovered by small studies.

The next two principles need no comment in the context of this chapter.

EU PRINCIPLE 6

- Pregnant or nursing women may not undergo medical research in which their health and/or that of the child would not benefit directly unless this research is aimed at benefiting other women and children who are in the same position, and the same scientific results cannot be obtained by research on women who are not pregnant or nursing.

EU PRINCIPLE 7

- Patients deprived of liberty may not undergo medical research unless it is expected to produce a direct and significant benefit to their health.

EU PRINCIPLE 8

- In an emergency situation, notwithstanding Principle 3, if a patient is unable to give prior consent, medical research can be carried out only when the following conditions are fulfilled:
  - •• The research must have been planned to be carried out in the emergency in question;
  - •• The systematic research plan must have been approved by an ethics committee;
  - •• The research must be intended for the direct health benefit of the patient.

This has most relevance in clinical nutritional problems and particularly with preterm low-birth-weight neonates. The guidelines are clear. It has been opined that ''informed consent from poorly educated parents entering a complex trial in stressful conditions is a sham'' (20). Ethics committees have been criticized for not appreciating the practicalities of doing trials in acutely sick newborns by insisting that investigators get the customary consent from parents, who might, however, be too upset to make clear judgments and who are particularly vulnerable to persuasion by investigators. It has been proposed that the Zelen procedure be followed in such circumstances, in that only parents whose infants were being given the novel intervention should be informed of the trial and asked for consent (21). This raises issues that are relevant to quantitative research in infant nutrition in nonacute as well as in acute circumstances.

Principles 9 to 11 cover issues that have been considered elsewhere.

EU PRINCIPLE 9

- Any information of a personal nature obtained during medical research should be treated as confidential.

EU PRINCIPLE 10

- Medical research may not be carried out unless satisfactory evidence as to its safety for the person undergoing research is furnished.

EU PRINCIPLE 11

- Medical research that is not in accordance with scientific criteria in its design and cannot answer the questions posed is unacceptable even if the way it is to be carried out poses no risk to the person undergoing research.

EU PRINCIPLE 12

- Medical research must be carried out under the responsibility of a doctor or person who exercises full clinical responsibility and who possesses appropriate knowledge and qualifications to meet any clinical contingency.

- The responsible doctor or other person referred to in the preceding paragraph should enjoy full professional independence and should have the power to stop the research at any time.

The competence and resources of the researchers are crucial to assessing the balance between risk and benefit of studies. In this respect, the Loi Huriet specifies that trials should be conducted "under the direction of a physician with appropriate experience, under material and technical conditions adapted to the trial and compatible with the strict scientific requirements for the safety of the persons participating in it" (9). These are reasonable specifications for the safe conduct of research (EU Principle 10). An absolute need for a physician to be in charge is questionable. Clearly, the expertise of the investigator is crucial to the assessment of the risk/benefit ratio, but the need for a medical qualification has to be gauged against the nature of the study and the risks involved.

To further guarantee or monitor the risk/benefit ratio, the possibility of unpredicted adverse outcomes should be addressed by clinical monitoring of all participants and perhaps by arranging independent scrutiny of study volunteers and of accumulating data, not only for adverse effects but also for beneficial effects, either of which could justify an early termination of the trial. In some circumstances it could be in the investigator's and sponsor's interests to use such a process.

EU PRINCIPLE 13

- Potential subjects of medical research should not be offered any inducement that compromises free consent. Persons undergoing medical research should not gain any financial benefit. However, expenses and any financial loss may be refunded, and in appropriate cases a modest allowance may be given for any inconvenience inherent in the medical research.
- If the person undergoing research is legally incapacitated, his legal representatives should not receive any form of remuneration whatever except for the refund of expenses.

The Committee of Nutrition of the French Pediatric Association was concerned that the selection for studies of children from poorly educated and economically disadvantaged families presented dangers in recruitment and declared that "one can only subscribe to the concept that studies carried out in children from deprived communities and who are not free to decide should be vigorously rejected, except if the disorder or disease to be combated exists only in those communities." One can sympathize totally with this viewpoint, but at the same time it is necessary to appreciate that some studies, such as the nutritional assessment of modifications of infant formulas, might need to be performed on representative populations.

In addition to inducements to participants' parents, the financial basis of studies and potential inducements for the investigators should be declared to ethics committees (22). It has been queried whether or not *per capita* payments for participation in pharmaceutical studies are ethically acceptable. In the development of infant formulas, there is a need to use multicenter studies and *pro rata* payments to accelerate the completion of studies. If this form of research funding were to be regarded as unethical, then the development of formulas or work to establish new information on infants and children with specific nutritional metabolic requirements would be seriously hampered.

EU PRINCIPLE 14

- Persons undergoing medical research and/or their dependents should be compensated for injury and loss caused by the medical research.
- Where there is no existing system providing compensation for the persons concerned, states should ensure that sufficient guarantees for such compensation are provided.
- Terms and conditions that exclude or limit, in advance, compensation to the victim should be considered to be null and void.

Trials should be covered by a contract between the sponsors and investigators defining the aims, methodology, and conditions of the trial, the outcomes to be expected, and the way the results are to be used. All studies should have adequate indemnity and insurance coverage, and ethics committees would be expected to check this on behalf of the subjects (1). The sponsors and investigators need to be insured, as does any participating health facility. An amendment to the Loi Huriet in 1991 enforced these provisions in France, and that law also makes it clear that the sponsor is responsible for ensuring that the trial conforms with the law (1,9).

EU PRINCIPLE 15

- All proposed medical research plans should be the subject of an ethical examination by an independent and multidisciplinary committee.

Ethical examination not only protects the children; it also protect the researcher, the sponsor, and the agency responsible for the location where the research takes place. The work of research ethics committees is increasingly demanding and responsible, and their competence and composition are of considerable concern (23). Most European guidelines expect committees to have a representative range of ages, members of both sexes, some lay members who are not directly associated with the health profession (ideally clergymen, lawyers, philosophers, and so on), a statistician, and members of health professions—certainly family practitioners, clinicians with experience in research, and if possible nurses and community caregivers. Most committees would not necessarily have a pediatrician and would therefore need to seek appropriate expert advice. There is a variable degree of autonomy for committees in EU member states (1), but some have national specialist ethics boards for central reference or review processes to smooth out variance between committees and to minimize inconsistency, particularly when this affects multicenter studies (24).

Another responsibility befalling ethics committees is to follow up the outcomes of previously approved proposals to ensure that the results are made available publicly (when possible), even if a study is abandoned (25). An applicant's record in this respect should be examined in any new proposal. The view that not to publish or use results is unethical is becoming widely appreciated (26).

EU PRINCIPLE 16

• Any medical research that is unplanned, or contrary to any of the preceding principles, or in any other way contrary to ethics or law, or not in accordance with scientific methods in its design and unable to answer the questions posed should be prohibited or, if it has already begun, stopped or revised, even if it poses no risk to the person(s) undergoing the research.

Pertinent issues arising from this principle have already been discussed. The ability of ethics committees to impose or propose sanctions if the guidelines are violated varies among the European member states. In France, there are penalties for those who transgress the guidelines: provision is made for imprisonment for periods of 6 months to 3 years and for fines of FF12,000 to FF200,000. Elsewhere, moral opprobium, rejection of work for publication, the displeasure of sponsors, and the possibility of not being able to get any subsequent research proposals approved or funded are considered sufficient disincentives to breaking guidelines. Additionally, anyone who might wish to pursue any miscreants for unethical conduct of clinical trials could initiate legal proceedings on the basis of assault or the breaking of contracts.

REFERENCES

1. Bankowski Z,, Levine RJ, eds. *Ethics and research on human subjects: international guidelines.* Geneva: Council of International Organisations of Medical Sciences, 1993.
2. Beecher HK. Ethics and clinical research. *N Engl J Med* 1966;274:1354–1360.
3. Pappworth MH. *Human guinea pigs.* London: Routledge and Kegan Paul, 1967.
4. Medical Research Council. *The ethical conduct of research on children.* London: MRC, 1993.
5. Department of Health and Social Security. *Supervision of the ethics of clinical research investigations and fetal research.* London: HSC (15) 153 DHSS, 1975.
6. Royal College of Physicians. *Research involving patients. Report of a Working Group.* London: Author, 1990.
7. World Medical Association. *Declaration of Helsinki. Recommendations guiding physicians in biomedical research involving human subjects.* Helsinki: Author, 1995.
8. British Paediatric Association. Guidelines to aid ethical committees considering research involving children. *Arch Dis Child* 1980;55:75–77.
9. Société française de pédiatrie. Comité de nutrition. Expérimentation et essais cliniques en nutrition pédiatrique. Obligations légales et règles de bonne conduite. *Arch Pédiatr* 1996;3:3–8.
10. Council of Europe. *Committee of Ministers Recommendation NoR(90)3 on Medical Research on Human Subjects.* Brussels: European Community, 1990.
11. Department of Health. *Report on Health and Social Subjects No. 47: Guidelines on the Nutritional Assessment of Infant Formulas.* London: HMSO, 1996.

12. Altman DG. The scandal of poor medical research. *Br Med J* 1994;308:283–284.
13. Oman AD. Checklists for review articles. *Br Med J* 1995;309:648–651.
14. Cook RJ, Sackett DL. The number needed to treat: a clinically useful measure of treatment effect. *Br Med J* 1995;310:452–454.
15. Jones B, Jarvis P, Lewis JA, Ebbutt AF. Trials to assess equivalence: the importance of rigorous methods. *Br Med J* 1996;313:36–39.
16. Gillon R. Recruitment for clinical trials: the need for public–professional co-operation. *J Med Ethics* 1994;20:3–4.
17. Thornton H. Clinical trials—a brave new partnership? *J Med Ethics* 1994;20:19–22.
18. Baum M. Clinical trials—a brave new partnership: a response to Mrs. Thornton. *J Med Ethics* 1994; 20:23–25.
19. Wager E, Tooley PJH, Emanuel MB, Wood SF. Get patients consent to enter clinical trials. *Br Med J* 1995;311:734–737.
20. Editorial. Your baby is in a trial. *Lancet* 1995;345:805–806.
21. Zelen M. A new design for randomised controlled trials. *N Engl J Med* 1979;300:1242–1245.
22. Evered D, Lazar P. Misconduct in medical research. *Lancet* 1995;345:1161–1162.
23. Harris J. The ethics of National Ethics Committees. *J R Coll Physicians Lond* 1994;28:323–324.
24. Harries UJ, Fentem PH, Tuxworth W, Hoinville GW. Local research ethics committees—widely differing responses to a national survey protocol. *J R Coll Physicians Lond* 1994;28:150–154.
25. Delamothe T. Whose data are they anyway? *Br Med J* 1996;312:1241–1242.
26. Pearn J. Publication: an ethical imperative. *Br Med J* 1995;310: 1313–1315.

DISCUSSION

Dr. Perman: Could you comment on the ethics of the sponsor wishing to review a manuscript prior to publication and perhaps engendering some censorship of the data and the nature in which they are going to be reported?

Dr. Aggett: If a study is done according to ethical review, then I think that if the sponsor did wish to exercise interference, it should be referred back to the appropriate ethics committee. In France, the law states there should be a specified contract between the researcher and the sponsor, and I think this type of contract could actually specify whether or not the company can censor the results. I don't think any academic institute or research body in the United Kingdom or elsewhere would accept a contract that allowed the sponsor subsequently to exercise interference or censorship.

Dr. Steenhout: I would like to ask a question concerning the independence of the ethics committee. When you submit a protocol to an ethics committee, you must put the name of the investigator and the name of the sponsor. When I see the composition of some ethics committees in Europe, I am apprehensive about their independence. I would like to ask this: don't you think that the names of the investigator and the sponsor should be withheld from the ethics committee, particularly in view of the fact that such committees may include a philosopher or a priest? And would it not be better if the ethics committee has the right to follow the outcome of the study later, especially in relation to ensuring the publication of all the results, even in the case of negative studies.

Dr. Aggett: Your second question is easier: yes, I think you are right. How one actually implements it, and how one provides the ethics committee with sanctions if data or papers are not published, is another issue. But it is becoming increasingly regarded as unethical not to publish data: results must be publicized in some form or another. When it comes to the independence of the ethics committee, I think there are times when the committee does need to know who is doing the study and to have some idea about the skills of the investigators, and they do also need to know the sponsorship of the studies. I cannot really sense what your anxiety here might be, but I think there are difficulties with the perceived expertise of ethics committees, and if that is a problem, then the resort that is available in many places now is national central referral committees or, in some cases, professional committees, and by professional, I mean ethics committees for psychiatrists, psychologists, pediatricians, and so on.

Dr. Rey: I am not in favor of a sort of blank proposal by a scientist to an ethics committee. I think that the ethics committee has a duty to discuss the project with the applicant and to try to improve his knowledge of ethics, if necessary, and also to understand fully what are the objectives of the research. As a member of the ethics committee of the Hôpital des Enfants Malades in Paris for many years, we were very pleased to discuss with the applicants the reason why they were proposing a particular piece of research. In France, it is mandatory to consult the ethics committee, but it is not mandatory to follow the opinion of the committee. So, the ethics committee has no right to follow the research afterwards. Finally, I think it is very important for pediatricians to discuss among themselves what ethical rules they should propose to the community. Sometimes, there is no pediatrician in an ethics committee, although it is important to have one when the committee is consulted on research involving children.

Dr. Aggett: I agree with all this. I think it might well be that we are going to see the evolution in due course of specialist ethics committees, committees for pediatric proposals, geriatric proposals, and so on, where people have appropriate expertise and experience in the requirements for the study, can understand the background science, and know whether the study is worthwhile, and then of course, be able to understand better the benefit and risk in the perspective of their own experience and that of the applicants.

Dr. Haschke: I am probably touching a critical issue: validation studies that are carried out by drug companies and infant-food-producing companies are probably unethical because "bad science is unethical." How can we eliminate the need for these validation studies? In the United States, there are clear rules—no validation studies are necessary. But in Europe, it is different: one country might not accept what has been shown in another country. It is even worse in Asia, and there might be also a problem in South America. How can we come to an agreement that we can at least reduce the number of these validation studies?

Dr. Aggett: What do you mean by a validation study?

Dr. Haschke: Once the drug has been tested in a clinical trial and has been found to be effective, it is probably allowed in that country, but in order for it to be marketed in other countries, further studies are required by their respective governments, although the data are already available from an adequate clinical trial. It may be that the companies are doing this for marketing reasons, but it is "bad science."

Dr. Aggett: I agree, that type of validation study is wrong: the science need not necessarily be bad, but it may be, as you imply, repetitious and not needed. Marketing trials, or marketing exercises masquerading as acceptability studies, are probably unethical.

Dr. Guesry: Although I agree with the principle that dictated your answer, I think we have to realize the implications of such an answer. We know that certain countries and certain governments are very protectionist. We also know that many prescribers of drugs or new foods are also protectionist. If we fulfill the rule and don't duplicate studies in other countries, this has at least two consequences and probably many others. If the study has been done in another country, then that means that the children in the protectionist country will not be able to benefit from new drugs or new formulas, and this may be detrimental. If we say, all right, in that circumstance, we will have to do all the research in the protectionist country, this means that scientists in other countries will be deprived of the possibility of doing research.

So, I would like more reflection on this issue. It is not simple, and a fast answer may not be the right one.

Dr. Aggett: My answer was an answer to the ethical aspect. I think your position is perfectly understandable from the point of view of the company; the solution, perhaps, lies elsewhere.

Dr. Lucas: There is an issue that I would very much like to hear some discussion on from both sides of the Atlantic, and that is to do with the complete reporting of clinical trials. Quite often in an ethically approved trial, a large amount of information is collected, and that is presented very selectively in scientific papers, often to prove a particular point, but the information that isn't reported is often very important from the point of view of the interpretation by others of the trial results, and it also could be an important basis for future work by other people. Now there would be a case for the complete results of an ethically approved trial being written up somewhere, and the important question here is one of property rights—whether the results of an ethically approved trial are in fact in the public domain, or whether the unpublished results remain the property of the investigators. Do you have any comments on that?

Dr. Aggett: We (i.e., Dr. Lucas, our colleagues in the U.K. COMA Panel, and I) have been involved in discussions on just this aspect. My personal view is that if people go to the trouble of collecting all this type of information, then it should be publicly available. If it is sensitive inasmuch as it relates to commercial development of a product, then indeed, there could be a 1-year, 2-year, or 3-year moratorium on this information. But one of the things that the United Kingdom Committee was considering was that it would be advantageous to have all such data deposited in a publicly available data base to which people could have access. We felt that all the data that have been acquired really should be in the public domain, and it should be part of the responsibilities of an ethics committee or review process to ensure that this actually happens by coming back to the investigators 2 or 3 years after the study. The other issue is whether or not one needs to find some way of being able to pool such data to offer the benefits of a much bigger data base for unanticipated benefits or unanticipated adverse effects, either in the 2 or 3 years after the study or, with our current interest, in the long-term effects of infant nutrition, for retrospective exploration, say, in 10, 20, or 30 years' time. To achieve this, we felt that there could well be an opportunity for basic core protocols to be undertaken giving guidance on how essential data, such as standardized weight, height, and length measurements, should be measured and recorded. In general, I think that once the data are collected, they should be in the public domain.

Dr. Lozoff: The comment was made that it is bad science to redo something that has already been done, but in fact, it takes a lot of studies to know something for certain. I was curious about what criteria you had in mind when you said that something was known. To give an example, the trials related to iron deficiency and development have produced different results. If you concluded that the effect was known after the first one, you would never have had the subsequent ones.

Dr. Aggett: I think it is the principle that is important. One doesn't go ahead and replicate a study with all its mistakes. I am sure that if one did look at various intervention studies, one would find anxieties with social class matching groups, how interventions are given, and things like that, and I am sure that one could find ways of benefiting from the previous study to improve on it. I think that is what is happening with the evolution of our understanding of iron intervention. So, I think that with good insight and with the right sort of people looking at the data, the appropriate questions can be generated.

Dr. Lozoff: My second question relates to your criterion of the purely breast-fed baby. I am a very strong advocate of breast-feeding, and I have some concern about the basis for that recommendation. I am aware of only one study on feeding practices that had a worldwide sample of nonindustrialized societies. In that study, one-third of such societies started supplementary foods before 1 month, one-third started between 1 and 6 months, and only one-third waited until after 6 months (1). So, if you were to establish a criterion of 4 to 6 months of pure breast-feeding, you would not be in harmony with practice in many traditional societies throughout the world.

Dr. Aggett: It sometimes worries me that we are perhaps being tempted to be politically correct in this context. The point that we are trying to make is that to come up with a product that matches human breast milk is not in itself a satisfactory outcome. What we would like to see would be that such a product has the long-term benefits observed in the baby fed predominantly on human breast milk. I don't think we are trying to be too pretentious about the ideal of breast-feeding.

Dr. Aeschlimann: I have to stress the distinction between collective ethics and individual ethics. This is an old debate published about 8 years ago in the *British Medical Journal* by Stuart Pocock (2), describing trials stopping early because one treatment was showing up as better than another. This was fine as far as individual ethics are concerned, and they stopped the trial, but then, what should the doctor do? The trial was not significant enough, and they continued to use the less-effective treatment. I think that ethics committees must continue to see what happens during the course of a trial and to give clear guidelines on whether to stop or not. Failure to achieve clear results is itself unethical.

Dr. Aggett: It is difficult to comment without knowing either the nature of the condition or the associated variables or even the number of subjects or even if the appropriate outcome is defined for that sort of study. But I agree that there is a risk that on occasions, the null hypothesis might be rejected because of inadequate numbers, and that was the point I was trying to make earlier, that if one has a well-characterized outcome, one should then be able to determine the numbers required to test the hypothesis.

Dr. Roche: In the context of randomized clinical trials, I want to make a heretical suggestion. Many companies producing infant formulas have been conducting clinical trials for years in very large numbers and have large amounts of control data. From an ethical point of view, is there any advantage in these accumulated control data? Can they be used to replace random controls in future clinical trials?

Dr. Aggett: They have not been fed the same product. If the basic formulas have different compositions, then one obviously cannot use the data as a reference.

Dr. Roche: Commonly, they have been collected in a standardized fashion and using the same reference formula. That is not the problem.

Dr. Aggett: It is an interesting suggestion.

Dr. Perman: Dr. Lucas, did you have a comment on the use of controls from previous studies?

Dr. Lucas: My own view is that while the sort of data that you are suggesting would be of immense value as reference data, and really should be available, they could never supplant a randomized clinical trial. The circumstances would always be different—you would never be able to use somebody else's control data to get at causation. So, I think it would be valuable, but it is not a complete answer.

Dr. Uauy: I would like to bring up the issue of double standards. We put all the burden of the ethics of medical acts on research activities, but the uncertainties linked with therapy in everyday practice are actually not subjected to ethical review.

Dr. Aggett: I think there is a lot of truth in that. Our experience is, for example, that something like 60% of the drugs we use are not licensed to be used in pediatric age groups.

I do not know the precise figure. There is a total lack of appropriate study or understanding of these problems.

Dr. Kauffman: It turns out that for the past 30 years in the United States, 80% of the drugs marketed have a labeling disclaimer for use in children; that is, only 20% of the drugs are approved for children. I have argued in a number of publications over the past 20 years that this is unethical. What is ethical is to do the studies under carefully controlled clinical trials in children under the purview of ethics committees; what is unethical is to continue this practice in medicine that is perpetuated by our regulatory system under which children are not given the same protection as their adult counterparts. So, I agree with you, it is a major problem.

Dr. Lucas: Unfortunately, the problem is one of industrial sponsorship: pediatric pharmacology is not very remunerative, and unless funding came from research bodies, it is very unlikely that clinical trials will be done.

REFERENCES

1. Nerlove S. Women's workload and infant feeding practices: a relationship with demographic implications. *Ethnology* 1974;13:207–214.
2. Pocock SJ. When to stop a clinical trial. *Br Med J* 1992;305:235–240.

Clinical Trials in Infant Nutrition, edited by
Jay A. Perman and Jean Rey, Nestlé Nutrition
Workshop Series, Vol. 40, Nestec Ltd.,
Vevey/Lippincott-Raven Publishers,
Philadelphia © 1998.

Ethical Aspects of Nutritional Research on Infants in Developing Countries

Roger G. Whitehead

MRC Dunn Nutrition Centre, Cambridge, United Kingdom

The primary ethical standards and procedures governing all types of research on human beings in developing countries must be exactly the same as for those of any more privileged country. At the same time, it should also be accepted, willingly, that extra requirements may well have to be imposed by ethics committees on investigators in developing countries, particularly where the proposed study is going to be carried out in a country with a general lack of elementary but essential clinical facilities. There are also likely to be sensitivities arising from social or religious traditions or even of a quasipolitical nature that need to be accommodated before any study is permissible. In this rather personal perspective on the subject, I contrast the basic rules and guidelines that my own institute has to follow before undertaking nutritional studies in the United Kingdom with how these are likely to be extended for any proposed studies, primarily in Africa but also in Asia. I quote extensively from the Medical Research Council's own policy document, *The Ethical Conduct of Research on Children* (1), as well as the British Paediatric Association's *Guidelines for the Conduct of Medical Research Involving Children* (2) and the MRC Dunn Nutrition Centre's specific ethical requirements for nutritional studies on children (3).

When I first started working for the Medical Research Council (MRC) in Uganda in 1959, there was no ethics committee as we would now know it. Ethical considerations were the direct responsibility of the senior clinician. There are no grounds for believing that this arrangement led to unwise investigations, but it did place a major onus of responsibility on this one individual. A few years later, the Ministry of Health in Uganda began to insist that before any new study was started, specific written permission had first to be received from them. This was mainly to protect Ugandan people, especially women and children, from visiting investigators who wanted to carry out nutritional and other types of human and clinical studies on malnourished people and who may have been resident in the country for only a very short time. Although most of these external research teams were highly principled, there were a few that accepted little or no responsibility for subsequent essential health action revealed by their findings once they had left the country. A closely associated safeguard was that before any work was published, the manuscript of the paper had also to be presented to the Ministry for prior approval. This was not an attempt at censorship, although it was occasionally interpreted as such. The Uganda Ministry of Health was very concerned that it should always be aware of research results that might have potential practical implications in terms of clinical and public health planning.

I return to this principle later, but it does raise another key issue when one considers the ethics of carrying out nutritional studies on anyone, but especially on babies and young children in developing countries. Approval should depend on the assurance that the work is of sufficient quality that it is publishable in a first-class, internationally available biomedical journal and that the results will be made readily available to all who need the information.

By 1973, when we began carrying out nutritional research in The Gambia, West Africa, the principles contained in the World Medical Association's Declaration of Helsinki, initially produced in 1964 and subsequently revised in 1975 and then again in 1983 and 1989 (4), were routinely being applied by all the research establishments of the British Medical Research Council. It was still essential, however, for the MRC and their colleagues in the Gambian Ministry of Health to go through the procedures of setting up an appropriate and properly constituted local, but nationally approved, ethics committee in that country, consisting not only of competent professionals but also of other responsible persons who would reflect and accurately represent the attitudes and sensitivities of the population at large.

THERAPEUTIC AND NONTHERAPEUTIC RESEARCH

In the British Medical Research Council's general guidelines, *The Ethical Conduct of Research on Children,* a distinction is made between therapeutic and nontherapeutic research. In the case of nutritional research on children in developing countries, in whom the incidence of subclinical and even clinically overt malnutrition may be high, the two entities are not, however, always readily distinguishable. The general term "therapeutic research" is used by the MRC to cover not only investigations into the treatment of disease but also its prevention, for example by vaccination, as well as research on diagnostic procedures. The MRC recognized that nontherapeutic research in children raises more complex ethical issues. A differentiation between therapeutic and nontherapeutic research was considered necessary because rather different safeguards and guidelines might be relevant in the two circumstances. It was concluded that children included in nontherapeutic research should be placed at no more than negligible risk of harm. Negligible risk was interpreted as meaning that the risks of harm anticipated in the proposed research are no greater, considering the probability and magnitude of physiological or psychological harm or discomfort, than those ordinarily encountered in daily life or during the performance of routine physical or psychological examination or tests. Although these sentiments are a valuable universal guide, it needs to be recognized that for those children living in developing countries, the risks encountered in daily life may well be much greater than we would ever wish to see introduced into a scientific study!

CONSENT

Age is an important consideration in defining when a child might be considered old enough to give informed consent. An important factor that may modify any age guideline is the degree of understanding a young person can be expected to have, taking into account both individual intellectual development and educational opportunity. Where the child is aged 16 years or over, the legal position in relation to therapeutic research is relatively straightforward in England and Wales. Under British family law, a person of the age of 16 has full power to consent to medical treatment, and because therapeutic research is closely linked to medical treatment, the MRC considers that such a person can reasonably consent to participate in this type of research. There is a rider, however, that is of considerable relevance insofar as the Third World is concerned. In circumstances where there is doubt as to the degree of understanding shown by a young person, it may be good professional practice to explain the research proposals primarily to the parents and to give any objections they have considerable weight. I believe this proviso to be especially important within the context of research in developing countries. Although this volume is primarily concerned with research into infants, nutritional research relevant to the health of the baby once he or she is born at least starts *in utero* and arguably before that, with the nutritional status of the mother. Many women in developing countries have their first babies by the time they are 16 or younger. Furthermore, educational opportunities and the broadening of experience that this should bring have often not been made available to them. Thus, not only the husband but, because of the closely knit family structure, also the young mother's parents and parents-in-law must also be considered key people to approach when obtaining consent to participate in a study.

In the United Kingdom, the situation for children under the age of 16 is less well defined: there are no strict legal precedents, but the MRC believes that the minor's capacity to make his or her own decisions depends on having sufficient understanding and intelligence to make the decision rather than on any judicially fixed age limit. When a child under 16 years of age is competent to consent, however, it is usually considered wise to complement this with the approval of the child's parents or guardian. It goes without saying that in developing countries, such a dual approach should be adopted only with the utmost care. The views of the parent are likely to be seen by them as paramount.

In the case of nontherapeutic research, the situation is somewhat different because that actual child may not receive any direct benefit from the research. For children aged between 8 and 16 years, the regulations set by the Dunn Nutrition Centre's own ethics committee, but based on general MRC guidance, are that although the child may not be able to understand the reasons for carrying out the investigation, any discomfort likely to occur during the course of the study should be fully explained both to the child and to the parents, and their consent must be obtained. For younger children, interpreted by us as meaning 3 to 7 years, it has to be assumed that, although they might be aware of what is happening to them, it is unreasonable to expect that child to understand the nature or scientific purpose of the investigation, and thus, it is impossible for them to give informed consent. Nevertheless, such children should receive an adequate explanation of the procedure, and their confidence be won. Furthermore, they should always be allowed to refuse to participate. Although these guidelines are primarily intended for the United Kingdom, the principles involved are not totally inappropriate for less scientifically aware communities. The critical issue has to be the ability of the person under investigation to understand.

In any community, children under the age of 2 cannot be expected to give any form of consent or voluntarily to cooperate in any procedure. In this case, the responsibility lies with the parents, who must be fully informed.

RISKS AND BENEFITS

Theoretical risks, however remote in practice, exist with many procedures, and this is most noticeably the case where the taking of blood is a necessary part of the research. We work under the general principle that investigations of this nature should not be undertaken on children if it is possible to do the studies in adults. It needs to be emphasized that, however necessary the taking of blood from children is, it is going to be a somewhat traumatic procedure, particularly for the younger ones. Care must always be exercised to reduce this trauma to an absolute minimum. Many of the risks to the child of blood taking are psychological in nature, arising from the perception that it is going to be a painful procedure. Transient pain of a venipuncture can be eliminated by the use of local anesthetic creams, and our investigators are encouraged to use such local anesthetics where possible. It is critically important that blood should be taken by venipuncture from children only by a wholly competent and experienced person. For this reason, and because of the special cultural sensitivities that can be associated with the taking of blood, in our work in Africa, this procedure is restricted to someone medically qualified or a senior qualified nurse. Additionally, we make a point of always having one of the parents present at the time of blood taking, so they are fully aware of what is going on. It is also essential that a mechanism be arranged for dealing with emotional disturbances that might occur during such a procedure.

RISK/BENEFIT BALANCE

The benefits that might accrue from the application of any investigative procedure in a study on young children will depend on the scientific nature of the proposals. Risks have to be balanced against benefits. One essential consideration for ethics committees must be the originality and scientific soundness of the work. In our United Kingdom–based work, a critical assessment of the scientific quality and unique importance of any proposed study is made directly by the ethics committee itself. In situations where the experimental design appears flawed, or where there is doubt as to any new scientific benefit that might accrue, approval to carry out the study will always be withheld until the ethics committee has been satisfied completely on this score. In The Gambia, all proposed work from anywhere in the world has first to go before the scientific coordination committee for an appraisal of the scientific content of the proposal. This occurs before the ethics committee ever sees the proposal and reevaluates it from the point of view of safety and other ethical issues.

These safeguards are crucial not only where pain and other possible traumas are involved. Studies can be invasive to privacy and happiness without blood being taken or some other physiological technique being performed. It is difficult to carry out a study without interfering with a person's normal life style. This can be justified only if soundly based scientific investigations are going to be carried out that will give rise to important and unique new knowledge.

The primary intention of all medical research must be to acquire knowledge that will be of benefit to humanity as a whole, both to those who are already ill and incapacitated and to those who might become so. Because therapeutic research is directly concerned with treatment, it can offer the potential of immediate benefit to the participant. By its very nature, the direct benefit to individual participants of nontherapeutic research is likely either to be long delayed or possibly never to occur at all. Nevertheless, for research in young children, it is essential that a case be made in the ethics proposal to justify the overall investigation on these grounds. The justification must also establish that this potential is relevant to the particular health problems of the community under investigation. Almost never can a study on one community of young children be justified on the basis that it could benefit another. I emphasize this because it is not unheard of for less scrupulous investigators to attempt studies in a developing country because they fear ethics permission will not be granted in their own country.

THE LEGAL POSITION

Quite apart from any international or national guidelines on the practice of ethics committees and their interpretation and amplification by local bodies, it needs to be recognized that, in many countries, there is actual legislation covering the protection of young people's rights. These differ significantly from country to country, however. For example, even within the United Kingdom, the law dealing with such things is not the same in England and Wales as it is in Scotland. With therapeutic research involving a child aged 16 or over in England and Wales, and also Northern Ireland, this individual has full rights in law to consent to medical treatment. In Scotland, however, the position depends on whether the child has reached the age of 12 in the case of a girl or 14 in the case of a boy. Below these ages, the children, known in law as "pupils," specifically cannot themselves give valid consent; it must be given on their behalf by a parent or registered guardian. Above these ages, up to 18, the child is called a "minor," and his or her ability to give valid consent depends on whether the child has sufficient understanding to consent. In other words, in Scotland, reaching the age of 16 has no legal significance in terms of medical procedures, whether in the form of treatment or otherwise. In the case of nontherapeutic research, there is no precise age in England, Wales, and Northern Ireland below which a child acquires legal capacity to consent. In Scotland, the position is the same as for therapeutic research.

Integrating national legal considerations with internationally accepted ethics guidelines is especially important when scientists from culturally different countries plan to carry out investigations elsewhere, particularly in a developing country. In the case of a previously dependent country, case law is often based on legal decisions made in the courts of the old colonial master, but it is no longer wise to take this for granted. New situations have required new attitudes and independent rulings.

For expatriate investigators, it is clearly not sufficient to depend on ethics approval from one's own institute's committee, as the members are unlikely to be fully conversant with the relevant legal requirements in the overseas country. It is essential that investigators work through a properly constituted local ethics committee. If one does not exist already, arguably it is the responsibility of those wishing to carry out research in that country to encourage and help with the setting up of such a committee before proceeding. This will inevitably cause delays and require much consultation with the appropriate authorities, but it will be worth it in the end. If it appears that such a venture is not going to be worth the time and effort involved, the only wise course of action is for the study to be carried out elsewhere.

In the case of the MRC's work in The Gambia, all ethics approval has to be obtained from such a local committee, although it does have access to a corresponding national body established by the Council in the United Kingdom, where advice on particularly complex investigative procedures can be obtained. In other countries where we have carried out investigations, it has been considered a wise precaution for the project to receive ethics approval both from the overseas committee and from our own in Cambridge. Issues that may not seem significant on the spot can worry a British ethics committee, and it is important that any differences be resolved before the investigation goes ahead.

It always needs to be borne in mind that ethics approval is necessary not only for the protection of the individual being studied but also for safeguarding the investigator from problems that might occur during the course of a study but that could not possibly have been foreseen beforehand.

STUDIES IN COUNTRIES IN WHICH THERE IS NOT A COMPREHENSIVE HEALTH SERVICE

In countries like the United Kingdom, it is reasonably easy to make appropriate arrangements before a study is begun about what will be done if—particularly in the case of nontherapeutic studies—something is discovered that is undesirable and that should be put right by appropriate treatment. Usually, it is sufficient for the subject's doctor to be informed in confidence about the matter so that he or she can take the appropriate professional action.

In many Third World countries, especially in rural areas, it is likely that no adequate facility of this nature exists. In my opinion, it then becomes the direct responsibility of the investigators themselves to do something effective about the problem. Identified serious health problems in a given individual just cannot be ignored by blaming any lack of action on shortcomings of the local health services. Knowledge brings with it responsibilities; these have to be accepted by the investigator.

Satisfying such exacting requirements is not easy for investigators contemplating only short-term studies. Where this proves impossible, however, it is far better for that research team to set up in a country where there is a more adequate indigenous health service rather than to compromise on essential ethical principles. Many years ago, I attended a meeting that established my philosophy toward community studies from then on. This meeting resolved to act by the general slogan "No survey without service." It has not been an easy path to follow, especially in an age when money is short and every attempt is made to cut budgets. In The Gambia, we operate our own rural clinic, which provides general-practitioner-type health care not only to the mothers and children we study but to the rest of their immediate family as well. When hospital admission is necessary, the patient can be transported to the coast where appropriate additional facilities exist. I regard this as an essential expense, and I have had to fight off any attempt at economies on this facility. Not only is this ethically essential from my point of view, but I believe this commitment has added greatly to the willing collaboration offered by the people we study.

STUDIES USING NOVEL TECHNIQUES

There is an understandable coolness on the part of most ethics committees in developing countries toward investigations that employ novel techniques, which may be seen as not having yet stood the test of time. An equivalent concern occurs when the use of experimental therapeutic procedures is contemplated, especially if these techniques or procedures have not already been fully tested in industrialized countries. There is the predictable suspicion that people in developing countries might be used as guinea pigs. Such a concern is especially valid where studies in young children, especially infants, are being contemplated.

Wherever possible, such studies should not be initiated in such an environment. Clearly, this is not always going to be possible, especially when one is dealing with a disease that is rare or totally absent in more affluent countries. But such instances are likely to be the exception rather than the rule. A good example of the principle of first using a technique in one's own country is afforded by the use of stable isotopes to measure important nutritional variables such as the breast milk intake of young babies and also their total energy expenditure and hence their energy requirements. Such data are notoriously difficult to obtain accurately in free-living subjects using classical procedures, and stable-isotope techniques offered us a novel way of doing so. We did not contemplate this, however, before our techniques had been evaluated and approved for use on British mothers and their babies. Furthermore, the Gambian ethics committee requested special reassurance from their British counterpart on this point.

PAYMENT OF VOLUNTEERS

Anywhere in the world, whether or not to pay volunteers is always a controversial decision. In the case of adults, and where people have to contribute a significant proportion of their time, it is sometimes appropriate to compensate them for out-of-pocket expenses. In developing countries, however, where salaries can be ridiculously low, decisions about compensation take on a quite different perspective. The danger is that people may be persuaded to participate in a scientific study, against their better judgment, just to make money. This is clearly ethically undesirable, and furthermore, it can place investigators in the invidious position of having to defend themselves against the accusation that they are exploiting impoverished subjects for their own research purposes.

In cases in which a parent is taking responsibility for consenting to investigations on behalf of a third person, it can never be justifiable to offer payment. With infants and very young children, this is especially true. As indicated above, in developing countries, the pressures on parents to obtain money from any source are especially great, and the rule of no payment should be sacrosanct.

The application of any rule, however, has to be tempered with common sense. In the Dunn Nutrition Centre's own scientific research on babies and young children, a major feature is the prospective longitudinal nature of our investigations. The same child may be seen and routinely examined clinically every month for at least the first 2 years of life as well as every time he or she falls ill. Furthermore, frequent visits may be made by the investigators to the subject's actual home. Inevitably, in such circumstances a close and friendly relationship becomes established. The wish to give the type of small gift, such as a child's dress or a ball, that one would normally give to someone you know well on birthdays, at Christmas, or on some other major feast day is understandable and is done. Nevertheless, it is highly desirable that the principle of giving such gifts should be contained in any ethical proposal, so that the authorizing committee can consider its appropriateness and provide general approval for such practices. Even at these times, I believe, however, that the gift should never be in the form of cash.

INVESTIGATIONS INVOLVING CONTROL SUBJECTS

In most investigations where an intervention is involved, it is necessary to have a control population that receives some form of placebo. Often this has to be given blind by a third person so that the scientist making assessments is unaware of exactly which type of subject he is investigating. This is to avoid the risk of any subconscious bias being introduced in favor of the hypothesis being tested. I have met, however, some reluctance on the part of ethics committees in developing countries to accept the concept of control groups. This is especially so with undernutrition or malnutrition, and where the subjects are known to be consuming levels of total food or specific nutrients that fall well below internationally set dietary guidelines. The argument is made that it is unethical to deliberately deny some subjects extra nutrients that would bring their intakes up to internationally suggested levels of adequacy when the investigators are in possession of the funds and facilities to do so. It is also pointed out that the administration of a placebo frequently costs at least as much as the experimental nutritional supplement.

Such arguments are not easy to counter. Clearly, where there are specific clinical signs of nutritional deficiency or malfunction, the placebo approach will rarely be justifiable. In other instances, however—and a good example in Africa would be calcium nutrition, where the functional consequences of a lifetime's intake of only a fraction of the internationally recommended dietary allowance does not seem to lead to any overt disorder—such an approach is more justifiable. Here, the target is to determine whether or not the redeployment of scarce financial resources at a national level, so that intakes of all the population could be brought up to theoretically derived reference levels of requirement, would be cost-effective.

It is important, however, for investigators working in developing countries to be conscious of sensitivities surrounding the selection of control groups. At the very least, it should be demonstrated to the ethics committee that every subject should benefit from participation, to a greater or lesser extent, including the control group. The improved well-being of no individual can be ignored just for the sake of scientific progress. This provides another sound justification for insisting on the philosophy of ''no survey without service'' and the provision in The Gambia by the Dunn Nutrition Centre and the MRC of the general medical care service for all persons participating in our studies.

In conclusion, an ethics committee should not be regarded as a necessary nuisance. It is there to protect us all: the subject being studied and, equally, the investigator. A good ethics committee can add greatly to the quality of research.

REFERENCES

1. Medical Research Council. *The ethical conduct of research on children. MRC Ethics Series.* London: Medical Research Council, 1991:1–21.
2. British Paediatric Association. *Guidelines for the ethical conduct of medical research involving children.* London: British Paediatric Association, 1992:1–18.
3. MRC Dunn Nutrition Unit. *Guidelines for research in children. Photocopied document produced by the ethics committee.* Cambridge: MRC Dunn Nutrition Unit, 1979, revised 1990.
4. World Medical Association. *The Declaration of Helsinki.* Ferney-Voltaire, France: The Association, 1964, revised 1975, 1983, 1989.

DISCUSSION

Dr. Perman: It does appear that certain ethical principles are universally applicable. That probably is not surprising, but at the same time, review of proposed research needs to be held at the local level. But is it appropriate for us to assume that these standards are universally applicable, or is this a view that certain of us are projecting on the world?

Dr. Kauffman: You have made a great issue of the generalizable applicability of the principles, and I certainly agree with those, but how close to this ideal do you think we are? I often hear statements to the effect that we are not going to site this study in the United States because we don't think we can do it here; we are going to do it in country X instead.

Dr. Whitehead: In The Gambia, we do receive requests of this type from people wanting to do research that they are unable to get approved at home. This is usually research on novel products—drugs or appliances—prompted by the belief that the standards are going to be very much lower. But I can only caution once again that ethics committees are there to protect the investigator as well as the person being investigated, and I think that anybody who is tempted to become involved in research like that ought to think twice. The only way to cover yourself is to make certain that you do research in countries where an appropriate ethical procedure has been established. If you want to work in a country over an extended period of time, and you believe that an adequate ethical procedure does not exist within that country, then the wisest thing to do is to set to work and help to organize one.

Dr. Uauy: Although practices vary from country to country, in many countries, it is the senior administrator—the head of service or the head of the hospital—who decides on his own whether a study is ethical or unethical. Sometimes, the study may touch on the administrator's own interests, so there is always the potential for conflict of interest. I think it is very important to give out the message that this group at least considers that even for occasional research, you should go through due processes, and the due process involves people from outside making the ethical decisions, as we have pointed out here. We must reinforce the need to apply the same standards everywhere, although practical aspects of this may vary. But I would like to point out one issue relating to research in developing countries. In many cases in such countries, the control group is in fact a deficient group in one or more nutrients, something that would not be ethical in developed countries, where the standards of care are so much higher. In a developing country, this may provide precisely the test situation that will eventually allow improvement to be obtained.

Dr. Whitehead: I agree with you completely, though the people who are making that sort of decision should be the indigenous people of the country. I think that the duty of the investigator is to spell out the potential benefits of the study in a simple way that does not require a huge knowledge of science.

Dr. Aggett: I believe that The Gambia is a Muslim country. Could you comment on how ethics committees operate in the context of different cultural and religious backgrounds. Are the guidelines similar, or are there other considerations that influence the way that people can get consent?

Dr. Whitehead: In the ethics committee, the great majority of people are Gambians, and most of them are Muslim. We also have an Imam, a religious leader, on this committee, just as in the United Kingdom, we would always try to have a priest of some description in ethics committees. Otherwise, the membership covers a wide cross-section of the educated population. The ethics committee insists that the procedures to be undertaken in the study can be described to the elders of the community in which you are going to work, and their approval will be necessary before any individual person or any individual family is approached.

Dr. Fisberg: I am a member of the ethics committee of my university, and some of my colleagues have raised an interesting concern. What happens when a child suffers as the result of ethical malpractice in a study that was approved by the ethics committee? Should the ethics committee be responsible because they gave approval to the study?

Dr. Whitehead: This is a very important point. I think that the fact that the study was approved by the ethics committee should afford the researcher some protection against litigation, but I would be interested to know what others think.

Dr. Lucas: In the West, as I understand it, ethics committees have no real legal standing, and, therefore, they do not protect investigators from any kind of liability. But in developing countries, the problem is that the legal systems for protecting subjects who have been damaged in research may not be adequate, and that puts an onus on investigators to set in motion some sort of compensatory maneuver if a subject is in fact damaged as a result of research.

Dr. Whitehead: Except I believe in France, it is absolutely true that strictly speaking ethics committees have no legal authority. But I think in terms of defense in circumstances such as we were discussing, the person would definitely be culpable if he was acting outside the limits of the ethics approval given. My guess is that, in the United Kingdom, if such an issue came before the courts, the judgment would be very important because it would then become part of common law, but I don't know whether or not that has ever been an issue.

Dr. Aggett: I think that increasingly people responsible for sites where research is performed—in the United Kingdom, this would be hospital authorities, etc.—are insisting that research does not take place on that site unless there is adequate insurance indemnity coverage. But there is still no regulatory enforcement for this sort of approach.

Dr. Klish: Our ethics committee, and I would assume most committees in the United States, put in a disclaimer as part of the informed consent, saying that neither the committee nor the institution is responsible for any injury that may occur as a result of the investigations. This has been routine. The problem with that is that this has never been challenged in the courts. Until that happens, at least in the Texas courts, we continue to assume that this is a legitimate way of absolving our responsibility.

Dr. Kauffman: There were two cases 15 or 20 years ago in the state of California where the Investigational Review Board (IRB) and investigator were sued, but I don't remember the outcome. I think one of them was successful. Regardless of what we do in terms of the indemnification statement, in the United States at least, there is always a lawyer who will take the case.

Dr. Whitehead: I am not aware of this disclaimer. Dr. Lucas or Dr. Clarke, are you aware of this within the United Kingdom?

Dr. Lucas: I am not aware of any equivalent, but I have always been told by ethics committees that they don't have legal standing and that one has to take out one's own insurance. This is precisely the point that concerns me, and there isn't this kind of cover for research in developing countries. That is an issue that needs to be thought about specifically.

Dr. Clarke: It has been explained already that, in the United Kingdom, the ethics committees that form the generality of the discussion today are within the National Health Service (NHS), and that is a cover-all service where all the drug work takes place and most of the clinical services. There are, however, difficulties with regard to doing research on food, because most of the studies are not done within the NHS. I don't know of a case where the ethics committee has had to hold itself responsible for a decision that might have been questioned subsequently, but with regard to foods, we are on new ground.

Dr. Meng: In China, money for research has to be used to provide payment to local government and to the doctors involved, but it is not thought advisable to give money to the participants. Many participants will not fully understand the aims of the research and will think that the money is being given because harm is going to be done to their children. This is not helpful for research. I agree with Dr. Whitehead that only small gifts should be given to the participants.

Dr. Whitehead: What you say is very interesting. I think one clearly has to be flexible. I don't think that the basic principles behind the Helsinki guidelines are so rigid that flexibility doesn't exist. What I am cautioning investigators—and we are all investigators—is not to allow ourselves to become involved in research that we could not justify to our own colleagues on the grounds of the Helsinki guidelines. Where flexibility has been exercised, investigators must convince themselves that that flexibility is justifiable and must feel able to discuss that flexibility and justify it with their colleagues. What we must not do is to allow ourselves to become involved in research in a place just because it creates opportunities that we would not have in countries where the laws and regulations are much more stringent.

Dr. Sorensen: If you have a project approved by the Gambian ethics committee, do you still request parallel approval by your home committee?

Dr. Whitehead: The Gambian ethics committee itself requested that all ethical submissions go first to them and to no other ethics committee. This principle had to be agreed to before research went ahead. However, in the great majority of the other work that we do, approval is sought from two ethics committees. For example, the work in China went to our own ethics committee and to an ethics committee established in China. In this particular case, our own ethics committee was rather concerned about one aspect of the work that did not worry the Chinese.

Dr. Sorensen: What is your policy regarding overhead that you might get for a project? I am concerned that very often, research is performed largely for the economic benefit of the developed country, and very little of that technology or money actually gets to the developing country.

Dr. Whitehead: In our own work in The Gambia, the overhead goes into running the medical service. We run a general clinic that operates twice every day, and when there are emergencies, those are also dealt with. The costs involved in emergency hospital admission are paid for by the Medical Research Council. Some overhead also goes toward the Ph.D. or M.Sc. training that we provide for Gambians, but mainly, it goes to help run the medical service.

Dr. Lozoff: On the issue of protection of human subjects in the United States, no federal dollar can be spent overseas unless it is cleared by OPRR (Office of Protection from Research Risks) regardless of what the local wishes are. Secondly, again for federally supported research for the United States, the direct cost of research in the foreign countries cannot get overhead, and that is written in regulations; but the direct costs of research—the grant support and the maintenance of rooms, and all of those things that we cannot charge in the United States—in fact, can be charged as direct costs in the developing country or in the foreign country that cannot receive overhead.

The question I want to ask is concerned with this guideline of what would be the ordinary life experiences of children. Several people have noted that this is a potentially hazardous standard. Whether it be in our inner cities or in war-torn countries around the world or in countries where there are very poor human rights records, the local standard may leave the door wide open for really quite unethical conduct. I wonder how you establish guidelines when local standards, which should be helpful, are really not protecting children.

Dr. Whitehead: I was not trying to minimize the importance of ethics committees in Europe or in the United States in terms of Third World research--obviously they are important. The main thing I was trying to get across was that it is absolutely essential also to put the project through a local ethics committee. What does one do when prevailing circumstances are unsatisfactory? It might be that your study wouldn't be looked on as hazardous within such circumstances, where if the same study were carried out elsewhere in the world, say in the United States, it would be looked on as hazardous. When investigators realize that this conflict exists, they should perhaps point out to the local ethics committee that this is a significant problem. Otherwise, that investigator is going to place himself at risk in colleagues' eyes if he is seen to be carrying out research that could not be carried out at home.

Dr. van't Hof: I have been cooperating for many years with countries in Africa. Their researchers come to The Netherlands, and we discuss their projects and send them back to collect the data. I completely agree with you that the basic rules are the same the world over, but in applying these rules, I have often encountered difficulties. For example, one of the best-known basic rules is the rule of informed consent, which we must always obtain in The Netherlands. In African countries, however, consent is never really informed. What is your opinion about that problem?

Dr. Whitehead: It is quite likely that the level of understanding of women living in the villages where we work in the west of Gambia would be similar to that of an equivalent group of women living in Cambridge. But there is also a procedure that you have to go through in explaining the project to the elders of the village and getting their basic approval, telling them what the advantages will be, both to them and to the sum of knowledge. From a public relations point of view, it is absolutely essential, and also just common courtesy, that if you are going to work with people over an extended period of time, you should take them into your confidence and try to explain things. I think people do appreciate this, even if they don't always have the basic background knowledge to be able to assimilate everything. People can understand most things if you really make an effort. We become very worried when people come for very short periods of time to do a study, and where this courtesy has not been exercised.

Clinical Trials in Infant Nutrition, edited by
Jay A. Perman and Jean Rey, Nestlé Nutrition
Workshop Series, Vol. 40, Nestec Ltd.,
Vevey/Lippincott-Raven Publishers,
Philadelphia © 1998.

Statistical Analysis: Significance Tests Versus Confidence Intervals

Stephen D. Walter

*Department of Clinical Epidemiology and Biostatistics, McMaster University,
Hamilton, Ontario, Canada*

Most research articles published in biomedical journals involve some form of statistical analysis, but there has been concern from some journal editors on the quality of statistical reporting. Reviews of published reports have shown a disturbingly high frequency of methodologic errors, some serious enough to jeopardize the study findings (1–4). One of the traditional methods of analysis, the statistical significance test, has come under particular scrutiny. Frequent misinterpretation of significance test p values has led to calls to discontinue this type of analysis (5,6).

Elsewhere, editorial requirements have been modified to encourage authors to present their data in other ways. For instance, the Vancouver style guidelines, to which many journals now adhere, advise potential authors on the use of statistical methods as follows:

> Describe statistical methods with enough detail to enable a knowledgeable reader with access to the original data to verify the reported results. When possible, quantify findings and present them with appropriate indicators of measurement error or uncertainty (such as confidence intervals). Avoid sole reliance on statistical hypothesis testing, such as the use of p values, which fails to convey important quantitative information (7).

Other journals have been even more explicit. The *British Medical Journal* (8) suggests that one should calculate confidence intervals "whenever the data warrant this approach," and the *American Journal of Public Health* states that "... use of confidence intervals would avoid many of the fallacies stemming from a mechanical use of significance testing" (9).

In this chapter, I review some of the key points involved in the significance testing and estimation (confidence interval) approaches to data analysis and also comment briefly on some other possible methodologies. Although I must confess to having no expertise in nutrition (except perhaps as a gastronome), I first put my work in the context of this conference by describing the current patterns of reporting statistical data in some major nutrition journals. Finally, we may reach some conclusions about the use of these and other methods in the future.

TABLE 1. *Summary of methods of statistical reporting by 100 research papers in four nutrition journals*

Type of report	Am J Clin Nutr		J Nutr		J Nutr Educ		Nutr Research	
	Abstract	Text	Abstract	Text	Abstract	Text	Abstract	Text
Nothing	9	0	7	1	11	3	10	1
p-Value only	7	1	14	2	13	4	10	5
SD only	0	0	0	0	0	1	1	1
SE only	1	0	0	0	0	2	0	1
p and SD	1	2	2	9	1	8	1	8
p and SE	7	21	2	13	0	5	3	9
p and CI	0	1	0	0	0	2	0	0
TOTAL	25	25	25	25	25	25	25	25

SD: Standard Deviation; SE: Standard Error; CI: Confidence Interval

CURRENT PATTERNS OF REPORTING STATISTICAL DATA IN NUTRITION JOURNALS

Recent issues of four journals *(American Journal of Clinical Nutrition, Journal of Nutrition, Journal of Nutrition Education,* and *Nutrition Research)* were examined to determine the current practices in reporting statistical data and findings. Original research articles in each journal were read and classified according to whether p values, standard deviations (SD), standard errors (SE), or confidence intervals (CI) were shown (a) in the abstract or (b) anywhere else in the main text. Articles were sampled by working back from the last 1995 issue of each journal until 25 articles from each journal had been obtained.

Table 1 indicates the distribution of statistical reporting by journal, and Table 2 shows the results for all journals combined, comparing the information shown in the abstract and text. Some type of statistical reporting occurred in almost all (96%) the articles. In the abstracts, the most common reporting method (44% of papers) was of p values only. (Papers that implicitly described significance tests, by using the term significant or similar, were also included in this category.) In the text, the

TABLE 2. *Type of statistical reporting in abstract and text of 100 nutrition research papers*

Abstract	Text				Total
	Nothing	p-Value only	SD/SE/CI	p and SD/SE/CI	
Nothing	4	6	5	22	37
p-Value only	1	5	0	38	44
SD/SE/CI	0	1	0	1	2
p and SD/SE/CI	0	0	0	17	17
Total	5	12	5	78	100

most common methods were combinations of *p* values with SEs (48%) or SDs (27%). Only three articles reported CIs, so it appears that the Vancouver guidelines have had little impact on nutrition research in this regard.

Papers that report at most *only p* values (16%, from Table 2) do not allow the reader to assess the variability in the component data or the magnitude or precision of outcome assessments. In some of these papers, it was not even possible to discern the *direction* of the treatment difference when only a "statistically significant difference" was declared; here, even the most basic scientific requirement of the reader is hidden.

The papers that show SDs and SEs do indeed present measures of variability in the data, but it is still difficult or impossible for the reader to construct CIs. Although the SD describes the variation between individual study subjects, and the SE describes the variation of quantities such as study group means, additional computation is required to understand the precision of study group means and (most importantly) of differences between study groups. In many cases, calculation of a CI for the treatment effect is impossible because of the nonavailability of the pertinent error variance, for instance, for within-subject changes in the response variable, or for the error in an analysis of variance (ANOVA) table.

Some differences between journals may be discerned in Table 1, and these may reflect their editorial instructions to authors, the relevant sections of which are:

> ... When possible, quantify findings and present them with appropriate indicators of measurement error or uncertainty (such as confidence intervals, SDs or SEMs). .... Avoid value judgments about the results of statistical analyses with phrases like "nearly reached significance." [*Am J Clin Nutr*] (10)

> ... describe statistical tests and indicate the probability level (*p*) at which differences were considered significant. .... In tables and figures, present the results of the analysis in the body or use superscripts to indicate significant differences .... Provide the appropriate statistics of variability. [*J Nutr*] (11).

> Methods section ... should describe ... statistical methods in enough detail for general readers to clearly understand what was done. [*J Nutr Educ*] (12)

> Tests of statistical significance should be identified. Statements about statistical significance of results should be accompanied by indications of the level of significance. [*Nutr Res*] (13)

The *American Journal of Clinical Nutrition* statement is similar to the Vancouver guidelines but specifically mentions SDs and SEMs as well as CIs. The *Journal of Nutrition* and *Nutrition Research* emphasize significance testing, whereas the *Journal of Nutrition Education* is the least directive. There are corresponding differences in the reporting patterns, especially in the abstracts, which might be regarded as containing the most important features of a study. For example, *p*-value-only abstracts were least common in the *American Journal of Clinical Nutrition* and most common in the *Journal of Nutrition*.

We turn now to a brief review of the methodologic features of the significance testing and CI methods of reporting. Further discussion of many of these points is available elsewhere (14).

SUMMARY OF TESTING AND ESTIMATION APPROACHES TO STATISTICAL REPORTING

Significance Testing

Significance testing is founded in the theory developed by R.A. Fisher, known today as the frequentist method. One begins by specifying a *null hypothesis* (H_0) to be tested, most usually that two (or more) study groups are equivalent in some respect. For example, consider a sample survey to assess the nutritional status of certain ethnic communities. It is intended to compare two ethnic groups and age subgroups with respect to nutritional energy intake using a 3-day dietary history (see, for example, ref. 15). Here we might define H_0: $\mu_1 = \mu_2$, where μ_1 and μ_2 are the mean daily energy intakes in the two ethnic groups.

One can define rejection regions for H_0 according to the possible outcomes in the study data actually observed. For instance, in the example, one might assume that the measured energy intake is normally distributed with a SD of approximately 500 kcal (15); the rejection regions are then defined as corresponding to differences in the group means for which the z statistic

$$z = \frac{\bar{x}_1 - \bar{x}_2}{\sigma \sqrt{\dfrac{1}{n_1} + \dfrac{1}{n_2}}}$$

exceeds 1.96 in absolute value. The numerator of z represents the sample mean difference for the outcome variable, n_1 and n_2 are the group sample sizes, and $\sigma = 500$ is the SD. Rejection will occur 5% of the time if H_0 is actually true. (The factor 1.96 is chosen so as to have 2.5% in each tail of the standard normal distribution.) Note that the use of 95% intervals in particular is somewhat arbitrary. The designated error rate (5% here) is denoted generally by α.

If $|z| > 1.96$, we conclude that the result is sufficiently different from what would be expected under H_0, that we reject H_0 and declare a significant effect. Alternatively, if $|z| \leq 1.96$, we fail to reject H_0. It is helpful to report the actual p value rather than simply whether or not it achieves significance.

If H_0 is really true and we reject it, a type I error occurs; we then falsely declare a difference between the study groups when none actually exists. In contrast, if H_0 is actually false and we fail to reject it, we make a type II error; we infer no significant difference when one actually exists (see Fig. 1). Of course, omniscience would be required to say for certain if H_0 is true or false, but if we were omniscient, we would not need to carry out the study in the first place.

Similar methods have been developed for many types of data. For instance, we can use the t test if the SD of the outcome above is not known, or the χ^2 test for the difference between two sample proportions p_1 and p_2. The main distinction between methods is in the mathematical form of the test statistic, but the underlying principles are the same.

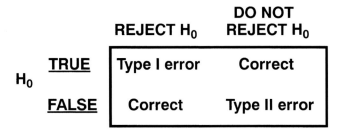

Ho: Null hypothesis

FIG. 1. Possible results from a statistical significance test. If H_0 is true but a significant result occurs, and H_0 is rejected, a chance type I error occurs. If H_0 is false but it is not rejected, a type II error occurs; lack of significance may sometimes be because of inadequate power.

Confidence Intervals

Instead of using the dimensionless probability metric, confidence intervals focus on the original units of measurement. For instance, in the previous example, suppose the mean difference in energy intake between ethnic groups is 320 kcal. One can also give the 95% confidence interval for the mean difference, such as (110, 530) kcal.

Calculation of the CI also involves distributional assumptions concerning the outcome variable; for instance, we might assume a normal distribution with either known or unknown SD. The CI is then constructed to have a probability of $1 - \alpha$ of including the true value in the population. Again, the conventional 95% level is arbitrary, and larger or smaller values may be selected, depending on the circumstances.

ISSUES ARISING IN THE INTERPRETATION OF SIGNIFICANCE TEST RESULTS

Significant/Not Significant Dichotomy

A frequent objection to the use of significance tests arises from a tendency to regard their results in a binary way, with "significant" results being equated to "important" and "not significant" to "unimportant." Thus, results that give $p < 0.05$ are viewed in one way, whereas p values just slightly larger than this magic value are disregarded.

This unfortunate tendency arises because of a failure to recognize the process that generates the p value. Nonsignificant results might occur, for instance, because of small sample sizes or measurement error. Unless the observations are extremely precise, small studies have little chance of rejecting H_0 except if the true effect is very large. The probability of rejection for nonnull cases is the "power" of the study, a feature that should be taken into account when the study is designed.

In a well-known paper, Freiman *et al.* (16) reported that a high percentage of clinical trials published with apparently "negative" results were underpowered because of small sample sizes and unlikely to detect even quite large treatment effects. Many studies were not inconsistent with substantial treatment effects. Thus, rather than concluding "no treatment effect," such studies might better be summarized in terms of their consistency with a range of possible effect sizes, including some with clinically meaningful implications.

Suppose Study A of a dietary modification program is intended to increase the percentage intake of the recommended daily allowance (RDA) for calcium in inner-city children, and the goal is to increase this percentage on average by 10%, a value that has been determined to be the smallest improvement of practical or clinical interest. Suppose the mean and CI for the difference between intervention and control groups are 4% and (-7%, 15%), with $p = 0.23$ (see Fig. 2). We would conclude that the intervention has an average benefit of 4% of the RDA but with a CI that includes the null value of zero. The nonsignificant results are compatible with a range of effect sizes from 7% deficit to 15% improvement. Although the target 10% improvement has not been achieved, the CI includes that value, so the results are compatible with it.

Suppose that in Study B, with a larger sample, the mean is again 4%, but the CI is now (2%, 6%), and $p < 0.001$. The narrower CI reflects the greater precision afforded by the larger sample. In this case, the CI excludes the null value, and the

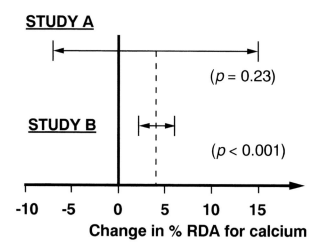

FIG. 2. Confidence intervals for two nutritional intervention studies. Study A has a nonsignificant mean effect size of 4%, with a wide CI that includes the null value of zero and the target value of 10% increase in % RDA for calcium. Study B has the same but significant mean effect size, with a narrow confidence interval that excludes both the null and target values.

finding is statistically highly significant. But the interval also excludes the target value of 10%, so one would conclude that the effect was less than effect sizes of any clinical interest.

The choices for α, sample size, and power can be formalized by considering the rates of type I and type II errors and their associated costs. For instance, one might imagine the costs of acting on a false-positive type I error from a nutritional intervention experiment with a statistically significant result. One might initiate nutritional intervention programs that have no actual benefit to participants, and further research would be required to eventually rescind the original result. On the other hand, a false-negative type II result might imply the abandonment of a beneficial intervention that happened not to give significant results in this study. The incorporation of such costing arguments into biomedical research would be difficult and would involve a level of formalism that does not currently exist in the way research studies are interpreted.

Misinterpretation of p Values

Many significance testers interpret the p value as the probability of having the right answer; for instance, if $p < 0.05$ in an experiment, they assert that there is a 95% probability that the experimental effect exists. This incorrect interpretation is widespread (5,6,17). The error in this interpretation is that it asserts an absolute (or unconditional) probability for the result, forgetting that the p value is calculated conditionally on H_0 assumed to be true. There may be little correspondence between the conditional and unconditional probabilities (18).

Substantive Versus Statistical Significance

Depending on the study sample sizes and the precision in the observations, one can obtain results that are discordant with respect to their statistical significance and their substantive impact. For instance, a study with very large sample sizes and precise observations is almost certain to declare statistical significance, even if the observed effect size is so small that it would be meaningless from a practical viewpoint (19,20). See Study B in Fig. 2 to illustrate this point.

The other type of discordance is where the results appear to be of interest to the investigator (substantively significant) but do not reach statistical significance. In the calcium example, results that showed a mean improvement of 25% of the RDA would be encouraging to the investigator because they exceeded the target of 10%, even if the effect was not statistically significant. A related concept is "data fragility," in which one considers the impact on interpretation of the results from the smallest possible change to the data (21,22).

The conclusion here is that one should not equate substantive and statistical significance. Again, this points to the deficiency of the p value as a measure of evidence from the study.

Significance Testing Versus Hypothesis Testing

Despite having proposed the 95% significance criterion himself, Fisher actually preferred to interpret p values in a flexible way. In contrast, the Neyman–Pearson philosophy of inference espouses a more formal decision-theoretic approach, involving testing of hypotheses rather than significance (23). Thus, whereas Fisher would use the observed p value as a guide to the importance of a study result, Neyman–Pearson adherents would limit themselves to declaring results "significant" or "not significant" at the chosen α level and would be indifferent, for instance, as to whether the actual p value was 0.04 or 0.0001. Paradoxically, it is the Neyman–Pearson philosophy that seems to have been more popular in the interpretation of biomedical research findings, even though the Fisherian approach is surely the preferred method in this context.

Logical Basis for Significance Tests

The p values are computed from the observed data, given an assumed null hypothesis H_0. The p value typically represents the tail area in the probability distribution for the data, given H_0, with the tail being defined as the set of outcomes that are as extreme as, or more extreme than, the outcome actually observed. (As we will see in a moment, even the definition of "extreme" is sometimes problematic.) The H_0 usually adopted assumes no difference between study groups.

A moment's thought reveals that H_0 is highly implausible. Even if an intervention does not produce a clinically meaningful impact, one still would not believe that the two study groups are exactly equivalent, as is required under H_0. Thus, the starting point for the significance test is inherently unpalatable from the scientific viewpoint. Furthermore, H_0 represents only the null situation (one that is of no scientific interest), and it does not directly consider any specific competing hypotheses. The alternative hypothesis, H_A, is usually framed so that there is some (unspecified) nonzero difference between the groups, for example, H_A: $\mu_E \neq \mu_C$.

A second difficulty is that the criterion for rejecting H_0 involves the probability of extreme values in the outcome distribution. These outcomes are not actually observed, and their relevance to what has been observed is questionable. This state of affairs has led a number of commentators to describe significance testing somewhat acerbically. Goodman and Royall (24) state: "The rarity of what we did see is assessed by combining it with the probability of results that didn't happen," and Jeffreys (25) indicates: "A hypothesis that may be true may be rejected because it has not predicted results which have not occurred."

Problems Defining Extremes

The possible study outcomes that are "more extreme" than the observed result are usually easy to define. For instance, if the observed difference between intervention and control groups with respect to daily energy intake is 320 kcal, then the more extreme results would be those with even larger differences.

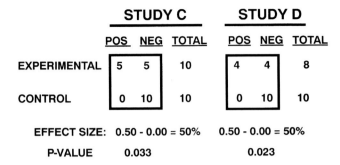

FIG. 3. Example of two studies in which a smaller sample size gives a more significant test result. Study D has a statistically more significant result than study C, even though it has a smaller sample size. The *p* values are from a two-sided Fisher's exact test. The outcome rates and the effect size are the same in both studies.

In a few cases, however, there are difficulties in defining the appropriate tail area for the test. For instance, consider the two study results in Fig. 3, showing the percentage of subjects who consume the RDA of fruit and vegetables in two experimental groups, with their associated *p* values from Fisher's exact test (26). In study C, the outcome rates are $p_E = 5/10$ and $p_C = 0/10$, giving a statistically significant result. In study D there are two fewer observations in the experimental group, but p_E is the same, at 50%. Despite having less data than before, and with identical outcome rates, Fisher's test in study D has a smaller *p* value. (The two-sided *p* values here are computed by adding the probabilities for all tables with probability no greater than the probability for the observed table.)

A second example makes a related point. For each of two studies, Fig. 4 shows the effect size $p_E - p_C$, and the *p* value from Fisher's test. The *p* value is smaller

STUDY E   STUDY F

	POS	NEG	TOTAL		POS	NEG	TOTAL
EXPERIMENTAL	15	5	20		18	2	20
CONTROL	1	4	5		2	3	5

EFFECT SIZE: 0.75 - 0.20 = 55%   0.90 - 0.40 = 50%

P-VALUE 0.0403   0.0377

FIG. 4. Example of two studies in which a smaller effect size gives a more significant test result. The experimental intervention in Study E has an effect size of 55%, larger than the effect size of 50% in Study F, yet Study F has the statistically more significant result (two-sided Fisher's exact test). Sample sizes are the same in both studies.

for study F, whereas study E has a larger effect size. Both studies have the same sample sizes. Thus, the more extreme findings are defined differently according to p value or effect size criteria, demonstrating that evidence on the effect size is not directly conveyed by the p value.

ISSUES ARISING IN THE INTERPRETATION OF CONFIDENCE INTERVALS

Misinterpretation of "Confidence"

A common error is to assert that because of the 95% confidence level, one is 95% certain that a CI contains the true parameter value or, equivalently, that there is a 95% probability of the interval containing the true value. This error arises from the common language interpretation of "confidence" and is similar to the misinterpretation of p values as absolute probabilities.

The confidence property is one of the method in general and not one possessed by specific intervals calculated from particular data. Indeed, once the data have been gathered and the CI calculated, the interval in truth either does or does not cover the true parameter value, so the coverage probability can only be 0 or 1. The confidence level applies to a series of repeated samples.

Identification of Plausible Parameter Values

One can claim 95% confidence for inclusion of the true parameter by the CI as a whole, but one cannot directly assert that values in the center of the interval are more likely than the values near the boundaries. To make such statements about particular parameter values, one must instead examine the likelihood function for the data, to develop likelihood ratios. This is not part of the methodology for frequentist CIs but is incorporated in the likelihood approach (24).

Use of CI as a Significance Test

Many readers of CIs will intuit a corresponding significance test by noting whether or not the null value of the parameter is included in the interval. Although this tactic does give a valid test, it ignores the additional information conveyed by the CI on the magnitude, direction, and precision of the effect estimate. The method also gives only a binary result to the implied test, that is, significant or not with the selected α error rate, and does not convey the exact p value.

OTHER POINTS AFFECTING BOTH SIGNIFICANCE TESTS AND CONFIDENCE INTERVALS

Nonstatistical Influences

It is important to remember that the nominal significance and confidence levels are typically based on numerous assumptions. For example, the *t* test assumes normality in the data. One also assumes that there is no selection bias in the sampling method, that there is no measurement bias, that there are no other confounding or interacting variables, and that the measurement errors are independent. Usually these assumptions are difficult to test, especially with limited data.

If any of these assumptions are violated, the validity of the analysis may be seriously in question. For example, if participants in a nutritional intervention study tended to drop out because of adverse side effects and were excluded from the analysis, a highly biased assessment of the treatment effect would occur.

Similar biases can emerge if the investigator manipulates the data in a variety of ways but reports only one final result. For instance, he might examine a wide variety of serum chemistry variables in study participants but report only the ones that seem to show positive effects of treatment. Similarly, one can try different categorizations of a continuous variable and report only the one that shows the greatest statistical significance (27). These forms of publication bias may be impossible to detect from the published study report.

These issues of bias are often forgotten when study findings are examined, but in fact they are probably the most important aspects of interpreting the data. In other words, one must be assured that these various issues of bias are taken into account before one can take the results of any statistical analysis literally.

Replication Paradox

Investigators who derive statistically significant results or reasonably narrow CIs from their data are usually encouraged, thinking that their scientific ideas have been vindicated. Surprisingly, however, even statistically significant findings are difficult to replicate. For instance, suppose one repeats a study that has given a *p* value just less than 0.05 (or equivalently one where the CI just excludes the null value), and for which the observed result (effect size) is exactly correct; it turns out that there is only a 50% chance that a new study will also give a significant result. Even if $p = 0.01$ in the first study (a highly significant result), there is only a 73% chance of significance (at the 5% level) in the replicate study (28).

This paradox is again rooted in the frequentist basis for the significance, and in particular a failure to distinguish between the pre-study α level and the *p* value from observed data. A corollary is that the average effect size observed in studies that produce statistical significance has to be considerably larger than the minimally significant difference.

The discrepancy between p values and lack of replicability again points to an inadequacy of the p value as a measure of support for the scientific hypothesis in question.

Consistency of Methods

The testing and estimation methods should be compatible, in the sense that if the test is significant, then the CI should exclude the null value. Occasionally, however, one may find discrepancies. An example is if Fisher's exact test is used for 2 2 table data, and a normal approximation is used to derive the CI for the odds ratio. The discrepancy can be resolved if the same distributional approach is used for both methods; so, for instance, an exact CI for the odds ratio will give results compatible with Fisher's test.

Equivalence Studies

Some trials are intended to demonstrate equivalence, rather than differences, between treatments. For instance, a new therapy may be thought to be as effective as a standard therapy, but at lower cost. In such cases, some modification is required to establish the appropriate null hypothesis and to correctly interpret CIs. The investigator defines a minimally important difference for the outcome, which is the smallest value that he would like to demonstrate, if it exists. Differences smaller than that would be clinically trivial, and the treatments would be regarded as equivalent. Accordingly, H_0 is now defined in terms of the (nonzero) minimally important difference.

One-Sided Versus Two-Sided Inference

If an investigator is interested in demonstrating effects in only one direction, then one-sided significance tests can be used. For instance, if he feels that an intervention can only improve outcomes, then he might use an alternative hypothesis such as H_A: $\mu_E > \mu_C$; then only positive effects of sufficient magnitude will lead to rejection of H_0. With a one-sided approach, smaller sample sizes are required for a given level of power.

The main objection to the one-sided method is that H_0 is not rejected if large differences occur in the opposite direction from that postulated by the investigator. Many observers feel that it is impossible always to predict the direction of study findings and that findings in the opposite direction from that postulated would be scientifically interesting and should not be ignored in the inferential process. Indeed, in some studies it might be unethical to ignore a contradictory finding.

Less well known is the option of one-sided confidence intervals. More generally, one can define test and estimation procedures with unequal but nonzero tail probabilities summing to α, for example 1% and 4%. There are examples of asymmetric CIs in bioavailability analysis (29) and of one-sided CIs in reliability estimation (30).

Other Issues

Space does not permit detailed discussion of several other methodologic points, such as allowance for multiple comparisons, sequential inference, and sample size calculations. Suffice it to say that although most of the literature on these points has been concerned with significance tests, there is a corresponding set of thinking for confidence intervals. For instance, one can base a sample size calculation on the expected width and coverage properties of a confidence interval rather than on the power of a significance test. Reformulation of such issues in terms of confidence intervals instead of significance tests may sometimes look appealing, but ultimately one should recognize that the same principles of the frequentist method still apply (31).

USE OF OTHER METHODS

As described earlier, there has been a move away from significance tests and toward greater emphasis on CIs in some areas of biomedical research. This focuses more clearly on the outcome in a scale that is relevant to the investigator; for example, one analyzes the data in units of energy intake rather than in the dimensionless probability metric.

Some methodologists have recommended the use of likelihood or Bayesian methods to replace the frequentist basis of both the testing and estimation approaches. Whereas the frequentist methods evaluate conditional probabilities of data given an assumed null hypothesis, likelihood methods instead evaluate the parameter space given the observed data. Likelihood provides direct comparisons (through likelihood ratios) of the support for competing scientific hypotheses, such as through the relative plausibility of various effect sizes, in a way that is not possible with tests or CIs. As data are accumulated, the likelihood method tends to add support to one hypothesis or another, so that the sample size becomes part of the measure of evidence. Likelihood methods will probably gain popularity as they become more familiar to applied scientists.

Bayesian methods are similar, except they require the specification of a prior distribution of belief about the parameter; Bayes' theorem is then used to evaluate the posterior distribution of the parameter, given the observed data. Bayesian methods are more controversial, mainly because of disagreement about how the prior distribution should be established.

CONCLUSIONS

We have seen that there are some basic problems of interpretation of p values, one of the traditional reporting mechanisms in biomedical research, including nutrition. Greater emphasis on the effect size by using confidence intervals may alleviate some of these difficulties and may make the statistical analysis more relevant to the applied investigator. Likelihood methods also hold promise in this direction for the future.

A role still remains for significance testing in many circumstances. For instance, some types of statistical analysis do not involve parameters directly, such as nonparametric rank analyses. Here, significance tests seem appropriate, whereas the use of CIs may be impossible or contrived. Significance tests also seem useful in complex analyses where construction of all the necessary CIs would be cumbersome; examples are the analysis of multidimensional contingency tables, multivariable regression modeling, and goodness-of-fit analyses. p values can also form a useful adjunct to CIs in some analyses (32).

Even if all the issues of statistical methodology could be resolved, little is known about the impact that the various forms of reporting have on readers. Some evidence suggests that readers can be influenced by certain features of graphic data presentation (33); also, the impact on clinicians by the same study results varies according to how they are presented numerically (34). At the moment, however, we have little idea how readers' belief in the validity of study findings is affected by p values versus confidence intervals or by other study features such as sample size or randomization.

Because, ultimately, the statistical analysis must be presented in concert with an underlying biological question, we need to achieve a better integration of the applied biological thinking and the statistical philosophy used to report the data. If this is successfully achieved, some of the mistakes and abuses of the past may be avoided.

REFERENCES

1. Schor S, Karten I. Statistical evaluation of medical journal manuscripts. *JAMA* 1966;195:145–150.
2. Altman DG. Statistics in medical journals: developments in the 1980s. *Stat Med* 1991;10:1897–1913.
3. White SJ. Statistical errors in papers in the *British Journal of Psychiatry. Br J Psychiatry* 1979;135: 336–342.
4. Gore SM, Jones IG, Rytter EC. Misuse of statistical methods: critical assessment of articles in *BMJ* from January to March 1976. *Br Med J* 1977;1:85–87.
5. Freeman PR. The role of *p* values in analysing trial results. *Stat Med* 1993;12:1443–1452.
6. Cohen J. The earth is round ($p < .05$). *Am Psychol* 1994;49:997–1003.
7. International Committee of Medical Journal Editors. Uniform requirements for manuscripts submitted to biomedical journals. *N Engl J Med* 1991;324:424–428.
8. Langman MJS. Towards estimation and confidence intervals [editorial]. *Br Med J* 1986;292:716.
9. Rothman KJ, Yankauer A. Editors' note. *Am J Public Health* 1986;76:587–588.
10. Editorial statement. Information for authors. *Am J Clin Nutr* 1995;61:166–170.
11. Editorial statement. Guide for authors. *J Nutr* 1995;125:1–9.
12. Editorial statement. Information for contributors. *J Nutr Educ* 1995;27:217–218.
13. Editorial statement. Instructions to authors. *Nutr Res* 1995;15(Dec):inside back cover.
14. Walter SD. Methods of reporting statistical results from medical research studies. *Am J Epidemiol* 1995;141:896–906.

15. Wu-Tso P, Yeh I, Tan CF. Comparisons of dietary intake in young and old Asian Americans. *Nutr Res* 1995;15:1445–1462.
16. Freiman JA, Chalmers TC, Smith H, Kuebler RR. The importance of beta, the type II error, and sample size in the design and interpretation of the randomized clinical trial. *N Engl J Med* 1978; 299:690–694.
17. Wulff HR, Anderson B, Brandenhoff P, Guttler F. What do doctors know about statistics? *Stat Med* 1987;6:3–10.
18. Wulff HR. Magic of *p* values [letter]. *Lancet* 1988;1:1398.
19. Gardner MJ, Altman DG. Confidence intervals rather than *p* values: estimation rather than hypothesis testing. *Br Med J* 1986;292:746–750.
20. Luus HG, Muller FO, Meyer BH. Statistical significance versus clinical relevance. Part II. The use and interpretation of confidence intervals. *S Afr Med J* 1989;76:626–629.
21. Feinstein AR. The unit fragility index: an additional appraisal of "statistical significance" for a contrast of two proportions. *J Clin Epidemiol* 1990;43:201–209.
22. Walter SD. Statistical significance and fragility criteria for assessing a difference in two proportions. *J Clin Epidemiol* 1991;44:1373–1378.
23. Goodman SN. *p* Values, hypothesis tests, and likelihood: implications for epidemiology of a neglected historical debate. *Am J Epidemiol* 1993;137:485–496.
24. Goodman SN, Royall R. Evidence and scientific research. *Am J Public Health* 1988;78:1568–1574.
25. Jeffreys H. *Theory of probability.* Oxford: Oxford University Press, 1961.
26. Fleiss JL. *Statistical methods for rates and proportions.* New York: John Wiley & Sons, 1981.
27. Altman DG, Lausen B, Sauerbrei W, *et al.* Dangers of using "optimal" cutpoints in the evaluation of prognostic factors. *J Natl Cancer Inst* 1994;86:829–835.
28. Goodman S. A comment on replication, *p* values, and evidence. *Stat Med* 1992;11:875–879.
29. Westlake WJ. Use of confidence intervals in analysis of comparative bioavailability trials. *J Pharm Sci* 1972;61:1340–1341.
30. Eliasciw M, Young SL, Woodbury MG, Fryday-Field K. Statistical methodology for the concurrent assessment of interrater and intrarater reliability: using goniometric measurements as an example. *Phys Ther* 1994;74:777–788.
31. Daly LE. Confidence intervals and sample sizes: don't throw out all your old sample size tables. *Br Med J* 1991;302:333–336.
32. Woolfson RF, Kleinman JC. Perspectives on statistical significance testing. *Annu Rev Public Health* 1989;10:423–440.
33. Walter SD. Visual and statistical assessment of spatial clustering in mapped data. *Stat Med* 1993; 12:1275–1291.
34. Forrow L, Taylor WC, Arnold RM. Absolutely relative: how research results are summarized can affect treatment decisions. *Am J Med* 1992;92:121–124.

DISCUSSION

Dr. Aggett: You have given us one-against-one types of comparisons. How does one use this approach in situations where we would traditionally be expected to use analysis of variance or other techniques? How does confidence interval reporting get used in these circumstances?

Dr. Walter: To take a simple example, if you had a one-way analysis of variance between different age groups in a study, for example, the significance testing route would allow you to first do an overall comparison to see if there are any differences between the groups and then, perhaps, to look at pairwise comparisons or other contrasts between the groups. There is a corresponding set of confidence intervals that you could construct to evaluate the mean difference between all the possible pairs of groups, and I think the same principles would apply about multiple significance testing versus multiple confidence intervals, for example.

Dr. Whitehead: Nutritional science is bedevilled by large studies in one community and equally large ones in another not giving the same answer on the basis of *p* values. I believe you indicated that if the *p* value is 0.05, there is a 50% chance of a replicate study coming up with the same positive finding, and if it is 0.01, there is a 73% chance. How widely known is this? Should it be more widely known that when somebody produces a public health intervention where the significance is, say, 0.05, then any repeat is only going to stand a 50% chance of coming up with the same answer statistically? If I have got this right, I think it is very important in terms of our understanding.

Dr. Walter: You have got it right and I don't think it is widely known. The calculation that I showed you is not original to me—there have been a number of articles about it, most particularly in the *British Medical Journal.* It is made on the assumption that the next person to do the replicate study is going to carry out that study with the same underlying difference in the means or the effect size, and with a study of exactly the same size, in other words, the same starting point as the original study. I think the trap that many people fall into with these *p* values—quite apart from the difficulty in replicating them—is that they will look only at the *p* values and say, ''Well, Jones's study was significant because his *p* value is less than 0.05, but Smith, who came along a year later, showed no significant effect,'' even though those results might be quite compatible when you look at the actual effect sizes. So in that way, particularly in the context of meta-analysis, people have proposed methods that have now become known as vote counting—so many positive and so many negative studies, according to the *p* values. I think this difficulty is probably better appreciated in the meta-analysis community than in the general community.

Dr. Guesry: When we do clinical studies in infants, we want to minimize the numbers involved, for many reasons—time, cost, limiting unnecessary studies, ethical reasons, and so on—and when we decide on the number of babies to be included in the study, taking into account the expected result and the standard deviation of what we know already, we have a tendency to overestimate the number of babies so as not to risk missing an important result. We have been told—and I don't know if this is true—that if we do intermediate analysis, we would have to increase the numbers by 50%. So why could we not use actuarial assessment of the results more often? This enables us to see when we have achieved a statistically significant result and that we can halt the study. What are the negative aspects of this technique?

Dr. Walter: To comment on your first remark, the problem that we have seen in many areas of the literature is not that people are using too many subjects but far too few. In fact, that is part of the rationale for meta-analyses, because you often find there have been a number of studies of intermediate or small size, none of which individually showed a significant effect, but that collectively may very well do so. Now, of course, as you add evidence—as you add further studies or further subjects—the *p* value will tend to get smaller: you tend to move further and further away from any null hypothesis, almost regardless of what it is, whether it is a zero null hypothesis or a nonzero one. So adding data makes the basic hypothesis that you are testing less plausible.

The rationale of the idea that you alluded to—that when you do an interim analysis, you are somehow penalized because you have to take more subjects—is that if you look at the data on multiple occasions, you have a greater chance of seeing a statistically significant result by chance. That is a difficulty that you have to live with if you are going to use the standard significance testing route. I don't think there is any way around that. It seems to me to be a very useful safeguard against early stopping of a trial, particularly if you can spend your type I error rate in the appropriate way. Often, of course, you arrange things so that the interim analysis is done with a very stringent type I error rate, perhaps at a level of 1% or less, so that most of the type I error rate is left to the final analysis.

On the other hand, if you go with likelihood methods, as I mentioned, the accumulation of evidence adds to one hypothesis or the other. It gradually draws you toward a conclusion, and within that framework, there is no penalty at all for looking on multiple occasions.

Dr. Lucas: If you calculate trial size at the beginning for, say, 80% power rather than for 50% power, so you have got twice as many subjects to start with, and you get a 5% significant result, is your calculation still true that 50% of subsequent studies will be negative; in other words, would you have expected on average better than a 5% significance result if you had calculated for 80% power and 5% significance.

Dr. Walter: The calculation I made assumed that the observed difference in the first study was absolutely right, and then, the replicate study has exactly the same size with the same underlying mean difference. So the power is not directly relevant; it is the same in both studies for the example I gave.

Dr. Lucas: Some people reduce sample size in their studies by using one-sided significance testing. Can you think of any legitimate reason for this? I have been brought up to believe that that is almost invariably a bad idea?

Dr. Walter: I have yet to be convinced of a situation where one-sided testing is very justifiable, unless scientifically you are completely uninterested in a result in the opposite direction from the one expected. If you can honestly say to yourself, "If it turns out that the two treatments are the other way round from the way I am expecting, I really don't care; it is the same as if there was no difference," then I think you could justify one-sided testing, but that is very much the exception. Actually, when you work out required sample sizes, going from one- to two-sided testing with everything else the same, the percentage increase in sample size is not that large.

Dr. Berlin: There is still a tendency in some journals to see *post hoc* power calculations: "We know the study was too small, and the only reason we didn't find a significant result was that the sample size was too small; here is the power of this study to detect the observed difference." What your 50% for $p = 0.05$ example shows is that when you observe a border-line statistically significant result in a study, if the study is repeated, you only have 50% power, even though what you just observed was a statistically significant result. So there is an inherent paradox that makes these *post hoc* power calculations meaningless. This is another argument in favor of confidence intervals rather than thinking strictly in terms of p values.

Dr. Walter: You can rationalize why the replication paradox works. Remember the scenario that I gave: the first study gives you a result that is exactly at the 5% significance level, and the second study is carried out under identical conditions; the truth is as observed in the first study. It is a 50–50 chance whether the result in the new study is greater than or less than the result in the first study—it is just random variation above and below that observed value. So that is where the 50% figure comes from, but it is a similar type of argument if you change the p value in the first study. Many people believe that if the p value is less than 0.01, the result is almost a certainty, but this turns out not to be true.

Dr. Aeschlimann: The main purpose of the confidence interval is, like p values, for posttrial calculations. We tend not to use pretrial calculations for study design and protocol writing. I think it is very important always to stress the medical and statistical hypothesis before the trial, not only for calculation of p values or confidence intervals but because you must check the hypothesis more precisely when you have expressed it before the trial, and I think all calculations done afterwards are only to prove the evidence. I think confidence intervals are the most useful for this. Most people have no hypothesis before a trial but many after it. If you have more than seven independent variables, you have a 50% chance that any positive result will be a chance finding. It is worth quoting Einstein, who said, "Investigators will have to focus more on scientific quality of the evidence and less on the statistical method of analysis and adjustment."

Dr. Walter: I agree, but I don't think that moving away from significance tests and doing everything by confidence intervals is going to solve the problem of multiple variables and multiple comparisons, because there is then a corresponding set of problems. People who are reporting using confidence intervals still have difficulty. They have a variety of intervals: some are wide, some are narrow, some are showing interesting results, others are not, and there is a lot of chance involved. I think what you said about defining all of this at the design stage—and specifically in the protocol—forms an enormous safeguard to the investigator because then, even if you find a somewhat surprising result, you can say, "This is what we were going to do at the outset."

It is interesting historically that this 5% significance rule—if it is a rule—actually came from R.A. Fisher, who was the inventor of many of the statistical methods that we use, and the way he wrote about significance testing was to emphasize that the *p* value should only be used as a guide, not as an absolute truth. I believe the 5% value was included only as an example because at that time, there were certain copyright restrictions that applied to the reproduction of the statistical tables for the *t* distribution, for instance, and so Fisher spoke about how one would use the 5% value as a guide, not as a method of formal decision making.

Dr. Uauy: There are massive amounts of data, especially with epidemiology–nutrition interactions, and we find a lot of problems in trying to make sense of these data. Can you comment on what we should be looking for with confidence intervals? I myself don't trust any odds ratios that are under 2. I see many studies where the magnitude of the effect of the odds is very small. Although they may be significant, you really wonder if this is a true effect. You find all sorts of interactions claimed by epidemiologists that really have very little biological basis unless you start speculating. Another issue is that you sometimes see ridiculous values, for example a ratio of 30 with a range of from 1.1 to 30.5, and that is supposed to mean something! I think we may be abusing odds ratios and confidence intervals, especially with epidemiologic data.

Dr. Walter: Some of the difficulties to which you refer come about because people are often looking at a lot of variables, so it is the same issue as multiple significance testing. I don't think it is important, however, whether one uses the odds ratio or some other measure, because the same principle applies. When you say that a result is statistically significant, but you don't believe it because it doesn't have a biological basis, that is reinforcing what we said earlier, that you have really got to integrate that biological thinking. If somebody is going to argue for a finding that seems implausible biologically, it would be much more convincing if they had the rationale worked out at the protocol stage rather than being just an incidental finding.

Dr. Roche: You have drawn attention to the limited replicability of *p* values. What about confidence intervals? Are they more replicable?

Dr. Walter: No, absolutely not. In fact, if you look at the confidence interval in the same way as significance testing, i.e., whether or not they exclude the null value, because of the consistency of a particular test with a particular confidence interval level, they will not be replicable. Even within the results portrayed by confidence intervals, you will see considerable variation in the width of those intervals from one study to the next.

Dr. Chouraqui: You can use *p* values and confidence intervals only if you assume that the data are of a normal distribution, and in most of the studies in nutrition, because of the small size of the samples, this is not the case. Do you think that then you can use a median instead of the mean, and what test do you use to prove that there is a significant difference?

Dr. Walter: You never prove there is significance! There either is or there isn't in a particular study, using the criterion (e.g., $p < 0.05$) to define significance.

The particular technical issue that you mentioned about an assumption that you have normal data when you use the *t* test was one of the things that I alluded to when describing the whole range of things that are in the background when you carry out a particular test. Thus, if you do a *t* test, and the data really are not normal, then the effects are sometimes a bit hard to predict. We do know that if you are comparing means in very large samples, you are all right because eventually the distribution of the sample mean will approach normality, even though you started out with observations that were very nonnormal. There are tests for normality, so on some occasions, you can actually verify these assumptions; but if you are uncomfortable about that, then I think the onus is on you to do an alternative type of analysis, the obvious one here being some kind of nonparametric test where you are not making such distributional assumptions. But even if you do all that, the same problems that I have mentioned about the interpretation of the results still apply.

Dr. Lozoff: Everybody seems very righteous about making the significance level more stringent if you are going to do multiple comparisons. I would be interested in your views about what you should do when a multiple set of comparisons fits a pattern that is what you have predicted *a priori.* In this case, I really don't understand about reducing the significance level.

Dr. Walter: You mean if, for example, you have a cluster of effects that you would expect to go together, then adjustment for multiple comparisons would not be appropriate. Is that your question?

Dr. Lozoff: Yes, sometimes statistical people argue you just always must.

Dr. Walter: I am not one of those people. I tend not to recommend multiple comparison adjustments, because I think there are many situations when you can quite reasonably ask scientifically independent questions of the same set of data. It is very reasonable to do that. I think the scenario that you have painted, though, is where you have a number of outcomes that might be correlated with one another, so it is unduly harsh to use, for example, a Bonferroni multiple comparison adjustment that makes it impossible to get a statistically significant result. A better strategy in that case would be to do a multivariate analysis so that you actually look at the vector—the set of outcomes for an individual—as a group, and you can assess the treatment or the intervention effect on that set of outcomes as a whole.

Dr. Lentze: You showed nicely that so many papers had only *p* values on them, so the question I want to ask is, does that mean that our knowledge of much of medicine, which is mainly dominated by *p* values, is now invalid?

Dr. Walter: That is a very serious question, and it relates to the problem of publication bias, where studies that show statistically significant results are much more likely to be published than ones that show apparently uninteresting results. So now there is a very serious attempt through organizations like the Cochrane Collaboration to go back and try to collect all the information on a particular intervention or a particular therapy and look at it in an unbiased way, if possible, including the unpublished studies as well. I think there are certain examples where we have indeed been misled by the literature that just happens to get into print.

Clinical Trials in Infant Nutrition, edited by
Jay A. Perman and Jean Rey, Nestlé Nutrition
Workshop Series, Vol. 40, Nestec Ltd.,
Vevey/Lippincott-Raven Publishers,
Philadelphia © 1998.

Selection of Variables, Timing of Examinations, and Retention

Alex F. Roche and Shumei Guo

*Department of Community Health, Wright State University,
Yellow Springs, Ohio, USA*

In any clinical trial, the selection of variables to be measured, the timing of examinations, and the retention of subjects form a triad of critical elements that in large part determine whether suitable data will be available for hypothesis testing at the end of the trial. These elements, which are particularly important in clinical trials of infants, must receive careful consideration during the development of the protocol. Because clinical trials involving infant nutrition are brief, there are only limited opportunities to modify these trials once they have begun.

The examples used in the present chapter relate to common measures of infant growth, but they are applicable to other measurements that might be made. Consideration of these examples can lead to the elaboration of some general principles and attitudes that are pertinent to the biochemical measures and to data relating to immunocompetence and health that are likely to be recorded and analyzed in clinical trials of infant nutrition.

It is assumed that a control group will be included in the trial. Usually, the control group and the experimental group will be constructed by random assignment, and the control group will receive a well-established infant formula. A comparison group of breast-fed infants can assist the interpretation of the findings, although it is difficult or impossible to standardize the intake and duration of breast-feeding, and there will not be random assignment involving the breast-fed group. In addition, comparisons are usually made with commonly used reference data to detect whether the growth status of some of the infants in the experimental group is outside the normal range. These latter comparisons should take covariates into account, but there are some limitations to the implementation of such adjustments. The current U.S. National Center for Health Statistics (NCHS) reference data for infancy were obtained from the Fels Longitudinal Study (1–3), and the data for matching covariates are incomplete and not readily available. It is expected that revised NCHS reference data will be published in 1997 and that data for covariates will be made available at that time for the infants in national surveys. These revised data will be based on national samples at birth and at ages older than 3 months. From birth to 3 months, however, they will be based on other data sets for white infants born at term (3–5). Adjustments for covariates will be difficult or impossible during these young ages.

SELECTION OF VARIABLES

In accordance with common practice, the measurements of infant growth are likely to be weight, length, and head circumference. These are good choices. Each of these measurements increases rapidly during infancy, particularly soon after birth. The more rapid the rate of growth, the more likely it will be modified by the infant formula being tested.

During the period from 1 to 12 months, the relative increases in the median values are about 145% for weight, 40% for length, and 26% for head circumference. Part of the much more rapid increase in weight is related to its three-dimensional nature. In the Fels Longitudinal Study, the coefficients of variation of increments, expressed as percentages of the means, are larger for weight (40%, 25%, and 16% for 1- to 2-, 2- to 3-, and 3- to 4-month increments, respectively) than for length and head circumference (about 20%, 15%, and 10%) for the same age intervals (6,7). For the increments from 10 to 11 and from 11 to 12 months, the coefficients of variation are 20% for weight, 8% for length, and 16% for head circumference. These differences between measurements reflect the fact that changes in weight tend to be much more rapid than those in length or head circumference. Therefore, significant effects of a formula being tested are more likely to be detected in weight than in length or head circumference.

Weight, which is the sum of the weights of all body components, is a less specific measure than length or head circumference. In the presence of disease, there may be extremely rapid changes in weight during a period of a few days, which usually reflect alterations in body fluids and are quickly reversed if the disease is treated effectively. Changes in adipose tissue stores, which become abundant at about 12 months, may be an important element in less rapid weight changes (8,9). If an infant has an unusual weight at birth, the centile levels for weight during infancy commonly change, so that they become closer to the medians. These changes, which are rapid from birth to 9 months, continue to 24 months (10) and may be large enough to be categorized as decanalization. They will not, however, meet the criteria for failure-to-thrive, which are basically a low centile level combined with a decrease in the centile level for weight.

Conceptually, the length of an infant is the sum of the lengths of many bones, and it reflects the past elongation of these bones during a period of months. Length cannot decrease. Therefore, any negative increments for length that are present in the recorded data must result from measurement errors. There may be changes in the relative levels for length during infancy that are not dependent on the type of feeding. For example, when the midparent stature, which is the average of the statures of the two parents, is large and the infant is short at birth, the centile levels for the length of the infant increase until about 12 months (11). Changes in the relative levels of length that are opposite in direction occur in infants who are long at birth and whose parents are short.

It is useful to interpret weight and length jointly. At older ages during childhood, weight and stature are frequently combined as the body mass index [BMI, weight (kg)/stature (m^2)]. The use of BMI, with the substitution of length for stature, is not recommended during infancy because the accurate measurement of length requires very careful attention to detail, and the effects of any measurement errors are increased when the square of length is calculated. During infancy, weight-for-length is the preferred combination of weight and length. Weight-for-length is described as age-independent throughout infancy and prepubescence, because for all practical purposes, the centile levels in one age group match the corresponding centile levels in the next older age group for matching lengths (12). As a result, weight-for-length centiles can be displayed conveniently in growth charts. This age independence also has advantages when the age of an infant is unknown, as may occur in developing countries. Some recent data indicate, however, that weight-for-length may increase with age from birth to 3 months (13).

When the centile levels of weight, length, and weight-for-length are considered for an infant, the size of the infant for each variable will be compared with reference data such as those of Hamill *et al.* (1,2). Some infants will be judged, for example, to be underweight and short but within the normal range of weight-for-length. The prevalence of these and other categories of infants can be compared between the experimental and the control groups.

The importance of head circumference derives from its close relationship to brain weight during infancy, when both the scalp and the cranium are thin (14,15). Small head circumferences are associated with reduced mental ability (16), and large head circumferences lead to concerns about possible hydrocephalus, particularly if the increments in head circumference are markedly greater than the median increments (17). When an unusual head circumference is noted in an infant, or there are rapid increases in head circumference, the cause should be sought. In some cases, an unusual head circumference is a familial trait that does not have functional significance.

Many other anthropometric variables could be recorded, but the measurement of these is recommended only for special circumstances. For example, it may be impossible to measure length and difficult to judge weight in an amputee. Alternative measures such as arm span, skinfold thicknesses, and circumferences can be considered. Skinfold thicknesses could be measured in all the trial infants at the triceps and subscapular sites. The measurement errors, relative to the means, would be particularly large from birth to 2 months because the subcutaneous adipose tissue layer is thin. Later in infancy, the relative measurement errors for these skinfold thicknesses may still be unacceptably large despite a thicker layer of adipose tissue. Midarm circumference can be measured with small errors, but this provides limited useful information if it is not combined with triceps skinfold thickness to calculate the cross-sectional area of adipose tissue and the combined cross-sectional area of muscle and bone at the same level. These estimates require that the triceps skinfold thickness be squared, which increases the effects of any measurement errors.

THE TIMING OF EXAMINATIONS

Because the word growth implies change, analyses of growth require serial data. If examinations are scheduled only at the beginning and the end of a clinical trial, the recognition of adverse effects would be delayed until the end of the trial, and brief effects may not be recognized. With such a protocol, few increments could be calculated for intervals matching those for which there are reference data. The recent North American sets of reference data for growth increments during infancy that are in common use are listed in Table 1. The examinations should be timed so that increments can be calculated for intervals matching those of the reference data. Although increments are important, not all analyses should be based on them.

It is necessary to compare serial recorded measurements with reference data for status to recognize decanalization (21) and to use reference data for both status and for increments to recognize failure-to-thrive (22,23). Decanalization, which is relatively common during infancy and pubescence, occurs when the serial plotted data for an individual cross two or more major centile lines on growth charts for status. This crossing may demonstrate an increase or a decrease in relative level. Decanalization can occur in length and head circumference but is most common in weight. Failure-to-thrive refers to a weight during infancy that is less than the median at one age and is followed by an increment in weight that is less than the fifth centile.

The timing of examinations is partly determined by the rates and patterns of growth during infancy. Growth is rapid in weight, length, and head circumference during early infancy, but these rates soon decelerate markedly. Consequently, the centiles of 1-month increments decrease rapidly from birth to 6 months and then

TABLE 1. *North American reference data for increments in weight, length, and head circumference during infancy*

Authors	Variables and intervals[b]	Age range
Guo *et al.* (5)[a]	W; 1-mo	Birth–6 mo
	W; 2-mo	Birth–12 mo
	L; 2-mo	Birth–6 mo
	W and L; 3-mo	Birth–24 mo
Guo *et al.* (6)	HC: 1-mo	Birth–12 mo
Roche *et al.* (7)	W and L; 1-mo	Birth–12 mo
Roche and Himes (18)	W, L, HC; 6-mo	Birth–36 mo
Baumgartner *et al.* (19)	W, L, HC; 6-mo	Birth–36 mo
Roche *et al.* (20)	W, L. HC; 1-mo	Birth–12 mo

[a] Also given in Fomon (4).
[b] W, weight; L, length; HC, head circumference; mo, month.

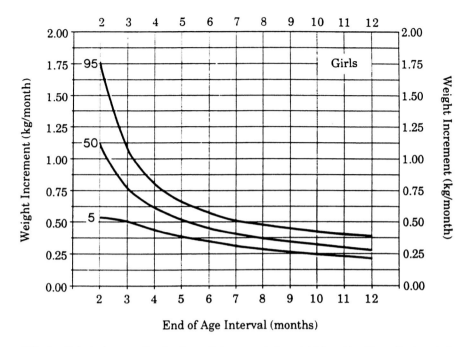

FIG. 1. Selected percentiles for 1-month increments in weight for girls. (From Roche *et al.*, ref. 7, with permission.)

decrease slowly throughout the remainder of infancy, as shown in Figs. 1 to 3. These figures, in which the increments are plotted opposite the ends of the intervals, display only the fifth, 50th, and 95th centiles because the expected measurement errors would make it difficult or impossible to distinguish among a more complete set of centile levels for an individual infant. The fifth centiles of these increments for girls are given in Table 2; these are slightly smaller than the corresponding values for boys, and, in each sex, the fifth centiles are almost the same as the tenth centiles.

It is recommended that the time intervals between examinations be long enough that the fifth centiles of the increments are larger than the technical errors (TE):

$$ TE = \sqrt{\frac{\sum\limits_{i=1}^{I} \sum\limits_{j=1}^{n_i} (x_{ij} - \bar{x}_i)^2}{\sum\limits_{i=1}^{I} n_i}} , $$

where x_{ij} is the *j*th measurement of the *i*th participant for $i = 1, 2, \ldots, I$ and $j = 1, 2, \ldots, n_i$. The TE for weight in infancy is about 10 g (S. Guo and A.F. Roche, *unpublished data*), which could lead to a suggestion that weight be measured daily to 6 months and then each second or third day for the remainder of infancy. There is, however, a biological variation in weight of about 100 to 250 g that is associated

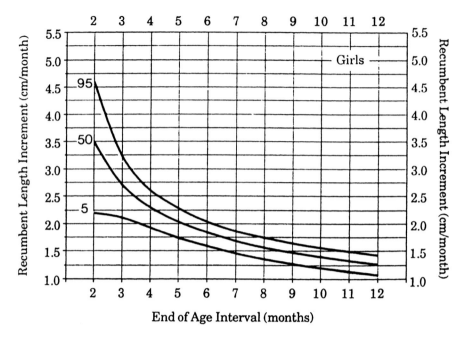

FIG. 2. Selected percentiles for 1-month increments in length for girls. (From Roche *et al.*, ref. 7, with permission.)

with feeding, defecation, and urination. In the absence of special arrangements to control this variation, intervals of 1 month between weight measurements are appropriate. The TEs for length during infancy are 0.3 cm, and for head circumference 0.2 cm (S. Guo and A.F. Roche, *unpublished data*). Even if the TEs for length are doubled because of incomplete quality control, the TE will still be less than the fifth centiles of the 1-month increments (Table 2). After 10 months, the TEs for head circumference that are attained with very good quality control are only slightly smaller than the fifth centiles for 1-month increments. Consequently, 1-month intervals between measurements of head circumference after 10 months are justified only if the quality control within the study is very good. In theory, if the TEs for length and head circumference were reduced to values smaller than those found by Guo and Roche, the measurements of these variables could be made at intervals shorter than 1 month. It would be difficult to achieve such reductions in the TEs, and more frequent examinations would be likely to place undue burdens on the mothers. Furthermore, there are no current reference data for intervals shorter than 1 month.

The calculation of increments can assist the statistical analyses and, in addition, can assist the identification of infants whose growth is unusual. One-month increments allow earlier recognition of serious decreases in growth rates than is possible from consideration of serial values for status. This is illustrated in Fig. 4, which displays theoretical serial weight data for two girls. The weight of each girl was

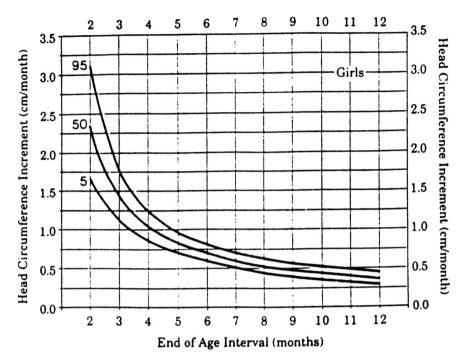

FIG. 3. Selected percentiles for 1-month increments in head circumference for girls. (From Guo *et al.*, ref. 6, with permission.)

TABLE 2. *Fifth centile increments during early infancy for girls[a]*

Age (mo)	Weight (kg/mo)	Length (cm/mo)	Head circumference (cm/mo)
1–2	0.54	2.21	1.9
2–3	0.50	2.10	1.2
3–4	0.44	1.92	0.9
4–5	0.38	1.72	0.7
5–6	0.35	1.58	0.6
6–7	0.31	1.45	0.5
7–8	0.29	1.35	0.5
8–9	0.26	1.26	0.4
9–10	0.24	1.19	0.4
10–11	0.23	1.12	0.3
11–12	0.21	1.07	0.3

[a] Data from Guo *et al.* (6) and from Roche *et al.* (7).

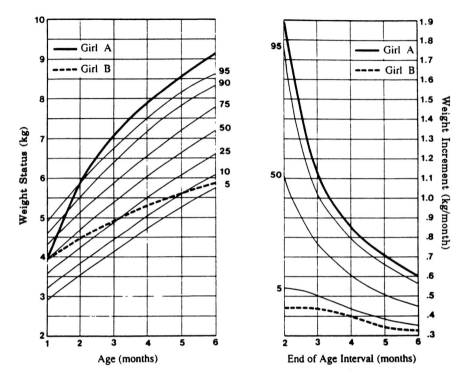

FIG. 4. Alternative plots of theoretical serial weights at 1-month intervals for girls A and B. In the **left panel,** serial status values are plotted against the NCHS reference data of Hamill *et al.* (1,2); in the **right panel,** 1-month increments are plotted against incremental reference data. (From Roche *et al.*, ref. 7, with permission.)

equal to the median at 1 month. Subsequently, the 1-month increments for girl A were slightly greater than the 95th centile, and those for girl B were slightly less than the fifth centile, as shown in the right panel of the figure. The serial status data for the two girls are plotted against the National Center for Health Statistics reference data of Hamill *et al.* (1,2) in the left panel. The status values for girl A reach the 95th centile at 2 months, when her rapid weight gain can be recognized. The status centiles for girl B decrease slowly with age; her unusually slow growth may not be recognized until 5 months. The 1-month increments in the right panel allow the unusual rates of growth for both girls to be recognized at age 2 months.

It is important that the TEs be as small as possible to increase the likelihood of significant findings from the statistical analyses. The TEs can be reduced by close attention to quality control with an emphasis on (a) the adoption of a standard protocol, particularly if there are multiple sites, (b) recruiting measurers who are interested in this task and anxious to do it as well as possible, (c) the selection of appropriate anthropometric instruments and the items needed for their calibration, (d) central training of physicians and measurers in measurement, calibration, and recording, (e) repeated training and the collection of reliability data throughout the trial, and (f) review by the pediatrician of the data recorded at each examination and discussion of these data with the measurer and the mother before the mother and infant leave the clinic. The procedures for the specific measurements should match those used by NCHS, which are in close agreement with the recommendations of a Consensus Conference (24,25). Lists of suppliers of anthropometric instruments are given by Lohman *et al.* (24) and Roche *et al.* (26).

The timing of examinations is set in the protocol as a series of target (scheduled) ages. In practice, there will, however, be some differences between these target ages and the actual ages at examinations. Although such differences are inevitable, they should be kept small by careful scheduling of appointments that takes into account the convenience of the mother and by rescheduling infants as soon as possible after missed appointments. No matter how large the differences in timing between the target ages and the actual ages at examinations, none of the recorded data should be excluded from consideration during the statistical analyses. The effects of the inevitable variations from the target ages can be overcome in some types of analyses by the use of exact age-specific centile levels that can be obtained using Epi Info software (27), although centiles are not metric. Analyses of ''1-month increments'' using the recorded data are likely to be misleading if the lengths of the intervals between measurements differ markedly from 1 month, particularly if these differences vary between groups. In such circumstances, the recorded data must be adjusted to the target ages either by fitting a function to the serial data for each infant or by regression of the experimental and control data sets on target ages. After the data have been adjusted to the target ages, they can be used to calculate values for fixed intervals.

RETENTION

Retention, within the context of clinical trials of infant nutrition, relates much more to interactions with the mother than to interactions with the infant, unless the trial is conducted on institutionalized infants. Retention in the trial is usually more difficult for teenage mothers and those who are single or have a language barrier. These mothers should not be excluded, but individual attention should be given to them and to other mothers with special needs, to increase the retention rate. The fathers should be involved in the trial. This can be done through a newsletter and by evening functions at the beginning and about 2 months after the start of the trial, to which both parents and all the siblings are invited. These functions should be pleasant and informative for the whole family and include the presentation of small gifts.

The convenience of travel to the clinic and of the appointments that are made is closely related to retention. Some mothers may desire appointments on Saturdays or evenings. Efforts should be made to meet these desires early in the trial; such efforts should not be delayed until there is a crisis. Preventive measures are always better than crisis management. The number of examinations will be set by the proto-col, but this number should not exceed what is really necessary. The provision of transportation increases the retention rate.

When the mother arrives with her infant for an examination, she should be greeted warmly and receive immediate attention. Ideally, the same few members of the clinic staff will manage all aspects of these examinations so that cordial relationships will develop between these staff members and each mother. Siblings should be made welcome at the clinic, and facilities for their play should be provided.

The mothers must be fully instructed about the trial so that they can give informed consent. In addition, mothers who fully understand the trial, including its aims and the potential benefits to society and to their infant, are more likely to be interested and compliant participants. This requires individual verbal explanations supplemented by a booklet that describes the trial and the changes that are usually noted in the variables being measured. This booklet should be brought by the mother to each examination, so that the pediatrician can make notes of the findings for her infant in spaces that the booklet provides. One excellent way to encourage continuing membership in the trial is to give the mother instant photographs of the infant that she can place in her booklet. At each examination, a stipend and travel expenses should be paid to the mother, and the infant should receive a toy. The distribution of bibs and carrying bags for diapers can help. Usually, the mother is given sufficient free formula to feed the infant until the next examination. This formula may weigh as much as 5 kg. If the mother uses public transport, special arrangements may be needed to move this formula to her home.

The previous paragraphs describe actions that relate specifically to the mother and father. The infant is important also. Invasive procedures should be kept to a minimum and should not precede the anthropometry. It is impossible to obtain accu-rate body measurements of an infant who is screaming because a blood sample has just been obtained or a vaccination performed. Similarly, infants who are upset because of hunger, thirst, or an uncomfortable diaper require attention to the cause of their distress before they are measured.

Complete retention is unlikely, despite all the efforts that may be made. Some guide to what can be achieved is provided by the data in Table 3. The data from the Fels Longitudinal Study are for infants born from 1985 to 1992. For the sake

TABLE 3. *The percentage retention in some studies of infants*

Study	Number enrolled (age)	Percentage retained at various ages (mo)					
		2	3	6	9	24	36
Fels Longitudinal Study (births 1985–1992)	47 (1 mo)	—	94	96	96	94	91
An unpublished clinical trial	352 (1 mo)	89	58	—	—	—	—
Sempé et al. (28)	542 (birth)	—	—	—	75	65	59

of simplicity, the data presented are for a subset of the examinations scheduled for these Fels participants. Retention was good, partly because of some special circumstances. A parent, and commonly a grandparent, of each infant has been included in the Fels Longitudinal Study since birth, and invasive procedures are not used before 36 months of age. One might expect that these advantages would be somewhat offset by the absence from the study of physical examinations and pediatric advice. The retention rate in one unpublished clinical trial of infant nutrition was not as high as in the Fels Longitudinal Study. The mothers of these infants did not have a preexisting commitment to the trial, and the protocol included some invasive procedures. Also, retention in this clinical trial could have been reduced by treatment failure—for example, inability to digest the formula—or by the application of exclusion criteria relating to changes that occurred after enrollment. Retention in the longitudinal study of Parisian infants, which was reported by Sempé *et al.* (28), was not as good as in the Fels Longitudinal Study. Invasive procedures were not included, but the mothers did not have a previous commitment to the study.

Attrition should be defined before the beginning of the trial, and its prevalence should be recorded for various categories of apparent causes (maternal refusal, change in place of residence, treatment failure, noncompliance in the feeding of the assigned formula or in the age at introduction of solid foods, noncompliance with the scheduled examinations, and maternal or infant diseases).

SUMMARY

The timing of examinations in a clinical trial of infant nutrition should be based on the rates of change in the variables measured, their technical errors, and the burden on the mothers. Consequently, the selection of the variables to be measured must precede decisions about the timing of examinations. The variables selected should be ones that are likely to show effects of differences in infant feeding on major dimensions of the body (weight, length), or on dimensions that have clear relationships to the size and function of an important organ (head circumference). Wise decisions about the timing of examinations and the choice of measures will be of little avail in the absence of unremitting efforts to maintain a high quality of data collection and to retain the mothers and infants in the trial.

REFERENCES

1. Hamill PW, Drizd TA, Johnson CL, Reed RB, Roche AF. *NCHS growth curves for children birth-18 years. United States. DHEW Publication No (PHS) 78-1650, Vital and Health Statistics, Series 11, No 165.* Washington, DC: US Government Printing Office, 1977.
2. Hamill PW, Drizd TA, Johnson CL, Reed RB, Roche AF, Moore WM. Physical growth: National Center for Health Statistics percentiles. *Am J Clin Nutr* 1979;32:607–629.
3. Roche AF. *Growth, maturation and body composition: the Fels Longitudinal Study 1929–1991.* Cambridge: Cambridge University Press, 1992.
4. Fomon SJ. *Nutrition of normal infants.* St Louis: CV Mosby, 1993.

5. Guo S, Roche AF, Fomon SJ, *et al.* Reference data on gains in weight and length during the first two years of life. *J Pediatr* 1991;19:355–362.
6. Guo S, Roche AF, Moore WM. Reference data for head circumference status and one-month increments from one to twelve months. *J Pediatr* 1988;113:490–494.
7. Roche AF, Guo S, Moore WM. Weight and recumbent length from 1 to 12 mo of age: reference data from 1-mo increments. *Am J Clin Nutr* 1989;49:599–607.
8. Rolland-Cachera MF, Sempé M, Guiloud-Bataille M, Patois E, Péquignot-Guggenbuhl F, Fautrad V. Adiposity indices in children. *Am J Clin Nutr* 1982;36:178–184.
9. Tanner J, Whitehouse R. Revised standards for triceps and subscapular skinfolds in British children. *Arch Dis Child* 1975;50:142–145.
10. Binkin NJ, Yip R, Fleshood L, Trowbridge FL. Birth weight and childhood growth. *Pediatrics* 1988; 82:828–834.
11. Smith DW, Troug W, Rogers JE, *et al.* Shifting linear growth during infancy: illustration of genetic factors in growth from fetal life through infancy. *J Pediatr* 1976;89:225–230.
12. Van Wieringen JC. *Seculaire Groeiverschuiving: Lengte and Gewicht Surveys 1964–1966 in Netherland in Historisch Perspectief.* Leiden: Netherlands Institute voor Praeventive Geneeskunde TNO, 1972.
13. Van't Hof MA. Weight for length in infants; application of survival analysis in the Eurogrowth Study. In: *Symposium on Problems and Solutions in Longitudinal Research.* Leeuwenhorst: Noordwijkerhout, 1996:21–23.
14. Cooke RWI, Lucas A, Yudkin PLN, Pryse-Davies J. Head circumference as an index of brain weight in the fetus and newborn. *Early Hum Dev* 1977;1/2:145–149.
15. Roche AF. Increase in cranial thickness during growth. *Hum Biol* 1953;25:81–92.
16. Gross SJ, Kosmetates N, Grimes CT, Williams ML. Newborn head size and neurologic status: predictors of growth and development of low birth weight infants. *Am J Dis Child* 1978;132:753–756.
17. O'Neill EM. Normal head growth and the prediction of head size in infantile hydrocephalus. *Arch Dis Child* 1961;36:241–252.
18. Roche AF, Himes JH. Incremental growth charts. *Am J Clin Nutr* 1980;33:2041–2052.
19. Baumgartner RN, Roche AF, Himes JH. Incremental growth tables: supplementary to previously published charts. *Am J Clin Nutr* 1986;43:711–722.
20. Roche AF, Guo S, Yeung D. Monthly growth increments from a longitudinal study of Canadian infants. *Am J Hum Biol* 1989;1:271–279.
21. Berkey CS, Reed RB, Valadian I. Longitudinal growth standards for preschool children. *Ann Hum Biol* 1983;10:57–67.
22. Bithoney WG, Rathbun JM. Failure to thrive. In: Levine MD, Carey WB, Crocker AC, Gross RT, eds. *Developmental-behavioral pediatrics.* Philadelphia: WB Saunders, 1983:557–572.
23. Ramsay M, Gisel EG, Boutry M. Non-organic failure to thrive: growth failure secondary to feeding skills disorder. *Dev Med Child Neurol* 1993;35:285–297.
24. Lohman TG, Roche AF, Martorell R, eds. *Anthropometric standardization reference manual.* Champaign, IL: Human Kinetics Publishers, 1988.
25. Najjar MF, Rowland M. *Anthropometric reference data and prevalence of overweight. United States. 1976–80. DHHS Publication No (PHS) 87-1688. Vital and Health Statistics, Series 11, No 238.* Washington, DC: US Government Printing Office, 1987.
26. Roche AF, Heymsfield SB, Lohman TG, eds. *Human body composition.* Champaign, IL: Human Kinetics, 1996.
27. Dean AG, Dean JA, Coulombier D, *et al. Epi Info, Version 6: A word processing, database, and statistics program for epidemiology on microcomputers.* Atlanta, GA: Centers for Disease Control and Prevention, 1994.
28. Sempé M, Pédron G, Roy-Pernot MP. *Auxologie. Méthode et séquences.* Paris: Laboratorie Théraplix, 1979.

DISCUSSION

Dr. Uauy: We can have normal infants who, in fact, are not growing for variable periods of time and then have variable growth spurts. How is this incorporated in individual follow-up?

Dr. Roche: I think the model is true. However, it appears to be true only during infancy—at least there is no proof of it being true at other periods. Points plotted on a growth chart do not show short-term pauses and succeeding spurts, because in order to recognize these little jumps, one has to measure the infant daily or every second day. But the fact that the jumps are happening means that they become a confounding variable—they add a little variance to the data. Thus, if you measure at monthly intervals, you are likely to have three or four of these little jumps and periods of stasis in between, so the 1-month increments that you observe will not be altered, but they will be smoother than the truth.

Dr. Rey: You say that it is difficult to detect the difference between the fifth and the tenth centile, but I never asked myself if there is a difference between the fifth and the tenth centile. Why do you ask this question?

Dr. Roche: I did not ask the question. These are the fifth and tenth centiles of increments we are talking about, and I drew attention to them for two reasons. One is to explain why the published graphs do not have a tenth centile—they only have three lines: the fifth, 50th, and 95th. Other centiles were published in tables. The second reason is that, in analyzing the results from a clinical trial, the FDA expects you to look at the increments in the experimental group and the control group, and, having looked at the increments, you can then make a comparison, a *t* test if you wish, or use confidence limits, between the increments in one group and the increments in the other; and you can also look at how many children in each of the groups are growing at a slow rate during each of the intervals for which you have data. What I am pointing out is that I would suggest you use the fifth centile, which is more meaningful to regulatory agencies. If you use the tenth centile, you will get almost the same answer. It is difficult to separate the fifth-centile children from the tenth-centile children because the interval is so small. In the revised NCHS status charts, it is still uncertain what the lower centiles will be. There will almost certainly be a third centile, but it is not certain whether there will be a fifth centile. They are likely to be too close together for the difference to be meaningful.

Dr. Walter: You have described the difficulty of estimating single increments in particular children or subjects, and this is really a matter of reliability in the measurement—the measurement variance is of the same order of magnitude as the day-to-day fluctuation and other things that will affect the actual weight or other variable. I wonder whether, instead of using single increments, you could perhaps look back at the history of the subject and use all the accumulated information that you have on that particular person up to that point—that would improve the reliability so that, for instance, you might observe a series of small increments that seem to deviate from the norm, which individually don't amount to very much but collectively could be very meaningful. I am thinking here of some of the indices referred to a tracking in cohort studies, where you can actually measure the tendency for individuals to stay on the same centile in the distribution over time or to move to a different point in the distribution.

Dr. Roche: These are very good points, and, in fact, we do that. We do fit functions to serial data for individuals and make comparisons between groups on the basis of the parameters of those functions if they fit the data well. We also look at the goodness of fit between the control and experimental groups. This is a similar approach to what you were suggesting.

Dr. Saavedra: Could you comment on the use of standard deviation scores, particularly when it comes to comparing populations across sex or across age, given the fact that the coefficients of variation change for the centiles over a period of time.

Dr. Roche: In the context of infancy, most of these growth variables are normally distributed, even for weight, though that is not the case later. However, in clinical trials, the populations are usually not general populations of infants—they typically exclude preterm infants, or else they are studies of preterm infants and low birth weight infants only. However, if all infants are included, one has nearly normal distributions. So, in these clinical trials, if we are dealing with a truncated distribution—truncated at 2500 g or 37 weeks of gestation or both—then, it is not appropriate to use standard deviations. A partial solution is to take the distribution and cut it in half, obtaining an SD for the upper half and an SD for the lower half and applying those, depending on whether the value you are describing is in the upper half or in the lower half. Those standard deviations will not be equal, which leads to statistical complications. Standard deviations have an advantage, however, in that, in theory, you can go to the extremes of the distribution. You can talk about children who are 4 or 5 standard deviations below the mean. Some inaccuracy is involved because such children are extremely uncommon in general samples, and most reference data are based on 200 to 500 per age and sex group.

Dr. Yetley: If you had two large enough groups of infants, one formula-fed and one exclusively breast-fed, would you see the same pattern of weight increments, or will they be different?

Dr. Roche: There are not much data that are convincing. The available data indicate that the breast-fed infants grow more slowly in weight for the first 12 months than formula-fed infants. The difference is not apparently as great as it probably was 20 to 30 years ago, when mothers using formula were giving larger amounts than they give now. There does not appear to be a difference in length or head circumference. The difference in weight appears to be subcutaneous adipose tissue rather than muscle. The best of the studies are those by Dewey (1), but some confounding variables were not taken into account.

Dr. Yetley: What ramifications does have that for using a breast-fed infant as control in a clinical trial of an infant formula, where your primary outcome measure is the weight increment?

Dr. Roche: The main problem with the breast-fed group is that it won't have been obtained by random selection. So if you do have only two groups, your experimental group and your breast-fed group, you would need to adjust for a lot of intervening variables, and, if you are dealing with small samples and many intervening variables, those adjustments will be quite uncertain.

Dr. Van't Hof: I may add in this respect that in a study on 2000 infants in Europe, we found that up to the age of 4 months, breast-fed infants grew better than formula-fed infants; later on, the formula-fed children were longer and heavier than the breast-fed children up to the age of 1 year. We don't yet know what happens after that.

Dr. Haschke: Is it recommended that one should measure length at intervals of 2 months, and the weight in monthly intervals?

Dr. Roche: For an individual, yes; for a group, I measure length monthly as well.

Dr. Rey: What is the minimum size of the sample, if we wish to demonstrate that there is no difference in growth between two groups of infants supplemented or not supplemented with anything?

Dr. Roche: I can't give you an exact answer to that. One would have to calculate it by picking certain powers and α values that you wanted to use. What you are asking for is a power analysis, and it could be done. The other thing is that you have to take into account the period of the study and whether you are going to analyze the sexes separately. Some people like to combine data for the two sexes, and this can be done if you get exact centiles for every status value, using a computer program that does exist. The problem then is that you base the further analyses on centiles, but centiles are not metric values—they are not evenly distributed. The difference between the 20th and 21st centile is not the same as the difference between the 80th and the 81st. So what you are asking about is a power analysis, and what you are calculating is how many you need at the end of the study, not how many you need at the beginning. You also have to decide what the outcome variable is going to be, whether it is the total growth from entry to exit, or whether you want to know whether this growth difference is significant month by month.

Dr. Walter: This is usually thought of in terms of an equivalent study design. I think Dr. Roche is correct to say that we need to factor in the usual thinking about type I and type II errors, but the inherent difference in that situation is that you must think about the smallest effect between the two groups that you would not like to miss—the smallest difference of clinical interest—and once you have done that, then you can indeed go through a formal sample size calculation. It is usually, but not always, the case that the result in sample size is larger in an equivalence design than in the usual situation where you are trying to demonstrate a difference.

Dr. Clarke: I would like to know to what extent you think that growth data and reference ranges should be ethnic-specific, and how specific? We are, at the moment, looking at growth data from groups of infants from the Indian subcontinent, and we are looking separately at the moment at Pakistani, Bangladeshi, and Indian infants. I recognize that differences may be culturally determined in terms of feeding patterns, but I am interested to know what you think about them being genetically determined and requiring separate examination.

Dr. Roche: I am aware of some of the British literature that shows big differences between the ethnic groups for individuals living in Britain. I don't know what the reason for those differences is—whether it is genetic or whether it is in some sense environmental. Your opinion as to whether it is genetic or environmental largely determines whether you support the use of ethnic-specific growth charts or one growth chart for all groups. If the cause is environmental, and there are differences between groups, the ideal is to improve the economic circumstances of the group that is growing poorly until they grow like the ones who are growing better. If the cause is genetic, you are imposing a hurdle that they are not likely to surmount. In the United States, it is believed that there are no clear signs of genetic differences among the major ethnic groups—and by that I mean the whites, the blacks, and the Hispanics—with one exception, and that is that during pubescence (but more markedly in girls than in boys), the Hispanics drop back quite markedly in stature in terms of centile level. It is not clear whether that is a selection effect or whether it is a real phenomenon. It seems to occur to a lesser extent in Mexico City, and evidence about whether this is a real phenomenon or a sampling artifact will come when the NHANES-III data are analyzed. Considering this in another context, it has been decided that the revised National Center for Health Statistics growth charts will not be ethnic-specific. The ethnic differences in the United States are not sufficiently large to justify different charts, irrespective of what the cause of the differences might be.

Dr. Van't Hof: You advised that, in clinical trials, one should measure weight, length and head circumference, but pediatricians do not see these as unidirectional variables: that is, excessive length gain may point to overestimation, high weight may point to obesity, and a very large head circumference may point to malformations. In such a situation, does the mean value have any meaning in the nutritional comparison between different groups?

Dr. Roche: I think the mean does still have some implications, but it is important to go beyond the mean and look at how many individuals there are in the group who are outside what is usually called the normal range and are, therefore, at risk of some of the conditions to which you refer. But that has to be done separately, variable by variable.

Dr. Van't Hof: So this doesn't mean that now that we have new measures such as impedance, we need to get rid of these simple measurements like length, weight, and head circumference?

Dr. Roche: No, because I don't know how you can use impedance in the absence of some of these measurements. You can't use impedance in the absence of height data, and you need other anthropometric values, in particular weight and, if you did get a predictive equation for infants, I would expect head circumference to be included, because head size is such a big factor in the size of an infant. When you talk about additional measures such as impedance, you are going beyond what I had contemplated that people would want to do in nutritional trials during infancy. There are some problems with impedance because with the usual tetrapolar placement of electrodes, one has to have the receiving electrode and the current-providing electrode separated by about 8 cm. It is difficult to do that in the wrist or ankle area of an infant; you just haven't got enough space.

Dr. Meng: China has its own national standards for growth and development. Are the NCHS standards good for the children in different countries, even in China? The national standards in our country are put together from populations from the different regions of the country. In your opinion, which would be best for evaluating the growth and development of children?

Dr. Roche: On the basis of population size, clearly the Chinese data have to be the best of all. These National Center for Health Statistics data are not standards; the word "standard" to me, and to a lot of other people, means a rather narrow range within which an individual ought to be. These are not standards, or limits to which people should be constrained; they are reference data, and they are describing what was the situation in the population of the United States in the late 1960s and early 1970s. It was a surprise to the people involved in constructing those charts when the World Health Organization encouraged other countries to apply them. WHO did that because they recognized them as reference data. They wanted a common set of reference data applied in all different countries, so they could be able to say that in such and such a country, 10% of the children are under the fifth centile, in another, 15% of the children are under the fifth percentile. It has no particular physiological significance. It is, however, true that children in the central part of the range, and you can define that as you wish, but somewhere from the tenth to the 90th or from the fifth to the 95th centile, are less likely to have diseases that interfere with growth or environmental circumstances that interfere with growth. Beyond that, they are nonspecific, and they are not standards. There are, however, data from about half a dozen countries indicating that upper socioeconomic groups come close to the NCHS reference data, which would suggest that the differences between the countries are more dependent on the environment than on genetics. But there is certainly still a genetic effect as well.

Dr. Rey: I am not sure that it is very useful to make these length or weight charts. What are we doing? We are just photographing a group, and if we try to make charts with different groups, we shall mix populations with low growth rate and populations with high growth rate. In the United States, for example, the percentage of obesity in children is too high. Should we use these people to establish weight standards for the United States or WHO? I think this would be a mistake. We should try to draw the ideal growth chart and try to compare populations with this ideal growth chart, if there is one. Finally, for a particular child, it is absolutely without interest to compare his growth with any chart; it is only interesting to compare the growth velocity of this child with his own genetic potential and to see if there is a deviance at one time or another. During the first month of life, the environment plays a very large role in weight increase and probably also in growth in length; we may have to wait 8 or 10 months before the child escapes from the environment. So it is difficult in infancy to be sure whether there is pathologic deviance of growth rate in a particular child; in any case, it is worthless to draw his particular growth rate on any chart.

Dr. Roche: If we talk about status values, you can plot serial data for a child and see whether a child is tracking—and by tracking, you mean: are those points running parallel to a nearby centile line on the chart? If you didn't have a chart, I wonder how you would recognize tracking for the individual child. Tracking in another sense means age-to-age correlations for groups. Now when you talk about the genetic potential, the only way in which this gets incorporated into the use of growth charts is to calculate what is sometimes called a target height or a target stature—you take the average of the two parents and adjust it for sex and then indicate the point on the chart that you hope the child will reach at 18 years. There is no equivalent for weight, and there is a lot of uncertainty—the confidence limit of getting to that target height is about plus or minus 15 cm.

REFERENCE

1. Dewey KG, Heinig MJ, Nommsen LA, *et al.* Breast-fed infants are leaner than formula-fed infants at 1 y of age: the DARLING study. *Am J Clin Nutr* 1993;57:140–145.

Clinical Trials in Infant Nutrition, edited by
Jay A. Perman and Jean Rey, Nestlé Nutrition
Workshop Series, Vol. 40, Nestec Ltd.,
Vevey/Lippincott-Raven Publishers,
Philadelphia © 1998.

Meta-Analyses of Clinical Trials

Henry S. Sacks

Clinical Trials Unit, Mount Sinai Medical Center, New York, New York, USA

Meta-analysis has become increasingly popular in recent years. Evidence of this is an article in the *New York Times* in 1994, which attempted to explain meta-analysis to the general public as follows: "A meta-analysis aims at gleaning more information from existing data by pooling the results of many smaller studies and applying one or more statistical techniques. The benefits or hazards that might not be detected in small studies can be found in a meta-analysis that uses data from thousands of patients" (1). Dr. Thomas C. Chalmers, one of the pioneers of meta-analysis, defined it as "the systematic analysis of data gathered in multiple research projects. Applied to the clinical trials field, it is the process of evaluating quality and combining the results of multiple randomized controlled trials" (T.C. Chalmers, *personal communication*).

The purposes of meta-analysis include the following: (a) to increase statistical power for primary endpoints and for subgroups; (b) to resolve uncertainty when reports disagree; (c) to improve estimates of size of effect; (d) to answer new questions not posed at the start of individual trials; and (e) to bring about improvements in the quality of the primary research. These functions are particularly applicable to randomized controlled trials because they are often undersized (2).

We conducted a survey in 1987 of 86 meta-analyses of randomized controlled trial reports in the English language literature and updated it in 1991 (3,4) (Table 1). The English language medical literature (from January 1966 to October 1986 for the first survey, and updated through July 1990) was searched for papers that pooled the results of controlled clinical trials. Papers were found in *Current Contents* and by computer searches of the National Library of Medicine (NLM) and Bibliographic Retrieval Services, Inc. (BRS) data bases, by looking for reviews of specific subjects and using the terms "meta-analysis," "pooled" or "pooling," and "combined" or "combining" in title, abstract, or, where available, full text. Other sources of papers included references in papers found by the above methods and by personal communication.

Our criteria for inclusion of papers in this analysis were that data from more than one study must be combined, and at least one of the studies pooled must be a

TABLE 1. *Comparison of quality features among meta-analyses*

	1955–1982 (n = 40): Number (%) adequate	1983–1986 (n = 66): Number (%) adequate	1987–1990 (n = 58): Number (%) adequate
Prospective design			
Protocol	5 (13)	2 (3)	13 (22)
Literature search	10 (25)	24 (36)	40 (69)
List of trials analyzed	37 (93)	56 (85)	54 (93)
Log of rejected trials	4 (10)	11 (17)	24 (41)
Treatment assignment	38 (95)	17 (26)	46 (79)
Ranges of patients	13 (33)	12 (18)	36 (62)
Ranges of treatment	20 (50)	25 (38)	39 (67)
Ranges of diagnosis	18 (45)	21 (32)	34 (59)
Combinability			
Criteria	17 (43)	26 (39)	39 (67)
Measurement	5 (13)	17 (26)	27 (47)
Control of bias			
Selection bias	0	0	7 (12)
Data-extraction bias	0	0	7 (12)
Interobserver bias	0	7 (11)	11 (19)
Source of support	17 (43)	14 (21)	16 (28)
Statistical analysis			
Statistical method	22 (55)	40 (61)	45 (78)
Statistical errors	15 (38)	31 (47)	38 (66)
Confidence intervals	14 (35)	27 (41)	49 (84)
Subgroup analysis	28 (70)	39 (59)	45 (78)
Sensitivity analysis			
Quality assessment	9 (23)	10 (15)	15 (26)
Varying methods	6 (15)	12 (18)	25 (43)
Publication bias	3 (8)	11 (17)	24 (41)
Application of results			
Caveats	37 (93)	31 (47)	41 (71)
Economic impact	0	2 (3)	3 (5)

randomized controlled trial. Each paper was evaluated independently by two investigators using a scoring sheet that lists what we consider to be the important elements of a meta-analysis. The evaluators were blinded as to the name of the journal and the authors of the papers.

RESULTS OF THE SURVEYS

We believe that the important qualities of any meta-analysis can be divided into six major areas: study design, combinability, control of bias, statistical analysis, sensitivity analysis, and problems of applicability. We divided the papers into three time periods, selected to give roughly equal numbers in each: 1955-82, 1983-86, and 1987-90.

Study Design

In meta-analysis, as in any other form of research, it is important to try to make the process as rigorous and as well defined as possible.

Protocol

As with any scientific endeavor, the questions to be answered, the criteria for inclusion in the study, and the methodology to be used should be established beforehand. There has been a slight improvement, but still only a minority of papers gave clear evidence that the study was conducted according to a predetermined protocol or research plan. Many more may have followed protocols, but it was not apparent to the reader. If retrospective meta-analyses are to be converted into prospective research, we believe writing of a protocol is an essential first step.

Literature Search

Because a valid meta-analysis should include as many relevant trials as possible, the authors should provide details of their search procedures. At present, it is insufficient to rely solely on computer literature searches, as they may yield fewer than two-thirds of relevant trials (5,6). A computer search can be supplemented by consulting *Current Contents,* reviews, textbooks, or experts in the particular field of study and by reviewing the references of the trials found. The proportion of papers clearly using such exhaustive searching methods has increased.

List of Trials Analyzed and Log of Rejected Trials

The report of a meta-analysis should provide a list of the trials analyzed, and most of the reports in all three periods did so. Just as important is an enumeration of the relevant trials excluded and the reasons why. This is analogous to the log of excluded patients in a clinical trial. We believe it is vital for the reader to be aware of any information that was not used, because the meta-analyst may have had a preconception or bias as to how the result should come out. The proportion of papers reporting excluded trials has steadily increased, but even in the latest period fewer than half did so.

Treatment Assignment

The most important question bearing on the validity of the data pooled is the method of treatment assignment in the primary study. It has been shown that results of trials using historical controls are more likely to favor the new treatment than results of the same treatment tested in randomized controlled trials (7). The proportion of papers using data only from randomized trials appears to have declined in recent years.

Ranges of Patients, Diagnoses, and Treatments

In order for the reader to judge the validity and generalizability of a meta-analysis, data should be provided on the patients, diagnoses, treatments, and endpoints in the original studies. It is not possible to provide more than broad general outlines here, but specific rules can, and should, be developed for each particular meta-analysis. The ranges of patient characteristics in all the trials analyzed—age, sex, relevant socioeconomic data, other diseases, etc.—should be included. Details on these items were given in only a minority of the meta-analyses in the first two time periods. The ranges of treatments should also be defined. Did all patients in all trials receive the same, or similar, treatment? In meta-analyses of drug treatments, were trials combined that used the same drug or the same class of drug? Dosage and route, as well as frequency and duration, of treatment in all the trials to be pooled should be available to the reader. This criterion was variably fulfilled in the papers analyzed. Similarly, data should be presented on the range of diagnoses in the pooled trials. Were diagnostic criteria the same in all trials? What stages or grades of disease were included? Such details on this important question were reported in fewer than half the meta-analyses in the first two time periods but in more than two-thirds in the third time period.

Combinability

A major issue in pooling data is whether the results of the separate trials can be meaningfully combined, and this should be explicitly addressed by the meta-analyst, in sufficient detail for the reader to determine that a useful and clinically relevant result will be obtained.

Criteria

What criteria were used to decide that the studies analyzed were similar enough to be pooled? The meta-analyst should note any differences in the primary studies and discuss how these differences affect the conclusions of the meta-analysis. Fewer than half of the meta-analysts in the first samples and 59% in the third detailed their criteria for pooling.

Measurement

Related to the problem of combinability is the statistical issue of heterogeneity. In addressing questions of combining estimates from different studies, statisticians distinguish between two possible models (8). In model 1, each study is considered to be a sample from the same population and provides an estimate of a single underlying true rate, with the differences resulting from experimental error (within study variability). In model 2, each study is considered to be from a different population, the rate varies from study to study, and their differences result from experimental error and from differences in the populations (between-study variability). There are several methods for deciding which of the above models is more appropriate (9). In either case, there are tests for homogeneity that help decide the degree of caution with which pooled results should be interpreted. Because of the heterogeneity of patients treated by practitioners who might be applying the results of meta-analyses, heterogeneity in the trials may not be so bad. Evidence of a statistical test for homogeneity was found in few of the meta-analyses in the first time periods but rose to nearly half in the most recent period.

Control and Measurement of Potential Bias

In performing a meta-analysis, as in any scientific endeavor, potential sources of unconscious bias should be controlled for where possible.

Selection Bias

To avoid bias in the selection and rejection of papers, the decision to include a paper should be made by looking only at its methods and not at its results, or looking at the two separately under coded conditions. This important source of bias was not reported in any of the meta-analyses reviewed for our first survey and in only 7% in the latest time period.

Data Extraction Bias

As with any other data-gathering process that requires interpretation, observers may disagree. When papers list a variety of subgroups, endpoints, exclusions, and so on, it is quite possible that readers may vary in how they extract the data from a particular study. The ideal way to control for this type of bias is to have the data extracted by more than one observer, each of whom is blinded to the various treatment groups through a coded photocopying process, and then measure the interobserver agreement. In none of the meta-analyses in the first time period was such agreement reported, but such reporting appears to be increasing recently. The data extraction process was blinded in none of the early papers and in only 12% of those in the latest period.

Source of Support

We feel that it is useful to the reader to know who financed a study when deciding how much credence to give to its conclusions. Potential conflicts of interest do not necessarily disqualify a study, but they should be clearly acknowledged. The source of support was specified in a minority of papers, and, if anything, the practice appears to have declined over time.

Statistical Analysis

This category deals with questions of statistical methodology.

Methods

We evaluated as "adequate" any recognized method of pooling except simple addition of successes across all trials to give an overall average, which was rated as "partial." An adequate method was used in well over half of the meta-analyses, and that proportion appears to have increased over time.

The most commonly used method was the Mantel–Haenszel test or a modification thereof. Other studies combined data by calculating a standardized average effect size; many also performed various types of regression analyses or significance tests, or a combination. A few papers used various other methods of pooling, and five papers did not specify the methods used. For further discussion of these various methods, see "Remaining Problems" below.

Statistical Errors

Fewer than half of the meta-analyses in the first two time periods showed an awareness of the potential problems of type I statistical errors (concluding that there is a difference when none exists) and type II errors (concluding that there is no difference when there is one). There has been some improvement in the last 3 years.

Confidence Intervals

It is often more useful to the reader to have an estimate with confidence intervals of the difference between the success rates of the treatments being compared than to have only the results of significance tests. Confidence intervals for major outcomes were given in fewer than half (43%) of the meta-analyses in the first periods, but this has risen to 84% recently.

Subgroup Analyses

One of the purposes of meta-analysis, as previously stated, is to increase the statistical power for subgroup analyses. Relevant subgroups were analyzed in the majority of papers.

Sensitivity Analysis

Depending on the test chosen, the same set of data can be combined to give different conclusions (9). Similarly, the results may vary depending on the overall quality of the primary trials and on whether certain trials, subgroups of patients, or other important variables are excluded or changed.

Quality Assessment

In a meta-analysis, the methodologic rigor and scientific quality of the papers to be combined should be assessed and considered in formulating recommendations (11,12). If the original methodology is poor, the resulting conclusion will be less reliable. Such features as the randomization process, the measurement of patient compliance, the blinding of patients and observers, the statistical analyses, and the handling of withdrawals in each primary study should be examined. This issue of quality was fully addressed in only a small proportion of the meta-analyses and was not even mentioned in nearly half. There was no evidence of improvement over time.

Varying Methods

Each meta-analysis should include in a sensitivity analysis data that show how the results vary through the use of different assumptions, tests, and criteria. This type of analysis was performed in only 15% of the meta-analyses reviewed in the first period but increased in use appreciably in the second and third.

Publication Bias

One of the criticisms sometimes made of meta-analysis is that there may be some unpublished studies that would contradict the results of published studies, and there is some evidence that negative studies are less likely to be published than positive ones (13,14). A simple method has been proposed for calculating the number of unpublished negative studies required to refute the published evidence (15), which is one possible measure of the strength of the published evidence. In only 8% of meta-analyses was publication bias considered in the first period, compared to 17% in the second and 41% in the third period.

Application of Results

Caveats

Once the results of the pooling process are available, the meta-analyst should attempt to put them into perspective, based on all of the considerations above. Does the new treatment seem to be established as more effective than the old one for all patients, for some subgroups, and so on? Or should the conclusions be taken only as suggestions for future study? Such caveats were included in the discussion in varying proportions of the papers, with, if anything, a decline over time.

Economic Impact

In today's climate of financial constraints on health care expenditure, it is increasingly important to consider the economic impact of adopting new methods of treatment or diagnosis. Although some may consider this a topic for other studies, we were disappointed that fewer than 5% of the meta-analyses included a thorough analysis of economic impact.

Of the 23 individual items, 7.63 $\pm$ 2.84 (mean $\pm$ SD) were adequately addressed in the 40 meta-analyses published between 1955 and 1982, 6.80 $\pm$ 3.86 were adequately addressed in the 66 published between 1983 and 1986, and 11.91 $\pm$ 4.79 were adequately addressed in the 58 published between 1987 and 1990 (F = 37.3, p < 0.001). Twenty-two of the 58 papers published in the last time period referred to our initial survey or to other similar guides for meta-analysis (which suggested that the guidelines were being used).

Discussion

An important development in the recent history of meta-analysis was the use by Chalmers and colleagues of cumulative meta-analysis (16,17). Cumulative meta-analysis pools the available data at successive points in time to determine when the combined evidence reaches various significance levels. This technique was applied to the question of thrombolytic therapy for myocardial infarction and showed that, by the early 1970s, there was sufficient evidence to conclude that the treatment saved lives. However, many more clinical trials were conducted over the next decade, and it was not until the mid- to late 1980s that textbooks and review articles began to advocate thrombolytic therapy. Thus, if cumulative meta-analysis had been applied to the evolving clinical trial data, the usefulness of this treatment could have been determined much sooner.

REMAINING PROBLEMS

The greatest problem is defining the role of meta-analysis. When should it be attempted, and how should its results be used? We believe that the best way to answer questions about the efficacy of new treatments or diagnostic methods is to perform well-designed, adequately sized randomized controlled trials. Meta-analysis may have a role when definitive trials are impossible or impractical, when trials have been performed but the results are inconclusive or conflicting, or while awaiting the results of definitive studies. Meta-analysis, like decision analysis, can give quantitative estimates of the weight of available evidence, which can be helpful in making clinical decisions. There is, however, a danger that meta-analysis may be used inappropriately or indiscriminately. As with many other types of analysis, the quality of the results depends on the quality of the input. Therefore, the question posed in each meta-analysis should be explicitly stated and clinically relevant.

Difficulty still exists in locating both meta-analyses and randomized controlled trials in the literature, because present literature-searching and indexing systems do not always distinguish primary studies and reviews from meta-analyses or randomized controlled trials from other clinical trials. Thus, it cannot be claimed that the papers found for these analyses are an exhaustive or representative sample. It is also quite likely that there are unpublished meta-analyses. Investigators will facilitate the process of recovery and integration of important clinical information if they insist on inclusion of the terms "randomized" and "meta-analysis" in titles and abstracts, so that indexing can be improved.

More attention also needs to be paid to statistical issues and to the advantages and disadvantages of the various pooling methods. A variety of statistical techniques have been developed for combining the results of separate studies. For example, there are several methods for combining the probability values or test statistics from individual studies (10). These methods, however, may not distinguish between small studies with large effects and large studies with small effects and do not yield an estimate of the size of the effect. The Mantel–Haenszel method (18) or a modification of that technique for combining separate 2×2 tables (19) (the Yusuf–Peto method) is becoming increasingly popular. These methods have several useful properties. They compare each treatment only with its own control and weight studies according to their sample size, and they can include a test for homogeneity as well as an estimate of the effect size. However, they may have some undesirable properties (see below). In the psychiatric literature, studies have been combined by computing effect sizes, defined as the mean difference between experimental and control groups, divided by the control group standard deviation (20). This method allows for the pooling of different endpoints because all findings are transformed into common units, but the conclusions may be difficult to interpret clinically; the validity of this process is thus open to question. A few papers have used multivariate methods or log-linear models to attempt to adjust for differences between studies.

Since publication of our first paper, there have been several important contributions to the statistical methods in meta-analysis. The validity of the Yusuf–Peto one-step method has been challenged (21). Simulations have confirmed this (22), and in those experiments the most valid method of determining variances has been that described by Robins *et al.* (23). When zero observations in one or both groups present a problem, the exact method, as modified and automated by Mehta *et al.* (24), is optimal. A Bayesian approach has been advocated (25). However, we encountered no published meta-analyses that used the last two methods.

Another important development in meta-analysis was a textbook entitled *Effective Care in Pregnancy and Childbirth* (26) with over 1000 individual meta-analyses.

These have not been included in our survey because they represent a special case—these studies were written on consignment by the editors and based on a data base of randomized controlled trials that had been collected in Oxford (27). Obviously, this approach needs to be replicated by the conduct of large numbers of meta-analyses in other fields of medicine.

Some meta-analysts believe that the only valid pooling of results should include the outcomes for all randomized patients regardless of how long (or even whether) they received the assigned treatment (the intention-to-treat method) (19). The authors of at least one paper apparently felt that dropouts and withdrawals should be excluded (exclusion method) (28). However, the data on withdrawals, dropouts, and so on are not always available. We believe that the results should be reported both according to the intention to treat and according to exclusion rules to facilitate evaluation of the differences. If there are none, there is no problem. If clinically important differences exist, the study may be difficult to interpret (29).

Because of the problem of publication bias, some meta-analysts choose to supplement their published data with unpublished trials or data. Unpublished results may be less reliable because they have not been found acceptable by peer reviewers and may not be collected with the same rigor or accuracy as published results (30). However, the potential problems inherent in unpublished results make it unclear whether both types of data should be given equal weight.

Greater uniformity in reporting meta-analyses would be helpful to readers. Many of the meta-analyses found were written in the standard format of scientific papers, with detailed methods and results sections, but several were editorials, leading articles, or letters to the editor with little detail on methodology. We believe that meta-analyses should be presented with sufficient information for readers to draw their own conclusions about the validity of the results.

With the growth in the number of published meta-analyses, there has been growing concern about their quality (31). Several national and international conferences have been held to develop and refine standards for meta-analysis (32,33). The Potsdam International Consultation on Meta-Analysis brought together proponents and critics of meta-analysis for a lively discussion, which was published in 1995 (33). It concluded with methodologic guidelines that should be consulted by anyone wishing to perform a meta-analysis. I quote here their guiding principles (34), which I endorse:

1. A systematic review must address a specific health care question. The question will determine which studies and data are relevant and how they should be synthesized.
2. Methodology must serve biology and the users and providers of health care. Therefore, a team with expertise in both the content area and methodology is ideally suited to conduct valid, useful systematic reviews.
3. A systematic review requires collaboration with the investigators who conducted the primary studies.
4. Systematic reviews are retrospective research and are potentially subject to many of the same biases that affect other retrospective studies; therefore, a systematic

review has to rely on both good randomized controlled trial methodology and good review methodology.

5. For several reasons, review methods may vary (for example, scarce resources may limit search strategies). Thus, the review methods actually employed must be described in detail.

6. The existence of unsatisfactory randomized trials, case-control studies, and cohort studies does not mean that any of these study designs should be abandoned; it means that they should be critically appraised, empirically studied, and improved. Overviews of observational studies require a great deal of methodologic development.

VALIDITY

A major unresolved issue is the validity of meta-analysis. Ingram Olkin, a statistician who has developed methodologies for meta-analysis, has proposed the following ranking of the validity of evidence from various study designs (35):

1. Anecdotal case reports.
2. Case series without controls.
3. Series with literature controls.
4. Analyses using computer data bases.
5. Case-control observational studies.
6. Series based on historical control groups.
7. Single randomized controlled trials.
8. Confirmed randomized controlled clinical trials including meta-analysis.
9. Meta-analysis with original data.

Others are much less optimistic. Alvan Feinstein complained that meta-analyses frequently violate scientific principles of precision, homogeneity, and consistency while focusing on the big process of aggregation but not on the overall small processes that produced the primary data (36).

We agree that a meta-analysis must be carefully done, according to the criteria discussed above, and that careful assessment of the primary data is a critical step. However, we believe meta-analysis can provide important and useful information on which to base clinical decisions. No question can ever be considered completely closed, and thoughtful physicians will always be searching for new data and revising their strategies.

META-ANALYSIS OF DIAGNOSTIC TESTS

Irwig *et al.* proposed methodologic standards for meta-analyses of diagnostic tests (37). They suggest that the process should include six steps:

1. Determine the objective and size of the meta-analysis. This should include a clear statement of the test of interest, the disease of interest and the reference standard

by which it is measured, and the clinical question and context; that is, is the objective to evaluate a single test or to compare the accuracy of different tests?

2. Retrieve the relevant literature. The literature retrieval procedure should be described with search and link terms given and inclusion and exclusion criteria stated.

3. Extract and display the data. Studies should be assessed by two or more readers. The authors should explain how disagreements between readers were resolved. The meta-analysis should give a full listing of diagnostic accuracy and study characteristic for each primary study.

4. Estimate diagnostic accuracy. The method of pooling sensitivity and specificity should take account of their independence. When multiple test categories are available, they should be used in the summary.

5. Assess the effect of variation in study validity on estimates of diagnostic accuracy. The relation between estimates of diagnostic accuracy and study validity of the primary studies should be examined for each of the following design characteristics: appropriate reference standard, independent assessment of the test or tests and reference standard, avoidance of verification bias. In comparative studies, were either all of the tests of interest applied to each patient, or were patients randomly allocated to the tests? Are analytic methods used that estimated whether study design flaws affect diagnostic accuracy rather than just test threshold?

6. Assess the effect of variation in the characteristics of patients and test on estimates of diagnostic accuracy (generalizability). Is the relationship between estimates of diagnostic accuracy and characteristics of the patients and test examined? Are analytic methods used that differentiate whether characteristics affect diagnostic accuracy or test threshold?

Irwig *et al.* (37) applied these standards to 11 published meta-analyses and found deficits both in the meta-analyses and in the primary studies on which they were based.

META-ANALYSES OF OBSERVATIONAL STUDIES

This is an area of much debate, where again a critical problem is the methodologic quality of the primary studies. Meta-analyses of observational studies have been done in many areas and have produced intriguing but controversial findings, including that chlorination of water supplies may slightly but significantly increase the incidence of malignancies of several organs (38) and that increased fat in the diet does not increase the incidence of breast cancer (39). It is clear that the danger of incorrect conclusions is higher than when results of randomized controlled trials are combined, but a distinguished group of researchers concluded that meta-analysis must not be limited to such trials (40). Nonrandomized controlled trial data make up the bulk of what is known regarding medical care. It is imperative that technology assessors, policy makers, clinicians, and patients have clear and explicit means for summarizing all sorts of published data. Policy makers cannot afford to ignore the vast majority of information available today merely because it does not fit the simple model of classical meta-analysis. Researchers must develop new methods and new models of analysis to assist those who must use today's imperfect data to make difficult decisions today.

META-ANALYSIS SOFTWARE

At least three computer software packages for meta-analysis are available. A detailed review and comparison was recently published (41).

CONCLUSIONS

In conclusion, if meta-analysis is to be accepted as a scientific tool, each meta-analysis should be conducted as a scientific experiment, beginning with a clear plan of the question to be answered and the methodology to be employed. Attention needs to be paid to intraobserver and interobserver variability, and attempts should be made to identify and minimize bias. Concerns have been expressed about the validity of pooling (42,43), but the process is increasingly used and frequently defended (44–47). We feel that a quantitative synthesis of the data in similar randomized controlled trials is more useful to the practicing physician than a traditional narrative review article, but such syntheses must be properly performed to warrant serious attention. We hope that the points raised here will stimulate discussion that will ultimately lead to better meta-analyses.

REFERENCES

1. Altman LK. Study shows wider utility for aspirin. *New York Times* 1994;Jan 7:A20.
2. Freiman JA, Chalmers TC, Smith H, Kuebler RR. The importance of beta, the type II error and sample size in the design and interpretation of the randomized controlled trial. Survey of 71 negative trials. *N Engl J Med* 1978;299:690–694.
3. Sacks HS, Berrier J, Reitman D, Ancona-Berk VA, Chalmers TC. Meta-analyses of randomized controlled trials. *N Engl J Med* 1987;316:450–455.
4. Sacks HS, Berrier J, Reitman D, Pagano D, Chalmers TC. Meta-analysis of randomized control trials: an update. In: Balder WC, Mosteller F, eds. *Medical uses of statistics,* 2nd ed. Boston MA: NEJM Books, 1992:427–442.
5. Poynard T, Conn HO. The retrieval of randomized clinical trials in liver disease from the medical literature. A comparison of MEDLARS and manual methods. *Controlled Clin Trials* 1985;6:271–279.
6. Dickersin K, Hewitt P, Mutch L, Chalmers I, Chalmers TC. Perusing the literature: comparison of MEDLINE searching with a perinatal trials database. *Controlled Clin Trials* 1985;6:306–317.
7. Sacks H, Chalmers TC, Smith H. Randomized versus historical controls for clinical trials. *Am J Med* 1982;72:233–240.
8. Laird N, Mosteller F. Some statistical methods for combining experimental results. *Int J Tech Assess Health Care* 1990;6:5–30.
9. Berlin JA, Laird NM, Sacks HS, Chalmers TC. A comparison of statistical methods for combining event rates from clinical trials. *Stat Med* 1989;8:141–151.
10. Rosenthal R. Combining results of independent studies. *Psychol Bull* 1978;85:185–193.
11. Chalmers TC, Smith H, Blackburn B, Silverman B, Schroeder B, Reitman D, *et al.* A method for assessing the quality of a randomized controlled trial. *Controlled Clin Trials* 1981;2:31–49.

12. DerSimonian R, Charette LJ, McPeek B, Mosteller F. Reporting on methods in clinical trials. *N Engl J Med* 1982;306:1332–1337.
13. Dickersin K, Chan S, Chalmers TC, Sacks HS, Smith H. Publication bias and clinical trials. *Controlled Clin Trials* 1987;8:343–353.
14. Simes RJ. Publication bias: the case for an international registry of clinical trials. *J Clin Oncol* 1986; 4:1529–1541.
15. Rosenthal R. The "file drawer problem" and tolerance for null results. *Psychol Bull* 1979;86: 638–641.
16. Lau J, Antman EM, Jimenez-Silva J, Kupelnick B, Mosteller F, Chalmers TC. Cumulative meta-analysis of therapeutic trials for myocardial infarction. *N Engl J Med* 1992;327:248–254.
17. Antman EM, Lau J, Kupelnick B, Mosteller F, Chalmers TC. A comparison of results of meta-analyses of randomized controlled trials and recommendations of clinical experts. Treatments for myocardial infarction. *JAMA* 1992;268:240–248.
18. Mantel N, Haentzel W. Statistical aspects of the analysis of data from retrospective studies of disease. *J Natl Cancer Inst* 1959;22:719–748.
19. Yusuf S, Peto R, Lewis J, Collins R, Sleight P. Beta blockade during and after myocardial infarction: an overview of the randomized trials. *Prog Cardiovasc Dis* 1985;27:335–371.
20. Glass GV, McGraw B, Smith ML. *Meta-analysis in social research.* Beverly Hills, CA: Sage, 1981: 21–56.
21. Greenland S. Quantitative methods in the review of epidemiologic literature. *Epidemiol Rev* 1987; 9:1–30.
22. Emerson JD. Combining estimates of the odds ratio: the state of the art. *Stat Methods Med Res* 1994; 3:157–178.
23. Robins J, Greenland S, Breslow NE. A general estimator for the variance of the Mantel–Haenszel odds ratio. *Am J Epidemiol* 1986;124:719–723.
24. Mehta CR, Patel NR, Gray R. Computing an exact confidence interval for the common odds ratio in several 2 × 2 contingency tables. *J Am Stat Assoc* 1985;80:969–973.
25. Eddy DM, Hasselblad V, Shachter R. A Bayesian method for synthesizing evidence: the confidence profile method. *Int J Tech Assess Health Care* 1990;6:31–56.
26. Chalmers I, Enkin M, Keirse MJNC, eds. *Effective care in pregnancy and childbirth.* Oxford: Oxford University Press, 1989.
27. Chalmers I, Hetherington J, Newdick M, Mutch L, Grant A, Enkin M, *et al.* The Oxford Database of Perinatal Trials: developing a register of published reports of controlled trials. *Controlled Clin Trials* 1986;7:306–324.
28. Levitt SH, McHugh RB, Song CW. Radiotherapy in the postoperative treatment of operable cancer of the breast. Part II. A re-examination of Stjernsward's application of the Mantel–Haenszel statistical method. Evaluation of the effect of the radiation on immune response and suggestions for postoperative radiotherapy. *Cancer* 1977;39(suppl):933–940.
29. Bhaskar R, Reitman D, Sacks HS, Smith H, Chalmers TC. Loss of patients in clinical trials that measure long-term survival following myocardial infarction. *Controlled Clin Trials* 1986;7:134–148.
30. Relman AS. News reports of medical meetings: how reliable are abstracts? [editorial]. *N Engl J Med* 1980;303:277–278.
31. Moher D, Olkin I. Meta-analysis of randomized controlled trials. A concern for standards. *JAMA* 1995;274:1962–1964.
32. Boissel JP, Sacks HS, Leizorovicz A, Blanchard J, Panak E, Peyrieux JC. Meta-analysis of clinical trials: summary of an international conference. *Eur J Clin Pharmacol* 1988;34:535–538.
33. Potsdam International Consultation on Meta-Analysis. *J Clin Epidemiol* 1995;48:1–169.
34. Cook DJ, Sackett DL, Spitzer WO. Methodologic guidelines for systematic reviews of randomized controlled trials in health care from the Potsdam Consultation on Meta-Analysis. *J Clin Epidemiol* 1995;48:167–171.
35. Olkin I. Statistical and theoretical considerations in meta-analysis. *J Clin Epidemiol* 1995;48: 133–146.
36. Feinstein AR. Meta-analysis: statistical alchemy for the 21st century. *J Clin Epidemiol* 1995;48: 71–79.
37. Irwig L, Tosteson AN, Gatsonis C, Lau J, Colditz G, Chalmers TC, *et al.* Guidelines for meta-analyses evaluating diagnostic tests. *Ann Intern Med* 1994;120:667–676.
38. Morris RD, Audet AM, Angelillo IF, Chalmers TC, Mosteller F. Chlorination, chlorination by-products, and cancer: a meta-analysis. *Am J Public Health* 1992;82:955–963.
39. Hunter DJ, Spiegelman D, Adami HO, Beeson L, van den Brandt PA, Folsom AR, *et al.* Cohort studies of fat intake and the risk of breast cancer—a pooled analysis. *N Engl J Med* 1996;334: 356–361.

40. Hasselblad V, Mosteller F, Littenberg B, Chalmers TC, Hunink MG, Turner JA, *et al.* A survey of current problems in meta-analysis. Discussion from the Agency for Health Care Policy and Research inter-PORT Work Group on Literature Review/Meta-Analysis. *Med Care* 1995;33:202–220.
41. Normand S-LT. Meta-analysis software. A comparative review. *Am Stat* 1995;49:298–309.
42. Elashoff JD. Combining results of clinical trials [editorial]. *Gastroenterology* 1978;75:1170–1172.
43. Goldman L, Feinstein AR. Anticoagulants and myocardial infarction. The problems of pooling, drowning, and floating. *Ann Intern Med* 1979;90:92–94.
44. Gerbarg ZB, Horwitz RI. Resolving conflicting clinical trials: guidelines for meta-analysis. *J Clin Epidemiol* 1988;41:503–509.
45. Wachter KW. Disturbed by meta-analysis? *Science* 1988;241:1407–1408.
46. L'Abbe KA, Detsky AS, O'Rourke K. Meta-analysis in clinical research. *Ann Intern Med* 1987;107: 224–233.
47. Thacker SB. Meta-analysis. A quantitative approach to research integration. *JAMA* 1988;259: 1685–1689.

DISCUSSION

Dr. Perman: You pointed out that the principal reason for doing meta-analysis is to be able to pool data from many smaller studies. Is the advantage of meta-analysis over multicenter clinical trials simply that somebody else has already done the work and sponsors have borne the cost, or is there something else that is inherently advantageous about meta-analysis over multicenter trials?

Dr. Sacks: I think the converse, that the best answers come from large-scale multicenter trials. However, it is not always practical to do that, so meta-analysis can be helpful either in the planning of definitive studies or in the interim, while awaiting the results of definitive studies when clinicians still need to make decisions about what they should do now. I think that any studies that are being done now should be designed and conducted in such a way that the results can be pooled with those of other studies.

Dr. Guesry: I feel very uncomfortable with the exponential trend to do meta-analysis rather than to do original work, for many reasons. The first and probably not the most important is the ethical reason: you take other people's work, usually without their permission, and make a paper of your own from it. But the most important reasons are really methodologic. There is bound to be inhomogeneity in the data: these studies have been done in different countries, with different investigators, different laboratories, and at different times, and many things could have changed in between. And of course, there are all the data that were not published because they were negative, which are not taken into account, so you introduce a very important bias when you do meta-analysis. Another factor that seems very important to me is that we pay more attention to studies that are made with large numbers of subjects, so by pooling together a lot of small studies, each of which would not be credible in itself, we create something that becomes credible simply by virtue of the numbers involved. Then, with the multiplication of meta-analysis, the same incredible study could be used many times. I think that we have to be very careful in the interpretation of meta-analysis, and it would be nice if the authors of the original study, if still living, could have a say in the interpretation.

Dr. Sacks: I agree with a lot of what you said. The strongest evidence comes from meta-analysis that combines the individual patient data, and that can usually be done only with the active collaboration of the original investigators. So that is probably the best way to synthesize the available information. I am less concerned than you are about the ethical issue. I believe there is also an important ethical obligation to the patients, and I think this is at least as important as the obligation to the authors of the papers. I certainly have no objection to trying to get the cooperation and collaboration of the primary authors, but if I thought that one could make it easier for some physicians to treat their patients, then I think that that would be at least as important for me as what was owed to the authors. The point about publication bias is a big issue, but it is an issue whether or not you are doing meta-analysis. Whether you are doing meta-analysis or looking at a single report of a clinical trial or reading or writing a traditional review, you still have to be concerned about publication bias. So I think that it is an issue not only for meta-analysis but for the medical literature in general.

Dr. Lucas: Let's suppose that you are interested in a nutritional intervention such as whether iron influences neurodevelopment, and there are five small trials in the literature with 50 subjects in them, all just about meeting the criteria for a meta-analysis but none particularly good in its own right. Investigator Bloggs comes along and decides that he is going to do this properly and does a study of 1000 subjects, a big study supported by a proper funding body, well designed, and so forth. Now, which would you rather rely on in your final conclusion of therapeutic efficacy, the stand-alone study on 1000 subjects or a meta-analysis that includes with those 1000 subjects the five small trials, so you now have 1250 subjects but with the noise of the less well conducted smaller studies? Olkin would suggest that the latter is more powerful than the former, but I intuitively feel that the 1000-patient study would be better.

Dr. Sacks: I am not advocating that a meta-analysis is superior to an adequately sized and well-designed single study. In fact, I emphasize that a lot of the work we have been trying to do is to establish criteria for meta-analysis so that it is not done sloppily. I think the critical issue is what the weight of the total evidence is. Meta-analysis will be most useful when a definitive study does not exist, either in planning a definitive study or in making an estimate where there is no definitive study.

Dr. Lucas: The problem is that in evidence-based medicine, people are now in the process of evaluating the literature to determine how they should best proceed, and it is a relevant question whether you should go for the big definitive study or the meta-analysis that includes the big definitive study with all the little ones as well. Olkin's categorization would suggest that anybody evaluating medical practice should in fact always give top priority to the meta-analysis, and I am just challenging that.

Dr. Sacks: I think it is more often the case that meta-analysis of small studies will agree with the definitive single trial than disagree, so there is not necessarily a conflict.

Dr. van't Hof: Also, if you are thinking in terms of evidence-based medicine, you have to read through all the literature. It is a good thing to have a structured review, as with meta-analyses—it saves you a lot of time.

Dr. Klish: I want to know whether or not meta-analysis can make discoveries that the original studies were not intended to discover. The particular meta-analysis I am referring to is one that you are probably aware of that was done several years ago (1,2), when all the clinical trials of dietary treatment of hypercholesterolemia were analyzed. It was found that the incidence of heart disease decreased, as was shown in the individual studies, but the overall mortality increased, and the increased mortality was from violent death, murder, suicide, and other things. I have always been disturbed by that study, and I would like your opinion.

Dr. Sacks: That is an interesting area. Meta-analysis can certainly be used to generate a hypothesis and identify areas that need further research; as to whether you can conclusively answer a question that was not intended to be answered by the original studies, I am not sure that you can. In terms of cholesterol, I think a recent analysis showed that the mortality benefit, not surprisingly, turned out to be greatest in the patients at highest risk (3), and now with the more active drugs, it is becoming clear that you can save lives overall with treatment of hypercholesterolemia. What was useful about those early studies was to raise the issue of the overuse of some of those drugs in low-risk patients, and maybe a little caution was appropriate for physicians prescribing those drugs. Another example of the value of meta-analysis to try to answer other questions was a study undertaken by a gastroenterologist (4) who used studies of corticosteroid versus placebo in the treatment of a variety of illnesses to try to answer the question of whether the incidence of peptic ulcer was increased by corticosteroid treatment. There were very small numbers in all the studies, but by putting them together, he was able to show that there was a statistically significant increase in peptic ulcer in people who were given steroids. So I think useful information can come from that sort of exercise.

Dr. Lozoff: Are there any techniques within meta-analysis for giving differential weight to better or worse studies by some standard set of methodologic criteria.

Dr. Sacks: There is not a clear answer to that. There have been some papers that have examined the weighting of studies by quality criteria, but it gets complicated for a variety of reasons, mostly because no one has agreed on what are the most important criteria of quality of the primary studies or on how to weight them. None of these criteria has been validated, so although there has been some work in that area, we don't really have an answer.

Dr. Lozoff: In one of your very early slides of magnitude of effects, you had a real outlier. What is the effect of having such an outlier in a meta-analysis?

Dr. Sacks: This is also a question that has received a lot of attention from statisticians and others, but without a definitive answer. There is, however, an argument for including such outliers: you could argue that if you include a variety of patient populations and still found a fairly consistent overall trend, that is actually stronger evidence than just including people between the ages of 35 and 37 studied in England, for example.

Dr. Ferry: When you put together a multicenter clinical trial, you design a variety of things into it that make the study reliable; you try to get centers that are comparable in many ways, and there are many techniques to try to produce a first-class study. When you look at meta-analyses, you do not have any direct information about biases and about the way some of those individual studies were conducted, so it seems to me it is a little hard to interpret their quality. On the other hand, accepting what you say, that most of these studies really do match good clinical trials, then in general, do meta-analyses make the data more generalizable? In other words, do they interpret across a broader range?

Dr. Sacks: I think they do. In response to the early part of your question about the standards of multicenter studies versus the standards of individual studies, I think there is a lot of variability in the former too. I don't think you can really say that multicenter studies are always done better than smaller studies. In general, that may be true, but there have been some famous examples, e.g., among breast cancer studies, where patients were included who should not have been, and various things were done that cast a great deal of doubt on the results on these multicenter studies. So I think it is important, whether in small studies, large studies, or multicenter single studies, to do as careful an assessment as possible of the quality of that study, and there are various criteria for doing this.

Dr. Walter: I was interested in the results in Table 1 comparing the quality of meta-analyses in three different time periods. Looking at those rather quickly, it seems to me that there was no obvious trend to improvement in the quality of reported meta-analyses, although some of the variables seemed to show a pattern in that the middle time period had a rather poor quality: for instance, the description of treatment assignment was 95% in the first time period, 26% in the second, and back up to 79% in the third. Is there perhaps a U.S. renaissance going on in the most recent time period?

Dr. Sacks: Our overall conclusion was that perhaps there was a slight trend toward improvement, but it was over a relatively short period of time, and it is something that needs to be looked at again. There seems to be a tremendous amount of variability in the quality of meta-analysis, and although there are some that I think have been done very well, there are many that have been done very poorly. So with the proliferation of meta-analysis has come a greater diversity in the quality of the individual meta-analyses.

Dr. Hamburger: Most meta-analyses are retrospective, but the studies that we generally prefer are prospective.

Dr. Sacks: I think the issue there is not so much the point in time at which the study starts but the way we try to address the issue. The closer a meta-analysis is done to a prospective study, the better it is going to be—in other words, the question must be spelled out clearly, and the inclusion and exclusion criteria for the meta-analysis properly defined at the outset.

Dr. Whitehead: Where people ignore these quality features, do they do it deliberately, or do they do it because the data do not allow them to include these features? In other words, does this reveal a primary problem with the raw data? If so, doesn't it cast a question mark over the whole procedure?

Dr. Sacks: We tried to define criteria that will be applicable to the meta-analysis, not just to the primary studies, but it is certainly true that if there are major deficiencies in the primary studies, that will weaken the conclusions of the meta-analysis. But that is a different issue. All those 23 standards that we thought were important were things that can be done by the meta-analysis, not by the primary studies. Most of those meta-analyses were done before we proposed the standards, and, as I tried to show, some of the standards have met with some acceptance, but many of them have not. So those are our opinions as to what the standards should be; we are not saying that those are gold standards.

Dr. Berlin: I have heard an argument that ethical committees ought to look at summaries of existing data before they approve new studies. In this context, my feeling is that we are really obligated to do some kind of quantitative summary if possible before we start new studies. The answer may be that the existing data are not conclusive for a variety of reasons, either because existing studies are of poor quality or because there is a lot of heterogeneity in previous results, but all this is important to know before we undertake a new study, in addition to getting estimates of the likely effect size that we are looking for. Another point relates to multicenter trials versus meta-analysis. There are several examples, but I will mention one. In general, we think that bigger is better, but a study being large does not necessarily make it more reliable. Magnesium after myocardial infarction is an example (ISIS-4): because of issues regarding the timing of administration of magnesium relative to thrombolytic therapy, it seems that the study was not done under optimal conditions. The fact that we can look at a meta-analysis of previous studies before ISIS and then at ISIS itself gives us a contrast that we could not necessarily have picked up from ISIS alone or from the other studies alone. So here is an example in which we may have learned something from the meta-analysis and also from a large clinical trial about how to design the definitive study.

Dr. Rey: I was interested in two of your examples. One was the comparison of rice-based antidiarrhea treatment and WHO oral solution, and the conclusion of the meta-analysis was that there is no advantage to rice-based treatment. My opinion is that it is cleverer to say that rice-based solutions are as effective and less costly than the WHO solution. So we can have a different approach to the same data. The second example is vitamin A. There are two meta-analyses, as you say, and practically all the data come from Southeast Asia; their conclusion is that vitamin A protects against infectious diseases. In other studies, it has also been said that vitamin A is protective against AIDS. But two recent studies in well-nourished children

(5,6) have shown that vitamin A supplementation has a deleterious effect, not only by causing intoxication (25,000 units of vitamin A causes a 10% incidence of side effects) but because the incidence of infectious disease or respiratory disease was found to be increased in well-nourished children treated with vitamin A. So it appears that we are using mathematical approaches to try to solve unsolved problems that may be unsolvable in this way. We don't need meta-analyses when we look at the effect of penicillin or to prove that ascorbic acid prevents scurvy or that vitamin D prevents rickets. We use meta-analysis only when we have no idea of the result. I think in such cases, it would be more useful to conclude that we don't know and that we should organize prospective multicenter studies to try to prove that there is an effect or no effect.

Dr. Sacks: I agree with much of what you say. Clearly, one does not need to be a meta-analyst to show that well-nourished children are more likely to be harmed than to be benefited by megadoses of vitamins. However, as I said, I still believe that there is a role for well-done meta-analyses in the planning of definitive trials, in providing interim answers, and in suggesting new areas for further study.

REFERENCES

1. Criqui MH. Cholesterol, primary and secondary prevention, and all-cause mortality. *Ann Intern Med* 1991;115:973–976.
2. Holme I. Relation of coronary heart disease incidence and total mortality to plasma cholesterol reduction in randomized trials: use of meta-analysis. *Br Heart J* 1993;69(1 suppl):S42–S47.
3. Smith GD, Song F, Sheldon TA. Cholesterol lowering and mortality: the importance of considering initial level of risk. *Br Med J* 1993;306:1367–1373.
4. Messer J, Reitman D, Sacks HS, *et al.* Association of adrenocorticosteroid therapy and peptic ulcer disease. *N Engl J Med* 1983;309:21–24.
5. West KP Jr, Katz J, Ram Shrestha S, *et al.* Mortality of infants <6 mo of age supplemented with vitamin A: a randomized, double-masked trial in Nepal. *Am J Clin Nutr* 1995;62:143–148.
6. Dibley MJ, Sadjimin T, Kjolhede CL, Moulton LH. Vitamin A supplementation fails to reduce incidence of acute respiratory illness and diarrhea in preschool-age Indonesian children. *J Nutr* 1996; 126:434–442.

Clinical Trials in Infant Nutrition, edited by Jay A. Perman and Jean Rey, Nestlé Nutrition Workshop Series, Vol. 40, Nestec Ltd., Vevey/Lippincott-Raven Publishers, Philadelphia © 1998.

Publication Bias in Clinical Research: Outcome of Projects Submitted to Ethics Committees

Jesse A. Berlin

Center for Clinical Epidemiology and Biostatistics, University of Pennsylvania School of Medicine, Philadelphia, Pennsylvania, USA

In evaluations of medical or social strategies aimed at treatment or prevention of disease, the published scientific literature almost always plays a central role. Such evaluations may involve either informal reviews of the literature or, as is increasingly the case, formal research syntheses or meta-analyses. Regardless of which type of evaluation is undertaken, scientists and policy makers assume, often implicitly, that the published literature contains either all, or at least a representative sample of, the available data (1). The selective publication of scientific findings based on the magnitude and direction of the results—termed publication bias—could lead to serious errors in the estimation (from research syntheses) of the potential benefits of interventions. The purposes of this chapter are: (a) to present a brief description of selected early research on publication bias to provide a historical perspective; (b) to describe several empirical assessments of publication bias based on projects reviewed by institutional review boards (ethics committees); and (c) to present a brief discussion of some proposed solutions to the problem of publication bias.

PREVIOUS RESEARCH

The existence of publication bias has been a concern for about two decades in the social science literature (2–7). For example, White (4) reviewed research on the correlation between socioeconomic status and academic achievement and showed that the highest correlations are published in books (average correlation $r = 0.51$), compared with journal articles ($r = 0.34$) and unpublished material ($r = 0.24$). Glass *et al.* (6) found systematic differences in the magnitude of effects between journal articles and dissertations in a variety of meta-analyses in psychology. Smith (5), in summarizing studies of educational innovations, found that effect sizes were considerably smaller for unpublished studies than for published studies. Coursol and Wagner (7) surveyed psychological researchers who had conducted studies of therapeutic outcome. They found that both the decision to submit an article for

105

publication and the editorial decision to accept or reject were associated with the results of the research, with statistically significant results favored at each step. Specifically, they found that 82% of articles with a significant outcome were submitted, compared with 43% for articles with a nonsignificant outcome. Among articles submitted, 80% of the significant articles were accepted versus 50% of the nonsignificant studies. A consequence of these findings is that inferences based on published literature may be biased away from the null hypothesis.

The early work on publication bias has led to increasing concern about its existence in the medical literature and evidence that it is a problem (8–12). One early approach to assessing publication bias used only published literature by exploiting the relationship between sample size and effect size (8–10). The authors argued that in order for studies with small sample sizes to achieve statistically significant results, those studies would have to show large effect sizes. Thus, if publication bias exists, one would expect to see large effect sizes, on average, in small studies, and smaller effect sizes in larger studies. Working with a consecutive series of published reports of cancer therapy, Begg and Berlin (8,9) found strong evidence of the anticipated relationship between sample size and effect size. In subsequent work, Berlin *et al.* (10) found that the apparent magnitude of publication bias, as evidenced by the strength of the association between sample size and effect size, depended on several study characteristics. A finding of particular interest was that randomized trials showed little or no evidence of publication bias; that is, there was only a weak association between sample size and effect size, whereas nonrandomized (but still comparative) trials showed considerable bias (10).

In some clinical fields, it is possible to use a sampling frame that is unaffected by publication bias. Simes (11,12) examined studies that compared single alkylating agent therapy with combination chemotherapy in the treatment of advanced ovarian cancer. He restricted the summary to randomized trials. Using several strategies, he found 20 published trials. He found an additional six studies through a data base maintained by the National Cancer Institute, the Compilation of Experimental Cancer Therapy Protocol Summaries (13). Three of the four significant trials were published but not registered, whereas all six unpublished trials yielded nonsignificant results. When Simes performed a standard meta-analysis using only published studies, he observed a significant improvement in survival with use of combination chemotherapy ($p = 0.02$). When the analysis was restricted to registered studies, for which data were available in 13 of 14, the observed improvement in survival was smaller, and the summary result was no longer significant ($p = 0.24$).

Following these studies, several empirical assessments of publication bias of a somewhat different nature were conducted (14–16). These four studies, described in three papers, involved the identification of projects that were submitted to institutional review boards (ethics committees) and follow-up of those projects to determine whether they had been published or not and whether they had obtained statistically significant findings. The design and results of these studies are the focus of the next section of this paper.

EMPIRICAL ASSESSMENTS OF PUBLICATION BIAS

The Oxford Study

The Oxford Study of publication bias was initiated in May 1990 and was reported in *Lancet* (14). The files containing all research protocols submitted to the Central Oxford Research Ethics Committee (COREC) between January 1, 1984, and December 31, 1987, provided the framework for this study. From those files, the investigators abstracted protocol titles and the names of the principal investigators. They wrote to all of the principal investigators explaining the purpose of the study and followed up with a telephone interview for information on the status of the study as of May 1990.

For projects that had actually begun, further information on the design, organization, results, and publication status of each study was obtained in the interview. Coinvestigators were contacted in the absence of, or at the request of, the principal investigator. The information requested included the source of funding of the study, the final sample size, the nature of the comparison group if one existed, and the main study findings, especially the attainment of statistical significance. Further information was requested regarding publications and presentations, papers rejected, planned, or still under review, and reasons for nonpublication. For clinical trials, a specific question was asked about the use of randomization.

The important specific definitions were as follows:

1. An *experimental study* was defined as one in which one or more variables were controlled by the investigator in order to study the effect on an outcome measure. This included *clinical trials,* in which a particular procedure or treatment was being studied, usually in comparison with another treatment or procedure.
2. Studies were considered *statistically significant* if the main outcome achieved a p value of 0.05 or less, as showing a *nonsignificant trend* if the difference or association carried a p value greater than 0.05, or as *null* if no difference was observed between the study groups or if no significant correlations were observed.
3. *Publication* implied acceptance by a journal but did not include book chapters or published meeting abstracts or proceedings.

The principal statistical analysis involved the use of logistic regression to examine predictors of the dichotomous outcome variable representing publication status. Separate analyses were conducted using the outcome "published or presented" and yielded similar results. A main question of interest was whether the magnitude of publication bias varied across different subgroups of studies, so appropriate interaction terms involving the "statistical significance" variable and each of several covariates were also examined.

The investigators identified 720 studies approved by the COREC during the 4-year period. Studies were excluded from further consideration if they had been subsequently withdrawn by the original investigators (n = 4); if they were not formal research studies (n = 5); if they were lost to follow-up because the principal investigator could not be contacted (n = 172); because the original investigators provided inadequate information (n = 15); or because the investigators failed to respond to the mailed questionnaire (n = 28), leaving 487 studies contributed by 216 investigators. Comparisons between those studies for which the investigator was found and interviewed and those for which the investigator was not located or did not respond revealed no significant differences in the year approved, the number of studies approved by the COREC per investigator, the main department of the study, or the type of study design.

As of May 1990, 287 studies had been partly (recruitment alone) or fully (recruitment and follow-up) completed; 100 had never started; 58 had been prematurely terminated or suspended; and 42 were still in progress. Only those studies that had been analyzed were considered to have the potential for being written up and published, so tests for publication bias were restricted to the 285 studies that had been analyzed, including 148 clinical trials.

By May 1990, 138 (48%) of the studies had been published. The unadjusted relationship between significance of the main outcome and publication status showed strong evidence of publication bias. Sixty-seven percent of published studies had statistically significant findings, compared with only 29% of studies neither published nor presented. Only 15% (23/154) of studies with significant results remained unpublished or unpresented compared with 44% (43/97) of those with null results. The unadjusted odds ratio (OR) for publication with a significant result versus a null result was 2.96 (95% confidence interval, CI: 1.68 to 5.21), indicating a higher likelihood of publication with a significant than with a null result. For the 148 clinical trials alone, the association was smaller, with an unadjusted OR of 2.10 (CI: 0.98 to 4.52). After adjustment for multiple other factors using logistic regression, the odds ratios for significant versus null studies were 2.32 (CI: 1.25 to 4.28) for all studies and 1.59 (CI: 0.70 to 3.60) for the clinical trials.

In the logistic regression analyses, other predictors of publication included sample size >20 (OR = 1.74; CI: 0.95 to 3.18) and funding source. Specifically, industry-sponsored studies were significantly less likely to be published (OR = 0.36; CI: 0.16 to 0.83).

Of the 78 unpublished studies, 23 (29%) had significant results. The most frequent reason given by the investigators for not publishing was that a paper had been written but not yet submitted, or submitted but not yet accepted (n = 35 of 175 reasons, 19%). For the 43 unpublished studies with null results, the presence of the null result was the most frequent reason for failing to write up the study. Editorial rejection was cited infrequently (9%) as the reason for studies remaining unpublished.

The authors also examined the association between the statistical significance of a study and the likelihood of it being *submitted* for publication. The adjusted OR of 2.94 (CI: 1.43 to 6.01) for submission was higher than the OR of 2.32 for publication, suggesting that the investigators of the original studies, rather than journal editors, play a major role in publication bias.

Differences in the degree of publication bias were examined between various subgroups of studies by testing the covariate statistical significance interaction terms in the logistic regression models. The only significant difference in the degree of publication bias between subgroups was related to study design. The adjusted OR for publication bias in observational and laboratory-based studies (including both comparative and noncomparative studies) was 3.79 (CI: 1.47 to 9.76), compared to only 0.84 (CI: 0.34 to 2.09) for randomized clinical trials. For clinical trials alone, randomized trials were significantly less susceptible to publication bias (OR = 0.73; CI: 0.28 to 1.91) than nonrandomized (but still comparative) trials (OR = 10.26; CI: 1.76 to 60).

Johns Hopkins Studies

Because the design of these investigations was so similar to that of the Oxford Study described above, I focus mostly on comparisons between the approaches. These studies were performed by Dickersin and colleagues at Johns Hopkins University (15). The original studies forming the basis for this research were those appearing on the records of the two institutional review boards serving the Johns Hopkins Health Institutions and approved in or before 1980. One board served several medical institutions (to be referred to as MED), and the other served the School of Hygiene and Public Health (referred to as PH). The logs of the two boards contained 1048 applications (MED, 766; PH, 282). Trained project staff were responsible for locating logged applications in files, for abstracting and recording information from the applications, and for classifying the study designs. The applications were read independently by two readers, and disagreements were adjudicated by a master reader.

Three hundred eleven applications were excluded because they were either withdrawn or not approved (MED, 28), were approved but not implemented (MED, 133; PH, 51), were classified as exempt from review (MED, 23), did not describe a research study (for example, applications for training) (MED, 26; PH, 6), or did not involve humans (MED, 19; PH, 25). The remaining studies were considered eligible for interview.

In 1988, the principal investigators of the 737 interview-eligible studies, or their surrogates, were contacted by trained interviewers in random order. The nature of the study findings was classified as in the Oxford Study (14) (statistically significant, suggestive trend but not statistically significant, or no trend or difference); however, for analytic purposes, significant studies here were contrasted with the combined group of trend and nonsignificant studies. (In the Oxford Study, significant studies were contrasted directly with the null studies.) Studies were classified as published if they were reported in journal articles, books or book chapters, monographs, or were available from medical libraries or from a public archive (for example, the National Technical Information Service). These authors did not examine publication in a journal as a separate outcome.

The results of the Hopkins studies were very similar to those of the Oxford Study (14). At the time of the interview, 277 (81%) of the 342 MED studies had been published, as had 113 (66%) of the PH studies. For MED, 89% of the significant studies had been published, compared with 69% of the nonsignificant studies (OR = 3.38; CI: 1.96 to 5.83). For PH, the values were 71% and 58%, respectively (OR = 1.78; CI: 0.94 to 3.39). Several other variables were predictive of publication status, including funding source. For both MED and PH, industry-funded studies had the lowest publication rates (65% and 50%, respectively), but the significance of that unadjusted result was not maintained in multiple regression analyses. Sample size ($\geq$100 versus <100) was not significantly associated with publication status in either MED or PH in logistic regression models.

The reasons for not publishing were similar in these studies to those in the Oxford Study (14). Over 90% (MED, 97%; PH, 93%) of the unpublished studies were not published because of the actions or inactions of the original investigators. Only a small proportion (MED, 3.1%; PH, 6.8%) of papers remained unpublished because they had been rejected by a journal.

National Institutes of Health Clinical Trials

The method for identifying eligible studies was different in this investigation from in the other two, but the strategy was similar. This study was also conducted by Dickersin and her colleagues at the Johns Hopkins University (16). Studies were identified from the magnetic tapes of the 1979 Inventory of Clinical Trials from the National Institutes of Health (17). A total of 986 trials were available on the tapes, 654 funded by the National Cancer Institute (NCI) and 332 by other institutes. The NCI studies were excluded because they were thought to include a large proportion of ''trials'' that were not stand-alone trials but were parts of ongoing programs. As in the other studies described above, principal investigators or their surrogates were contacted and interviewed about study characteristics and outcomes. Definitions of variables were essentially the same as those used in the Johns Hopkins studies.

Of 332 trials listed on the tapes, 293 (83%) were eligible for interview. Complete interviews were obtained for 217 (74%) of the trials. The 198 trials for which there was publication information form the basis of the analysis. These studies were found to be comparable on several dimensions to the studies for which incomplete or no information was available. A large proportion (184/198, 93%) of the trials had been published. Publication was more likely for trials reporting a statistically significant finding than for those with a nonsignificant finding (OR = 7.04; CI: 1.90 to 26). No other trial or author characteristic was associated with publication status. However, publication bias appeared to be absent in multicenter trials (OR = 0.84; CI: 0.07 to 9.68) but severe in single-center trials (OR = 21; CI: 2.60 to 172).

Meta-Analysis of All Four Studies of Publication Bias

Dickersin and colleagues (16) performed a meta-analysis of the four studies described above. The results are summarized in Fig. 1. The combined, unadjusted OR

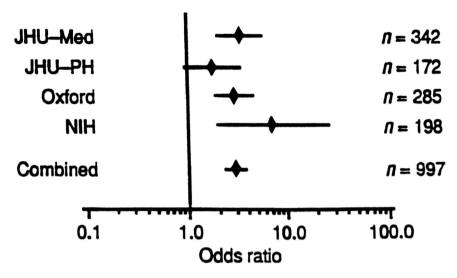

FIG. 1. Meta-analysis of four studies [Johns Hopkins Medicine (JHU-Med) (15); Johns Hopkins Public Health (JHU-PH)(15); Oxford (14); NIH (16)] examining the association between significant results and publication: unadjusted odds ratios and confidence intervals (with permission from Chapman & Hall publishers).

was 2.88 (CI: 2.13 to 3.89). There was little evidence of heterogeneity of the odds ratios across studies of publication bias.

SOLUTIONS TO THE PROBLEM OF PUBLICATION BIAS

The existence of publication bias is clearly demonstrated by the studies described. Thus, the potential for obtaining biased summaries from research syntheses based solely on published studies is real and of concern. Various methods have been proposed to estimate the potential magnitude of publication bias in the context of performing a meta-analysis, to correct for the bias analytically, and to prevent its occurrence. I describe each of the approaches briefly in this section.

A simple and practical technique for assessing the potential for publication bias is the "funnel plot," first proposed by Light and Pillemer (18). This method involves plotting the measure of effect (for example, the log odds ratio) against a measure of study size, either the actual sample size or the inverse of the variance of the effect measure. In the absence of publication bias, the points should produce a funnel shape such that the values of the effect size are scattered symmetrically around the true estimate, with that scattering narrowing as the sample size increases. Figure 2 (19) shows an idealized funnel plot. If publication bias exists, there may be few or no points around the point estimate, indicating no effect (for example, a log odds ratio of 0) for the small studies. Alternatively, points may appear to be missing on one side of the plot.

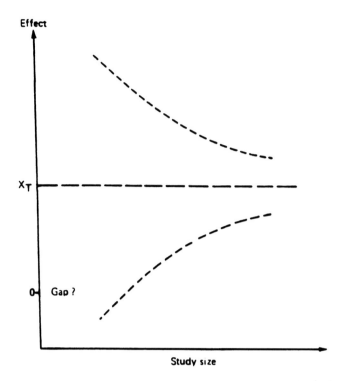

FIG. 2. Idealized funnel plot of expected scatter of study results according to study size. X_T indicates a true positive effect; 0 indicates a null effect; and "Gap" indicates the expected lack of published results in the event of publication bias (19).

Figures 3 and 4 show two funnel plots representing studies of psychoeducational programs for surgical patients (18,20). In the first plot, only the published studies are included, and the funnel appears to have a gap where the small studies showing no effect of these programs should be. The second plot includes unpublished studies, and the former gap is filled by those studies.

A recent method proposed to assess publication bias involves the use of a modified version of the ordinary Kendall's τ rank correlation procedure (21). It is a direct statistical analog of the funnel plot described above. Although this test is based on the appealing analogy with the funnel plot and is relatively free from restrictive assumptions, it is not very powerful statistically when the number of studies is 25 or fewer.

An early approach to quantifying publication bias in a given data set was developed by Rosenthal (22). He proposed the calculation of a quantity he called the "fail-safe N" when the results of a meta-analysis are statistically significant. His method uses the Z statistics from the individual studies included in the meta-analysis to calculate the number of unpublished studies showing no effect—that is, with a Z statistic of zero—that would have to exist to render the overall combined Z statistic

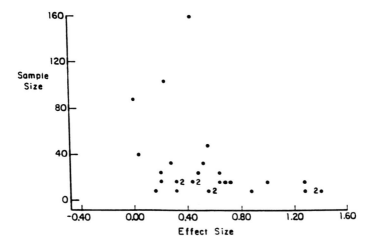

FIG. 3. Funnel plot for published studies only: analysis of data from Devine and Cook's (20) review of psychoeducational programs for surgical patients. (From Light and Pillemer, ref. 18, reprinted by permission of the publishers. Copyright 1984 by the President and Fellows of Harvard College.)

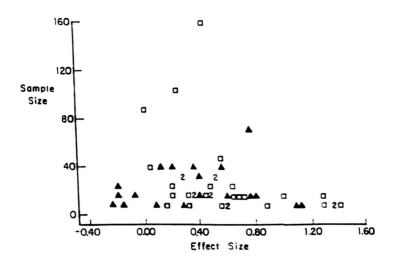

FIG. 4. Funnel plot for published (□) and unpublished (▲) studies combined: analysis of data from Devine and Cook's (20) review of psychoeducational programs for surgical patients. (From Light and Pillemer, ref. 18, reprinted by permission of the publishers. Copyright 1984 by the President and Fellows of Harvard College.)

(including both published and unpublished studies) nonsignificant. If the number of unpublished null studies required to overturn the significant result is small, then the meta-analysis should be interpreted with some caution. If that number is large, then the conclusions of the meta-analysis are unlikely to change even if a few unpublished studies do exist. In general, this approach is of limited utility for two reasons: first, because it uses only Z statistics and ignores quantitative estimates of effects (for example, odds ratios); and second, because the assumption that all the unpublished studies have a Z statistic of exactly zero is unrealistic.

Methods of correcting for publication bias deal specifically with the issue of estimating bias-corrected effect sizes but make some fairly strong assumptions about the underlying mechanisms leading to the bias. For example, a method proposed by Iyengar and Greenhouse (23) examined two particular functional forms relating the p value attained by a study to its probability of publication. They assume in one approach, for example, that the probability of publication is proportional to the t statistic for each study when the study is not statistically significant and that all statistically significant studies are published. The available data are used to estimate both the average effect size—corrected for publication bias using weighted distributions—and the probabilities of publication. A similar but more recent approach relaxes some of the assumptions about the selection mechanism (24). This method still assumes that the p value is the primary determinant of publication; however, it does not assume a particular shape for the relationship between the p value and the probability of publication. The authors propose this method as an exploratory technique, intended as an informal tool to assist in establishing the likelihood that publication bias is a serious problem in a given meta-analysis. They suggest, however, that when bias is identified by their approach, one should be very cautious about using their model (or any other) to correct it. They argue that attention should instead be directed toward identifiying the causes of the bias, perhaps by initiating a search for missing studies (24).

Because none of the available methods is entirely satisfactory for correcting publication bias, efforts should be directed at its prevention. One way to avoid publication bias would be to obtain unpublished studies. In some cases, unpublished data can represent a large proportion of the available data. For example, in the Early Breast Cancer Trialists Collaborative Group meta-analysis (25), 20 of the 92 studies (22%) providing data for the meta-analysis were unpublished. It is often impracticable, however, to identify unpublished studies (26). Further, some investigators have chosen not to include unpublished studies in a meta-analysis because those studies have not usually been peer-reviewed (27). A survey of authors of meta-analyses, meta-analysis methodologists, and editors showed that most (78%) of the meta-analysts and methodologists favored the inclusion of unpublished material in meta-analyses under some conditions, whereas only 47% of the editors favored the inclusion of unpublished data (28).

In the clinical trials field, there has been some movement toward the prospective registration of all initiated studies (29–33). This would provide a sampling frame that would identify studies independently of their findings, much along the lines of the Simes (11,12) study described above. Funding for such registries has been difficult to obtain and seems to remain an issue. Various institutes within the National Institutes of Health support registries of studies involving human beings (31,32). The systems of ethics committees and institutional review boards in place in many countries could provide a convenient framework for such registration.

CONCLUSIONS

The empirical studies of publication bias, coupled with previous research, show that publication bias is a potentially serious problem when a meta-analysis is performed or even when individual studies are evaluated. Although there is some evidence that publication bias is not as severe for randomized trials as for nonrandomized trials, the potential for bias to exist should not be dismissed solely on the basis of the presence of randomization. In any meta-analysis, funnel plots or related analytic approaches should be used to evaluate the potential for publication bias. If there is evidence of publication bias, results of the meta-analysis need to be interpreted extremely cautiously. Because it is not clear that current analytic corrections for publication bias are entirely satisfactory, the best solution to publication bias is prevention. One prevention strategy is to try to obtain unpublished studies, but this is not always feasible without registries of trials and is not universally viewed as desirable, given the lack of peer review for unpublished studies. Registries—perhaps using the framework of existing ethics committees or institutional review boards—represent a promising strategy.

REFERENCES

1. Sterling TD, Rosenbaum WL, Weinkam JJ. Publication decisions revisited: the effect of the outcome of statistical tests on the decision to publish and vice versa. *Am Stat* 1995;49:108–112.
2. Sterling TD. Publication decisions and their possible effects on inferences drawn from tests of significance or vice versa. *J Am Stat Assoc* 1959;54:30–34.
3. Greenwald AG. Consequences of prejudice against the null hypothesis. *Psychol Bull* 1975;82:2–12.
4. White KR. The relation between socioeconomic status and academic achievement. *Psychol Bull* 1982;91:461–481.
5. Smith ML. Publication bias and meta-analysis. *Eval Educ* 1980;4:22–24.
6. Glass GV, McGraw B, Smith ML. *Meta-analysis in social research.* Beverly Hills, CA: Sage Publications, 1981.
7. Coursol A, Wagner EE. Effect of positive findings on submission and acceptance rates: a note on meta-analysis bias. *Profess Psychol* 1986;17:136–137.
8. Begg CB, Berlin JA. Publication bias: a problem in interpreting medical data. *J R Stat Soc A* 1988; 151(part 3):419–463.
9. Begg CB, Berlin JA. Publication bias and dissemination of clinical research. *J Natl Cancer Inst* 1989;81:107–115.
10. Berlin JA, Begg CB, Louis TA. An assessment of publication bias using a sample of published clinical trials. *J Am Stat Assoc* 1989;84:381–392.
11. Simes RJ. Confronting publication bias: a cohort design for meta-analysis. *Stat Med* 1987;6:11–29.
12. Simes RJ. Publication bias: the case for an international registry of clinical trials. *J Clin Oncol* 1986; 4:1529–1541.
13. US Department of Health and Human Services. *Compilation of experimental cancer therapy protocol summaries. NIH Publication No 83-1116,* 7th ed. Washington, DC: US Department of Health and Human Services, 1983.

14. Easterbrook PJ, Berlin JA, Gopalan R, Matthews DR. Publication bias in clinical research. *Lancet* 1991;337:867–872.
15. Dickersin K, Min YI, Meinert CL. Factors influencing publication of research results: follow-up of applications submitted to two institutional review boards. *JAMA* 1992;267:374–378.
16. Dickersin K, Min YI. NIH clinical trials and publication bias. *Online J Curr Clin Trials* [serial online] 1993;Apr 28:Doc No 50.
17. National Institutes of Health. *NIH inventory of clinical trials: fiscal year 1979* (unpublished). Datatapes obtained from the Division of Research Grants, Research and Evaluation Branch, Bethesda, MD, 1980.
18. Light RJ, Pillemer DB. *Summing up: the science of reviewing research.* Cambridge, MA: Harvard University Press, 1984.
19. Vandenbroucke JP. Passive smoking and lung cancer: a publication bias? *Br Med J* 1988;296: 391–392.
20. Devine EC, Cook TD. Effects of psycho-educational interventions on length of hospital stay: a meta-analytic review of 34 studies. In: Light RJ, ed. *Evaluation studies review annual,* vol 8. Beverly Hills, CA: Sage, 1983.
21. Begg CB, Mazumdar M. Operating characteristics of a rank correlation test for publication bias. *Biometrics* 1994;50:1088–1101.
22. Rosenthal R. The file drawer problem and tolerance for null results. *Psychol Bull* 1979;86:638–641.
23. Iyengar S, Greenhouse JB. Selection models and the file-drawer problem. *Stat Sci* 1988;3:109–117.
24. Dear KBG, Begg CB. An approach for assessing publication bias prior to performing a meta-analysis. *Stat Sci* 1992;7:237–245.
25. Early Breast Cancer Trialists Collaborative Group. *Treatment of early breast cancer. Vol I. Worldwide evidence, 1985–1990.* New York: Oxford University Press, 1990.
26. Hetherington J, Dickersin K, Chalmers I, *et al.* Retrospective and prospective identification of unpublished controlled trials: lessons from a survey of obstetricians and pediatricians. *Pediatrics* 1989;84: 374–380.
27. Chalmers TC, Berrier J, Sacks HS, Levin H, Reitman D, Nagalingam R. Meta-analysis of clinical trials as a scientific discipline. II. Replicate variability and comparison of studies that agree and disagree. *Stat Med* 1987;6:733–744.
28. Cook DJ, Guyatt GH, Ryan G, Clifton J, Buckingham L, Willan A, *et al.* Should unpublished data be included in meta-analyses? Current convictions and controversies. *JAMA* 1993;269:2749–2753.
29. Meinert CL. Toward prospective registration of clinical trials. *Controlled Clin Trials* 1988;9:1–5.
30. Dickersin K. Report from the panel on the Case for Registers of Clinical Trials at the Eighth Annual Meeting of the Society for Clinical Trials. *Controlled Clin Trials* 1988;9:76–81.
31. Dickersin K. Why register clinical trials?—Revisited. *Controlled Clin Trials* 1992;13:170–177.
32. Making clinical trialists register (Noticeboard). *Lancet* 1992;338:244–245.
33. Dickersin K. Research registries. In: Cooper H, Hedges L, eds. *The handbook of research synthesis.* New York: Russell Sage Foundation, 1994.

DISCUSSION

Dr. Aeschlimann: Because of the bias toward publishing positive results, I am afraid that if I want to do a meta-analysis on safety data from published results, the final result will be unreliable.

Dr. Berlin: Safety issues are also complicated by the fact that we are often looking at very small event rates, particularly with adverse effects of drugs, and those are very hard to detect in individual studies. So you are dealing with an added complication that the studies, in general, are going to be too small to look at the issue properly, and then, there is also a zero event rate in both groups, which is quite often the case in some of the safety studies. One suggestion is that we really need larger safety studies to begin with.

Dr. Guesry: There may be an additional publication bias because of the problem of publication in little known journals. I suspect that the visibility of the journal in which the study is published is very different depending on whether the results are significant or nonsignificant. Some of the thousands of publications are barely available in libraries.

Dr. Berlin: Dickersin looked at that in the Johns Hopkins study, and your suspicion was correct: the significant studies were more likely to be published in a high-visibility journal. A Scandinavian study (1) also looked at the issue of reference bias: when you look at a review article that summarizes the existing literature, and you examine the references that are cited by that article, and then do your own search to find all of the existing literature, then there seems to be preferential citation of the significant results. I think part of the issue here is that scientists need to get promoted; and to get promoted, you have to publish; and to publish, you have to find significant results—it's a vicious cycle. One point I didn't make clearly enough is the focus on p values; if we had started out looking at likelihood methods or even confidence intervals, then we might have avoided a lot of publication bias—it is the focus on p values and $p < 0.05$ that is really the issue here.

Dr. van't Hof: Although I am convinced of the existence of publication bias, I wonder if you have overestimated it because the quality of the study itself may be a confounder in this situation. If the quality of the study is bad, the results will not be good, or there will be no useful result, so in this case, you hesitate to publish.

Dr. Berlin: I think you are asking whether statistical significance, publication status, and study quality are confounding variables. Even after you adjust for various measures of study quality, you still see this publication bias effect. I think the more interesting question is probably the interaction question; that is, are poor-quality studies subject to a different degree of publication bias than good-quality studies? What we are suggesting, and are not really able to prove from one example, is that higher-quality studies and particularly randomized trials seem to be less prone to publication bias than others. They are not immune from publication bias—in fact, you can find examples of groups of randomized trials where there is some evidence of publication bias.

Dr. Madden: The idea of an electronic journal is intriguing. Would it be peer-reviewed? Do you see this is as a trend? And also, could you say something about your thoughts on a registry?

Dr. Berlin: Henry Sacks is the editor of the one journal that I know about, which is the *On Line Journal of Current Clinical Trials.* It is to my knowledge the only existing electronically published journal. It is peer-reviewed. There was discussion *ad nauseam* when we were setting the journal up about the issue of peer review, and let me reassure you that if anything, we are erring on the side of too much peer review because of potential criticism. There is a risk with any kind of electronic medium that proper peer review will not be implemented. As to the registry issue, I think the idea of a registry is fairly widely accepted in the clinical trials community in principle, but the problem has been that nobody wants to pay for a registry, and that is part of the impetus for the Cochrane collaboration. What is happening is that people in the Cochrane collaboration are in effect creating their own registries, at least of published trials, using their own resources and their own time. This is something that we are moving toward, whether or not anybody wants to pay for it.

Dr. Uauy: I would encourage the model of the Cochrane data base, where people register their protocols before they have results, and at the present time, they are providing data from all of the registered studies, whether they are published or not. I think that is going to be the only way of addressing this problem in the long run. The other point I would like to make is that in the literature, and I think this model is true for a lot of pediatric interventions, there are usually several small to medium-sized trials showing effects, and then you do a collaborative prospective randomized trial, and you have no effect; we have at least three or four in the neonatal literature over the last few years—intravenous immunoglobulin, comparisons of corticosteroids for the prevention of various conditions, and so on—and we find that the large control trials show no effects. So I think that the publication bias in favor of positive results is affecting clinical practice in a deleterious way, and we should be more demanding about what we accept as necessary evidence to modify clinical practice, whether it is published or not.

Dr. Berlin: One point I didn't make clear enough is that when I spoke about registration, I was really talking about *prospective* registration, that is, registration before the conduct of the study—so before you know what the answer is, you register the trial, so that even if you never finish the trial, somebody knows that it existed or should have existed. That is the only way of avoiding any kind of selection bias in the registry itself. I think you are touching on an issue about the fundamental process of how medical research takes place. In fact, it is not a random process at all—the statistical models all have some assumptions about random sampling. The kind of process that you are referring to reflects the fact that it is the positivity or possibly the negativity of preceding research that stimulates new studies. The whole statistical framework of the null hypothesis is bogus in that context, because nobody would really undertake a study based on the belief that the null hypothesis was true.

There is a statistical framework that says, "here is the null," but what I am really trying to do is to knock down the null hypothesis. However, if I didn't have some reasonable prior suspicion that the null is not true, why would I bother spending all that money and all that time? I think the situation relating to how studies get done is probably more chaotic than we like to believe, and it may be an argument for prospective meta-analysis. One reason why the FDA has not gotten more involved in meta-analysis as a way of evaluating the evidence is that it is a retrospective process, and we don't know why the research got done or how it got done. In fact, what we should be doing is sitting down right at the beginning and saying here are the clinical issues, here are the subgroups that are important, so what is the best way to design not the first trial but the next five trials that you are going to need to provide the evidence that will convince us one way or the other that the treatment works or doesn't work?

Dr. Clarke: The title of this chapter was "Publication bias in clinical research," and yet, you have dealt almost exclusively with clinical trials, and of course that doesn't cover the full range of clinical research, which also makes a very helpful contribution in straightforward observational clinical work and sometimes in retrospective assessment of clinical data and that sort of thing—it doesn't always have to be trials. I am the most avid supporter of everything you should do about trials—randomizing, double-blinding, etc.—but I do sound a slight note of caution. For those of us who have to make policy decisions on the available data, sometimes the controlled trials don't come up with the best answers, so far as one can assess. If you take, for instance, folic acid supplementation in the prevention of neural tube defect, the only prospective controlled trial comes up with a value of 800 μg of folic acid per day, whereas I think universally now the value advised is 400 μg, and that is based almost entirely on retrospective data. I wonder if you could comment?

Dr. Berlin: I may have emphasized the clinical trial aspect of publication bias studies, but in fact, the Oxford Study covered the entire range of studies. In terms of retrospective studies, I think that if you get into retrospective versus randomized studies in a given clinical area, there are going to be strengths and weaknesses to each. In breast cancer screening, for example, there are some obvious strengths to the large randomized trials, but there are some obvious weaknesses also in terms of compliance and crossover and contamination of groups. So I would not dream of saying that the only thing we should base our clinical decisions on is randomized trials—clearly, in some cases, it is not feasible to do randomized trials. I think the point that you are making is that somebody has to make a decision on the basis of the data, and those data may be better in some cases than in others.

Dr. Rey: The story of folic acid and neural tube defects is more complicated than Dr. Clarke stated. First of all was the MRC study, the secondary prevention study in women who had already given birth to a child with a neural tube defect. In this, they used 4 or 5 mg a day. Then there was the Hungarian study, a primary prevention study using 700 μg/day with other vitamins added, and it is not clear to this day whether folic acid alone is sufficient to prevent neural tube defects in primary prevention. It is also amusing to remind ourselves that an ethics committee at the beginning of the 1960s rejected a double-blind versus placebo study, which was finally realized by the MRC 10 years later. So the actions of an ethics committee may also be a possible source of bias! I know another story of bias introduced by the peer-review system: the original research of Weijers and van de Kamer on the role of gluten in celiac disease was rejected by an American journal because, in the opinion of the reviewer, it was impossible that bread could be responsible for celiac disease. This is the reason why they published all their papers, except one, in *Acta Paediatrica Scandinavica.*

Dr. Roche: Could you clarify what you mean when you ask a principal investigator whether he has published the results of his study. Many studies are multifaceted, and results could easily be published that are not central to the major hypothesis addressed by the study. He could still say he published the results, even if this was only a description of the recruitment process.

Dr. Berlin: We had to take their word for it; there was no way of looking at every publication.

Dr. Lucas: I think we have all accepted today the aphorism that it is unethical to do a badly designed study. Would we also accept the aphorism that it is unethical not to register or make available the results of a clinical trial, regardless of the findings? If we actually regarded it as unethical, then this could be a duty for ethics committees rather than just something that they might or might not take care of; in other words, it should be a specified duty that was regulatory. Is that something that could come out of this meeting?

Dr. Berlin: I would say clearly, yes. In fact, we are preparing a chapter for a Cochrane collaboration book, and we managed to get hold of an as yet unpublished manuscript from Iain Chalmers, who was arguing that very thing, that ethics committees are not fulfilling their obligation if they do not insist on registration and publication of results of studies.

REFERENCE

1. Gøtzsche PC. Reference bias in reports of drug trials. *Br Med J* 1987;295:654–656.

Clinical Trials in Infant Nutrition, edited by
Jay A. Perman and Jean Rey, Nestlé Nutrition
Workshop Series, Vol. 40, Nestec Ltd.,
Vevey/Lippincott-Raven Publishers,
Philadelphia © 1998.

Design of Randomized Clinical Trials: Review of Criteria for Patient Inclusion in Trials of Infant Nutrition

Frank L. Iber

Loyola University, Gastroenterology Section, Edward Hines Jr. Hospital, Hines, Illinois, USA

The randomized controlled trial is the most desirable design to test issues of infant nutrition because it is most free of bias and, through experience, has had the greatest influence in changing delivery of health care. In this chapter, I draw on my experience in studies in this field over the last 10 years and emphasize some of the unique problems of conducting studies in infants.

Randomized controlled trials (RCT) of infant nutrition vary widely in their goals, which in turn largely influence the study design and the criteria for selection of subjects. Nearly all goals in trials in infant nutrition relate to growth and development. A few trials concerned with novel products focus on adverse effects that are common in infants with selected inborn errors of metabolism and infrequent in others. Table 1 lists common goals that are the basis for undertaking trials. Prominent features of setting and reaching the goal are establishing just what will be measured to determine the outcome and which types of infants will be studied.

Growth and development are among the most common and important outcomes of infant nutritional studies. Changes in body weight, length, and head circumference, as well as motor and psychological maturation, are among the most widely used measures, but many surrogate outcome markers are used in order to dissect some biologically appropriate change of maturation or to shorten the period of observation. The commendable desire to shorten the length of intervention required to establish differences in growth and development has led to unestablished methods being used to define the primary outcome. Experience with the variability and rates of change in normal growth of each of these markers largely determines the duration of a study and influences the size of the sample. Roche and Guo *(this volume)* provide excellent norms for time of change of body weight and head circumference. Unfortunately, many other markers of growth and development are not well characterized for variability and rate of change, and without such information, protocol planning is impaired.

To accomplish the goal of the study, many secondary issues influence the trial

TABLE 1. *Purpose of trials in infants of various nutritional treatments*

Normal growth and development (1,2)
Catch-up growth in low-birth-weight and short-gestational-age infants
Catch-up growth in diseased infants (3,4)
Maintenance of growth and development
With or following diarrhea (5)
Operation (6)
With impaired diets (7)
Growth and development with special diets (8)
Growth and development in inborn errors of metabolism (9,10)
Measurement of a highly specific function of development or biochemistry (11)
Assessment of toxicity

---

design and subject selection. Prominent examples of these are listed in Table 2 and are elaborated in this section.

ISSUES OF TIME

Interventions reaching the outcome in a few days or weeks make it easier to enroll subjects and are often conducted with all interventions tightly controlled in the clinic or study unit, thus leading to better compliance. Much longer interventions require more cooperation of the parents and raise problems of compliance with the intervention. Failure to continue the intervention—or to limit feeding to the desired intervention—and failure to obtain the essential outcome measure increase with the length of study. To lessen the loss of subjects, features of the caregiver become increasingly important as entry criteria. When recruitment is prolonged over many months or

TABLE 2. *Secondary considerations influencing entry criteria and study design*

Issues of time
    Time to complete a single intervention
    Time to complete recruitment
    Time to complete study
Restrictiveness of entry criteria and exclusions
    High restrictiveness may exclude a responsive group of subjects
    Comparability of study group to population targeted for the treatment
    Availability of sufficient subjects
Issues of parent or caregiver
    Extra requirements for parent
    Pain, annoyance or risk to infant
    What is given up or interdicted by study
    Duration
    Conflict with food lore or societal mores
Issues of compliance
    Adherence to the feeding requirements
    Providing primary endpoints
    Methods of statistical treatment of data

---

years, there is the possibility that changing routine practice patterns or other factors may make those entering the study in the second half quite different from those enrolled initially. Initial entrants often take part in a study because of the enthusiasm of their doctors and the staff over a novel treatment, but this effect is lost after a year or so. Many studies handle lagging recruitment by relaxing entry criteria or adding centers that may be less committed to the study protocol. Extremely long studies often suffer from changes in study coordinators and other key personnel.

ISSUES OF RESTRICTIVE ENTRY CRITERIA

All studies estimate the magnitude of the outcome that must be observed to be meaningful and use this to set the sample size. The sample size is always smaller when the entry criteria are extremely strict and a very homogeneous group of subjects is studied. Such restriction slows recruitment and may limit the generalizability of the results when the admission features are to be extrapolated to the larger population with the condition, who may indeed be quite different. Such restriction often excludes the most severely impaired, who may have the most to gain from the intervention. The restrictiveness of the entry requirements may force the study to be multicentered in order to be completed in a reasonable time.

ISSUES OF THE CAREGIVER

Infants require extensive care, and investigative protocols always place some additional burden on the caregiver. Administration of the diet, obtaining supplies, and transporting the child to the study site for essential observations cannot be avoided, but the bother to the family can be minimized. The longer the study, the more important the continued enthusiastic cooperation of the caregiver becomes. The outcome measures, particularly those involving blood samples or prolonged immobility, often alarm the caregiver because they cause discomfort to the infant. The overall duration that each infant is in a study directly influences the rate of dropout. Because parents differ greatly in their willingness to undertake studies, parental characteristics often enter into the recruitment criteria for more prolonged studies. Increasingly, longer studies involving parents as coinvestigators in all aspects of the study require frequent communication through newsletters and support groups to ensure continued cooperation. The characteristics of the contact staff and the involvement with the study families are important adjuncts to continued participation. Issues of what the child is giving up by participating in the study assume importance in long interventions. The exclusion of all food supplements, the opportunity to travel with the child using locally obtained formula, participation in family celebrations, and so on often determine participation. Particularly in studies in developing countries or immigrant groups, respect for the traditions and mores of infant feeding may influence recruitment. There is a growing belief that the relationship of the research staff with the caregiver is among the most important factors in determination of both compliance with and continuation in the study until the primary endpoint is attained.

ISSUES OF COMPLIANCE

A run-in period or short trial of an intervention is one of the proven ways to determine short-term compliance. Markers of diet utilization, frequent home visits or phone calls, and occasionally measurements of unique changes produced by the experimental diets are sometimes employed. To assure endpoints in a high proportion of the subjects, frequent measurements of the outcome variable are obtained, so that subjects may be included for the months that the intervention was employed and the outcome obtained, notwithstanding the fact that some patients may adhere to the protocol longer than others. The best-planned studies define exactly what will be done with missing data. Most studies are analyzed on the basis of endpoints obtained, ignoring those who disappeared; this is a setting for potential bias. Patients who drop out and have no endpoint may be healthier than those who remain or may in other ways be different.

There is a consensus among infant feeding experts that breast-feeding is most desirable and optimal among all feeding choices (12–14). Although this is the gold standard of infant feeding, breast-feeding is seldom used in a randomized controlled trial because of the major maternal factors that enter into the decision on whether to breast-feed. A common design adds a nonrandomized comparison group made up of infants similar to the study group whose mothers choose to breast-feed and are willing to undertake the outcome observations. In the best studies, only a single component is different between the two diets, and double-blinding can be accomplished. As a compromise, many studies compare an established diet derived from industrialized nations with the local customary diet, and these cannot be blinded.

Spilker (15), in reviewing quality-of-study issues largely derived from short-term testing of pharmaceutical agents in infants, identified important issues influencing studies, and these are modified in Table 3 to be appropriate to nutritional studies.

REPRESENTATIVE STUDIES IN NORMAL PRETERM AND FULL-TERM INFANTS

Agostoni *et al.* (16) addressed neurologic development assessed by the Brunet–Lezine psychomotor score in 60 well-characterized term newborns. Subjects were randomized to formula with or without polyunsaturated fatty acids (PUFA). A third nonrandomized group of breast-fed infants was included. Data were analyzed on the basis of endpoints obtained in 95% of the subjects, and the breast-fed and PUFA-supplemented subjects were more advanced in development than the controls. Carlson (17) and Uauy *et al. (this volume)* provide insight into improvement of study design in evaluating PUFA in infant feeding. These designs have been largely

TABLE 3. *Considerations in designing protocols and interpreting trials on infants*[a]

Issues in the newborn
  Details of labor and delivery
  Medication, smoking, illicit drug use in pregnancy and labor
  Gestational age
  Apgar scores at 1 and 5 min
  Congenital defects
  Length and weight at birth
  Length and weight at enrollment
  Diet until entry if any
If breast-feeding under study
  Smoking, medications, drugs used by mother concurrently
  Adequacy or exclusivity of breast milk
  Supplements if any for infant
Issues during first year of life
  Gestational age
  Birth weight
  Percentile of length and weight at enrollment
  Breast, bottle, and solid feeding durations
  Nature and amount of feedings
  Caregiver availability for feeding, observations, travel to study facility
  Age of siblings, other household members

[a] Modified from Spilker (15), Tables 87.18 and 87.19.

responsible for the large body of data strongly supporting the need for these fatty acids in selected infants.

Wasserhess *et al.* (18) investigated the effects of supplemental taurine on the neutral and acidic sterols in stools. Groups of six infants, stratified on gestational age and weight for age, were randomly assigned to taurine supplements in a crossover design. Feedings were of 6 days' duration, with fecal samples collected on days 4 to 6 and 10 to 12. All studies were completed in a hospital unit, and all 30 subjects completed all outcome observations. The results showed that taurine supplements in both preterm and small-for-gestational-age infants led to a significant increase in bile acid excretion and an increased absorption of long-chain fatty acids. This study was extremely well done.

Pichichero *et al.* (19) tested serum and stool responses to rotavirus vaccine given orally to infants aged 2 to 5 months. Spillage of live virus in the stool and development of protective titers of serum antibody were major endpoints; secondary endpoints included the effect of mode of feeding on these outcomes. These investigators showed that infants fed mothers' milk had a significantly blunted serum antibody response. Stool samples were supplied in fewer than 70% of the cases. Fuchs *et al.* (20) assayed fecal blood loss in infants fed cow's milk versus several different formulas for at least 6 months. Blood samples were obtained at enrollment and 9 and 12 months of age. Stools were obtained monthly. Fecal blood measurements and blood iron indices were the outcome measurements. Although none of the diets proved different, blood endpoints were available in 90% and stools in 60% to 70%. Analysis was performed only on the endpoints obtained.

A study of 40 infants with cow's milk intolerance compared an elemental diet with hydrolyzed whey formula (21). All subjects were full term and enrolled an average of 10 weeks after birth. Food diaries were kept, and growth and plasma proteins were the outcome variables. Only two-thirds of the enrollees completed 24 weeks of the diet and were the basis of the evaluation. Among the subjects completing evaluation at 24 weeks, growth was increased, and plasma albumin was higher for the whey than the elemental diet, but the differences were not significant. The groups studied were highly heterologous, the entry allergy was not confirmed, the compliance was poor, and the outcome measures were limited. This limited study is representative of much in the field of special diets for atopic infants (22).

STUDIES IN ACUTE AND CHRONIC DIARRHEA

Diarrhea is most widely studied in the nonindustrialized world, where it is a particular problem and is often associated with malnutrition. Diarrhea is mostly identified by a history of frequent or watery stools, and studies on diarrhea usually separate cases with duration less than or greater than 7 days. Stool weight is rarely measured. Issues of compliance with the diet under study, availability of the diet, precision of the measurements, and the traditions and mores of the population under study interact to determine the exact nature of the study. Short-term studies are often carried out entirely in a clinic-based study unit, but longer ones involve the home and caregivers.

Maulen-Radovan *et al.* (23), in a research unit in Mexico City, studied 87 boys aged 5 to 36 months with diarrhea less than 96 hr in duration and associated dehydration. Patients were excluded if they had had diarrhea within the previous 14 days, had systemic infection, or were breast-fed. Children whose postrehydration weight for length was less than 2 SD below the median of the U.S. National Center for Health Statistics were also excluded. Nine percent of the subjects did not complete 5 days of observations. All subjects were rehydrated with WHO solution and then randomly assigned to a puree of chicken, brown beans, and carrots or to a soy formula (Isomil, Abbott Laboratories). Treatment failure was defined as continued or recurrent diarrhea in the 5 days of study and occurred in six patients, all of whom received the soy diet ($p < 0.01$). The overall duration of diarrhea and the stool volume the first day of feeding were significantly less in the children fed the puree, and the weight gain after 5 days was significantly more. The study was highly conclusive, and the observations were made in a study unit, but commonly encountered diarrhea cases were among those excluded.

Darling *et al.* (24), working in a study unit in Dar es Salaam, Tanzania, compared three locally available infant feedings given at weaning. The conventional porridge was prepared with 66 g corn flour, 28 g peanuts, and 906 g water to provide 39 kcal/100 g. Germinated grain from sorghum was sun-dried, then mixed with 123 g corn flour and 858 ml water to provide an energy density of 58 kcal/100 g. One preparation was fermented for 24 hr; the other was boiled promptly to destroy the amylase.

Selected children were aged between 6 and 25 months, largely weaned, with a history of diarrhea of <14 days. Only infants requiring a nasogastric tube, those with kwashiorkor, or those studied for less than 1 day were excluded. Children were fed five times daily with all diets, which were weighed and recorded, but many were also breast-fed, and these feedings were not quantified. Of 75 children entered, six were excluded. The groups studied proved similar in weight and the presence of other diseases. The group fed amylase-digested porridge ate 42% more food during the 4 days of study than those fed the conventional porridge, but the duration of diarrhea was similar.

This study, much less restrictive in its entry criteria, was carefully controlled in stool frequency but not stool weight. The information on dietary intake was flawed by the absence of recorded volumes of mothers' milk. The study was too short in duration to show a beneficial effect on malnutrition of the predigested corn flour. The stunting in growth in diarrhea has been addressed in open parallel studies given supplements and can be partially reversed (25).

A highly important group of patients were studied in Dhaka (Bangladesh) by Rahman *et al.* (26). Severely malnourished children aged 5 months to 5 years, whose weight for age was less than 60% of the median for the U.S. National Center for Health Statistics, were studied after their diarrhea and associated diseases had been treated in hospital. Two diets were compared: one used a wheat-based porridge, and the other the same porridge preincubated with an amylase-rich flour to make the diet more digestible.

All children and mothers were instructed and observed in the hospital in the preparation and feeding of the assigned diet, which was given for 5 days. Exclusion criteria included diarrhea during the observation period in hospital and children who had bacteremia or pneumonia during the initial evaluation. Eighty-one children were enrolled, and all but three (with severe diarrhea) were considered in the initial 5-day study. The important result is that the total energy ingested in those on the amylase-predigested diet was 33% more than in those on the nondigested diet. The predigested diet was particularly effective in infants aged 6 to 11 months. This study, though short-term, is quite convincing. A much longer follow-up of similar patients is needed.

Persisting diarrhea (defined as symptomatic for more than 2 weeks) was the basis of a study in Dhaka, Bangladesh, reported by Ray *et al.* (27). Twenty-six boys aged 4 to 18 months passing more than two liquid stools daily for more than 14 days were selected. Exclusions were breast-feeding with no intention to introduce supplements, presence of cholera, *Salmonella,* or *Shigella,* systemic infections, and kwashiorkor. Twenty-five age-matched healthy controls who were treated for acute diarrhea at least 4 months previously with no subsequent diarrhea were included. Both groups were fed a rice-based diet containing egg white, soybean oil, and glucose for 7 days of detailed observations. Of the patients with persisting diarrhea, 81% recovered within a median time of 4 days. Among those whose diarrhea ceased, much less energy, nitrogen, and fat was recovered in the stools than in those whose diarrhea did not stop. Those in whom diarrhea stopped improved rapidly in nutrition, whereas those with continued diarrhea did not. This study showed an important impairment of gut absorption in the malnourished infants, the impairment being greatest in those with the most malnutrition. In marked contrast, an industrialized nation approach to intractable diarrhea involved the development of an enteral feeding plan based on an audit of 29 patients and tested in the next 16, randomized into two treatment groups. This showed a diminution in time needed for parenteral nutritional support and fewer days in hospital (28). In another study, a somewhat similar group was randomized to total enteral versus parenteral treatment, and the authors concluded that enteral treatment was advantageous (29).

Brown, in reviewing the contemporary issues of dietary treatment of diarrhea (30), including study design, emphasizes directions for new studies. Brown's group (31), in a study performed in Lima, Peru, found the addition of fiber produced a prompt reduction in watery diarrhea but did not change any of the other measured variables, including stool weight, nutrient absorption, and dietary intake. Allen and Uauy (32) discuss the common problem of stunting of linear growth and its nutritional treatment. They review the genetic factors, the intrauterine and postnatal nutrient supply, the importance of infection, and the need to investigate and control for each of these. Many suggested controls, enrollment investigations, and even measurements to be made are presented.

STUDIES IN PARENTERAL NUTRITION

Although the studies are usually conducted in the hospital, and many of the outcome observations are the same as those required for the control and safety of the treatment, the clinical trials are often flawed. The infants in whom partial or total parenteral nutrition is required vary markedly in their conditions, duration of the requirement, and in the previous growth and disease characteristics.

Thus, McIntosh and Mitchell (33), in a study of 68 neonates given partial or total parenteral nutrition in the first week of life, stratified them by birth weight above or below 1000 g. Subjects requiring parenteral nutrition less than 5 days were excluded after randomization—a total of 20 patients. Two different compositions of parenteral amino acids were studied; body weight, head circumference, and plasma amino acids were the outcomes. No differences were found, but the loss of 20 of the randomized subjects and the absence of the blood endpoint in one-third of the analyzed subjects were major weaknesses. One arm had sicker infants and more deaths. Rosenthal *et al.* (34) also compared two amino acid formulations in all infants requiring parenteral nutrition. Seven of 39 infants were excluded after randomization for various reasons. Most infants less than 32 weeks of gestation had idiopathic respiratory distress; most over 32 weeks had surgery. Although differences were identified, the small groups, the marked differences in diseases, and the few infants requiring treatment for 21 days or longer rendered the results unconvincing.

A much better study was completed by Hammerman and Aramburo (35), who studied 42 neonates less than 1750 g in birth weight with respiratory distress syndrome randomized to parenteral solutions with or without lipid. On days 3 and 5, retinopathy was assessed by electroretinograms, and blood prostaglandins were assayed. The results showed clearly that the lipid-infused infants had a more prolonged requirement for ventilatory support and supplemental oxygen, higher grades of bronchopulmonary dysplasia, and more severe retinopathy. It was concluded that lipids should be withheld in this group. The selection criteria were strong, and the exclusions carefully preplanned. The endpoints were obtained in all of the patients, and meticulous clinical follow-up provided many of the statistically significant differences.

CONCLUSIONS

Table 4 sets forth my conclusions regarding a review of controlled trials in infant nutrition published in the last 10 years. These are organized to educate clinical investigators about the frequent shortcomings in study design from otherwise well-motivated and well-intentioned persons.

There are many studies that simply should not have been done. The chapters in this volume by Whitehead and Kauffman support the notion that a study that cannot answer the hypothesis or purpose for any reason should not be carried out. In various publications, the primary outcome measurement is simply too new for there to be established criteria of reliability and variability, condemning the study to failure. In a desire to provide measurement of growth or development within a week or two

TABLE 4. *Comments on randomized controlled infant nutrition trials published in the last decade*

Studies that should not have been done
Unclear hypothesis
Primary outcome measure not established as valid
No estimate of sample size; reasonable estimates indicate no possibility of reaching a conclusion
Inadequate size of study population
Weak and inconclusive studies
Relaxed or changed entry requirements
Primary endpoint not obtained in large numbers
No measure of adherence to complex regime
Rare events discussed in a conclusive manner when sample size is inadequate
Common design shortcomings
Failure to blind treatments
Subjective criteria evaluated by unblinded observers
No measure of compliance
Analysis does not consider "intention to treat" limited to primary endpoints obtained
Inadequate staffing or training to promote retention and compliance
Well-designed and -executed trials
Substantial statistical input in planning
Multicentered
Ample support staff
Blinded at all levels

of the intervention, indirect or surrogate markers (36) of growth are used. In many studies, there is no estimate of sample size or discussion of the magnitude of change that is being sought, and reasonable guesses of a meaningful outcome simply exclude useful information based on the size of the samples. With encouragement, consultation with statisticians at the time of planning, and stronger function of human study committees, these should largely disappear.

Slightly stronger studies emerge with very inconclusive results. The two most common reasons are that patient selection is too broadly based to be meaningful and the primary endpoint was unattained in more than one-third of the patients. Both of these problems can be overcome by better planning and appropriate staffing to obtain more primary endpoints. In many cases, each of these solutions requires funding that is often not available but is essential to convert inconclusive studies into those with a much higher likelihood of success.

Many studies that are both adequately designed and of sufficient power to answer the intended goal or hypothesis have shortcomings that introduce potential bias. Some of the common difficulties are noted in the absence of ready solutions. Diets available in developing countries are often compared with formula diets from industrialized countries to be certain of including all reasonable nutrients, but blinding is impossible. There is no satisfactory method of fully handling subjects who fail to provide the primary endpoint.

Finally, there are many state-of-the-art studies. These are most commonly well supported to allow for careful planning of the study and its measurements and adequately staffed to diminish dropouts and to increase compliance. Granting agencies, university research departments, and industry could assist in improving the quality of studies by underwriting the costs of statistical planning with clinical investigators.

We should also reexamine the major commitment to randomized, blinded, controlled trials. A properly carried out study is extremely expensive, and there are other methods of research design that are sometimes more feasible and may allow the inclusion of larger numbers and greater varieties of patient to give an even more conclusive result. Very infrequent events, such as serious side effects, cannot be studied by randomized blinded controlled trials. Other designs include single-patient assignment to randomized treatment of variable duration and crossover designs in small numbers of patients. The advantages and disadvantages of each of these have been discussed (15).

REFERENCES

1. Stettler N, Schutz Y, Micheli JL, Jéquier E. Energetic and metabolic cost of growth in Gambian infants. *Eur J Clin Nutr* 1992;46:329–335.
2. Davies PS, Gregory J, White A. Energy expenditure in children aged 1.5–4.5 years: a comparison with current recommendations for energy intake. *Eur J Clin Nutr* 1995;49:360–364.
3. Vaisman N, Leigh T, Voet H, Westerterp K, Abraham M, Duchan R. Malabsorption in infants with congenital heart disease under diuretic treatment. *Pediatr Res* 1994;36:545–549.
4. Unger R, DeKleermaeker M, Gidding SS, Christoffel KK. Calories count. Improved weight gain with dietary intervention in congenital heart disease. *Am J Dis Child* 1992;146:1078–1084.

5. Bhutta ZA, Molla AM, Issani Z, Badruddin S, Hendricks K, Snyder JD. Nutritional management of persistent diarrhea: factors predicting clinical outcome. *Acta Paediatr [Suppl]* 1992;381:144–148.
6. Rickard KA, Loghmani ES, Grosfeld JL, Lingard CD, White NM, Foland BB, *et al.* Short and long-term effectiveness of enteral and parenteral nutrition in reversing or preventing protein–energy malnutrition in advanced neuroblastoma. A prospective randomized study. *Cancer* 1985;56: 2881–2897.
7. Dagnelie PC, van Dusseldorp M, van Staveren WA, Hautvast JG. Effects of macrobiotic diets on linear growth in infants and children until 10 years of age. *Eur J Clin Nutr* 1994;48(Suppl 1): S103–S112.
8. Paganus A, Juntunen-Backman K, Savilahti E. Followup of nutritional status and dietary survey in children with cows milk allergy. *Acta Paediatr* 1992;81:518–521.
9. Legido A, Tonyes L, Carter D, Schoemaker A, DiGeorge A, Grover WD. Treatment variables and intellectual outcome in children with classic phenylketonuria. A single-center based study. *Clin Pediatr* 1993;32:417–425.
10. Thomas E. Dietary management of inborn errors of amino acid metabolism with protein modified diets. *J Child Neurol* 1992;7(Suppl):S92–S111.
11. Sullivan PB, Lunn PG, Northrop-Clewes C, Crowe PT, Marsh MN, Neale G. Persistent diarrhea and malnutrition—the impact of treatment on small bowel structure and permeability. *J Pediatr Gastroenterol Nutr* 1992;14:208–215.
12. Dewey KG, Peerson JM, Brown KH, Krebs NF, Michaelsen KF, Persson LA, *et al.* Growth of breast fed infants deviates from current reference data: a pooled analysis of US, Canadian and European data sets. World Health Organization Working Group on Infant Growth. *Pediatrics* 1995;96:495–503.
13. Dewey KG, Heinig MJ, Nommsen LA, Peerson JM, Lonnerdal B. Breast-fed infants are leaner than formula-fed infants at 1 yr of age: the DARLING study. *Am J Clin Nutr* 1993;57:140–145.
14. Dewey KG, Heinig MJ, Nommsen LA, Peerson JM, Lonnerdal B. Growth of breast-fed and formula-fed infants from 0 to 18 months: The DARLING study. *Pediatrics* 1992;89:1035–1041.
15. Spilker B. *Guide to clinical trials.* New York: Raven Press, 1991.
16. Agostoni C, Trojan S, Bellu R, Riva E, Giovannini M. Neurodevelopmental quotient of healthy term infants at 4 months and feeding practice: the role of long chain polyunsaturated fatty acids. *Pediatr Res* 1995;38:262–266.
17. Carlson SE. Lessons learned from randomizing infants to marine oil-supplemented formulas in nutrition trials. *J Pediatr* 1994;125:S33–S38.
18. Wasserhess P, Becker M, Staab D. Effect of taurine on synthesis of neutral and acidic sterols and fat absorption in preterm and full-term infants. *Am J Clin Nutr* 1993;58:349–353.
19. Pichichero ME, Losonsky GA, Rennels MB, Disney FA, Green JL Francis AB, *et al.* Effect of dose and a comparison of measures of vaccine take for oral rhesus rotavirus vaccine. *Pediatr Infect Dis J* 1990;9:339–344.
20. Fuchs G, DeWier M, Hutchinson S, Suundeen M, Schwartz S, Suskind R. Gastrointestinal blood loss in older infants; impact of cow milk vs formula. *J Pediatr Gastroenterol Nutr* 1993;16:4–9.
21. McLeish CM, MacDonald A, Booth JW. Comparison of an elemental with a hydrolysed whey formula in intolerance to cows milk. *Arch Dis Child* 1995;73:211–215.
22. Zeiger RS. Dietary manipulations in infants and their mothers and the natural course of atopic disease. *Pediatr Allergy Immunol* 1994;5(Suppl 6):33–43.
23. Maulen-Radovan I, Brown KH, Acosta MA, Fernadez-Varela H. Comparison of a rice based, mixed diet vs a lactose-free soy protein isolate formula for young children with acute diarrhea. *J Pediatr* 1994;125:699–706.
24. Darling JC, Kitundu JA, Kingamkono RR, Msengi AE, Bduma B, Sullivan KR, *et al.* Improved energy intakes using amylase-digested weaning foods in Tanzanian children with acute diarrhea. *J Pediatr Gastroenterol Nutr* 1995;21:73–81.
25. Lutter CK, Mora JO, Habicht J-P, Rasmussen KM, Robson DS, Sellers SG. Nutritional supplementation: effects on child stunting associated with diarrhea. *Am J Clin Nutr* 1989;50:1–8.
26. Rahman MM, Islam MA, Mahalanabris D, Biswas E, Majid N, Wahed MA. Intake from an energy dense porridge liquefied by amylase of germinated wheat; a controlled trial in severely malnourished children during convalescence from diarrhoea. *Eur J Clin Nutr* 1994;48:46–53.
27. Ray S, Akramuzzaman SM, Haider R, Khaatun M, Akbar MS, Eckels R. Persistent diarrhoea: efficacy of a rice based diet and role of nutritional status in recovery and nutrient absorption. *Br J Nutr* 1994; 71:123–134.

28. Orenstein SR. Enteral vs parenteral therapy for intractable diarrhea in infancy: a prospective random-ized trial. *J Pediatr* 1986;109:277–286.
29. Smith AE, Powers CA, Cooper-Meyer RA, Lloyd-Still JD. Improved nutritional management reduces length of hospitalization in intractable diarrhea. *J Parent Ent Nutr* 1986;10:479–481.
30. Brown KH. Dietary management of acute diarrheal disease: contemporary scientific issues. *J Nutr* 1994;124:1455S–1460S.
31. Brown KH, Perez F, Peerson JM, Fadel J, Brunsgaard G, Ostrom KM, *et al.* Effect of dietary fiber (soy polysaccharide) on the severity, duration and nutritional outcome of acute watery diarrhea in children. *Pediatrics* 1993;92:241–247.
32. Allen LH, Uauy R. Guidelines for the study of mechanisms involved in the prevention or reversal of linear growth retardation in developing countries. *Eur J Clin Nutr* 1994;48(Suppl 1):S212–S216.
33. McIntosh N, Mitchell V. A clinical trial of two parenteral nutrition solutions in neonates. *Arch Dis Child* 1990;65:692–699.
34. Rosenthal M, Sinha S, Laywood F, Levene M. A double blind comparison of a new pediatric amino acid solution in neonatal total parenteral nutrition. *Early Hum Dev* 1987;15:137–146.
35. Hammerman C, Aramburo MJ. Decreased lipid intakes reduces morbidity in sick premature neonates. *J Pediatr* 1988;113:1083–1088.
36. Fleming TR, DeMets DL. Surrogate endpoints in clinical trials: are we being misled? *Ann Intern Med* 1996;125:605–613.

DISCUSSION

Dr. Hamburger: Could I ask you to comment further on what can be done to neutralize the loss or the negative effect of large numbers of dropouts.

Dr. Iber: One technique that readily identifies the dropout patient is a run-in period. For many studies, a 1- or 2-week period to allow the formula or the intervention to be tried, combined with more than one visit for physical examination, is a way to identify the extremely weak of heart who will drop out very promptly. I think that that should be done in many studies if it can be built into the design. Otherwise, I think that trained staff and proper planning of the study are more important in diminishing dropouts than almost any other feature.

Dr. Lucas: We agreed that it is unethical to do a badly designed study, and one of the aspects of bad design is a high dropout rate, and particularly for certain sorts of study. In neurodevelopmental outcome studies, selective dropout rates can have such a major impact on the interpretation of the results that they become meaningless if the dropout rate reaches, say, 10% to 20%, so for certain types of study, it is important to define circumstances where a low dropout rate is going to be achieved. This means ensuring that patients can be traced, and much more sophisticated tracing techniques are required than are often employed at present—it shouldn't be left to random chance. There are certain types of study that simply can't be done in particular countries, where there are very diffuse and mobile populations, if you really want to achieve a good follow-up. So as part of the ethics of designing a study, it is very important to consider whether the dropout rate you are likely to achieve will, in fact, make it an ineffective study; for a neurodevelopmental outcome study, for instance, a 30% or 40% dropout rate is completely unacceptable.

Dr. Iber: I agree entirely. One of the frustrations in planning a study is that often the popula-tion you most need information on may be the most difficult both to find at a later time and to influence to continue the intervention. I applaud continued efforts to tackle better studies in the target groups that need better studies. In America, many of the people with poor medical care and living in poor circumstances are avoided like the plague by investigators because of the traditionally very high dropout rate, and yet, information is desperately needed in these groups.

The great success of the data on fertility control came about in large part because it had a built-in safety net and was very effective in people who weren't completely compliant.

Dr. Guesry: My first point is that you mentioned the tendency to do shorter studies, taking the baby into hospital for 2 weeks to ensure a compliance. This is fine if the baby is admitted because of pathology, but to admit a healthy baby to hospital for 2 weeks just to do a clinical study would not pass our ethics committee. My second point is related to the paper by Agostini that you cited as an example of a good study. As far as I know, the 4-month data were published only as a letter in *Lancet*. The statistics were doubtful, and Mr. Baumgartner, who is one of our statisticians, found that the statistical significance was obtained only because there were two outliers in the breast-fed groups. Third, and this is my main point, the choice of the endpoint is very important. To use the development quotient at 4 months of age as the endpoint is dubious when you take into account the difficulties of doing such tests—in particular, the huge individual variability. What I say was confirmed last May in München when Agostini himself presented results showing that at 1 year of age, there was no difference whatsoever among the three groups.

Dr. Iber: Thank you for your comments.

Dr. Uauy: I tend to agree with Dr. Guesry. However, Agostini's paper was fully published in *Pediatric Research* (1). I also agree that long-term effects are what we should be looking for, but we should not neglect the possibility that there may be transient effects. A transient effect is still a valid observation.

Dr. Iber: I would emphasize that I only looked at papers in my review, not letters.

Dr. Haschke: Alan Lucas calculated the sample size that is needed in neurodevelopmental outcome studies to be 80 in each group, and in the Agostini study, we have only 20.

Dr. Lucas: If you take the breast milk model, the advantage in cognitive development for breast-fed over formula-fed babies, which is purported by some people to be related to the LCPs in breast milk, is around a third of a standard deviation, which is about 5 DQ points. If you wanted to test the hypothesis that all of the difference was caused by LCPs, then you would need 144 subjects per group for 5% significance and 80% power, but of course, if you hypothesize that only half of the difference between breast-fed and formula-fed babies was linked to LCPs, then you would need groups of over a thousand.

Dr. Whitehead: It is incredibly difficult in a community-type study to control for everything, and anybody who carries out such studies is fully aware of the shortcomings of their studies and the assumptions that have to be made. It might make it easier for fellow scientists to follow these arguments if the editorial boards of various journals were rather more tolerant of people spelling out the shortcomings of their studies. I know about the big demand for space and so on, but if you look back at very early reports in journals like *Lancet,* there was a tremendous amount of discussion of this sort of thing. Now you just never see it, and I think that is creating problems—indeed investigators are often blamed for oversimplifying the presentation of their results when all the pressures are on them to oversimplify and it is difficult for them to be truly honest.

Dr. Iber: I think multicenter controlled trials often have methodologic papers that appear in *Controlled Trials*. The policy of that journal is to recognize the importance of allowing the designers to include extensive discussion about areas of uncertainty, or where they made compromises to keep cost within reasonable limits or widened their expectations so that the power of the study fitted the anticipated budget. I think that that is the only place I have seen such discussion published.

Dr. Salle: You pointed out that it is very important to look at the effect of nutrition on growth parameters. Don't you think that it is also important to look at the quality of growth, particularly in premature babies? We have many tools now for measuring quality of growth, DEXA and indirect calorimetry for example, and it seems to me that it is now very important to do this so that we can assess precisely the effect of different low-birth-weight formulas. Would you comment on that?

Dr. Iber: I think you are correct in a certain type of protocol, for example, where you are looking at correction of nutritional injury imposed by surgery or an acute infectious illness, where it is important to document the immediate response to the maximum amount of nutrient that can be accepted. I think that we need to focus on a hypothesis. In certain studies, the issues you raise would be important; in others, they may well not be.

Dr. Hamburger: I would agree with you. Wherever you can add quantitation, your result is going to be easier to interpret.

Dr. Glinsmann: Would you speak a little bit about the intention-to-treat analysis: how often should it be used, and what do you think its usefulness is when you do, in fact, have a poor study with a large dropout rate?

Dr. Iber: I think we have all become addicted to the randomized blinded controlled trial. The emphasis to avoid bias is on a completely blinded randomization, and only by using that blinded randomization in analyzing the data is one continuing the strength of the controlled trial system. As soon as you statistically analyze only the endpoints that you have, ignoring the dropouts other than to record them, you introduce an influence of factors that lead to dropout and factors that may influence efficacy. These may be correlated; there are data suggesting that poor compliance is a precursor to dropout, and therefore, the dropped-out people might be a very different population and will, because you have no endpoint, be ignored. The difficulty is that when you are talking about growth, where you need two points, if you don't have that second point, you have to make assumptions of what would happen if it had been zero, or what would happen if it had been the same as the rest of the patients. There are statistical adjustments, but they are all relatively poor guesses, and when the dropout rate approaches 50%, as it does in a fair number of studies for the primary endpoint, you really need to think of another design. We need to devote more thought to innovative designs. Crossover studies have great strength, even though the child is developing and growing. Multiple endpoints provide another way of handling the problem, but if you put too much burden on the caregiver and the subject, you will have major recruitment problems.

Dr. Hamburger: Our secret weapon for compliance and dealing with dropouts was our nurse coordinator, who, in several of our studies, developed personal relationships with every single participant so that compliance increased, and when we had the expected dropouts, she was able to find them and follow up adequately.

Dr. Lucas: On the question of dropouts, I think we may have confused what we mean here. Let's say that we are doing a randomized intervention study of two formulas. Subjects may drop out of the short-term limb because they develop some problem on the formula, but that doesn't mean that they necessarily drop out of the follow-up. It is extremely important to follow up such ''dropouts''; it is only when the persons actually refuse to have the long-term follow-up, which they had originally agreed to do, that you have a serious problem. So what you need to do is to analyze with your primary outcome all the subjects, regardless of whether they have been on the treatment or not. That is very different from what has been described as dropping out.

Dr. Iber: I agree with that.

Dr. Ferry: One of the problems with dropouts is, of course, noncompliance: patients who fall out because they don't keep appointments, or who don't stay on whatever the therapeutic product is, or what have you. I think this comes back to the issue of truly adequate and thoroughly thought out inclusion criteria, because that is the point at which you really need to think about all the variables that may cause patients to be noncompliant. There are many issues you can take into account right from the start, and this will—at least to some extent—help decrease the number of noncompliant patients.

Dr. Iber: I would agree that planning and staff training make a tremendous difference in all studies, and certainly in some studies, these issues have not been given enough attention. However, restricting entry to patients who have characteristics that lead to high compliance may well restrict the applicability of the study results when they are finished because individuals who are the most compliant are a modest subset of the population. I don't think that compliance can be the only thing that determines the design of a study.

Dr. Fisberg: I am very concerned about the economic impact, especially when you calculate a very high level of dropouts. These subjects will be exposed to the same measures as the others, but the data will be abandoned. Don't you think it would be wiser to take these studies to other countries or populations with less chance of dropout, especially in underdeveloped countries?

Dr. Iber: We must consider what you are trying to accomplish. There are some studies that, because of the uniqueness of the illness or the population or the partial deficiency, can be carried out only in the less developed portions of the world, and though you could have a much higher assurance of compliance and a lower dropout rate by doing a study in an industrial country, this would never allow you the numbers you need. We agreed that poor science is unethical, and I think that many of these problems can be anticipated with planning or perhaps, in a very large study, with a preliminary trial. And one can have a factual data base to suggest what the needs are, what the follow-ups are, and so forth. The multicenter studies funded by the National Institutes of Health often require a small feasibility study of maybe 100 subjects, and then, when they undertake the main multicenter study, they will initially fund two or three centers a year ahead of everyone else to work out the problems and allow a bit of experimentation to determine pitfalls and unanticipated problems before the study spreads to 15 centers, or 25, or what have you.

Dr. Hamburger: I would like to ask some of the statisticians, and Dr. Walter particularly, how often they are consulted in the design of a study, in contrast to how often they are asked to look at the results and try to bail out some findings that are inexplicable.

Dr. Walter: I would like to make two comments about some other issues first. First, on the crossover design that was suggested as a possible solution, it is true that such designs have a lot of appeal because you can compare the treatments within subjects, and that generally leads to a more efficient comparison, but only if you get the observations. I think that the problems of dropout and compliance are going to be more severe in a crossover design because participants have to commit themselves to two treatments rather than one at a minimum if it is a two-period study. So you need to think very carefully about that, quite apart from all the other issues introduced by using a crossover design, such as a carryover effect, which is important. My second comment is that these very high dropout rates that have been mentioned of up to 50% are much larger than any I have experienced in the fields that I work in. But one proposal that has been made in this situation is to look at ''drop out'' as an outcome, because it may be that the fact of dropping out is some kind of indication of acceptability of the treatment, and that is certainly something you would want to know about if you were thinking about using a particular nutritional therapy in the future. If it is unacceptable to 50% of the people to whom it is offered, then that obviously has some implications about its clinical usefulness. So I think dropout itself can be analyzed as an outcome in some circumstances. And then, to respond to Dr. Hamburger's question, I suppose people's circumstances differ enormously. In my institution, I think we have our clinicians relatively well trained, and they do tend to come along quite early; we encourage a longer-term relationship with investigators and actively discourage the people who come at the last minute.

Dr. Uauy: Every experimental design is a compromise between the ideal and the real. We have to be ready to do our best in the planning stage, but we also have to be willing to do the best analysis and the most critical review of our results. I would not dismiss data that have been carefully planned just because they did not meet the ideal. Moreover, most ideal studies become unfeasible because one would like to include, for example, mechanisms behind the observations, and usually in nutritional research that means blood drawing, invasive procedures, or whatever, and that interferes with compliance. So in any design, there will be compromise. My plea is that we stick to reality and judge that there is really no ideal study. We learn in the process to do better studies, but we must also judge the level of the field we are working with: initially you are going to have stage 2 studies, which will be limited and do not pursue the aim of changing clinical practice. Where we need very clearly defined standards is when we feel that the level of knowledge has come to a point where it might change a clinical practice or a feeding practice. But many studies are done in a preliminary phase to provide a better hypothesis or mechanism.

REFERENCE

1. Agostoni C, Troján S, Bellú R, *et al.* Neurodevelopmental quotient of healthy term infants at 4 months and feeding practice: the role of long-chain polyunsaturated fatty acids. *Pediatr Res* 1995;38:262–266.

Clinical Trials in Infant Nutrition, edited by
Jay A. Perman and Jean Rey, Nestlé Nutrition
Workshop Series, Vol. 40, Nestec Ltd.,
Vevey/Lippincott-Raven Publishers,
Philadelphia © 1998.

Pediatric Gastroenterology Collaborative Research Group (PGCRG) Success and Failures in Multicenter Clinical Trials

George D. Ferry

Gastroenterology and Nutrition, Texas Children's Hospital, Houston, Texas, USA

Multicenter clinical trials offer great opportunities to answer clinical research questions through greater access to patients and pooling of data from multiple institutions. Unfortunately, these benefits are accompanied by many challenges in dealing with different sites and different investigators (1). Even the most experienced investigator and sponsor may find surprises and problems in selecting collaborators and in the recruitment of patients. In pediatrics, collaborative research is often a necessity because so many problems we encounter are relatively uncommon. Although placebo-controlled trials can reduce the number of patients needed, they are not always an option for studies involving children. The American Academy of Pediatrics has outlined appropriate instances for placebo trials (2), but pediatricians often are reluctant to enter children in such studies because of potential or perceived harm from offering no treatment.

In addition to greater patient access, multicenter trials offer a number of other advantages (Table 1) (3). Broad patient representation may be a requirement for some protocols, and collaboration regionally, nationally, or internationally can answer this need. Selecting study sites in different clinical settings is another way to add validity and generalization to the results. The choice of a private practice setting rather than an academic setting might be more representative of real-life situations and give a study added significance.

Although the need for a multicenter trial may seem obvious, the sponsoring agency and the principal investigator must clearly define the benefits to attract qualified and productive participants. Because multicenter studies are time-consuming and often generate extra paperwork, it may take a considerable effort to maintain interest and active participation throughout the study. One way to create this enthusiasm and a sense of ownership in a study is to include investigators from the very beginning of a new protocol. The following sections explore some of these issues in more detail. The outline used by our Pediatric Gastroenterology Collaborative Group to develop a multicenter clinic is shown in Table 2. A sample budget is shown in Table 3.

TABLE 1. *Selected advantages and disadvantages of multicenter clinical trials[a]*

A. Advantages
  1. More rapid patient recruitment
  2. More complex protocols may be able to be conducted because of additional resources utilized for certain large trials
  3. Less opportunity for one person's biases to influence the design or conduct of the clinical trial
  4. Greater likelihood that data processing and analysis will be conducted at a high standard
  5. Greater likelihood that a heterogeneous patient population will be enrolled
B. Disadvantages
  1. Administrative arrangements and management details are more complex
  2. Costs are usually greater for the clinical trial than if the same total number of patients was studied at a single site
  3. Statistical data analyses would be stronger from a single site
  4. Some Ethics Committees/IRBs[b] may insist on changes to the protocol that create major delays or are unacceptable to the sponsor or other Ethics Committees/IRBs
  5. Individual investigators in large multicenter trials receive little recognition through the publication of results

[a] Reprinted from Spilker (3), with permission.
[b] IRB, institutional review board.

ACCESS TO PATIENTS

The need for a large number of patients is one major reason for collaborative research. Unfortunately, the number of subjects available for study is often hard to confirm. Clinicians often think they have patients who meet the criteria for participation, only to find that either the inclusion and exclusion criteria are too strict or that patients are unwilling to participate. In an ideal setting, an investigator would know ahead of time how many study patients might exist at each potential collaborative site. Our Pediatric Gastroenterology Collaborative Research Group has 13 centers in the United States and Canada. We have addressed this problem using computer-generated information from billing data maintained by clinic or hospital billing services. This type of data is limited and sometimes inaccurate, but it can give the number of patients with a specific diagnosis, their ages, dates of visits, and associated activities, such as procedures and laboratory tests ordered. Variables that might give a better representation of potential patients, such as severity and length of illness, current status, treatment, and so on, are not available through charge data. Another large data base in many managed care settings is the pharmacy record. These computer data may include past and current medications on all patients in a given plan. For drug studies, this can help in determining patient eligibility.

Our collaborative group also has developed a software program that will allow each participating institution to gather the same data on all children with inflammatory bowel disease (IBD). Because the main research interest of the group is IBD, we think this data base will allow us to estimate the number of potential patients for future studies as well as the number of centers needed and the time frame for

TABLE 2. *The Pediatric Gastroenterology Collaborative Research Group's outline for development of multicenter clinical trials*

1. Protocol development
   a. The person with the greatest interest writes the first draft of the protocol and serves as Principal Investigator (PI)
   b. This first draft should:
      i. Define the problem
      ii. Review the current literature
      iii. Show why a multicenter study is needed
      iv. Outline inclusion/exclusion criteria, how the study will be carried out (methodology), compliance criteria, statistics, etc.
   c. The group meets to review the protocol and address the following issues:
      i. Is the protocol of interest and of value?
      ii. What are the clinical endpoints? What findings will be considered clinically significant?
      iii. Are diagnostic criteria acceptable?
      iv. Is the study feasible? Are there enough patients?
      v. How many centers will be needed to provide the required number of patients (the dropout rate is often 10% or more)?
      vi. Is the statistical analysis appropriate?
      vii. How much data to collect—do not overburden collaborators with too much paperwork
      viii. Determine who will handle statistical analysis.
      ix. Who will control data, and how will data be shared?
      x. Who has publication rights?
      xi. Pick the coordinating center or organization (usually the same as PI)
      xii. Who will set up randomization and be responsible for shipping drugs?
      xiii. Decide on authorship
         (1) PI should be first author
         (2) List others by the number of patients enrolled
         (3) Do not include if only one or two patients enrolled
      xiv. Where will the results be published?
      xv. Consider an advisory board to monitor the study and provide advice and expertise
   d. The PI revises the protocol for final acceptance
   e. The PI submits the protocol to his or her Institutional Review Board for approval of the study and consent forms to be sure there are no significant ethical problems
2. The PI and group then picks the appropriate centers
   a. Choice based on:
      i. Adequate patient numbers
      ii. Time, interest, and appropriate facilities
      iii. Research nurse available
   b. Each center must sign a letter of intent to carry out the study and follow the protocol
   c. All centers obtain IRB approval of the study and consent form
3. Funding
   a. The PI develops a budget for the coordinating center and collaborating centers
   b. The PI and other members of the group develop a strategy and identify potential sources for funding
      i. The PI makes initial contacts and sends the protocol for review
      ii. If pharmaceutical or governmental funding is sought, seek their advice and suggestions about the protocol early

(continued)

TABLE 2. *The Pediatric Gastroenterology Collaborative Research Group's outline for development of multicenter clinical trials (continued)*

---

4. Investigator meeting when funding available
   a. The PI or coordinating center develops case report forms, an algorithm of how the study is carried out, and a short handbook of instruction
   b. All investigators and research nurses should be brought together to review the protocol and learn what will be needed to complete the trial
      i. Inclusion/exclusion criteria
      ii. Algorithm of visits, lab procedures, etc.
      iii. Case report forms
      iv. How drug is to be delivered and monitored
      v. Recruiting techniques
      vi. Reporting adverse events
5. Enrollment of patients
   a. Research nurse works in clinic, contacts patients, recruits, explains consent forms
   b. Frequent contact between PI and coordinating center and participating centers
      i. Encourage enrollment
      ii. Answer questions
      iii. Stimulate interest
   c. Update all centers on progress of study every 3 months
   d. Share any problems so all centers benefit as the study progresses
   e. Site visits very helpful if funds available
6. Collection and sharing of data
   a. Coordinating center collects all data and initiates the appropriate data base and data entry, sent by mail, FAX, or e-mail
   b. If the PI is recruiting patients, he or she must be blinded to data entry codes
   c. Site visits or telephone calls periodically to keep interest high and to check recruitment efforts and validity of data
   d. Any missing data are tracked immediately with the participating center
   e. Date base is set up so that a percentage of data entry is evaluated for accuracy of entry, and parameters are established so incorrect values cannot be entered
7. Payments to collaborating centers
   a. Pay after a predetermined number of visits or after the patient has completed the study
   b. Bunch payments to avoid excess work
8. Publication
   a. Should be prompt
   b. Acknowledge all who participated but are not listed as authors
   c. Acknowledge support

---

completing new studies. Abstracting the information into this new data base is time-consuming and duplicates clinic chart entries. We hope that our effort will be of value in the development of future electronic medical records. If what we have learned can be transferred to these new systems, data retrieval for research purposes will become much easier and, we hope, more accurate.

PICKING THE RIGHT CENTER

Because institutions vary greatly in patient mix, facilities, and expertise, care must be taken in determining what type of setting is most likely to provide the right mix

TABLE 3. *Sample of clinical research budget*

Total costs, year 1

Title of Study: _____

Personnel	Effort (%)	Hours/ week	Salary	Total cost
Principal investigator Nurse coordinator Data manager Secretarial support Total Salaries				
Consultant Costs	Amount			
Policy board, two meetings/year				
Supplies	Amount			
Binders for patient data Miscellaneous supplies Total supplies				
Travel	Amount			
Investigators' meetings Travel for presentation of data Site visits Total travel				
Patient costs (outpatient)	Number of patients	Number of times	Cost per test	
Drug dispensing/mailing Clinic visits List specific tests Total patient costs				
Other expenses	Amount	Number of visits		
Honorarium (per patient per visit)[a] Postage Telephone/fax Total other expenses				
Total direct costs				
Indirect costs (university overhead)				
Total costs				

[a] To reimburse the center for successful study completion.

and an adequate number of patients. The choices between academic and private practice settings, between managed care and capitation, hospital and outpatient, regional and local, and between national and international offer a variety of types of patients and patient care settings. In multinational collaboration, and in some regional cooperative studies, issues of language, regulatory laws, clinical practice, other drug availability (including over-the-counter drugs), patient acceptance, genetics, frequency of disease, and definitions of disease are critical issues. Even with careful selection of study sites, a randomized clinical trial may lead to results that are too specific and are valid for only one or two centers. The danger in this is that the results may not be generalizable to real-life situations (4).

Any multicenter study must have a protocol that can be accepted by physicians with diverse backgrounds and practices. If a potential collaborator has trouble compromising and accepting the study design, he or she should not be encouraged to participate. Investigators must be enthusiastic about a study or they will not actively recruit patients. Over this past year, I have had the opportunity to work with the European Pediatric IBD study group in the development of a joint drug protocol for Europe and the United States. The two major issues that emerged early on were the diversity in definitions of disease and disease activity and the differences in standard medical practice. It took considerable compromise to resolve these issues, but once everyone agreed, most other issues were accepted with a good consensus.

It is not always possible to define which setting will give the best advantage for patient recruitment. A good example of this is our Pediatric Gastroenterology Collaborative Research Group experience in testing the effects of treatment on growth failure in children with Crohn's disease. This study began with large academic teaching centers because we expected these centers to attract patients with significant growth problems. What we discovered was that many smaller institutions and private practice settings were more successful because of better patient mix and fewer commitments by the collaborator. In addition, several centers in this study were primarily referral centers and had very little long-term follow-up. Because patients came from long distances, it was impossible for them to return as required by the protocol.

Comparability among centers can be a major factor in the success and validity of multicenter studies. Different study sites need a similar level of personnel training, facilities, laboratory expertise, and treatment philosophy. Unfortunately, this type of information is rarely mentioned in publications, and a reader has to make the assumption that each center followed the protocol in the same way. Both in small studies (5,6) and in articles using meta-analysis (7), authors tend to avoid discussion of how participants were similar or different and what potential biases might have existed. This need not necessarily be the case. In a recent study of long-chain polyunsaturated fatty acids in infant formulas, multiple sites in several European countries were involved (8). There were multiple complex biochemical measures, neurologic evaluations, repeated anthropometric measurements, and varying feeding practices. The results could have been strengthened significantly by including how personnel were trained in feeding and anthropometry, describing who carried out the neurologic and visual tests, and documenting how many laboratories were used and their levels of expertise. Although the article's conclusions may be correct, the study could have significant flaws. It is impossible for the reader to evaluate the validity of the observations. In contrast, a study in 1993 on cow's milk and gastrointestinal blood loss included significant details on the choice of study sites, how patients were followed monthly, and the patient mix (9). This gives the reader a real advantage in evaluating the significance of the findings.

There are other good examples of center variability and how studies might be influenced positively or negatively. In a study of low-protein formula in chronic renal disease, carried out by the Southwest Pediatric Nephrology Study Group, the authors described possible center differences in the way children were fed and how this might have influenced differences in observed growth (10). The authors also pointed out another problem in the study—refusal to follow the protocol as a result of parent and physician reluctance to carry out invasive procedures. Specifically, several investigators and parents refused use of a nasogastric tube in spite of the patient meeting the criteria for tube feeding, needing the extra nutrition, and its being part of the accepted protocol and consent form. In our Gastroenterology Collaborative Group, we have had a similar problem with follow-up flexible sigmoidoscopy in the treatment of ulcerative colitis. In spite of signing a consent form and agreeing ahead of time to the procedure, both physicians and parents often refused (11). The results in both cases were influenced by these protocol violations, although the basic studies still had validity in all other respects.

Participating centers must be screened carefully to be sure they can comply with the protocol and recruit the patients needed. It is important to be sure that collaborating centers have no commitments to conflicting protocols and that they have the resources to recruit patients and keep up with the paperwork. Conflicting studies will decrease the number of patients enrolled and may bias the results, depending on how patients are randomized. If the research staff does not have time to recruit patients into multiple studies, patients may never hear about the study, or record keeping may suffer.

HOW MANY CENTERS ARE NEEDED?

The number of centers to include in a collaborative study is always a major question. More centers should mean a study should get done more quickly. The problems that arise in recruiting a larger number of centers are the significant increase in workload and the increased cost in terms of overheads, travel, and monitoring. The more centers involved, the more difficulties arise in monitoring quality and in promotion of the study to keep investigators committed.

In choosing sites for a collaborative trial, the principal investigator and sponsor must be sure each potential participant understands the minimum number of patients expected and the time period for enrollment. If some sites do not perform well and only enter an occasional patient, the final patient sample may be very unrepresentative, and the results less significant. When centers are slow to enroll patients and a study is extended, there is a much greater chance for bias (12). This is especially true if the study is extended beyond 3 or 4 years. Patients entered early may not be the same as patients entered late, or methods of enrollment may vary as personnel change. New drugs or formulas may alter the patients who can be used for a trial. If the investigators' preferences change, there may be more and more reluctance to continue the study. Adding extra centers to make up for any underperforming centers might be helpful, but the best choice is to pick centers with a high probability of success.

REASONS FOR PARTICIPATION

There are many reasons why investigators might be interested in joining a multicenter trial, but a few of the more important include: (a) a high scientific or clinical interest; (b) the study product having the potential for significant benefits to patients; (c) possible benefits of academic prestige for individuals belonging to the group doing the study or of additional patients to the center; if the group is small authorship and publication; and funding from the study, which may allow support for other activities or provide a significant honorarium for the investigator.

A high degree of scientific interest and potential patient benefit have been the major stimuli for our Pediatric Gastroenterology Collaborative Group to work together and develop research protocols. To maximize this interest, all members are involved in the planning of protocols. This allows each investigator to take some ownership in the protocol and helps maintain a high level of interest throughout the study. It also gives an opportunity to discover potential problems with a protocol early on: Is it too complicated? Does it vary from standard practice? Is it uninteresting? Is there too much paperwork or high risk? Are there enough patients? If these issues are not addressed at the very beginning, it may be difficult to find collaborators, and the success of the study may be in jeopardy before it ever starts.

Benefits for patients can be a good motivation for participation in multicenter trials, especially if a new product has consumer interest, potential significant improvement over existing treatment, or fewer side effects. If new products are minimally different, patients may not see much benefit in participating, and it may be hard to motivate investigators. Ideas that are too new or radical may also meet with some resistance from physicians. In a recent protocol review of a new elemental formula, the investigators expressed much concern because there were too many changes in the formula. Although patients might benefit, no one could figure out how to analyze the results in terms of what new ingredient might make a difference. The scientific interest was in more thorough testing of the individual additives before combining them into one ''super'' formula.

In small collaborative group studies, coauthorship and the right to claim membership in a group or study may be important. Authorship and publication rights should be established early on in discussions among collaborators and between collaborators and sponsors. Who will write the paper? Who will be the first author, and in what order will investigators be listed? It is also critical to clarify all issues regarding ownership and analysis of data. Investigators and sponsors need to understand who is responsible for what in the interpretation, presentation, and publication of data.

PROTOCOL DEVELOPMENT, COORDINATION, AND MONITORING

Most of the physicians in our collaborative group like to develop a protocol independently, or in cooperation with a sponsor. They also like to analyze data separately. The general feeling is that a protocol written by an investigator will be less biased and will carry more weight academically. Whether a protocol is developed by an investigator or is company sponsored, there is an advantage in having potential collaborators meet early on during the planning stage. Advice and input from potential collaborators helps build a real partnership between the sponsor and the investigators. Nurturing this partnership to the advantage of both sides gives a protocol the best chance for success.

In those cases where there is an interest in approval from the Food and Drug Administration or other regulatory agencies, the quality of safety and efficacy data are the top priority. We have found it useful to meet the appropriate section of the FDA in planning pediatric drug studies where we would like to see a drug approved for pediatric use. Although working with the FDA in protocol development is no guarantee that the results will lead to agency approval, at least all of the data considered useful are planned for ahead of time. Unfortunately, rules often change, so that even the most careful planning may not lead to the anticipated approval.

In designing a protocol, it is important to collect an adequate amount of information, but too much data discourages investigators and consumes too much time. There is always a concern among investigators that data not collected might lead to some important opportunity being missed. On the other hand, narrowing the scope of a study is often more realistic when it comes to protocol compliance and getting a study done. Trying to balance the right amount of scientific data without missing important information is critical to the success of any study. This may become an even greater problem with the increasing emphasis on data regarding cost analysis, functional status, and quality of life. All of these issues are important, and we will need to find the appropriate tools and develop the methodology in pediatrics to incorporate these data without overburdening our collaborative research efforts.

When individual investigators come together to collaborate, a single institution must become the coordinating center and be responsible for all aspects of the study. This is a great responsibility and requires adequate staff and the time commitment to keep the study moving. The principal investigator must take the lead to interest other collaborators, organize pretrial meetings and follow-up, and provide ongoing motivation for participants. In our Gastroenterology Collaboration Group, my center in Houston has been the coordinating center for all of our protocols, but we have encouraged different members to act as principal investigators for different studies. This has created some confusion with sponsors, especially in terms of funding. In one instance, we split a percentage of funds between the coordinating center and the principal investigator's institution. The contract for this type of arrangement was difficult to write, but the split funding provided real benefits academically to the principal investigator. At the same time, it allowed our coordinating center to handle the data, monitor the study, and support the principal investigator.

It is critical that each center have a coordinator who will take responsibility for the study. Enrolling patients and completing data collection forms is time-consuming, and most physicians are too busy to guarantee daily attention to a study protocol. It is helpful if the coordinator has some experience in clinical trials, but if not, a pretrial meeting to review the protocol is essential to help the coordinators and the investigators understand their responsibilities.

For large multicenter trials, monitoring of study sites and data is the key to running a high-quality study. This requires careful planning as to what will be monitored and who will do the monitoring. Will it be done on site or from a distance, and how often will data be evaluated? Monitors must promote enrollment, check for accuracy of records, ensure that adequate personnel are present in each center, determine if the protocol is being followed as written, and look at all adverse reactions and their appropriate reporting. Failure in any of these areas can lead to serious quality issues that will undermine a good study.

Because of expense and training and time commitments, our collaborative group has depended on telephone monitoring and careful review of data collection forms for all of our studies. This is not ideal, but it has been difficult to find funding for on-site visits for the protocols we have written. In the future, we would prefer on-site monitoring to check for accuracy of data collection and adherence to protocols. In addition, on-site visits will give us a better opportunity to stimulate continued interest and patient enrollment.

Finally, we have found that an advisory board can be of help in evaluating the progress of a study. We have a pediatric gastroenterologist, someone trained in clinical trials, and a pediatrician to monitor results. This group has the authority to stop a trial if there is any problem regarding safety and efficacy. They can also do an interim analysis to see if data suggest a study should continue or be terminated for any other reason. We are also considering a steering committee for future studies. This group would include study investigators from different regions so that they can work with centers that are geographically close. Their role will be to promote the study, maintain enthusiasm, and help with any recruiting problems.

SUMMARY

Once a decision is made that a multicenter clinical trial is desirable, various questions should be addressed before starting. How many centers will be needed? What setting will work best? How many patients must each center recruit? Is the protocol of sufficient interest to attract other investigators? Do potential collaborating centers have appropriate patients in appropriate numbers? How long will it take to get the study done? Who will serve as principal investigator? What about publication rights and authorship? How will the study be monitored? How much data is absolutely necessary to answer the question? Once these issues are addressed, the sponsor and investigators can begin the task of picking the collaborators and progressing to a successful conclusion.

REFERENCES

1. Pocock SJ. *Clinical trials—a practical approach.* Chichester: John Wiley & Sons, 1983:134–138.
2. American Academy of Pediatrics Committee on Drugs. Guidelines for the ethical conduct of studies to evaluate drugs in pediatric populations. *Pediatrics* 1977;60:91–101.
3. Spilker B. *Guide to clinical trials.* New York: Raven Press, 1991:283–286.
4. Spriet A, Dupin-Spriet T, Simon P. *Methodology of clinical drug trials,* 2nd ed. Basel: Karger, 1994: 140–147.
5. Boehm G, Bierbach U, Moro G, Minoli I. Limited fat digestion in infants with bronchopulmonary dysplasia. *J Pediatr Gastroenterol Nutr* 1996;22:161–166.
6. Koo WWK, Krug-Wispe S, Neylan M, Succop P, Oestreich AE, Tsang RC. Effect of three levels of vitamin D intake in preterm infants receiving high mineral-containing milk. *J Pediatr Gastroenterol Nutr* 1995;21:182–189.
7. Gavin N, Merrick N, Davidson B. Efficacy of glucose-based oral rehydration therapy. *Pediatrics* 1996;98:45–51.
8. Ghraf R, Jelinek J, Lehwalder D. Status of clinical trials with the long-chain polyunsaturated fatty acid infant formula Aptamil with Milupan. *Eur J Clin Nutr* 1994;48:S31–S34.
9. Fuchs G, DeWier M, Hutchinson S, Sundeen M. Gastrointestinal blood loss in older infants: impact of cow milk versus formula. *J Pediatr Gastroenterol Nutr* 1993;16:4–9.
10. Uauy RD, Hogg RJ, Brewer ED, Reisch JS, Cunningham C, Holliday MA. Dietary protein and growth in infants with chronic renal insufficiency: a report from the Southwest Pediatric Nephrology Study Group and the University of California, San Francisco. *Pediatr Nephrol* 1994;8:45–50.
11. Ferry GD, Kirschner BS, Grand RJ, Issenman RM, Griffiths AM, Vanderhoof JA, *et al.* Olsalazine versus Sulfasalazine in mild to moderate childhood ulcerative colitis: results of the Pediatric Gastroenterology Collaborative Research Group clinical trial. *J Pediatr Gastroenterol Nutr* 1993;17:32–38.
12. Spilker B. *Guide to clinical trials.* New York: Raven Press, 1991:615–636.

DISCUSSION

Dr. Perman: What are your thoughts about incentives for individuals to participate in multicenter studies? Clinical investigators are committed to producing new knowledge, and that is, and probably should be, reward in itself. But the reality is that publications arising from multicenter studies are simply not given the same kind of recognition as work that reflects the creativity of the individual investigator. So what have you done to allow the recognition of individual participation in a study while at the same time asking individuals to work as a group?

Dr. Ferry: The main thing that we have done is to have our group very involved in protocol development. We also insisted that someone from our group be a principal investigator for the protocol, even if the project originates from the industry. That usually works well, though not in every instance—it depends on the goals of the particular study. We have tried to spread around our authorship to help younger investigators. This gives them a chance to be involved in one or more publications through participation in a multicenter study.

Dr. Hamburger: There could be 13 authors?

Dr. Ferry: We do not all participate in every study, but, in fact, we have had 13 authors. That certainly dilutes the recognition, but in talking to some of the young investigators, they feel their participation has been helpful to them in their own academic promotions. Another incentive is the need of investigators for more help. In doing multicenter studies, a big motivator is funding for a coordinator or research nurse. We have tried to provide some funding to allow for a proportion of someone's time for each study.

Dr. Lucas: You touched on the question of what you mean by a "clinical investigator." We have done about 15 large-scale multicenter trials now in infant nutrition, and we have tried very hard to achieve 100% follow-up or near to that, with very little loss of data. The only way that has been possible is by not relying on clinicians to do anything at all. We rely on clinical investigators to be part of the intellectual process, but we don't rely on them in any other way—either clinical nurses or medics—to collect data or do anything practical in the study, because they are always too busy, and indeed they should put their clinical responsibility before their research responsibility. So we have found that the only way to run big clinical trials is for them to be fully staffed with totally committed staff. Obviously, when the results come out, we can decide how the publications are going to be divided among investigators, and so on. But I am interested that you actually manage to get clinicians to do effective work reliably in multicenter trials.

Dr. Ferry: We do have our problems, and we have had some major protocol difficulties—as an example, one of our studies required an invasive procedure as a follow-up. We could hardly get any of the investigators to do the follow-up or get the parents' permission. So we do have difficulties that we have not solved. However, we do not expect our investigators to actually do very much of the work, and we communicate mostly with the coordinator or research person. The clinical investigators have to be committed though; if they are not enthusiastic, you won't get the patients.

Dr. Steenhout: I think it is true that some investigators don't always read the protocol, but in multicenter trials, it is also the responsibility of the principal investigator to check that the others have really understood and read the protocol. With regard to data storage, I agree with Alan Lucas that it must be the same group or person who inputs the data into the data base to ensure that it is done in the same way throughout and to minimize problems during the statistical analysis. My question is about the statistical aspects of such big trials, because clearly, your cases are different from center to center, and the way people work is different. What must we do when we design a protocol for such a trial to avoid too many differences between centers and ensure that we don't introduce too much bias?

Dr. Ferry: I am not sure I have an answer to this question. We work with academic and nonacademic centers. We picked the centers in that way hoping that the studies would thus gain in generalizability, at least in the respect that the patients and clinicians come from many different areas of the United States and Canada. But the centers are truly quite different, and in any given study, there may be certain centers that fail to produce any data. For example, one of our centers is such a large referral center that they see mostly very complex patients who rarely fit our studies. So the only way you can deal with that is to ask the right questions about each group ahead of time and then make a decision as to whether you do truly want similar centers or whether you want a variety. Sometimes, it is better to be different than to be the same.

Dr. Berlin: If we are talking about randomized trials, I think most people would agree that randomization would need to take place within a center, so that you are stratifying everything else, and whatever clinical variability there is is controlled for. You then have unconfounded treatment in the center and in theory, at least adjustment for centers is probably not going to make much difference. Once you move away from randomized trials, things are much messier, and that is the next 6 months of a statistics course.

Dr. Whitehead: You emphasized the great importance of the study coordinator. Could you spell out what you think are the key attributes of such a person?

Dr. Ferry: The ideal is someone who has had experience in doing clinical studies and understands the importance of accurate data collection. Such people are not easy to find, however, because personnel come and go. We are constantly training new people. A very important quality is organizing ability, particularly attention to detail, so that the person recognizes when information is missing and knows how to go out and obtain it before that patient is lost because of missing data. I also think good communication skills are important. Your success in getting patients to participate and keeping them in the study really depends to a large extent on the coordinator's good relationship with patients.

Dr. Lentze: I was interested about your comment about disease-specific data bases. I think this is very important, and we all want them. But how do you assess that the data base is fueled by the centers? We had faced this problem with diabetes and cystic fibrosis, and the data bases are only theoretical because they are not properly fueled. In theory, it is wonderful, but in practice, people don't provide the data. How do you overcome this problem?

Dr. Ferry: We use a common outpatient visit form to collect the same data. It is a checkoff sheet that can be used for data entry. What we don't have is every blank on the page filled in as we would like, and I think it is going to take some time to convince people that when something is missing, we really have a problem. However, one of the advantages of using this form is that at least everyone is gathering most of the same data in the same way in the clinic setting.

Dr. Aggett: Can I ask you about your experience and practice in ensuring good quality control when it comes not only to the collection of data but also to the methods that are applied if there are serial measurements and, of course, also laboratory measurements?

Dr. Ferry: In terms of clinical measurements, some of our studies have been following growth in inflammatory bowel disease, and here, we have requested that each of our centers must use a stadiometer, and they must average more than one measurement. We do try to standardize as much as we can. In terms of laboratory work, we haven't done studies where this has been very critical. What we have found is that the cost of doing such studies is enormous at most hospitals and academic centers, but we haven't been involved in the kind of study where you have to have very highly trained laboratory personnel to do specific tests.

Dr. Rey: I am puzzled by your presentation. You presented all the difficulties that can arise in multicenter trials, but at the end, I had the feeling that there was no pilot in the plane! Can you give us an example of one of your studies that was well done with a simple answer to a simple question? I can give you an example of the reverse: a very famous study in the United States—the PKU collaborative study, involving at least 30 centers. There were two steps: the first was to determine the IQ of the patients at 4 years of age—the answer was clear, the IQ was around 100; the second was to compare two treatment groups, one treated with a phenylalanine level between 1 and 5 mg per 100 ml, and the other between 5 and 10. After a few months, it was apparent that there was no difference in the dietary score index between the two groups, so it was impossible to answer the question (1). But the principal coordinator continues to cross the world every year to present data--not on the IQ of the two treatment groups but on the consequences of the loss of dietary control, which is a completely different question from the initial one. So he is giving a false response to a true question, and I find myself asking whether there is really a place for multicenter trials in gastroenterology.

Dr. Ferry: What I tried to do today was to give an overview, both from the sponsors' and from the investigators' side, on how to attract the right people to do studies, and what you should be looking for in coordination and data gathering. One of our first studies was a drug study in inflammatory bowel disease involving one of the newer 5-aminosalicylic acid drugs. There was great interest in the pediatric gastroenterologic community about whether this drug was as good as existing treatments, so we decided to do a comparative study. We hypothesized that there shouldn't be very much difference in response, so what we looked at was whether this drug had fewer side effects. Our group of investigators met together, made an assessment of how many patients might be available, and began to develop a protocol and criteria for the kinds of patients to include. We did our statistics ahead of time and knew what sample size was needed; we built in an interim analysis to look at the study as it went along; we had an advisory group to look over our shoulder and make sure that we weren't causing any problems for the patients; and we structured the study so that it could be done in 2 years. Each participating center signed a letter of intent and named a study coordinator. As the study progressed, the enrollment rate was slower than we had wanted, but we did get to a point toward the end of the 2 years when we had enough patients to look at the safety issues. It turned out that the new drug wasn't nearly as effective as the comparison drug, and we decided to stop the study. In all multicenter studies, you have to do the following: develop an interesting and valuable protocol, share it with all investigators for their input, determine whether it is feasible, determine whether there will be enough centers and patients, set the inclusion and exclusion criteria firmly, but not so strictly that you can't find the patients, and establish your statistics and questions ahead of time. Once you get into the study, you must carefully monitor all the data and constantly encourage centers to actually enroll patients.

Dr. Walter: We have done a number of multicenter trials in childhood development, and we have had to involve centers for whom research is not part of their culture. They are providing important clinical services, but they are not routinely involved in research. So, like you, we have had to invest very heavily in research coordinators to make sure the data are being collected appropriately and in a consistent manner. I was, therefore, a little surprised to hear you say that you thought the quality of data would go up when you add centers to a trial. In our experience, it is very difficult to maintain the quality under these circumstances because of the diversity of situations in which people work. It can be done, but it takes a great deal of continuing effort during the life of the trial. My second comment relates to the point that Dr. Berlin made about center-by-treatment interactions. And this is a very controversial problem in the analysis of multicenter trials. Quite apart from the statistical strategy that you might use for the analysis, our experience has often been that as a reward for taking part in a multicenter study, individuals are often interested to know if their center is doing better or worse than average. There is an expectation that there will be center-level results provided to them, and you have to be very careful to explain that that is a dangerous path to go down because of the obvious difficulties in looking at relatively small subgroups. An extreme case of that is in the situation where the trial comes out with essentially negative results, or no difference between interventions. We had that experience a few years ago, where a surgical trial showed that a particular intervention is not really beneficial, but there was serious income involved on the part of the surgeons, so all sorts of cases were made to us to try to persuade us to consider exceptional subgroups, and often their centers, in particular, where their patients would do better.

Dr. Ferry: Large multicenter studies provide greater generalizability of data, but in fact, monitoring is more difficult, and quality may be an issue. We do try to have enough subjects in each center so that there can at least be some randomization within the center itself. If we can get a center to enroll six patients over a year or a year and a half, we are very happy with that; it is the center that enrolls only one patient that creates difficulties with data.

Dr. Tsang: The question of creativity in multicenter trials is a real one. We are involved in multicenter trials with NIH in regard to intensive care units. One of the things we noticed very quickly was that the investigators became very uncreative. Most of the questions have already really been asked, and the multicenter trial is more of a confirmatory study than anything else, so the investigators quickly got bored because they all had to agree to a very common protocol, which was rather bland. The other investigators in the institution were also turned off because they felt that this was only a data-collecting exercise, and there was no creativity. The real problem is for young investigators: young people get really put off because they are participating in a study with no hope of academic recognition or advancement, and no input from them. For example, when multicenter trials first started to be done, the NIH had very strict criteria that ensured that the minor people had no input and were never invited to participate at the planning stage. I think this is a real problem that needs to be tackled, especially as we are about to train new investigators, and we want to get clinical investigators excited about the investigations, young investigators especially. So a balance has to be found between trying to establish enough data, enough data bases, statistics, etc., and allowing a reasonable amount of creativity. Tag-on studies are one way to do this, but we must encourage the drive that drove us into clinical investigation.

REFERENCE

1. Holtzman NA, Kronmal RA, van Doorninck W, *et al.* Effect of age at loss of dietary control on intellectual performance and behavior of children with phenylketonuria. *N Engl J Med* 1986;314: 593–598.

Clinical Trials in Infant Nutrition, edited by
Jay A. Perman and Jean Rey, Nestlé Nutrition
Workshop Series, Vol. 40, Nestec Ltd.,
Vevey/Lippincott-Raven Publishers,
Philadelphia © 1998.

Nutrition, Diet, and Infant Development: Long-Chain Polyunsaturated Fatty Acids in Infant Neurodevelopment

*†Ricardo Uauy-Dagach, *‡Patricia Mena, and †Dennis Hoffman

Institute of Nutrition and Food Technology, University of Chile, Santiago, Chile; †Retina Foundation of the Southwest, Dallas, Texas, USA; and ‡Clinical Nutrition and Neonatal Unit, Hospital Sótero del Rio, Santiago, Chile

Lipids are the predominant source of dietary energy for infants and young children and constitute the major energy stores in the body. There is a growing interest in the quality of dietary lipid supply in early childhood as a major determinant of infant growth, development, and long-term health. Thus, the selection of dietary lipid supply during the early stages of postnatal life is considered of great importance.

Lipids are structural components of all tissues and are indispensable for cell membrane synthesis; the brain, retina, and other neural tissues are particularly rich in long-chain polyunsaturated fatty acids (LC-PUFA). These fatty acids serve as specific precursors for eicosanoid production (prostaglandins, prostacyclins, thromboxanes, and leukotrienes). Eicosanoids are powerful autocrine and paracrine regulators of numerous cell and tissue functions (for example, thrombocyte aggregation, inflammatory reactions and leukocyte functions, vasoconstriction and vasodilation, blood pressure, bronchial constriction, uterine contraction). Dietary lipid intake also affects cholesterol metabolism at an early age and is associated with cardiovascular morbidity and mortality in later life. More recently, lipid supply, especially the provision of LC-PUFA, has been shown to affect neural structural development and function.

BRIEF SUMMARY OF ESSENTIAL FATTY ACID METABOLISM, LC-PUFA SYNTHESIS, AND BASIS FOR ESSENTIALITY

George and Mildred Burr in 1929 introduced the concept that specific components of fat may be necessary for proper growth and development of animals and possibly humans (1). They proposed that three fatty acids be considered essential: linoleic acid ($18:2\ n-6$), arachidonic acid ($20:4\ n-6$) and α-linolenic acid (LNA; $18:3\ n-3$) (1). The essentiality of $n-6$ and $n-3$ fatty acids for humans is best explained by the inability of animal tissues to introduce double bonds in positions

Dietary EFA source

$$n\text{-}3 \quad 18:3 \xrightarrow{\Delta 6} 18:4 \longrightarrow 20:4 \xrightarrow{\Delta 5} 20:5 \longrightarrow 22:5 \quad 22:6$$

α - LINOLENIC   EPA   DHA

24:5 $\xrightarrow{\Delta 6}$ 24:6

$$n\text{-}6 \quad 18:2 \xrightarrow{\Delta 6} 18:3 \longrightarrow 20:3 \xrightarrow{\Delta 5} 20:4 \longrightarrow 22:4 \quad 22:5$$

LINOLEIC   GLA   AA   DPA

24:4 $\xrightarrow{\Delta 6}$ 24:5

$$n\text{-}9 \quad 16:0 \longrightarrow 18:0 \xrightarrow{\Delta 9} 18:1 \xrightarrow{\Delta 6} 18:2 \longrightarrow 20:2 \xrightarrow{\Delta 5} 20:3$$

palmitic   stearic   oleic   ETA

De Novo Synthesis and Diet

FIG. 1. Long-chain polyunsaturated fatty acid (LC-PUFA) and essential fatty acids (EFA) metabolism. Parent EFA are derived from dietary sources for both $n - 3$ (18:3, LNA) and $n - 6$ series (18:2, LA). *De novo* synthesis is able to produce only $n - 9$ LC-PUFA. Elongation occurs two carbons at a time and Δ-desaturases introduce double bonds at 9, 6, and 5 carbons from the carboxylic end of the fatty acid chain. The final step in the formation of $n - 3$ and $n - 6$ end products is catalyzed by a peroxisomal β-oxidation. PUFA of interest include 18:3 $n - 6$ (GLA), 20:4 $n - 6$ (AA), 22:5 $n - 6$ (DPA), 20:3 $n - 9$ (ETA), 20:5 $n - 3$ (EPA), and 22:6 $n - 3$ (DHA). EPA, AA, and 20:3 $n - 6$ are immediate precursors of prostaglandins (PG) and other eicosanoids.

before carbon 9, counting from the methyl or n terminus. Essential fatty acids (EFA) were considered of marginal nutritional importance for humans until the 1960s, when signs of clinical deficiency became apparent in infants fed skimmed-milk-based formula and in those given lipid-free parenteral nutrition (2,3). These infants presented with dryness, desquamation, and thickening of the skin and growth faltering as frequent manifestations of linoleic acid deficiency. More subtle clinical symptoms appear in $n - 3$ essential fatty acid deficiency. They include skin changes unresponsive to linoleic acid supplementation, abnormal visual function, and peripheral neuropathy (4).

Parent EFA (linoleic acid and LNA) are further elongated and desaturated by mammals, generating a family of compounds for each (Fig. 1). As shown in the figure, arachidonic acid can be formed from linoleic acid; it becomes essential only if the capacity for elongation and desaturation of linoleic acid is limited. This occurs in the cat and other felines. Further information can be found in recent reviews (5,6). The competitive inhibition of the desaturation step of the respective precursors (for $n - 3$, LNA; for $n - 6$, linoleic acid; and for $n - 9$, oleic acid) by Δ^6-desaturase is of major significance because this is the controlling step of the pathway. If $n -$ 3 fatty acids are absent or deficient in the diet, the elongation/desaturation of the

$n - 6$ compounds generates a significant increase in docosapentaenoic acid (DPA; $22:5$ $n - 6$); if both EFA are lacking, eicosatrienoic acid (ETA; $20:3$ $n - 9$) accumulates (5). The triene/tetraene (ETA/arachidonic acid) ratio may be used as an index of essential fatty acid deficiency but is not valid as a marker of isolated $n - 3$ deficit. An increased ratio of DPA to docosahexaenoic acid (DHA) has been suggested by us and others to serve as a useful index of $n - 3$ deficiency.

The LC-PUFA arachidonic acid, eicosapentaenoic acid (EPA; $20:5$ $n - 3$), and DHA ($22:6$ $n - 3$) are important membrane components and precursors of potent bioactive oxygenated products. Eicosanoids such as prostaglandins, leukotrienes, and epoxides derived from arachidonic acid and EPA modulate or are required in numerous physiological processes; a myriad of clinical correlates associated with deficient or excessive essential fatty acid intake have been observed. The conversion of parent EFA to LC-PUFA is under active regulation; therefore, the effects of providing arachidonic acid, EPA, or DHA are not replicated if the equivalent amount of linoleic acid or LNA is provided (7,8). The uniqueness of feeding human milk relative to essential fatty acid metabolism is based on the direct supply of LC-PUFA bypassing the regulatory step of the Δ^6-desaturase. Excess dietary linoleic acid associated with some vegetable oils, particularly safflower, sunflower, and corn oils, may decrease the formation of DHA from LNA because the Δ^6-desaturase is inhibited by excess substrate. In addition, arachidonic acid formation is reduced when excess linoleic acid or LNA is provided (5–8). The inhibitory effect of EPA on Δ^5-desaturase activity has been considered in part responsible for the lower arachidonic acid observed when marine oil is consumed. Excess linoleic acid, as seen in infants receiving corn oil or safflower oil as the predominant fatty acid supply, will inhibit the elongation/desaturation of the parent EFA and thus lower the LC-PUFA supply necessary for membrane synthesis. Marine PUFA provide minimal preformed arachidonic acid and substantial amounts of preformed $n - 3$ LC-PUFA such as EPA and DHA (9).

The biochemical and functional evidence indicates that in early life, C_{18} $n - 3$ precursors are not sufficiently converted to DHA. Thus, not only linoleic acid and LNA but also DHA should be considered essential nutrients for normal eye and brain development in the human.

ASSESSMENT OF CLINICAL TRIALS ON LC-PUFA SUPPLEMENTATION

The dry weight of the human brain is predominantly lipid; 22% of the cerebral cortex and 24% of white matter consist of phospholipids. Studies of several animal species and recent evidence from humans have established that brain phospholipid arachidonic acid and DHA decrease, whereas $n - 9$ and $n - 7$ mono- and polyunsaturated fatty acids increase, when linoleic acid and LNA are deficient in the diet (10–12). Typically, $n - 3$ fatty acid-deficient cells have decreased DHA and increased levels of the end product of $n - 6$ metabolism, DPA. Within the subcellular organelles, synaptosomes and mitochondria seem to be more sensitive to a low dietary $n - 3$ supply, as evidenced by the relative abundance of DHA and the changes in composition of these organelles in response to dietary deprivation (10–12). The animal data accumulated over several decades strongly support the essential nature of EFA for humans, and particularly a need for LC-PUFA in early life. Direct information from humans is limited because human investigation in this area is just a decade old. In this chapter we review randomized clinical trials addressing the putative effects of LC-PUFA on neurodevelopment.

How to Define and Design the Diet to be Tested (the Independent Variable)

The Human Milk Model

A good starting point is to mimic the composition of human milk. Unfortunately, human milk does not have a uniform lipid composition; the type of fatty acid in human milk is affected by mother's diet during pregnancy and lactation and varies according to postpartum age, preterm or term delivery, and maternal diseases affecting lipid metabolism such as diabetes, cystic fibrosis, and abetalipoproteinemia. Arachidonic acid is the main $n - 6$ and DHA is the most significant of the $n - 3$ series of LC-PUFA found in human milk. The ratio of total $n - 6$ to $n - 3$ is $5:1$ to $10:1$, ranging up to $18:1$ if oils high in linoleic acid are consumed. The ratio of arachidonic acid to DHA is most commonly $1.5:1$ to $2:1$. The variability in LC-PUFA in human milk is high and determined mainly by diet. Eicosapentaenoic acid is found in minimal amounts except in populations consuming high intakes of fish; it is always lower than the DHA content (13,14). The DHA levels range from 0.1% in Germany to 1.4% in Inuits of North America. Typical values range from 0.3% to 0.4%; however, higher concentrations are found in human milk from women consuming non-Western diets (13). Recently, Gibson et al. reported a longitudinal reduction in the DHA content of human milk from Australian women on Western diets from 0.32% in 1981 to 0.21% in 1995 (15).

The question of what amounts of specific fatty acids to feed is not answered just by deciding to follow the human milk model. Should one select a value in the upper range of LC-PUFA content, the lower range, or the midpoint? If the effort is focused primarily on demonstrating functional efficacy, selecting a value in the upper range is preferable. On the other hand, if safety concerns are the main objective of study, selecting a value in the lower range might be more appropriate. In our initial studies, we did not have access to pure LC-PUFA sources; thus, in order to provide DHA, we were obligated to include EPA because the available marine oil had a ratio of EPA/DHA of $2:1$. No sources of arachidonic acid were available for commercial use; thus, we could not include this fatty acid, which is recognized as of potentially critical importance. We chose to provide 0.35% DHA in both the preterm and term infant studies (16–18). This value is in the mid- to upper range of the mean DHA content derived from combined data on human milk composition of omnivorous

TABLE 1. *Observational studies of dietary LC-PUFA intake and neurodevelopmental function*

Author, year (ref.)	Subjects, age at evaluation	Main outcome variables	Test diets	Main results
Birch, 1993 (22)	Term infants, 3 years	DHA plasma PL <1 year OPL visual acuity OPL stereoacuity, HOT recognition	HM or term formula	HM better stereoacuity and better recognition DHA at 4 months + correlated with stereoacuity at 3 years
Bjerve, 1993 (23)	VLBW infants, 1 year	Bayley MDI and PDI DHA and EPA serum PL	Not characterized	DHA + correlated with PDI EPA-correlated with MDI
Makrides, 1993 (24)	Term infants, 5 months	VEP visual acuity DHA and LA in RBC PL	HM or term formula	HM better acuity DHA + correlated with acuity
Innis, 1994 (25)	Term infants, 3 months	TAC visual acuity FAs in plasma and RBC PL	HM or term formula	No differences
Courage, 1995 (26)	Term infants, 18 months	TAC visual acuity	HM or cow's milk formula	HM better acuity at 3, 6, and 18 months
Jorgensen, 1996 (27)	Term infants, 4 months	TAC visual acuity DHA, AA, EPA in RBC PL	HM or term formula	HM better acuity

women. Other investigators have studied premature infants given 0.2% to 0.5% DHA (19,20) and term infants given 0.1% to 0.36% (21), as shown in Tables 1 through 3.

What Sources of LC-PUFA to Use in the Test Formulas

Vegetable oils derived from maize, safflower, and sunflower contain predominantly linoleic acid and little or no LNA. Oils derived from soybean and linseed contain ample LNA. This latter fatty acid has higher concentrations in green leaf vegetables than in vegetable seeds. Thus, products from animals fed in the wild have higher $n - 3$ fatty acids than grain-fed animals. This is of interest in terms of the higher DHA content of eggs from range-fed chickens. The use of evening primrose oil or black current oil provides $18:3$ $n - 6$ γ-linolenic acid (GLA), bypassing the controlling step, Δ^6-desaturase, necessary for arachidonic acid formation. γ-Linolenic acid has been added by some manufacturers as an alternative to arachidonic acid, with limited benefits. The main source for the *de novo* synthesis of $n - 3$ fatty acids in the aquatic environment is marine autotrophic bacteria, microalgae, and protozoa, which constitute the zooplankton and phytoplankton (38,39). Fish, higher in the food chain, incorporate the $n - 3$ PUFA and further elongate them to form EPA and DHA. Thus, fish will concentrate EPA and DHA as triglycerides, mainly in the adipose tissue and in the fat of muscle and visceral organs. The higher the fat content of fish, the higher its content of $n - 3$ fatty acids (40,41).

Another important source of LC-PUFA used in infant diets is egg yolk phospholipid. The concentrations of PUFA are different depending on the feed given to

TABLE 2. *Randomized controlled trials of biochemical and functional effects of LC-PUFA supplementation*

Author, year (ref.)	Subjects, age at evaluation	LC-PUFA source	LA (% total)	LNA (% total)	AA (% total)	EPA (% total)	DHA (% total)	Main outcome variables
Uauy, 1992 (16–18)	VLBW infants, bw 1000–1500 g, 57 weeks PCA[a]	Marine oil	20–21	2.7	0.1	0.65	0.35	FA composition plasma, RBC, and cheek cells Rod and cone ERG, VEP, and FPL visual acuity Growth, bleeding time Membrane fluidity
Carlson, 1992 (19, 28, 29)	VLBW infants, bw 748–1398 g, 9 months	Marine oil	19–33	3.2–4.9		0.3–0.7	0.2–0.4	FA composition plasma and RBC TAC visual acuity Growth Development (Bayley)
Agostoni, 1995 (30)	Term infants, 4 months[a]	Egg phospholipids	11	0.3	0.44	0.05	0.3	FA composition Cholesterol Development (Brunet–Lezine)
Makrides, 1995 (31)	Term infants, 30 weeks[a]	Marine oil, primrose oil	17	1.6	0.01 and 0.27	0.58	0.36	FA composition VEP visual acuity
Carlson, 1996 (32, 33)	Preterm infants, bw 747–1275 g, 12 months	Marine oil	21	2.4	GLA	0.06	0.2	FA composition Growth TAC visual acuity
Mena, 1996 (34)	Preterm infants, bw 1000–1950 g, 18 months[a]	Animal phospholipids	11–15	1.1–1.4	0.8–0.9		0.5	FA composition Growth Rod and cone ERG, VEP, and FPL visual acuity BAER Sleep–wake cycle, heart rate variability
Carlson, 1996 (35)	Term infants, 12 months[a]	Egg phospholipids	22	2.2	0.43	0.0	0.1	FA composition Growth TAC visual acuity

[a] Study includes a human-milk-fed reference group.

TABLE 3. *Randomized controlled trials of biochemical effects of LC-PUFA supplementation*

Author, year (ref.)	Subjects, age at evaluation	LC-PUFA source	LA (% total)	LNA (% total)	AA (% total)	EPA (% total)	DHA (% total)	Main outcome variables
Koletzko, 1995 (36)	VLBW infants, 3 weeks[a]	Egg phospholipids	14	0.8	0.5	0.03	0.30	FA composition of plasma PL
Ghebremeskel, 1995 (20)	VLBW infants, bw <2200 g, 8 weeks[a]	Egg phospholipids	14	1.0	0.12	0.01	0.51	FA composition of plasma and RBC
Clandinin, 1992 (37)	VLBW infants, bw <1500 g, 4 weeks[a]	Freshwater fish	14	1.6	0.21	0.20	0.35	FA composition of plasma and RBC

[a] Study includes a human-milk-fed reference group

chickens: ample use of fish meal in chicken feed results in increased egg yolk DHA (42,43). LC-PUFA products for blends in infant formulas can be successfully produced if chicken feed is carefully monitored and if refined lipid extraction procedures are used. This is presently an important LC-PUFA source used in some infant formulas. Bacterial strains and microalgae isolated from the intestinal content of some fish have a remarkably high content of EPA and DHA (41). Efforts to grow these microorganisms in natural or artificial seawater to obtain DHA for nutritional or pharmacologic use have been successful. In addition, selected fungal strains produce concentrated arachidonic acid that is suitable for human consumption. The industrial production of arachidonic acid, EPA, and DHA from strains of these single-cell organisms has been successful; their expanded use will depend on price and demand relative to the concentrates obtained from marine oils. Single-cell oils offer a promising new source of LC-PUFA provided mass production becomes commercially feasible (38).

Rigorous purity and toxicologic testing should be conducted on fatty acid sources intended for use in commercial infant formula. Currently there is insufficient knowledge on the implications of using these novel LC-PUFA sources in infant formula. Initial studies used a mixture of vegetable oils to supply linoleic acid and LNA, and marine oil as a source of $n - 3$ LC-PUFA (17,19). More recent studies, including our own, have used nearly pure DHA from marine oil fractions or DHA and arachidonic acid from single-cell oils. Most published work to date is based on infant formulas enriched with marine oil, marine oil fractions, or egg phospholipids as LC-PUFA sources.

Defining the Correct Balance Between Fatty Acid Species for Optimal Endogenous LC-PUFA Biosynthesis

Metabolism of LC-PUFA is greatly affected by the interaction of various fatty acids. This may determine the final effect of the diet being fed. Excess linoleic acid, a high linoleic acid/LNA ratio, and possibly other fatty acids may affect the endogenous synthesis of DHA and arachidonic acid. Because the choice of oil mixes to be used in formulas was traditionally based on fat digestibility, a high linoleic acid was considered beneficial. Furthermore, LNA was usually not included in order to decrease peroxidative potential. The linoleic acid/LNA ratio in the older formulations was often 50:1 and sometimes as high as 100:1. These ratios are in sharp contrast with human milk, where the linoleic acid/LNA ratio is close to 5:1 and at most 10:1. In addition, when marine oil sources are used, EPA is also included. If the concentration of EPA is sufficiently high, it will interfere with arachidonic acid biosynthesis and compete for incorporation into phospholipids.

The alternative fates of dietary linoleic acid and LNA are (a) mitochondrial oxidation to yield energy, (b) esterification and incorporation into membranes or circulating lipid moieties, and (c) serving as precursors for arachidonic acid and DHA biosynthesis. The relative effects of these alternate pathways on the size of the LC-PUFA pool are difficult to quantify, yet it can be anticipated that several dietary factors will affect them. In addition, even if preformed arachidonic acid and DHA are provided, they can also be oxidized as fuels or undergo peroxidation before incorporation into phospholipid or other functionally relevant cellular pools. Thus, in evaluating the effect of lipid composition of the diet, one should consider not only the arachidonic acid and DHA content of the formulation but also the balance of LC-PUFA precursors, antioxidants, and other fatty acids that may affect LC-PUFA metabolism.

Controlling Major Diet-Related Confounders

Energy Balance

Energy balance and the provision of energy substrates are major determinants of fatty acid oxidation rates. If the infant is in negative energy balance, a greater proportion of the absorbed linoleic acid and LNA will be oxidized. The provision of medium-chain triglycerides may be critical to spare EFA and LC-PUFA from oxidation. The full extent of this phenomenon has not been evaluated, but the available information indicates that LNA is preferentially spared from oxidation, while C_{16} and shorter-chain fatty acids are readily oxidized (5).

Overall Organ Function

The elongation and desaturation pathway is dependent on intact function of several cellular organelles. The endoplasmic reticulum is responsible for the desaturation steps, whereas elongation requires availability of activated acetate from mitochondrial energy metabolism, and the final partial β-oxidation necessary to form DHA occurs in peroxisomes. Potential physiological or pathologic conditions that affect the function or maturation of these organelles may also affect the biological response to a given essential fatty acid or LC-PUFA intake. In addition, desaturation and elongation enzyme systems are dependent on the availability of a variety of cofactors. Metals such as iron, zinc, and copper and cofactors such as coenzyme A, cytochrome C, NADP, and NADPH are all necessary for the endogenous synthesis of arachidonic acid and DHA from linoleic acid and LNA. The selection of human subjects in terms of gestational age, energy balance, micronutrient status, disease condition, and liver and other organ function may all be critical in determining the biological response to dietary essential fatty acid supply.

Need for Antioxidant Protection

The need for antioxidant protection is increased according to the number of double bonds present in the fatty acid. Thus, the balance of PUFA + LC-PUFA to tocopherol and ascorbate is important to preserve the unsaturated bonds. This should be considered in designing the formula product as well as in the evaluation of biological effects. Sufficient antioxidants must be present in the formula and in the body to minimize peroxidation of the LC-PUFA. If peroxidation of LC-PUFA is not prevented, these compounds will be lost, and potential damage to membranes by the products of peroxidation may occur.

Digestibility of Fat Sources and Specific Fatty Acids

Further considerations need to include limited bioavailability of LC-PUFA in formula compared to human milk. Because human milk contains bile-acid-stimulated lipase capable of enhancing LC-PUFA digestion and assimilation into tissue phospholipids, addition of LC-PUFA in excess of that in human milk or addition of human milk lipase to formula may need to be considered (19). This issue also affects the source of LC-PUFA, where positional isomerization of the acyl group can influence metabolic utilization. Thus, overall digestibility and specific LC-PUFA utilization should be considered in evaluating the effect of diet on an infant's LC-PUFA status. Recent evidence suggests that LC-PUFA in formula are better absorbed than in fortified pasteurized human milk (44).

Controlling Major Clinical Confounders

The selection of subjects is a critical issue in the design of studies to define the effects of LC-PUFA on neurodevelopment. Randomized controlled clinical trials using identical study formulas except for the addition of the test fatty acids are necessary to establish effects. The evaluation of human-milk-fed infants in comparison to formula-fed infants should not be used to support a relationship between a specific compound present in human milk, such as LC-PUFA, and developmental outcome.

Using "Healthy" or Truly Representative Experimental Subjects

Selection of relatively healthy infants has the advantage of providing results that are not confounded by intercurrent illness or morbidity, which may affect the developmental outcomes or metabolic handling of EFA. On the other hand, if the study is intended to address the needs of preterm infants, selecting a "healthy" subgroup may not reflect the population of interest, limiting the external validity of the study. If a representative sample of a clinically heterogeneous population is used, the variability in developmental outcomes will most likely be greater; this should be considered in the estimation of sample size. Initial studies to explore the relationship between diet and neurodevelopment may consider using select subgroups, but if the purpose is to modify feeding practices, a true representative sample with very few exclusion criteria is necessary to establish efficacy and safety of a new feeding regimen. Randomization methods need to assure that the chance to enter the experimental or control groups is truly random. Specific gestational age and possibly birth weight strata as well as gender should be considered to assure randomness in the distribution of these intervening variables. If in the course of a randomized controlled clinical trial, a new treatment that significantly modifies survival or complications becomes available, the randomization scheme should block subjects according to time of entry in order to assure that interactions are appropriately evaluated. The randomized controlled clinical trial is indeed the only way to scientifically define optimal feeding on the basis of safety and efficacy.

The Human-Milk-Fed Reference Group

It is important to define reference groups if the experimental diet is better, the same, or worse than the standard feeding regimen. The human-milk-fed infant appears to be an obvious reference control group to compare the relative effects of diet on growth and development. Unfortunately, it is not possible to randomize infants to human milk feeding because this practice requires the cooperation of the mother, and success is not always achieved. Most studies that use human-milk-fed reference controls match the groups by the main confounding variables of birth weight, sex, gestational age, and presence of morbidity. Maternal characteristics that affect growth and central nervous system (CNS) development, such as maternal height, socioeconomic status, and educational level, are recorded and used in *post hoc* analysis. Unfortunately, these confounders are usually biased in favor of the human-milk-fed group. Covariance adjustments are performed but cannot truly correct for group differences. A truly randomized trial of human milk feeding to define a reference population is ideal but not feasible.

Term Infants as a Reference Group in Studies of Preterm Infants

In evaluating developmental outcomes of premature infants, the use of controls born at term provides another valid reference group. The preterm group given the experimental treatment can be compared with the preterm control group and also with a full-term group at the equivalent postconceptional age. The goal in feeding preterm infants is to achieve similar development to full-term infants of similar postconceptional age. In this approach, the experimental group is compared to a randomly assigned control group and to two reference groups—a human-milk-fed group and, in the case of preterm infant, a term human-milk-fed reference control. The underlying assumption is that the human-milk-fed term infant provides the best possible developmental outcome.

Defining Outcome Variables

The selection of outcome variables is another key step in determining the effect of LC-PUFA on infant neurodevelopment. Biochemical and functional responses may be used to define biological effects. If both are compared in a correlation analysis, one can use biochemical effects as a proxy to predict functional outcomes. The timing of measurements is crucial because effects may be found only within a given developmental time interval. The duration of the effect should also be characterized; enhancing or accelerating a maturational or developmental milestone may not necessarily be better. The true validation requires either a reference group or a sufficiently long follow-up to assure that the final outcome is indeed modified. In the following sections, we analyze the most common outcome variables used in LC-PUFA clinical trials.

Changes in Plasma and Red Blood Cell Membrane Composition

The effect of feeding lipids with specific fatty acid compositions will usually result in measurable differences in plasma lipid composition. For example, the fatty acid composition of triglycerides in plasma will reflect the fatty acid composition of recent lipid dietary intake, but plasma phospholipid composition will more probably reflect tissue pools with functional significance. The selection of plasma phospholipid or red blood cell biochemical indices of fatty acid intake is based on the fact that under deficiency conditions they have been found to be correlated to tissue composition and can readily be measured. The triene/tetraene ratio (that is, $20:3\ n - 9$ to $20:4\ n - 6$) is useful for defining the overall essential fatty acid deficit. The DPA–DHA ratio ($22:5\ n - 6$ to $22:6\ n - 3$) has been related to overall $n - 3$ deficit. The use of absolute concentrations will better reflect true changes in blood lipid composition; on the other hand, values expressed as percentages of total lipids may be better indicators of available tissue pools. For example, the relative content of arachidonic acid and DHA blood lipids (percentage of total) drops markedly postnatally in formula-fed infants, yet the absolute concentrations per unit of volume fall only slightly after birth in formula-fed infants and rise in the human-milk-fed infants (45).

Composition of Neural Tissues

The composition of neural tissues such as the retina or brain cortex is clearly of greater interest but cannot be measured in humans. The study of infants who died suddenly of an unexplained cause has served to document a good correlation between the composition of the brain cortex and red blood cell total lipids (46). Two studies have examined neural tissue levels of LC-PUFA in formula-fed compared to human-milk-fed term infants (46,47). Farquharson and colleagues found 25% lower levels of DHA in cerebral cortex phospholipids from formula-fed infants than in those from human-milk-fed infants (47). Makrides *et al.* reported significantly lower levels of DHA in red blood cells and cortex but not in retina or basal ganglia of formula-fed term infants than in human-milk-fed infants. The DHA in cortex was dependent on age and duration of breast-feeding (46). The results indicate that DHA supply for brain accretion is critical during the first months of life: LNA conversion to DHA appears to be insufficient, although linoleic acid conversion to arachidonic acid is sufficient, based on compositional data (47,48).

Functional Response of the Retina and Brain Cortex

The functional response of the retina and brain cortex can be measured by electrophysiological or behavioral methods. The latter outcomes are potentially of greater interest but are more variable and difficult to measure. The selection of these indices should be based on the developmental stage being evaluated and the sensitivity and specificity of the response. If the wrong outcome measure is selected, no effect may be found. For example, behavioral assessment of visual acuity (by forced-choice preferential looking, FPL) is highly variable and is difficult to obtain before 40 weeks postconceptional age. On the other hand, visual evoked potential (VEP) acuity measurements can be obtained as early as 36 weeks; furthermore, these later acuity estimates are less variable. The VEP measurements may reveal a significant effect of diet, whereas the FPL assessment may yield no effect. Careful selection of specific times to conduct infant testing is critical; the test must be given at a time when rapid development is occurring, and nutritional influences will affect the function being examined. The need for normative data obtained with rigorously defined testing protocols is essential if subtle differences in visual outcome are to be detected. Most studies to date have been limited to retinal function and indices of visual development. Some studies have included measures of mental and motor development at 12 and 18 months. Studies of the effect of LC-PUFA on sleep–wake cycle development, sympathethic tone, auditory evoked responses, and activity levels are under way in our laboratories. In these investigations we have verified that sleep state, an often ignored factor, is an important determinant of electrophysiological responses such as electroretinography (ERG) and VEP (49,50).

SUMMARY OF EFFECTS

Recent clinical trials convincingly support modifications in the LC-PUFA composition of preterm infant formulations to reflect that of human milk. Comprehensive clinical studies have shown that dietary supplementation with marine oil results in increased blood levels of DHA as well as an associated improvement in visual function in formula-fed premature infants to match that of human-milk-fed infants (16–19).

Published observational studies comparing functional outcomes of human-milk- and unsupplemented formula-fed infants are summarized in Table 1. Randomized controlled studies that have included only biochemical measures are summarized in Table 2. We focus our discussion on published results of randomized controlled clinical trials that have included both biochemical measures and functional assessment of neurodevelopment, summarized in Table 3.

Preterm Infant Studies

In our studies, preterm infants received human milk or were randomized to one of three formulas. The formulas were based on: (a) corn (maize) oil, which provided 24% of total fat as linoleic acid ($18:2\ n-6$) and 0.5% LNA; (b) soybean oil, 21% linoleic acid and 2.7% LNA; and (c) soybean and marine oil, 20% as linoleic acid, 1.4% as LNA, 0.65% as EPA, and 0.35% as DHA. The corn oil and soybean oil diets provided no LC-PUFA, and the marine oil diet provided no arachidonic acid. Significant results of this study included a marked inability of the corn oil formula to support the necessary accumulation of LC-PUFA in plasma and red cell lipids. Supplementation of $n-3$ LC-PUFA was sufficient to increase red cell DHA concentrations in the marine-oil-fed group to levels two- to fivefold higher than in the corn oil and soybean oil groups (17,18). The functional impact of this fatty acid modification included significant maturation of ERG responses in marine-oil-fed infants compared to the corn oil and soybean-oil-fed infants at 36 weeks postconceptional age (Fig. 2). Equivalent ERG thresholds (the minimum amount of light required to elicit a given retinal response) were found in the marine-oil- and human-milk-fed infant groups. The soybean-oil-fed infant group presented intermediate values. By 57 weeks postconceptional age, a time when retinal development is nearly complete, the corn-oil-fed group recovered in most indices of retinal function except in oscillatory potentials (Fig. 3). Visual acuity tests that measure higher neural activity such as cortical function (for example, pattern-reversal VEP) or cortical plus motor function (for example, FPL) were less mature in the corn oil and soybean-oil-fed groups throughout the 6-month study (17,18). The LC-PUFA-supplemented marine oil group had significantly better visual acuity as measured by VEP and FPL than the $n-3$-deficient corn oil formula group, whereas visual acuity in the soybean-oil-fed group was intermediate (Figs. 2 and 3). Highly significant correlations were found for both VEP and FPL visual acuity when compared to the level of DHA in multiple lipid fractions from study infants (Figs. 4 to 6). No significant differences in growth indices were evident among the three groups despite reduced levels of arachidonic acid in the marine oil group, probably attributable to EPA accumulation (two- to fourfold higher than other groups). Body length and weight in the LC-PUFA supplemented group were not reduced (16), in contrast to the observations of Carlson (28). The lower arachidonic acid levels, in part related to fish oil supplementation in her studies, were associated with poorer growth. Differences in subject selection criteria and in formula composition (higher linoleic acid and insufficient mineral and vitamin content), as well as the longer duration of LC-PUFA provision in her study (9 months versus 4 months), may explain the differences in the results.

Carlson's randomized clinical study in preterm infants supplemented with 0.2% DHA/0.3% EPA showed that there was better visual acuity (measured by the Teller acuity card tests) in infants up to 4 months of age. After this, control infants "caught up" in visual function measures. These investigators also report evidence of more rapid visual processing, as measured by the Fagan test of visual recognition at 6 to

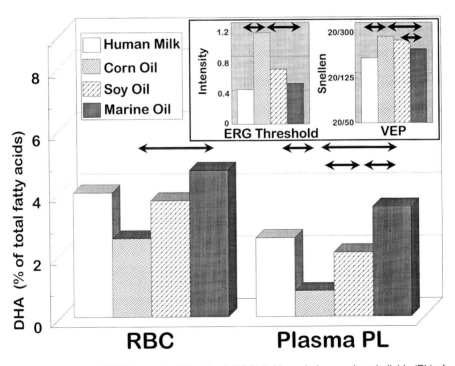

FIG. 2. Content of DHA in total red blood cell (RBC) lipids and plasma phospholipids (PL) of preterm infants on study diets at 36 weeks postconception. **Inset:** Rod ERG thresholds (intensity units are in log scotopic troland-seconds) and VEP visual acuity in Snellen equivalents in infants studied at 36 weeks. *Arrows* indicate significant differences between diet groups using Newman–Keuls multiple comparison analysis ($p < 0.05$).

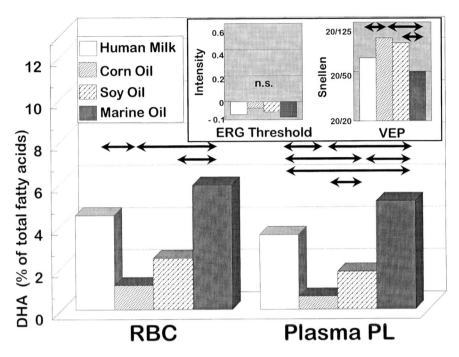

FIG. 3.   Content of DHA in total RBC lipids and plasma phospholipids (PL) of preterm infants on study diets at 57 weeks postconception. **Inset:** Rod ERG thresholds (log scotopic troland-seconds) and VEP visual acuity (Snellen equivalents) measured in study infants at 57 weeks. *Arrows* indicate significant differences between diet groups using Newman–Keuls multiple comparison analysis ($p < 0.05$).

12 months of age in LC-PUFA-supplemented infants (29). The reduction in blood lipid levels of the $n - 6$ LC-PUFA, arachidonic acid, when fish oil was provided as a source of $n - 3$ fatty acids was a significant finding in this study. The reduction in arachidonic acid was associated with reduced weight and length growth ($r = 0.27$ to 0.53, $p < 0.05$) (28). Similar correlations have been reported by others, yet no study has specifically tested this hypothesis prospectively (51,52).

The issue of a direct benefit to visual and cognitive function of specific DHA formula enrichment (using low-EPA marine oil) has been addressed in Carlson's second preterm infant study, where infants were fed for up to 2 months corrected age (32). This study showed improved visual development at the 2-month follow-up and a 10-point IQ difference favoring the DHA-supplemented group at 12 months. No significant drop in arachidonic acid or deleterious effects on growth were observed when low-EPA marine oil was used. The DHA-supplemented group had shorter look times in the novelty preference test at 9 months, suggesting better visual processing. Weight-for-length indices and head growth were lower in the DHA-supplemented infants (33). We are presently completing a study using formulas containing DHA and DHA plus arachidonic acid to confirm whether DHA supplementation by itself is sufficient or if DHA plus arachidonic acid is needed to optimize efficacy and prevent deleterious effects.

Additional preterm infant studies by other laboratories confirm the need for LC-PUFA enrichment of formula to maintain blood levels of $n - 3$ and $n - 6$ LC-PUFA in these ''at-risk'' infants (20,36,37). These data are summarized in Tables 1 through 3. Pending issues regarding LC-PUFA provision to preterm infants currently include defining the following:

1. The need to supplement with both DHA and arachidonic acid, and whether there are other fatty acids that could replace them.
2. The amount of LC-PUFA to include in the formula.
3. Duration of supplementation.
4. What sources of LC-PUFA should be used, considering safety and costs.

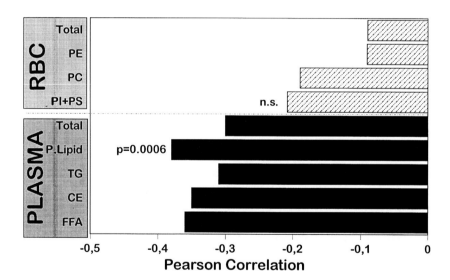

FIG. 4. Correlation coefficients of rod threshold measured at 36 weeks postconceptional age and DHA relative concentration in red blood cell and plasma lipid fractions. PE, phosphatidylethanolamine; PC, phosphatidylcholine; PI + PS, sum of phosphatidylinositol and phosphatidylserine; P.Lipid, total phospholipids; TG, triglycerides; CE, cholesterol esters; FFA, free fatty acids. Higher concentrations of DHA in plasma lipid fractions were associated with lower rod threshold values (light intensity required to elicit a 2-μV b-wave response)—that is, less light was needed.

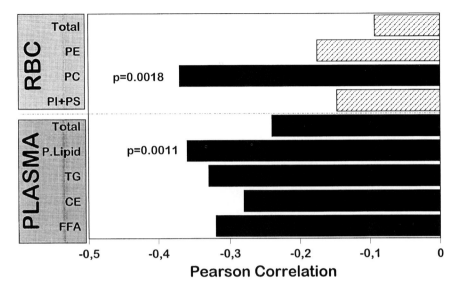

FIG. 5. Correlation coefficients for visual evoked potential (VEP) acuity measured at 36 weeks postconceptional age and DHA relative concentration in red blood cell (RBC) and plasma lipid fractions. PE, phosphatidylethanolamine; PC, phosphatidylcholine; PI + PS, sum of phosphatidylinositol and phosphatidylserine; P.Lipid, total phospholipids; TG, triglycerides; CE, cholesterol esters; FFA, free fatty acids. Higher concentrations of DHA in RBC PC and in plasma lipid fractions were associated with lower values for minimum angle of resolution, that is, better visual acuity.

Term Infant Studies

The controversy regarding the possible need for $n - 3$ and $n - 6$ LC-PUFA in human milk or term infant formula has gained increasing attention over the past year. The primary issue involves the putative need for LC-PUFA supplementation in the diet of an otherwise healthy term infant and whether this modification would promote optimal development of visual function.

Initial observational studies by us in Dallas were the first to compare visual outcomes of full-term infants fed exclusively on human-milk- or corn-oil-based formula. We documented significantly better VEP acuity (20/65 versus 20/83) and FPL acuity (20/107 versus 20/129) in the human-milk-fed group at 4 months of age (22). We also reported follow-up results on 3-year-old children in whom diets were controlled throughout the first year of life on a dietary regimen of human-milk- or corn-oil-based formula. In a series of near and far visual recognition tests and operant FPL acuity test, all human-milk-fed infants tended to have better acuity than formula-fed infants, but the results did not achieve statistical significance ($p < 0.1$). More

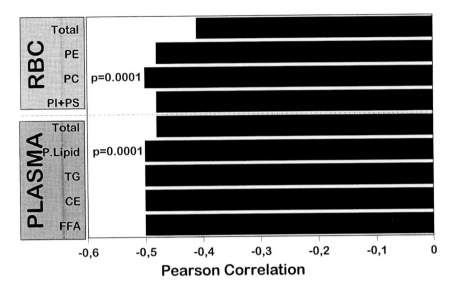

FIG. 6. Correlation coefficients of rod threshold measured at 57 weeks postconceptional age and DHA relative concentration in red blood cell (RBC) and plasma lipid fractions. PE, phosphatidylethanolamine; PC, phosphatidylcholine; PI + PS, sum of phosphatidylinositol and phosphatidylserine; P.Lipid, total phospholipids; TG, triglycerides; CE, cholesterol esters; FFA, free fatty acids. Higher concentrations of DHA in RBC and plasma lipid fractions were associated with lower values for minimum angle of resolution, that is, better visual acuity.

refined visual tests using random dot stereoacuity and HOT letter matching were significantly better ($p < 0.05$) for the human-milk group, indicating an association between early feeding and more advanced visual function later in life. A parallel observational study by Makrides *et al.* reported that full-term human milk-fed infants at 6 months of age had better VEP acuity (20/52 versus 20/110) than formula-fed infants (24). Similarly, red cell DHA concentrations were also higher in the human-milk-fed group (6.16% versus 3.31%) and were significantly correlated with VEP acuity ($r = -0.65; p < 0.01$).

Several research groups have recently reported results of controlled trials comparing infants fed formulas with and without LC-PUFA supplementation. Makrides *et al.* compared in a controlled randomized study infant groups that had received human milk for more than or less than 16 weeks or formula either with LC-PUFA supplementation or without LC-PUFA (24). Infants given formula supplemented with 0.36% DHA, 0.58% EPA, and 0.27% GLA had significantly higher red cell DHA concentrations than standard-formula-fed infants at 6, 16, and 30 weeks of age. The VEP acuity was significantly better in the supplemented group at 16 weeks (20/63 versus 20/110) and 30 weeks (20/18 versus 20/56), with no evidence of "catch up" by the LC-PUFA-deficient infants. Red cell DHA concentrations and VEP acuity were significantly correlated at 16 weeks (R^2 = 0.23) and 30 weeks (R^2 = 0.12). A dietary supply of DHA was recommended for the first 6 months of life because infants receiving less than 16 weeks of human milk had significantly poorer VEP acuity at 30 weeks of age than those fed human milk throughout their first 6 months (31).

In another controlled study of early cognitive function, Agostoni *et al.* compared full-term infant groups fed human milk, standard formula, or formula enriched with 0.3% DHA, 0.4% arachidonic acid, and 0.3% 18:3 *n* − 6 (30). At 4 months of age, red cell DHA concentrations in the standard-formula-fed group were significantly lower than those of the human-milk and LC-PUFA-supplemented groups (1.8%, 4.1%, and 4.1%, respectively). These investigators found significantly worse scores at 4 but not at 12 months in the Brunet–Lezine psychomotor development test for the DHA-deficient formula-fed group (30,53). In this study, LC-PUFA added to the formula originated from egg yolk phospholipids; thus, formulas differed in cholesterol content and in choline phosphoglycerides. Carlson recently reported that infants receiving formula supplemented with 0.1% DHA and 0.43% arachidonic acid had better visual acuity than an unsupplemented formula group at 2 months (20/220 versus 20/315) but not at 4 months according to the Teller acuity card (TAC) procedure. Thus, the DHA-deficient infants are able to "catch up" with the LC-PUFA-supplemented infants. No differences in acuity were found at 6 and 12 months between groups (35).

Several other investigators have presented early results of observational studies of human milk versus formula-fed term infants. A consensus finding is that both DHA and arachidonic acid concentrations are reduced in formula-fed infants; however, there are conflicting results regarding the potential benefits to visual function of human milk feeding in full-term infants compared to formulas not containing LC-PUFA. Courage *et al.* report that infants receiving an evaporated cow's-milk-based formula had significantly poorer visual acuity as measured by the Teller acuity card test than human-milk-fed infants at 3, 6, and 18 months and that there was no evident catch-up phase by the *n* − 3–deficient group (26). There was a trend toward lower acuity in standard formula-fed infants compared to human milk-fed infants in each age group. Jorgenson and colleagues report better Teller card acuity at 2 and 4 months but not at 1 month for human milk-fed infants compared to a formula-fed group (27). Higher red cell DHA concentrations in the human-milk group paralleled better visual acuity. Innis reported trials comparing Teller-card-derived acuity in human-milk-fed and standard-formula-fed groups (25,54). In a prospective non-randomized study, infants receiving a controlled formula had a reduction of DHA levels in red cell phosphatidylethanolamine of 47% compared to human-milk-fed infants at 3 months of age (25). Teller visual acuity was 20/152 in the human-milk group and 20/126 in formula-fed infants. In a second prospective study, term infants provided formulas with two levels of LNA (4.7% or 1.9%), with linoleic acid/LNA ratios of around 8:1, were compared to a human-milk-fed group. Although plasma and red cell DHA concentrations were significantly lower in the formula-fed groups, visual acuity, as measured with the Teller acuity card procedure, was not influenced by diets at 3 months of age. In a third retrospective study, 327 infants receiving human milk in graded duration from less than 1 month to 9 months were compared to 38 mixed formula-fed infants by the Teller acuity card procedure and Fagan recognition test (55). No significant differences were found between the groups in visual acuity or cognition; however, boys had significantly better visual acuity, and girls scored better on the Fagan infant test.

Results obtained by Neuringer *et al.* and Auestad *et al.* have been contradictory (21,56). Infants in a yet unpublished trial received (a) standard formula, (b) formula supplemented with 0.2% DHA from low-EPA marine oil, or (c) formula with 0.12% DHA and 0.43% arachidonic acid. No significant differences could be detected among the three diet groups by ERG at 4 months or by the Bayley Scales of Infant Development test at 12 months. Furthermore, a negative correlation was demonstrated between red cell DHA at 4 months and language development assessed by the MacArthur Communicative Development Inventory given at 14 months. Language development skills in these infants were negatively correlated with red cell DHA concentrations ($r = -0.20$ to $-0.37, p < 0.05$) (21). This finding could be associated with the source of DHA, but a clear interpretation is lacking, and it warrants further investigation.

Assessment and analysis of these divergent vision and cognitive function developmental test results are complex and confounded by differences in experimental design and other methodologic issues addressed previously. The most frequent confounders are the selection of test diets and the definition of outcomes measures of neurodevelopment.

Studies reviewed in this chapter provide evidence that dietary $n - 3$ fatty acid deficiency affects eye and brain function of preterm infants as measured by ERG, cortical VEP, and behavioral testing of visual acuity. Preterm infants require DHA in their diet because they are unable to form long-chain derivatives in sufficient quantity from LNA provided by soybean-oil-based formula products. Provision of dietary $n - 3$ and $n - 6$ LC-PUFA results in discernible differences in the fatty acid composition of plasma and red cell membrane lipids. Changes in membrane chemical structure are probably responsible for the observed functional effects. Preliminary evidence from term infants suggests that DHA supplementation is also required by this group.

BIOLOGICAL SIGNIFICANCE OF THE EFFECTS

The presence of an effect does not in itself make it of biological significance. As pointed out, diet-induced changes in triglyceride composition are of little consequence except to validate compliance with study formulas. Moreover, tissue fatty acid pools, particularly those required for retinal and CNS neural membrane formation, may not be reflected by plasma or even red blood cell fatty acid composition.

For example, we have found that in response to a low–$n - 3$ diet, the DHA concentration in plasma and red cells falls steadily during the first 6 months postnatally; however, though the diet-induced alteration in rod b-wave threshold measured by ERG can be documented early (that is, at 36 weeks postconceptional age), after 4 months on the $n - 3$–deficient diet, threshold values are similar to those of the control group receiving DHA or of a human-milk-fed reference group. The biochemical effects cannot be used as surrogates for functional measures; only in the presence of established correlations could one use the biochemical indices as predictive.

The selected outcome measure will ideally be clinically relevant, but the sensitivity of clinical responses is usually low; thus, functional responses are considered valid to define biologically significant outcomes. In the case of LC-PUFA supplementation, growth is affected only in extreme $n - 6$ fatty acid deficiency and thus is not considered a sensitive measure of $n - 6$ sufficiency. The effects of $n - 3$ fatty acids on sensory maturation and cognitive development are the outcomes of greater interest in studies of $n - 3$ supplementation.

The duration and reversibility of diet-induced effects is another important consideration. In evaluating diet-induced changes in developmental outcomes, there may be transient effects that reflect the acceleration or the slowing of a maturational process with a fully normal final outcome. This is of special relevance during the first few months of life, when visual maturation is progressing rapidly. Several studies have shown significant effects of the dietary LC-PUFA on visual maturation in the first 4 months of life, but in most cases the delayed response becomes normal at 6 months or at most by 1 year of age. Should we dismiss this phenomenon as being transitory and of limited significance or assume that we failed to detect a significant change at a year because our tools were not sensitive enough or that other related functions are indeed affected? In the same example, we failed to detect differences in visual acuity at 6 months, but space perception, assessed by stereoacuity responses, was different at 3 years of age. These examples illustrate that unless sensitive outcome measures are used and sufficient follow-up time is provided, there may actually be long-term consequences of early developmental effects.

Evidence of potential beneficial long-term effects of DHA supplementation on brain development of term infants is suggestive; however, proof is lacking. The resolution of this issue should be forthcoming because controlled clinical trials of DHA and DHA–arachidonic acid supplementation in term infants are now being completed. The follow-up of these infants beyond infancy should help to address the question of long-term effects.

CONCLUSIONS

The LC-PUFA have demonstrable benefits during development. The effects on neural development are of particular interest. Human milk is the best and only time-proven source of fat and EFA in the infant diet. Technological procedures based on chemical and physical separation of the unsaturated fatty acids have permitted the elaboration of concentrated DHA and arachidonic acid for clinical use. The development of single-cell oil sources has allowed the provision of novel forms of LC-PUFA delivery. Before the 1990s, low LNA was found in most infant formulas; by now virtually all infant formulas in developed countries are supplemented with LNA, and several manufacturers in Europe and in Japan have added DHA or DHA plus arachidonic acid, and some have included GLA in preterm and term formulas. Efficacy seems less well established. The need for comprehensive safety evaluation is underscored before the practice of LC-PUFA supplementation can be advocated. Safety issues have been addressed in small to medium-size studies; larger-sample-size trials are required to identify potential side effects that are of low prevalence. Moreover, the public health implications of the beneficial effects need to be fully evaluated in order to support the practice of supplementing infant formula and possibly maternal diets on a global scale.

REFERENCES

1. Burr GO, Burr MM. A new deficiency disease produced by rigid exclusion of fat from the diet. *J Biol Chem* 1929;82:345–367.
2. Caldwell MD, Johnson HT, Othersen HB. Essential fatty acids deficiency in an infant receiving prolonged parenteral alimentation. *J Pediatr* 1972;81:894–898.
3. Hansen AE, Wiese HF, Boelsche AN, Haggard ME, Adam DJD, Davis H. Role of linoleic acid in infant nutrition: clinical and chemical study of 428 infants fed on milk mixtures varying in kind and amount of fat. *Pediatrics* 1963;31:171–192.
4. Holman RT Johnson SB, Hatch TF. A case of human linolenic acid deficiency involving neurological abnormalities. *Am J Clin Nutr* 1982;35:617–623.
5. Sprecher H, Luthria DL, Mohammed BS, Baykousheva SP. Reevaluation of the pathways for the biosynthesis of polyunsaturated fatty acids. *J Lipid Res* 1995;36:2471–2477.
6. Willis AL. Essential fatty acids, prostaglandins, and related eicosanoids. In: Olson, RE, ed. *Present knowledge in nutrition.* Washington, DC: The Nutrition Foundation, 1984:90–113.
7. Innis SM. Essential fatty acids in growth and development. *Prog Lipid Res* 1991;30:39–103.
8. Galli C, Simopoulos AP, Tremoli E, eds. Effects of fatty acids and lipids in health and disease. *World Rev Nutr Diet* 1994;76:1–149.
9. Brockenhorff H, Ackman RG, Hoyle RJ. Specific distribution of fatty acids in marine lipids. *Arch Biochem Biophys* 1963;100:93–100.
10. Menon NK, Dhopeshwarkar GA. Essential fatty acid deficiency and brain development. *Prog Lipid Res* 1982;21:309–326.
11. Bourre JM, Durand G, Pascal G, Youyou A. Brain cell and tissue recovery in rats made deficient in $n - 3$ fatty acids by alteration of dietary fat. *J Nutr* 1989;119:15–22.
12. Bourre JM, Francois M, Youyou A. The effects of dietary alpha-linolenic acid on the composition of nerve membranes, enzymatic activity, amplitude of electrophysiological parameters, resistance to poisons and performance of learning tasks in rats. *J Nutr* 1989;119:1880–1892.
13. Jensen RG. The lipids in human milk. *Prog Lipid Res* 1996;35:53–92.
14. Innis SM. Human milk and formula fatty acids. *J Pediatr* 1992;120:S56–S61.
15. Makrides M, Simmer K, Neumann M, Gibson R. Changes in the polyunsaturated fatty acids of breast milk from mothers of full-term infants over 30 weeks of lactation. *Am J Clin Nutr* 1995;61:1231–1233.
16. Uauy R, Hoffman D, Birch EE, Birch DG, Jameson DM, Tyson J. Safety and efficacy of omega-3 fatty acids in nutrition of very low birth weight infants: soy oil and marine oil supplementation of formula. *J Pediatr* 1994;124:612–620.
17. Uauy R, Birch DG, Birch EE, Tyson JE, Hoffman DR. Effect of dietary omega-3 fatty acids on retinal function of very low birth weight neonates. *Pediatr Res* 1990;28:485–492.
18. Birch EE, Birch DG, Hoffman DR, Uauy RD. Retinal development in very low birth weight infants fed diets differing in omega-3 fatty acids. *Invest Ophthalmol Vis Sci* 1992;33:2365–2376.

19. Carlson SE, Werkman SH, Rhodes PG, Tolley EA. Visual acuity development in healthy preterm infants: effect of marine oil supplementation. *Am J Clin Nutr* 1993;58:35–42.
20. Ghebremeskel K, Leighfield M, Leaf A, Costeloe K, Crawford M. Fatty acid composition of plasma and red cell phospholipids of preterm babies fed on breast milk and formulae. *Eur J Pediatr* 1995; 154:46–52.
21. Auestad N, Montalto MB, Hall RT, Fitzgerald KM, Wheeler RE, Connor WE, *et al.* Visual acuity, erythrocyte fatty acid composition, and growth in term infants fed formulas with long chain polyunsaturated fatty acids for one year. *Pediatr Res* 1997;41:1–10.
22. Birch E, Birch D, Hoffman D, Hale L, Uauy R. Breast-feeding and optimal visual development. *J Pediatr Ophthalmol Strabismus* 1993;30:33–38.
23. Bjerve KS, Brubak K, Fougner KJ, Johnsen H, Midthjell K, Vik T. Omega-3 fatty acids: essential fatty acids with important biological effects, and serum phospholipid fatty acids as markers of dietary $n - 3$ fatty acid intake. *Am J Clin Nutr* 1993;57:801S–806S.
24. Makrides M, Simmer K, Goggin M, Gibson RA. Erythrocyte docosahexaenoic acid correlates with the visual response of healthy, term infants. *Pediatr Res* 1993;33:425–427.
25. Innis SM, Nelson CM, Rioux MF, King DJ. Development of visual acuity in relation to plasma and erythrocyte $n - 6$ and $n - 3$ fatty acids in healthy term gestation infants. *Am J Clin Nutr* 1994; 60:347–352.
26. Courage M, Friel J, Andrews W, McCloy U, Adams R. Dietary fatty acids and the development of visual acuity in human infants. *Invest Ophthalmol Vis Sci* 1995;36:S48.
27. Jorgensen MH, Hernell O, Lund P, Holmer G, Michaelson KF. Visual acuity and erythrocyte docosahexanoic acid status in breast-fed and formula-fed term infants during the first 4 months of life. *Lipids* 1996;31:99–105.
28. Carlson SE, Werkman SH, Peeples JM, Cooke RJ, Tolley EA. Arachidonic acid status correlates with first year growth in preterm infants. *Proc Natl Acad Sci USA* 1993;90:1073–1077.
29. Werkman SH, Carlson SE. A randomized trial of visual attention of preterm infants fed docosahexanoic acid until nine months. *Lipids* 1996;31:91–97.
30. Agostoni C, Troján S, Bellú R, Riva E, Giovannini M. Neurodevelopmental quotient of healthy term infants at 4 months and feeding practice: the role of long-chain polyunsaturated fatty acids. *Pediatr Res* 1995;38:262–266.
31. Makrides M, Neumann M, Simmer K, Pater J, Gibson R. Are long-chain polyunsaturated fatty acids essential nutrients in infancy? *Lancet* 1995;345:1463–1468.
32. Carlson SE, Werkman SH, Tolley EA. Effect of long chain $n - 3$ fatty acid supplementation on visual acuity and growth of preterm infants with and without bronchopulmonary dysplasia. *Am J Clin Nutr* 1996;63:687–697.
33. Carlson SE, Werkman SH. A randomized trial of visual attention of preterm infants fed docosahexanoic acid until two months. *Lipids* 1996;31:85–91.
34. Mena P, Nieto S, Hoffman, Gil A, Uauy R. *Red blood cells (RBC) fatty acids (FA) composition in preterm infants fed human milk or formulas with different LC-PUFA composition.* Paper presented at the AOCS Conference on PUFA, Barcelona, November 1996.
35. Carlson SE, Ford AJ, Werkman SH, Peeples JM, Koo WWK. Visual acuity and fatty acid status of term infants fed human milk and formulas with or without docosahexaenoate and arachidonate from egg yolk lecithin. *Pediatr Res* 1996;39:882–888.
36. Koletzko B, Edenhofer S, Lipowsky G, Reinhardt D. Effects of a low birth weight infant formula containing human milk levels of docosahexaenoic and arachidonic acids. *J Pediatr Gastroenterol Nutr* 1995;21:200–208.
37. Clandinin MT, Parrott A, VanAerde JE, Hervada AR, Lien E. Feeding preterm infants a formula containing C_{20} and C_{22} fatty acids simulates plasma phospholipid fatty acid composition of infants fed human milk. *Early Hum Dev* 1992;31:41–51.
38. Iwamoto H, Sato G. Production of EPA by freshwater unicellular algae. *J Am Oil Chem Soc* 1986; 63:434–438.
39. Cohen Z, Norman HA, Heimer YM. Microalgae as a source of $n - 3$ fatty acids. *World Rev Nutr Diet* 1995;77:1–31.
40. Ackman RG. Structural homogeneity in unsaturated fatty acids of marine lipids. A review. *J Fish Res Board Can* 1964;21:247–254.
41. Akimoto M, Ishii T, Yamagaki K, Ohtaguchi K, Koide K, Yazawa K. Production of eicosapentaenoic acid by a bacterium isolated from mackerel intestines. *J Am Oil Chem Soc* 1990;67:911–915.

42. Simopoulos AP, Salem N. Egg yolk as a source of long-chain polyunsaturated fatty acids in infant feeding. *Am J Clin Nutr* 1992;55:411–414.
43. Sawatzki G, Georgi G, Kohn G. Pitfalls in the design and manufacture of infant formulae. *Acta Paediatr [Suppl]* 1994;402:40–45.
44. Picaud JC, Lapillonne AL, Chirouze V, Claris O, Salle B. Fatty acids intestinal absorption in very low birth weight infants fed fortified own mother's milk or preterm formula enriched with docosahex-anoic acid [abstract]. *Pediatr Res* 1996;39:317A.
45. Foreman-van Drongelen MMHP, van Houwelingen AC, Kester ADM, *et al.* Long-chain polyene status of preterm infants with regard to the fatty acid composition of their diet: comparison between absolute and relative fatty acids amounts in plasma and red cell phopholipids. *Br J Nutr* 1995;73: 405–422.
46. Makrides M, Neumann MA, Byard RW, Simmer K, Gibson RA. Fatty acid composition of brain, retina, and erythrocytes in breast- and formula-fed infants. *Am J Clin Nutr* 1994;60:189–194.
47. Farquharson J, Cockburn F, Patrick WA, Jamieson EC, Logan RW. Infant cerebral cortex phospho-lipid fatty-acid composition and diet. *Lancet* 1992;340:810–813.
48. Farquharson J, Jamieson EC, Logan RW, Patrick WJA, Howatson AG, Cockburn F. Age- and dietary-related distributions of hepatic arachidonic and docosahexanoic acid in early infancy. *Pediatr Res* 1995;38:361–365.
49. Peña M, Uauy R, Birch E, Peirano P. Effect of the early human development on the modulation of the sleep states on electrophysiological response [abstract]. *FASEB J* 1996;12:A323.
50. Apkarian P, Miranda M, Tijssen R. Effects of behavioral state on visual processing in neonates. *Neuropediatrics* 1991;22:85–91.
51. Koletzko B, Braun M. Arachidonic acid and early human growth: is there a relation? *Ann Nutr Metab* 1991;35:128–131.
52. Leaf AA, Leighfield MJ, Costeloe KL, Crawford MA. Long chain polyunsaturated fatty acids and fetal growth. *Early Hum Dev* 1992;30:183–191.
53. Agostoni C, Troján S, Bellu R, *et al.* LC-PUFA status and developmental quotient in term infants fed different dietary sources of lipids in the first months of life. In: Bindels JC, Goedhart AC, Visser HKA, eds. *Recent developments in infant nutrition.* Norwell, MA: Kluwer Academic Publishers, 1996:212–217.
54. Innis SM, Dierson-Schade DA, Akrabawi SS. Prospective evaluation of preferential looking acuity in healthy term infants fed infant formula or breast-fed [abstract]. *Pediatr Res* 1995;37:310A.
55. Innis SM, Nelson CM, Lwanga D, Rioux FM, Waslen P. Feeding formula without arachidonic acid and docosahexanoic acid has no effect on preferential looking acuity or recognition memory in healthy full-term infants at 9 mo of age. *Am J Clin Nutr* 1996;64:40–46.
56. Neuringer M, Fitzgerald KM, Weleber RG, Murphey WH, Giambrone SA, Cibis GW, *et al.* Electrore-tinograms in four month-old full term human infants fed diets differing in long chain $n - 3$ and $n - 6$ fatty acids. *Invest Ophthalmol Vis Sci* 1995;36:S48.

DISCUSSION

Dr. Aggett: In what way would you regard the development of research protocols for looking at LC-PUFAs as a paradigm for many of the issues we have been addressing? For example, Dr. Lozoff has told me that if we had totally accepted some of the first studies on iron intervention, we would not necessarily have followed it up and pursued it more closely.

Dr. Uauy: Our knowledge is at various degrees of advancement; in fact, it is only this year that we have been able to say with certainty that DHA can be formed from α-linolenic acid. Thus, even the biology of today is different from what we were learning 5 years ago, so study design has to reflect these rapid changes. We now have stable isotopes to see if we can enhance DHA formation from α-linolenic. That question has been partly answered by Bill Heird and his group; they showed that no matter how much α-linolenic they gave, they were unable to provide sufficient DHA for biochemical normality. So that is the first step, but there still needs to be more work before we do a definitive clinical trial. Now as to outcome, I would use state-of-the-art electrophysiological measurements to look at visual acuity. I would include state-of-the-art noninvasive methods to look at electroretinography. After I have those outcomes properly established, I would then look at the long-term effects. I think we are still not ready to do the definitive clinical trials.

Dr. Klish: In Houston, Heird and Jensen have shown that the elongation of the $n - 3$ and the $n - 6$ series shares the same enzyme system and, as a result, there is competition between those two cascades (1). That brings up the question of the potential for toxicity if the ratios of those two groups of fatty acids are not correct. There are also data that suggest there is a potential for growth retardation in term infants (2). So, knowing this new biology, how comfortable do you feel at this point about using long-chain polyunsaturated fatty acids in clinical trials before we actually understand the relationship between these ratios?

Dr. Uauy: The evidence we have from preterm infants indicates that if we provide a DHA source with low EPA, we do not have any adverse effect on growth. There are at least three studies that support what I am saying (3–5). If you give a very high linolenic acid intake, which is the model that Bill Heird uses, then you may compromise growth, or if you use high-EPA marine oil, then you also have a drop in arachidonic acid, which is the most likely mechanism. It is not a new finding. If you go back to Hansen's original data, low arachidonic acid compromised growth in infants in 1954, when he studied them.

Dr. Klish: What you are really saying is that there is a pharmacologic effect, and what we don't know is the window of safety. We have some studies that are in the normal range and some that appear outside that range, and there are different ways of supplementing these fatty acids, none of which totally controls the ratios.

Dr. Whitehead: I wonder if I could just ask you about the term "pharmacologic effect." Are you looking on this as pharmacology, or are you looking on it as nutrition?

Dr. Uauy: I didn't use the term pharmacologic effect. I think Dr. Klish meant outside the range found in human milk, but I had problems convincing the NIH reviewers that the safety components of the study needed to be included because, in fact, we were using amounts that are present in human milk.

Dr. Guesry: Your paper showed very clearly that there is no need to add arachidonic acid, even in premature babies, provided that you don't give too much DHA and that you give as little EPA as possible, but then in your comment, you said, "You can add arachidonic acid if you like." I realize you want to be nice, but why?

Dr. Uauy: This is a very important issue. Until we have data on DHA alone, low-EPA DHA, and DHA plus AA (arachidonic acid), I cannot provide you with the definitive answer, because there are other people saying that if arachidonic acid is in breast milk, then it should be added. I think the stable isotope work that I showed you will probably give us the answer, because accretion of arachidonic acid by the infant is double what is provided by human milk; the human milk-fed infant is synthesizing at least 50% of the arachidonic acid from linoleic acid. The functional data that we have, using carefully defined groups, show that the drop in arachidonic acid that we get, which is about 20%, has no influence on growth. But I have to accept that, in Carlson's study, in which infants also had low zinc and low vitamin A and were as small as 700 g, the adverse effect on growth was apparently associated with the low arachidonic acid rather than the DHA supplementation.

Dr. Hamburger: Are you not implying by what you just said that you would have to have the exact proportions of all the lipids that are found in breast milk in order to not deviate from what the baby may be doing in the way of processing?

Dr. Uauy: The breast milk model offers you a wide range: you can go as low as 0.1 or as high as 1.2 with DHA, and as low as 0.2 or as high as 2.5 with AA. So human milk does not offer you exact numbers, but it provides a range, especially if you take the omnivorous woman as a model, against which you can test your biochemistry and your function and hope to get a good answer.

Dr. Rey: I don't understand why you continue to study the effect of corn oil or soybean oil or marine oil in preterm and term infants. It is known that the best ratio of $n - 6$ to $n - 3$ is around 6:1 to 10:1. Why don't you only compare human milk with formulas with that ratio? Why are people working in this field continuously trying to prove that there is an advantage in a formula that differs so much from human milk? My second question is, what are the long-term effects you suggest?

Dr. Uauy: The studies we are doing at present are exactly as you have suggested; the only difference is that we are now using a pure DHA source or DHA plus AA to try to get the answer. There is no purpose in just adding AA. So our present studies include DHA only, with appropriate α-linolenic and appropriate linoleic acids, a DHA plus AA, and a formula that has no LC-PUFAs and has the right balance. The preliminary data show that we do not have an effect of the addition of AA, we have functional effects of DHA, and we have no additional beneficial effects of DHA plus AA. Now, to your other question regarding long-term effects. The infants we studied in Dallas are now about 8 years of age. Out of the 80 infants we studied, we have been able to trace only ten by conventional methods. We are paying a private detective to try to find the subjects. In the urban United States, in a county hospital, getting a 7-year follow-up is not an easy job; I would say it is an impossible job. We need those long-term studies, and it is only the people who already have systems that will allow them to follow up for 7 or 8 years who will provide us with the answers.

Dr. Crozier: I find it difficult to reconcile the evidence that the baby is capable of synthesizing his fatty acids with the evidence that the baby needs a dietary source. You have mentioned that the relative contribution of synthetic and dietary arachidonic acid was roughly 50:50. Do you have any kind of estimate of what these numbers would be for DHA? And how does the high conservation of DHA in the retina and other neural tissues factor into this equation.

Dr. Uauy: The stable isotope work is very limited. With the amino acid, we know the precursor enrichment, but here, we really have no tool to evaluate precursor enrichment, especially at the tissue level, so we have to make a lot of assumptions. We are assuming that what we measure in the plasma reflects tissue equilibrium. We are assuming that we have steady-state conditions so that the kinetic models can be applied. And third, we have no measure of oxidation rates because we have no tool at the present time to measure how much of what we give is oxidized. So any figures that I could give you are really the minimum conversion, but for DHA, only 3% of the label appears as long chain over a 6-day period, as opposed to 60% of the label when linoleic acid is fed. The other source of data is the accretion data. These data show that it is impossible for a baby who is fed human milk to get all the arachidonic acid he or she needs from human milk. So that is a different set of observations. My view is that the amount of DHA in human milk is enough to satisfy 100% of the accretion need. From the accretion data and the stable isotope work, it looks as though the $n - 3$ component is the most limiting. Your other question is crucial, because our data suggest that even when there are very small amounts of DHA in the plasma, the retina seems to manage perfectly well. We know from studies of turnover that if you inject labeled DHA in an eye, 99.5% of the label remains in the eye and does not enter the circulation. So the eye definitely traps it. We know there is recycling of segment and pigment epithelium, so that the cell turnover takes up all the DHA that is released with the segment renewal, which happens on a daily cycle. So the brain, and especially the retina, is very well protected; once it loads up with DHA, it is hard to lose it, that is why you don't find DHA deficiency in mature animals or mature humans, no matter for how long they are given a low-DHA diet.

Dr. Lucas: I have a comment about the mimicability of human milk. The first thing to say is that the presence of something in breast milk doesn't imply that it is important; the most prevalent component of human milk is lactose, present at 70 g per 1000 ml, and not considered to be an essential nutrient. But as far as human milk goes, there are 160 fatty acids, over 100 triglycerides, a unique stereo isometric structure, fat globules with a complex glycocalix over them, and so on; human milk is completely unmimicable, and the fats that we have available to add LC-PUFAs are unphysiological ones that are not present in milk, for instance containing three arachidonates or three DHAs on the triglyceride molecule, which you will never have in human milk. So that does pose a problem. If you want to hypothesize that adding DHA to humans would improve visual development, what you would do is to look at the comparison of breast-fed and bottle-fed babies. There have been about 12 studies of this type, and as far as I can see, it is only in the studies where there has been a low linolenic acid content in the formula that there has been a difference between the breast-fed and the formula-fed group. When there has been a linolenic acid content greater than 0.7% of energy, then differences have not been observed. So on the basis of published data, would you in fact hypothesize that there would be a difference from adding DHA as opposed to the precursor?

Dr. Uauy: Our data using visual evoked potentials do show an effect, so with more subtle tools, you can pick up differences between formulas relating to α-linolenic acid content. But there is really no long-term study; you are correct. I fully agree that trying to mimic human milk is impossible, though you can vary the degree of closeness of matching.

Dr. Crozier: From the industry point of view. I feel I have to ask some questions about feasibility, and particularly in relation to the sourcing of these fatty acids. Professor Klish mentioned synthetic fatty acids, and I think he was referring to the single-cell oils that are enriched sources of fatty acids but, of course, are not pure sources—they are accompanied by a number of other compounds, for example, phytosterols and other fatty acids, which may interfere with the metabolism of these particular fatty acids. Do you have any comments about the safety of these sources?

Dr. Uauy: The sources need to be tested in all aspects: biological activity, toxicity, animal work, adult human work, and eventually infant work. We need more safety data, and the safety data will have to be obtained from sources that are economically feasible and industrially available. I agree with you: you first have to define a source and then test it and do your clinical trials.

Dr. Rey: The Scientific Committee for Food (SCF) of the European Union has prepared guidelines on the safety of novel foods. It is clear that DHA and AA prepared from single cells should be considered as novel ingredients according to these guidelines. This DHA was accepted in Holland, but I would not say what the opinion of the SCF would be regarding the acceptability of such fatty acid sources in the European Union. The use of novel ingredients in infant nutrition cannot be accepted without all the guarantees of safety.

REFERENCES

1. Sauerwald TU, Hachey DL, Jensen CL, *et al.* Effect of dietary α-linolenic acid intake on incorporation of docosahexaenoic and arachidonic acids into plasma phospholipids of term infants. *Lipids* 1996;31: S131–S135.

2. Jensen CL, Prager TC, Fraley JK, *et al.* Functional effects of dietary linoleic/α-linolenic acid ratio in term infants. *J Pediatr* (in press).
3. Uauy R, Hoffman D, Birch EE, *et al.* Safety and efficacy of omega-3 fatty acids in nutrition of very low birth weight infants: soy oil and marine oil supplementation of formula. *J Pediatr* 1994;124: 612–620.
4. Mena P, Nieto S, Hoffman D, *et al. Red blood cells (RBC) fatty acids (FA) composition in preterm infants fed human milk or formulas with different LC-PUFA composition.* Paper presented at AOCS Conference on PUFA, Barcelona, November 1996.
5. Faldella G, Govoni M, Alessandroni R, *et al.* Visual evoqued potentials and dietary long chain polyunsaturated fatty acids in preterm infants. *Arch Dis Child* 1996;75:F108–F112.

Clinical Trials in Infant Nutrition, edited by
Jay A. Perman and Jean Rey, Nestlé Nutrition
Workshop Series, Vol. 40, Nestec Ltd.,
Vevey/Lippincott-Raven Publishers,
Philadelphia © 1998.

Long-Term Outcome Trials of Early Nutrition on Later Health and Development

Alan Lucas

*MRC Childhood Nutrition Research Centre, Institute of Child Health,
London, United Kingdom*

In therapeutic research, the principal objectives are generally to establish robust data on *efficacy* (benefit) and *safety* (risk) for any proposed intervention. If we are to apply these principles to infant nutrition research, we must address several key questions: What do we mean by "efficacy" or "safety" in a nutritional context? And what sorts of benefits or risks of early nutrition are biologically plausible? Is it practical to apply to infant nutrition the "therapeutic intervention" experiment—notably the randomized clinical trial? If so, what are the best windows of opportunity to do so? What are the practical issues in conducting such trials, and are researchers using this tool effectively? And, most importantly, are such clinical trials proving their worth by changing our biological perspectives and our practice of infant nutrition?

In this chapter, I touch on these issues in a general way and then use some of our own research findings on the long-term consequences of infant nutrition to illustrate key points.

"EFFICACY" IN NUTRITIONAL STUDIES: A HISTORICAL PERSPECTIVE

Over the past two centuries, there has probably been more research on infant nutrition than on any other area of pediatrics. By 1953, Macy *et al.* (1) were able to collate over 1500 publications on the composition of breast milk, just one small area of infant nutrition research. Yet, despite the massive scientific effort, fundamental issues in infant nutrition practice remain unresolved, resulting in confusion among both health professionals and parents and in inconsistent, inadequately supported recommendations and standards of practice. When such uncertainty exists in the presence of such a large body of research and knowledge, it is reasonable to challenge whether the right questions have been addressed.

To throw more light on this, it is instructive to examine how other fields of therapeutic intervention have generally evolved. Usually, this has been a three-stage process (2). In stage I, anecdotal observations raise the question, "Is there anything in this?" In stage II, epidemiological and physiological research provides descriptive and mechanistic data that raise testable hypotheses concerning the potential impact of a therapeutic intervention. Finally, in stage III, formal intervention experiments test the efficacy and safety of the treatment and practice. Thus, if we take the analogy of research into high blood pressure, stage III research tells us if intervention with antihypertensive drugs improves long-term health (reduced risk of stroke, improved survival, and so on) at an acceptable cost to the patient (for example, acceptably low incidence of side effects such as depression or impotence). The ability of antihypertensives simply to lower blood pressure (stage II research) has meaning for us only if in doing so they improve outcome (stage III research).

When I entered the field of infant and childhood nutrition some 20 years ago, it seemed that the field had mainly become stuck in stage II. Research largely focused on collection of physiological and epidemiologic data on growth, nutritional status, metabolic response to feeding, energetics, nutrient absorption and retention, composition of foods, prevalence of nutritional disorders, and so on. It is true that considerable earlier efforts had been made to define intakes that would prevent overt nutritional deficiency, and that was, of course, of obvious clinical importance. However, formal experimental stage III research on whether early nutrition mattered in terms of critical outcomes such as long-term health and development was seldom undertaken and usually poorly conceived. Whereas the outcome effects of blood pressure lowering are what now govern practice in that field, the corresponding data on the outcome of our practices in infant nutrition have usually not been available. Official bodies have had to make theoretical recommendations largely on the basis of short-term, stage II, studies. Clearly, however, parents and health professionals should be more concerned about whether our nutritional policies are formally proven to affect health and development (stage III research) than whether they affect, say, if the infant grows on the 25th rather than 75th centile, has a higher energy expenditure, retains more calcium in bone, or incorporates more ^{13}C-glycine into protein (stage II research)—though if outcome effects of early nutrition are established, such stage II findings become important in providing insight into mechanism.

SAFETY

Safety in nutritional studies has received even less attention than efficacy. In many nutritional trials, safety is a real issue. In preterm infants, nutritional management policies could result in necrotizing enterocolitis (see below), infection, and death. Trial size for detecting adverse effects may need to be greater than for testing efficacy because a relatively large sample may be needed to detect differential incidence between groups of a relatively rare event.

Safety monitoring in clinical trials of infant nutrition is frequently relegated to trivial consequences of feeding, under the general umbrella of "acceptability," including observations on minor spitting up, stool color, stool frequency, and so on.

Not infrequently, however, significant risks are not factored into the trial design. The long-chain polyunsaturated fatty acid (LC-PUFA) supplementation trials provide a good example. There are around ten published efficacy trials, with neurodevelopment or visual endpoints, on preterm and term infants, though several more trials are in progress. The average sample size in these trials is 25 per group. Although Uauy *et al.* (3) do measure some "safety" aspects (for example, bleeding time, red cell membrane stability), none of the published studies was large enough to have addressed safety in any realistic way. Yet here is a group of lipids, linked to the ubiquitous prostaglandins, that may have wide ranging effects, for instance on gene expression (4,5), hemostasis (3), blood pressure (6), insulin resistance (7), calcium metabolism (8), and immune function (9). The latter is of particular concern. In Carlson's second study (10) of LC-PUFA supplementation in preterm infants, 94 babies were randomized into two equal groups, and of these 95 babies, 35 were withdrawn before 2 months; five of the control babies were withdrawn because of infection ($n = 2$) or necrotizing enterocolitis (NEC; $n = 3$) versus 14 withdrawals because of infection ($n = 5$) or NEC ($n = 9$) in the LC-PUFA-supplemented group. These are worrying findings that require confirmation (Carlson herself recognized that a larger sample was needed to test the hypothesis that infection or NEC was *individually* influenced by the use of marine oil). Were these risks to be confirmed, most neonatologists would be more concerned about NEC (with its 20% to 40% mortality) or (potentially life-threatening) sepsis than they would be about transient promotion of visual acuity (10). We are currently exploring this question in three large preterm trials. Also, numerous small human milk fortification trials in preterm infants have focused principally on stage II–type outcomes (calcium retention, weight gain, and so on). In our own neurodevelopmental outcome study on 275 infants (11), we identified in the short term an increased overall risk of systemic infection (diagnosed on clinical plus hematologic grounds with or without bacteriologic confirmation) in the fortifier group. Bacteriologically confirmed systemic infection and NEC (together, but not separately) were also significantly more common in the fortifier group. The possibility that adding fortifier powder to human milk could reduce its antiinfective properties (previously shown *in vitro*) is just as relevant (if not more so) to the clinical decision-making process as the knowledge that fortifiers may confer a small short-term benefit for weight gain (11).

EARLY NUTRITION AND LATER HEALTH AND NEURODEVELOPMENT

If, after all, our infant nutrition policies ensure freedom from immediate nutritional deficiency and ill health at the time, devising policies that optimize health and development would seem an important target. But is it plausible that such effects could occur? This question is part of a more general one as to whether there are sensitive or critical periods in early life when events may have lasting significance.

To describe this general phenomenon, some years ago, I proposed the term "programming" (12,13), the concept that a stimulus or insult, when applied at a critical or sensitive period of development, could result in a permanent or lasting effect on the structure or function of the organism. We now know of numerous examples of endogenous and exogenous triggers of a physiological or unphysiological nature (including hormones, drugs, physical stimuli, and so on) that may operate during windows to produce lifetime effects (12,13). Such early programming appears to be a normal part of development and, in some circumstances, might allow the organism to fine-tune its later biology in response to early environment.

A key question here is whether infant nutrition could operate in this programming way. Since the 1960s, the evidence on this from experimental studies in animals, including primates, has been extensive (14–20). What an animal is fed during a brief period in infancy may, in adult life, influence numerous outcomes that would be of major clinical and public health significance in humans. These include lifelong "programming" effects on intermediary metabolism, blood lipids, tendency to diabetes, body size, body fatness, blood pressure, and atherosclerosis. Smart (16) reviewed 165 animal studies on the impact of early nutrition on later learning and behavior, with a predominance of studies showing long-term or lifelong effects; and numerous parallel studies show that early nutrition may have lasting effects on the physical development of the brain.

As often occurs, application of knowledge from animal studies to humans has taken time, and only recently has the priority for equivalent nutritional intervention studies in humans been recognized. This need has been further heightened by nonexperimental, epidemiologic data (21–23) suggesting that early nutritional factors might be important in man. For instance, potential markers of early nutrition, notably size at birth and in infancy, are more highly predictive of death from ischemic heart disease and its risk factors (diabetes, high blood pressure, hyperlipidemia, central obesity) than most risk factors for vascular disease identified in adult life.

RANDOMIZED TRIALS IN INFANT NUTRITION: GENERAL CONSIDERATIONS

Clearly, public health and clinical policy would be most soundly based on experimental rather than epidemiologic studies. In the light of this, 15 years ago, I elected to devote the major attention of my research group to developing the use of the infant nutritional intervention experiment in a formal way to explore the concept of nutritional programming in humans and to underpin nutritional practice. The elements of this program, which, collectively, were novel at that time, included the following in each clinical trial:

1. Formal randomized nutritional intervention in infancy, with planned long-term follow-up;
2. Carefully calculated size to detect differences between groups for a key targeted health or developmental outcome ("efficacy") with adequate power; and

trials large enough to detect differences in adverse outcomes (''safety'') between groups;
3. Trials conducted in a similar manner to a pharmaceutical intervention trial employing what are now termed ''good clinical practice'' guidelines;
4. Cohort details documented to facilitate long-term (or lifetime) follow-up.

There are several windows of opportunity for infant nutritional intervention experiments that are feasible and ethical. (a) Preterm infants can be randomized to diet to test the importance of the perinatal period for nutrition. Some years ago, milk banking was commonly practiced in neonatal care, so that for babies whose mothers did not provide their own milk, it was possible, among other interventions, to randomly assign infants to human milk (from unrelated donors) or formula, a key ''experiment'' that would be difficult to achieve in full-term infants. (b) Formula-fed full-term infants could be randomly assigned to formulas of different nutrient contents to test ways in which early infancy might be critical for nutrition. These interventions can also be targeted to full-term infants growth-retarded at birth, who have been shown epidemiologically to be at long-term risk for growth and neurodevelopmental deficits and for ischemic heart disease and its antecedents. A key question is whether early nutritional intervention could ''reprogram'' these infants following poor intrauterine growth and ameliorate risk. (c) Infants can be randomly assigned to different weaning foods to test whether nutritional sensitivity extends into infancy.

Specific interventions depend on the hypothesis but may involve the use of ''whole diets'' (for example, multinutrient-enriched formulas) or supplementation of specific factors of hypothesized benefit for outcome, such as iron or LC-PUFAs. In 15 major outcome studies now, we have around 5000 infants and children in all of these categories, in various stages from the intervention period to long-term follow-up, the oldest subjects followed prospectively now to 14 years.

One important objective in these outcome studies has been to use them to identify medium-term outcomes that have predictive value for long-term health and development, so that valuable data in future studies can be collected within a practical period. For cognitive development, for instance, we find scores at 18 months have some correlation (around $r = 0.5$) with scores later in childhood. However, by age 7 to 8, formal cognitive tests, for example, WISC-R IQ, are highly correlated with adult performance (24). Thus, in a study designed to test the hypothesis that an infant nutrition intervention has a permanent impact on cognitive function, follow-up to 18 months would provide suggestive evidence only, but follow-up to 7.5 to 8 years, compelling evidence. We are also attempting to identify childhood health measures that have predictive value for adult health. For instance, at what point does bone mineral content determined, say noninvasively, by dual x-ray absorptiometry, begin to predict peak bone mass and hence adult osteoporosis—a disease that could, theoretically, be influenced by infant nutrition (25). When does endothelial dysfunction, assessed noninvasively by vascular ultrasound, predict risk for adult atherosclerosis? When does children's blood pressure or blood lipid pattern have good predictive value for adult measurements? New information here will help to define the duration of follow-up needed to demonstrate lasting benefits or adverse effects from early nutritional interventions convincingly. To achieve this, the first studies, like our own, may need to be conducted into adult life.

Another important principle in such studies is to use them as a vehicle for concomitant explanatory physiological research, so that mechanistic physiology can be related to outcome and not studied in isolation in circumstances where the significance of the findings may remain unknown.

After a study has been designed with adequate size, a major problem in published follow-up studies is attrition in sample size. In our experience, this is largely avoidable with good tracing techniques and the use of noninvasive measurement endpoints. The consequences of failing to achieve near-complete follow-up of the sample in some studies is serious. For instance, in one of our neurodevelopmental outcome studies involving 424 preterm infants randomly assigned to the diet given in the neonatal period (26), we achieved a follow-up rate of 89% at 18 months postterm. The 11% loss to follow-up was to a large extent linked to a temporary staffing problem in one center. We reported major differences between groups in neurodevelopment (see below for a presentation of the findings). However, we found no difference between groups in neuromotor impairment (''cerebral palsy''). At our 7.5- to 8-year follow-up on the same cohort, we resolved to achieve near-complete follow-up. We traced and saw 98% of survivors still resident in Britain (though now widely dispersed). At this follow-up, we noted a significant and potentially important difference in neuromotor impairment (to be published). This should have been detected at the 18-month follow-up but was not because the relatively small loss of subjects turned out to be a selective one. Many reported follow-up studies have losses well in excess of 30%, and one can only speculate on the possible loss of data and distortion of findings.

LONG-TERM FINDINGS FROM INTERVENTION STUDIES

A review of long-term outcome data from our own and other studies is beyond the scope of this chapter, and I shall be selective. From our own most long-standing trials on preterm infants, for instance, we have published evidence that a randomized nutritional intervention for on average 1 month, with blind evaluation at follow-up, had a major impact on health and developmental outcomes. Bone mineral content 5 years after random assignment to human milk rather than formula was higher in the former, despite the low mineral content of human milk for preterm infants in the newborn period (25). These data could imply that early nutrition programs later bone metabolism, and we are currently completing a study on around 400 of these children aged 9 to 12 years to explore whether these findings persist and could have relevance for the development of adult peak bone mass and hence osteoporosis risk. We also conducted in preterm infants what we believe to be the only prospective and strictly randomized study (in term or preterm infants) comparing the effects of human milk (from unrelated donors) and cow's-milk-based formula on the later incidence of allergic and atopic disease (27). Brief early exposure to cow's milk "programmed" a range of allergic and atopic phenomena (notably eczema) in those infants with a positive family history of allergy but appeared marginally beneficial in those without a family history, indicating an important interaction between genes and environment in the development of atopy.

The most important findings from our trials, however, are those relating to the impact of early diet and later neurodevelopment. These unique findings, discussed in more detail in the following section, have influenced clinical practice, provide major justification for the long-term ("stage III") nutritional intervention trial approach, and illustrate a number of the general points I made earlier.

EARLY DIET AND LATER NEURODEVELOPMENT

Numerous studies have addressed whether suboptimal nutrition in early life, at a critical or vulnerable phase of early brain development (15,28–32), could affect later cognitive function. Most studies have been on malnourished children in developing countries, where malnutrition is so closely associated with poverty, poor social circumstances, and lack of stimulation that it has been difficult to extricate influences of these factors from any potential long-term effect of nutrition itself (32,33). Although evidence supporting the view that early nutrition influences later cognitive development in humans is accumulating (34), firm conclusions are still hampered by lack of randomization in the great majority of studies. Yet unequivocal data on the later effects of early nutrition on brain development would be of critical public health and clinical importance.

In humans, the so-called critical brain growth spurt is between the third trimester and 2 years postterm (31). We have designed a series of strictly randomized prospective studies that test the vulnerability of the human brain to nutrition during specific periods of the brain growth spurt. Our most long-standing series of studies, started in 1982, were on preterm infants (26,35) and were therefore designed to test the effects of diet in the earliest part of the brain growth spurt—the period before full term; it is these studies that I report here. In the early 1980s, diets available for preterm infants varied grossly in nutrient content (26), and it was ethical and feasible to randomly assign these diets because there was considerable uncertainty at that time on the best nutritional strategies. In our prospective randomized five-center trials on the effects of diet on long-term growth and development in infants weighing less than 1850 g at birth, 926 infants were randomly allocated to their diet in the neonatal unit, as shown in Fig. 1.

Study 1 was conducted in three centers that had donor breast milk banks; infants were randomly allocated to (A) banked donor breast milk or (B) preterm formula, with 159 infants in the sole diet group and 343 in the supplement group. In study 2, the random allocation was to (A) standard term formula or (B) preterm formula,

Informed consent from parents

Does the mother wish to provide her own expressed breast milk for her baby?

	No			**Yes**	
	↓			↓	
	Randomise (Sole diet study)			Randomise (Supplement study)	
	Trial A	**Trial B**		**Trial A**	**Trial B**
Study 1	banked donor breast milk	preterm formula		banked donor breast milk	preterm formula
Study 2	term formula	preterm formula		term formula	preterm formula

FIG. 1. Study design.

with 160 in the sole diet group and 264 in the supplement group. The major nutritional constituents of these diets are shown in Table 1. The values for human milk are mean values for 6000 pooled samples. The donor breast milk was donated by breast-feeding mothers in the community who collected milk that dripped from the contralateral breast as they fed their own infants. The preterm formula was designed (by us) to meet the calculated nutritional requirements of preterm babies. Study details are described elsewhere (26). Many of the infants required initial parenteral nutrition, and the median time to attain full enteral feeds was 7 days in study 1 and 9 days in study 2. Intake of trial diet in the supplement trials depended on the mother's success in providing her own milk; median intake in study 1 was 47% of the infant's feed volume and 53% in study 2. The assigned diet was given (for a median of 4 weeks) until the baby attained a weight of 2000 g or was discharged

TABLE 1. *Nutrient compositions of breast milk and formulas*

Component (per 100 ml)	Preterm formula	Term formula	Mother's expressed breast milk	Banked donor breast milk
Protein (g)	2.0	1.5	1.5	1.3
Fat (g)	4.9	3.8	3.0	1.7
Carbohydrate (g)	7.0	7.0	7.0	7.1
Energy (kcal)	80	68	62	<50
Na (mg)	45	19	23	16
Ca (mg)	70	35	35	35
P (mg)	35	29	15	15

TABLE 2. *Growth data from a five-center feeding trial on 926 infants: growth measurements are between regaining birth weight and hospital discharge*

	Mean weight gain (S.E.) (g/kg per day)	Mean head circumference gain (S.E.) (mm/day)
Study 1		
Trial A (sole diets)		
BBM[a] (*n* = 83)	12.6 (0.4)	1.28 (0.05)
PTF (*n* = 76)	17.2 (0.6)***[b]	1.49 (0.05)*
Trial A plus trial B		
(supplement to EBM)		
BBM (*n* = 253)	13.4 (0.3)	1.30 (0.03)
PTF (*n* = 249)	16.0 (0.3)***	1.46 (0.04)**
Study 2		
Trial A (sole diets)		
TF (*n* = 79)	13.0 (0.6)	1.21 (0.10)
PTF (*n* = 81)	16.6 (0.5)***	1.53 (0.08)**
Trial A plus trial B		
(supplement to EBM)		
TF (*n* = 211)	13.3 (0.3)	1.33 (0.05)
PTF (*n* = 213)	15.8 (0.3)***	1.45 (0.04)

[a] BBM, banked breast milk; TF, standard term formula; PTF, preterm formula; EBM, mother's own expressed breast milk.
[b] Significance, * $p < 0.05$; ** $p < 0.01$; *** $p < 0.001$.

from the neonatal unit, whichever was sooner. After discharge from the neonatal unit, mothers fed their babies as they and their advisers chose. Follow-up staff were blind to the original dietary assignment.

Data on the characteristics and clinical status of this cohort have been published elsewhere (26). Two aspects are reported here for reasons discussed below. These are growth and necrotizing enterocolitis. Growth data in Table 2 show that in both study 1 and study 2, the babies both in trials A and A–B (a combination of trials that preserves randomization) fed preterm formula had faster weight gain and faster head circumference gains and therefore faster brain growth (36).

Among the major, and potentially diet-related, causes of morbidity, we monitored the incidence of NEC. Previous inconclusive evidence tentatively linked human-milk feeding to a lower incidence of NEC (37–39). The only trial in which we could test this in a randomized comparison was study 1, trial A, in which we found 1/83 confirmed cases of NEC on banked breast milk and 4/76 cases on preterm formula (odds ratio 4.7; 95% confidence interval, CI, 0.5 to 43) (40). The sample in this trial was too small for anything less than a tenfold difference in NEC to be detected. However, we then split the entire cohort of 926 infants into three groups: formula alone (preterm or term formula); formula plus mother's milk; and human milk alone (banked milk or banked milk with mother's own milk). In these three groups, the incidence of confirmed NEC was 17/236 (7.2%) in the formula-only group, which was significantly higher than in the formula plus mother's milk group, 11/437 (2.5%;

TABLE 3. *Bayley Mental Development Index (MDI)*
and Psychomotor Development Index (PDI) at 18 months corrected age[a]

Developmental test	Milk formula		Advantage for preterm formula (95% CI)
Study 1	BBM	PTF	
Trial A	$n = 62$	$n = 52$	
MDI	94.8 (2.1)	95.3 (2.7)	0.5 (-6.2 to 7.1)
PDI	93.0 (1.8)	94.2 (2.2)	1.2 (-4.4 to 6.8)
Trial A plus B	$n = 196$	$n = 191$	
MDI	99.9 (1.3)	101.5 (1.4)	1.6 (-2.3 to 5.5)
PDI	94.7 (1.1)	94.4 (1.2)	-0.3 (-3.4 to 2.8)
Study 2	TF	PTF	
Trial A	$n = 55$	$n = 59$	
MDI	92.6 (2.7)	98.6 (2.4)	6.0 (-0.4, 12.6)
PDI	84.2 (2.1)	98.9 (2.2)	14.7 (8.7, 20.7)***
Trial A plus B	$n = 156$	$n = 154$	
MDI	99.6 (1.6)	102.2 (1.6)	2.6 (-1.7, 6.9)
PDI	89.6 (1.4)	95.8 (1.4)	6.2 (2.4, 10.0)**

[a] Tests exclude those with cerebral palsy. BBM, banked breast milk; TF, standard term formula; PTF, preterm formula; ** $p < 0.01$; *** $p < 0.001$.

odds ratio 3.0; 95% CI 1.4 to 65; $p < 0.005$); and also higher than for human milk alone, 3/253 (1.2%; odds ratio 6.5; 95% CI 1.9 to 22; $p < 0.001$).

At long-term follow-up of this cohort, the principal targeted outcome was neurodevelopment. Within each study (26,41), calculated sample size was for one-third of a standard deviation (5 quotient points) for trials A–B combined and half a standard deviation (8 quotient points) for trial A alone. The subjects were seen at 18 months corrected age and at 7.5 years. Only data from the 18-month follow-up are published so far and are shown in Table 3. For study 1, despite the low nutrient content of banked breast milk, infants did not have lower scores than those fed preterm formula. However, in study 2, babies in trial A fed standard formula had a 6-point lower mental development index (close to 5% significance) and a 15-point lower psychomotor score ($p < 0.001$); and in trials A–B ($n = 310$; a balanced addition, preserving randomization) a 6-point lower psychomotor score ($p < 0.01$), despite the blunting effect of mothers' milk usage (trial B) in both randomized groups.

Recently, we confirmed that the significant developmental disadvantage seen in preterm babies fed a standard term formula, which we now recognize does not meet the nutrient needs of this group, is also seen at 7.5 years, when verbal IQ was significantly depressed *(unpublished)*.

DISCUSSION

These data are considered in greater depth elsewhere. However, I have juxtaposed here short-term data on growth and NEC with longer-term data on neurodevelopment to illustrate concepts developed earlier in the chapter. First, in study 2, we showed that a brief period of dietary manipulation in the neonatal period (4 weeks on average), using a nutrient-enriched rather than a standard formula, significantly influenced neurodevelopment at 18 months. Our further follow-up at 7.5 years *(unpublished),* when IQ is more predictive of that in adults, indicates that the disadvantage for the standard-formula-fed group had persisted and could now, therefore, represent a permanent effect. These data provide some of the only evidence from a large long-term randomized trial that early diet, during a "critical" or vulnerable period, could "program" neurodevelopment.

Surprisingly, in study 1, despite the poor nutrient content of donor breast milk, outcome of those individuals fed on it in the neonatal period was no worse than that seen with preterm formula (we have published data suggesting this may reflect a beneficial effect of factors in donor milk on development that ameliorate the potentially adverse effect of its low nutrient content).

Given these outcome findings, it is pertinent to reconsider the neonatal growth data. Short-term growth has been measured as a key outcome in nearly every neonatal nutrition trial. Yet here, neonatal growth did not have any predictive value for the main long-term outcome. Compared with babies fed preterm formula, those fed term formula grew poorly and had poor neurodevelopment at follow-up. However, infants fed donor milk grew particularly poorly compared with those fed preterm formula in the neonatal period, but at follow-up, developmental scores in these two groups were the same. Our unpublished data also show that early diet, with its major effect on short-term growth, had no effect on any aspect of body size at 18 months or 7.5 years. Although it is possible that at future follow-up we may identify some factor for which early growth is predictive, we have not done so yet, perhaps illustrating the weakness, discussed earlier, of relying on short-term (stage II) physiological findings.

Our findings indicate that the risk of NEC, a life-threatening complication, is greater in formula-fed than in breast-milk-fed infants. This conclusion was based on nonrandomized comparison of formula- and human-milk-fed groups, but the data are compelling. If this was confirmed, breast milk would emerge, at least from the present findings, as the diet of choice for babies not fed their mother's milk. As it happens, the HIV scare has resulted in closure of most milk banks so that the use of donor milk is not usually an option, and there are other aspects of unsupplemented donor milk that are unsatisfactory. But as an exercise in using research data to support practice, we can summarize the situation for babies not fed their own mother's milk as follows: if only stage II research had been done (growth), we would reject banked milk and term formula and choose preterm formula. If a randomized outcome trial with neurodevelopment as an endpoint was undertaken, we would reject term formula but could not distinguish between banked milk and preterm formula. If, however, we do an outcome study, as we have done, with safety monitoring (that is, we incorporate as suggested above, both efficacy and safety in our trial), we might then choose banked breast milk—the opposite conclusion to that derived from a stage II study.

OVERVIEW

Formal stage III intervention experiments in infant nutrition are only recently gaining acceptance to explore the impact of infant nutrition on clinically relevant short- and long-term outcomes. I have illustrated the value of such trials in approaching the critical issue of whether early nutrition affects later health and development. Ultimately our public health and clinical recommendations would be most secure if based on such an approach. Indeed, it is possible that recommendations based on more conventional physiological ("stage II") work could turn out to be inappropriate (as illustrated above), bearing in mind the lack of predictive value some short-term physiological findings may have for later outcome.

Unfortunately, clinical trials are still being used suboptimally in many circumstances, with targeted outcomes of unproved clinical relevance (for example, short-term growth), inadequate and uncalculated sample size, inappropriate blinding procedures, inadequate follow-up duration, and incomplete follow-up.

The current regulatory climate is likely to impose more rigorous standards on researchers and a need to prove efficacy and safety for new advances in infant nutrition. The clinical efficacy trial is not, of course, a new development—it is simply that in the past, infant nutrition researchers, funding bodies, and industry have been resistant to the use of this powerful tool.

EPILOGUE ON HUMAN MILK AND NEURODEVELOPMENT

Although randomized trials are an ideal in infant nutrition research, some are not possible or ethical. Our inability to do randomized outcome studies of breast-milk-fed versus formula-fed infants poses problems, particularly because the breast-fed infant is used as a model for performance.

The major problem of interpretation of studies of breast milk versus formulas, at least in more recent decades, is that mothers who choose to breast-feed have higher education, higher socioeconomic status, and show a greater degree of positive health behavior (42). Because these factors may independently influence many of the outcomes of interest in infant nutrition research—notably neurodevelopment—comparative studies are generally confounded.

At least 17 studies (for example, 42–49) have now addressed whether breast-fed and formula-fed infants differ in cognitive outcome or in visual development. A few have failed to observe any differences between these groups. Most have found advantages for the breast-fed group, some even after attempts to adjust for sociobiological confounding. In other cases, such adjustments have eliminated the apparent advantage. Where advantages for the breast-fed group have existed, they have generally been of the order of 0.25 to 0.5 SD of cognitive scores. The advantage has perhaps been less in term infants than in preterm infants.

The problem has been how to get at causation. This pursuit has been revitalized recently by those who cite the cognitive advantage of the breast-fed infants as evidence in favor of an essential role for dietary LC-PUFAs in neurodevelopment (LC-PUFAs being found in breast milk and not in formula).

In Popperian terms, repeated verification of findings is not an optimal approach; and certainly, there are enough studies showing a cognitive advantage for breast-fed babies, even after adjustment for confounding, for there to be limited value in repeating that exercise.

A more useful approach is to identify novel circumstances in which the causation issue can be examined afresh. One such approach is to study populations in which it is the mothers with lower education and socioeconomic status who breast-feed. Recently, Gale and Martyn (50) published such a study and found that the previously breast-fed group, now in adult life, still performed more highly on cognitive tests despite their social disadvantage. Gale did a subsequent regression analysis and concluded that the apparent breast-feeding effect was associated with dummy (pacifier) use, though this has been debated. More studies of underprivileged breast-feeders might be valuable.

Our own approach has been to explore this issue in premature babies, where the problems of confounding can be tackled in a new way. The two major proposed sources of confounding in this area are: (a) that the breast-feeding effect might be caused by the act of breast-feeding itself affecting mother–infant interaction and hence development and, (b) as discussed above, the sociobiological advantage of modern breast-feeders. We have devised two studies, each of which avoids one of the above types of confounding. The first study (42) involved the follow-up of 300 children from the five-center study described above (Fig. 1) and divided them according to whether or not they had received their own mother's milk. According to the WISC-R intelligence quotient (IQ) test at 7.5 years, those whose mothers provided breast milk had a 10-point higher IQ. Adjustment for mother's education (as a proxy for mother's IQ), social class, and sex reduced the difference to 8.3 points.

This residual 8.3-point difference in IQ at 7.5 years was large, though it might, at least in part, still have been explained by residual social and education confounding. However, the novel circumstance that assists the causation issue here is that we cannot argue that any advantage was conferred by breast-feeding itself, because these infants were too immature to suck and were fed by nasogastric tube. Indeed, an analysis on those babies who received breast milk (for an average of 1 month in hospital) but did not go home breast-feeding showed they still had a near 8-point advantage in subsequent IQ.

The second study (41) was perhaps even more compelling. At the 18-month follow-up, Bayley scores were not different (in study 1, trial A) between children previously fed donor milk versus preterm formula. This was surprising because the term formula versus preterm formula comparison (study 2, trial A) had shown the importance of providing the preterm baby with a formula that met the increased needs of this population. Yet, babies fed donor breast milk, with its low nutrient content for preterm infants (see Table 1), did not appear disadvantaged. We speculated that this might be because donor breast milk contained a factor or factors that

TABLE 4. *Bayley psychomotor development (PDI)[a] in infants whose mothers chose not to provide breast milk*

PDI			Difference (95% CI)
Study 1	BBM[c] ($n = 62$)	PTF[c] ($n = 52$)	
	93.0 (1.8)[d]	94.2 (2.2)	1.2 (-4.4 to 6.8)
Study 2	TF[c] ($n = 55$)	PTF ($n = 59$)	
	84.2 (2.1)[d]	98.9 (2.2)	14.7 (8.7 to 20.7)[b]

[a] Excluding cerebral palsy.
[b] $p < 0.001$
[c] BBM, banked (donated) breast milk; PTF, preterm formula; TF, standard term formula.
[d] Advantage for BBM over TF (95% CI), 8.8 (3.3 to 14.3), $p < 0.02$.

ameliorated the effect of its poor nutrient content. However, a fairer comparison was between donor milk (from study 1, trial A) and term formula (from study 2, trial A), where the diets compared have more similar nutrient contents (Table 1). For clarity, data illustrative of PDI scores have been extracted from Table 3 and placed in Table 4. The comparison between trials of banked-milk-fed and term-formula-fed infants is legitimate because the same preterm formula acted as an internal standard between trials. The babies fed banked milk had a significant near 9-point advantage in PDI over those fed term formula. The novel circumstance of this study is that none of these infants had mothers who chose to provide breast milk, so that the usual sources of sociobiological confounding did not apply, yet the breast-milk-fed group was still advantaged.

These two studies were done on preterm infants, and although they provide perhaps more compelling evidence than previously for an effect of breast milk itself on later cognitive function, it is possible that the findings cannot be extrapolated to the term infant born during a less rapid stage of brain growth. It should be emphasized, however, that if there is a breast milk advantage, it cannot necessarily be ascribed to the presence of long-chain polyunsaturated fatty acids—there are indeed many candidate factors in human milk (thyroid hormone, growth factors, and so on) that might exert a biological effect (42). Demonstration of a clear long-term effect on neurodevelopment of any of these candidate factors in a randomized formula supplementation study would provide important collateral evidence for any beneficial effect of breast milk. Because the cognitive advantage of breast-fed versus formula-fed babies has been seen during midchildhood, when cognitive tests are predictive of those in adulthood, supplementation studies in formula-fed babies would need to have at least a several-year follow-up period. Currently, the trials of LC-PUFAs, important in this regard, are generally small, with relative short-term follow-up, and do not yet contribute convincingly to the intriguing question about breast milk and long-term cognitive function.

REFERENCES

1. Macy IG, Kelly HJ, Sloan RF. *National Academy of Science, Publication No 254: The composition of milk.* Washington DC: National Research Council, 1953.

2. Lucas A. Does diet in preterm infants influence clinical outcome? *Biol Neonate* 1978;52:141–146.
3. Uauy R, Birch DG, Birch EE, Hoffman D, Tyson J. Visual and brain development in infants as a function of essential fatty acid supply provided by the early diet. In: *Lipids, learning and the brain: Fats in infant formulas: Report of the 103rd Ross Conference on Pediatric Research.* Columbus, OH: Ross Laboratories, 1992:215–232.
4. Danesch U, Weber PC, Sellmayer A. Arachidonic acid increases c-fos and Egr-1 mRNA in 3T3 fibroblasts by formation of prostaglandin E_2 and activation of protein kinase C. *J Biol Chem* 1994; 269:2758–2763.
5. Clarke SD, Jump DB. Dietary polyunsaturated fatty acid regulation of gene transcription. *Annu Rev Nutr* 1994;14:83–98.
6. Toft I, Bonaa KH, Ingebretsen OC, Nordoy A, Jenssen T. Effects of $n - 3$ polyunsaturated fatty acids on glucose homeostasis and blood pressure in essential hypertension. A randomized controlled trial. *Ann Intern Med* 1995;123:950–952.
7. Storlien LH, Jenkins AB, Chisholm DG, Pascoe WS , Khouri S, Kraegen EW. Influence of dietary fat composition on development of insulin resistance in rats. Relationship to muscle triglyceride and omega-3 fatty acids in muscle phospholipid. *Diabetes* 1991;40:280–289.
8. Claassen N, Coetzer H, Steinmann CM, Kruger MC. The effect of different n-6/n-3 essential fatty acid ratios on calcium balance and bone in rats. *Prostaglandins Leukotrienes Essent Fatty Acids* 1995;53:13–19.
9. Sperling RI, Benincaso AI, Knoell CT, Larkin JK, Austen KF, Robinson DR. Dietary omega-3 polyunsaturated fatty acids inhibit phosphoinositide formation and chemotaxis in neutrophils. *J Clin Invest* 1993;91:651–660.
10. Carlson SE, Werkman SH, Tolley EA. Effect of long-chain $n - 3$ fatty acid supplementation on visual acuity and growth of preterm infants with and without bronchopulmonary dysplasia. *Am J Clin Nutr* 1996;63:687–697.
11. Lucas A, Fewtrell MF, Morley R, Lucas P, Baker B, Lister G, Bishop N. Randomized outcome trial of human milk fortification trials and developmental outcome in preterm infants. *Am J Clin Nutr* 1996;64:142–151.
12. Lucas A. Role of nutritional programming in determining adult morbidity [annotation]. *Arch Dis Child* 1994;71:288–290.
13. Lucas A. Programming by early nutrition in man. In: Bock GR, Whelan J, eds. *The childhood environment and adult disease (CIBA Foundation Symposium 156).* Chichester: Wiley, 1991:38–55.
14. Smart JL. Critical periods in brain development. In: Bock GR, Whelan J, eds. *The childhood environment and adult disease (CIBA Foundation Symposium 156).* Chichester: Wiley, 1991:109–128.
15. Dobbing J. Nutritional growth restriction and the nervous system. In: Davison AN, Thompson RHS, eds. *The molecular basis of neuropathology.* London: Edward Arnold, 1981:221–233.
16. Smart J, Undernutrition, learning and memory: review of experimental studies. In: Taylor TG, Jenkins NK, eds. *Proceedings of XII international congress of nutrition.* London: John Libbey, 1986:74–78.
17. Snoek A, Remacle C, Reusens B, Hoet JJ. Effect of a low protein diet during pregnancy on the fetal rat endocrine pancreas. *Biol Neonate* 1990;57:107–118.
18. Hahn P. Effect of litter size on plasma cholesterol and insulin and some liver and adipose tissue enzymes in adult rodents. *J Nutr* 1984;114:1231–1232.
19. Lewis DS, Bartrand HA, McHahan CA, McGill HC, Carey KD, Masoro EJ. Preweaning food intake influences the adiposity of young adult baboons. *J Clin Invest* 1986;78:899–905.
20. Mott GE, Lewis DS, McGill HC. Programming of cholesterol metabolism by breast or formula feeding. In: Bock GR, Whelan J, eds. *The childhood environment and adult disease (CIBA Foundation Symposium 156).* Chichester: Wiley, 1991:128–174.
21. Barker DJP, Gluckman PD, Godfrey KM, Harding JE, Ownes JA, Robinson JS. Fetal nutrition and cardiovascular disease in adult life. *Arch Dis Child* 1993;341:938–941.
22. Fall CHD, Barker DJP, Osmond C, Winter PD, Clark PMS, Hales CN. Relation of infant feeding to adult serum cholesterol concentration and death from ischaemic heart disease. In: Barker DJP, ed. *Fetal and infant originals of adult disease.* London: BMJ Publishing Group, 1992:275–288.
23. Barker DJP, Martyn CN, Osmond C, Hales CN. Growth *in utero* and serum cholesterol concentrations in adult life. *Br Med J* 1993;307:1524–1527.
24. McCall RB. The development of intellectual functioning in infancy and the prediction of later IQ. In: Osofsky JD, ed. *The handbook of infant development.* New York: Wiley, 1979:707–741.
25. Bishop NJ, Dahlenburg SL, Fewtrell MF, Morley R, Lucas A. Early diet of preterm infants and bone mineralization at age five years. *Acta Paediatr* 1996;85:230–236.
26. Lucas A, Morley R, Cole TJ, *et al.* Early diet in preterm babies and developmental status at 18 months. *Lancet* 1990;335:1477–1481.

27. Lucas A, Brooke OG, Morley R, Cole TJ, Bamford MF. Early diet of preterm infants and development of allergic or atopic disease: randomised prospective study. *Br Med J* 1990;300:837–840.
28. Gardner JM, Grantham-McGregor SM. Physical activity, undernutrition and child development [review]. *Proc Nutr Soc* 1994;53:241–248.
29. Pollitt E, Gorman KS, Engle PL, *et al.* Early supplementary feeding and cognition: effects over two decades. *Monogr Soc Res Child Dev* 1993;58(7).
30. Grantham-McGregor SM, Powell CA, Walker SP, *et al.* Nutritional supplementation, psychosocial stimulation and mental development of stunted children: the Jamaican study. *Lancet* 1991;338:1–5.
31. Husaini MA, Karyadi L, Husaini YK, *et al.* Developmental effects of short term supplementary feeding in nutritionally at-risk Indonesian infants. *Am J Clin Nutr* 1991;54:799–804.
32. Grantham-McGregor SM. Field studies in early nutrition and later achievement. In: Dobbin J, ed. *Early nutrition and later achievement.* London: Academic Press, 1987:128–174.
33. Richardson SA. The relation of severe malnutrition in infancy to the intelligence of school children with different life histories. *Pediatr Res* 1976;10:57–61.
34. Smart JL. Malnutrition, learning and behavior: 25 years on the from the MIT symposium. *Proc Nutr Soc* 1993;52:189–199.
35. Lucas A, Gore SM, Cole TJ, *et al.* Multicentre trial on feeding low birthweight infants: effects of diet on early growth. *Arch Dis Child* 1984;59:722–730.
36. Cooke RWI, Lucas A, Yudkin PLN, Pryse-Davies J. Head circumference as an index of brain weight in the fetus and new-born. *Early Hum Dev* 1977;1/2:145–149.
37. De Curtis M, Paone C, Vertrano G, *et al.* A case control study of necrotizing enterocolitis occurring over 8 years in a neonatal intensive care unit. *Eur J Pediatr* 1987;146:398–400.
38. Kleigman RM, Pittard WB, Fanaroff AA. Necrotizing enterocolitis in neonates fed human milk. *J Pediatr* 1979;95:450–453.
39. Kosloske AM. Pathogenesis and prevention of necrotizing enterocolitis: hypothesis based on personal observation. *Pediatrics* 1984;74:1086–1092.
40. Lucas A, Cole TJ. Breast milk and neonatal necrotising enterocolitis. *Lancet* 1990;336:1519–1523.
41. Lucas A, Morley R, Cole TJ, Gore SM. A randomised multicentre study of human milk versus formula and later development in preterm infants. *Arch Dis Child* 1994;70:F141–F146.
42. Lucas A, Morley R, Cole TJ, Lister G, Leeson-Payne C. Breast milk and subsequent intelligence quotient in children born preterm. *Lancet* 1992;339:261–264.
43. Hoefer A, Hardy MC. Later development of breast fed and artificially fed infants. *JAMA* 1929;92:615–619.
44. Rogerson BRC, Rogerson CH. Feeding in infancy and subsequent psychological difficulties. *J Ment Sci* 1939;85:1163–1182.
45. Broad B. The effects of infant feeding on speech quality. *NZ Med J* 1972;76:28–31.
46. Taylor B. Breast versus bottle feeding. *NZ Med J* 1977;85:2385–2387.
47. Morley R, Cole TJ, Lucas PJ *et al.* Mother's choice to provide breast milk and developmental outcome. *Arch Dis Child* 1988;63:1382–1385.
48. Rodgers B. Feeding in infancy and later ability and attainment: a longitudinal study. *Dev Med Child Neurol* 1978;20:421–426.
49. Silva PA, Buckfield P, Spears GF. Some maternal and child development characteristics associated with breastfeeding: a report from the Dunedin multidisciplinary child development study. *Aust Paediatr J* 1978;14:265–268.
50. Gale CR, Martyn CN. Breastfeeding, dummy use, and adult intelligence. *Lancet* 1996;347:1072–1075.

DISCUSSION

Dr. Aeschlimann: I have a comment about safety. You say assessment of safety needs an adequate sample size, but it is necessary to be precise about the sample numbers. If you have only 30 infants in a trial and see no adverse reactions, you can only say with 95% confidence that the incidence of adverse reactions is less than one in ten; and if you have 3000 people with no adverse reaction, you can only say that the incidence is less than one in 1000.

Dr. Lucas: Recent test cases in court, for example the Debendox case, show that it is almost impossible to have a large enough safety trial to pick up all the rare effects. Nevertheless, I think that we have to do a realistic job here, and in situations where safety issues are testable. For instance, several of the potential effects of LC-PUFAs in premature babies, such as infection and necrotizing enterocolitis, are not so rare that we can't reasonably test the hypothesis that there is a differential incidence between groups—and we should do it. There are many more postmarketing questions that need to be addressed as far as minor safety is concerned, but I would still say that not only are we bad at looking at premarketing safety in clinical trials, we are equally bad, if not more so, at looking at postmarketing surveillance techniques to examine safety.

Dr. Haschke: Without going into details, could you comment a little more on the long-term outcome in the LC-PUFA studies? You mentioned you had 2000 infants in different studies, with different designs of course. Could you give us a preliminary idea of the outcome of those studies? We are struggling with studies with a sample size of 50, and we are discussing effects in the very short-term range.

Dr. Lucas: We have six LC-PUFA studies at various stages. The first one to be completed has over 400 subjects in it, but we are only doing a preliminary analysis on it at the 9-month follow-up; our targeted follow-up is 18 months. I can say at this very preliminary stage—because we have now been allowed to do an analysis although we have not actually broken the code—that there is no impact on development and growth between LC-PUFA-supplemented infants and nonsupplemented infants, using both AA and DHA, at 9 months. However, we clearly need to look at our 18-month follow-up data before drawing any definite conclusions. At 18 months, test scores are verging on showing reliable correlations with later scores, although by no means definitively; for example, the correlation coefficient between the Bayley score at 18 months and the WISC-R score at $7\frac{1}{2}$ to 8 years would be about 0.5, but it is obviously better in populations than in individuals. If we find differences at 18 months, then clearly they need to be followed up; if we fail to find differences at 18 months, we still need to do longer-term follow-up because the early tests may not be sophisticated enough to pick up effects. So in these studies, we really are committed to follow-up into childhood, but we may get some important clues in the second year of life.

Dr. Haschke: My second question is related to long-term outcome in growth. Was there any long-term effect on growth, in particular in those infants who were fed breast milk versus the preterm formula?

Dr. Lucas: We have failed to find a consistent relationship between early growth and later neurodevelopment up to $7\frac{1}{2}$ to 8 years. We have also found absolutely no relationship between early diet, which has a profound effect on neonatal growth, and body size up to $7\frac{1}{2}$ to 8 years later. So it appears that early neonatal growth is far less predictive of anything than we might have imagined.

Dr. Tsang: You have identified an important problem, but it is a moving target. You just told us that your banked breast milk is no longer being used, your term formulas are no longer being used, and your preterm formulas are not the same, so all three things you studied are no longer in existence. Because of the long duration of your studies, every time you present your data, they are out of date and no longer relevant. How do you face this new challenge?

Dr. Lucas: I totally disagree that it is irrelevant! The issue that we need to address, which is unknown, is whether early nutrition *per se* matters for long-term outcome. If we decide that feeding babies suboptimally makes a difference to long-term outcome, then that is of immediate clinical importance in 1996 because premature babies are frequently fed suboptimally—they may not be fed on term formulas or banked breast milk, but they are frequently fed suboptimally. So we are establishing whether nutrition matters. Now obviously in these long-term studies, you will have some degree of redundancy if you like. Nevertheless, as we discover that more medium-term outcomes have predictive value for later outcomes, then we can get much closer to our target in subsequent studies. Neonatal intensive care has been extremely fast moving over the last 20 years, and it is likely to stabilize in the next few years. I think we will very shortly be getting data that are of current relevance.

Dr. Hamburger: At the very least, you have convinced people that it is worth paying for long-term study!

Dr. Lozoff: Many of us in this room are physicians, and we have generally been quite content to use outcome measures such as Bayley or IQ tests, but if we were to present these data to behavioral scientists, they would be horrified. They would say these are very crude measures, they tell us nothing about process, they don't correlate with function, IQ measurements are horribly confounded by measurement and culture bias, and we don't know what intelligence is, and so on.

Dr. Lucas: These are all valid points. First, what psychologists are generally interested in is cognitive measures in an *individual,* but what we are looking at is differential effects on cognitive function between large randomized *populations.* That cancels some of their criticisms. In populations, intelligence quotient is certainly correlated with academic performance, and I don't think any of us, or even your most critical psychologists, would like to lose 5 IQ points as a result of early diet. I have presented data on the Bayley and IQ tests simply because I felt they would be most amenable to a general audience. We are in fact doing a lot more sophisticated testing on these children and have done all the way through; in our adolescent follow-up, we will be able to do some really very sophisticated tests on these children. So I agree with you, but nevertheless I think that the Bayley and WISC-R IQ have such general acceptance that they are worth measuring—but other things as well.

Dr. Whitehead: You said at the beginning of your talk that your hope was there would be a lifetime follow-up on your work. What do biomedical scientists like yourself, who are interested in this kind of topic, need in order to ensure that such a follow-up does occur, because if it does not occur, then we are not delivering the goods that science expects us to deliver.

Dr. Lucas: This is a practical issue. I would make the general point that we have heard some important comments from statisticians, and the statistics of these clinical trials are of course very important, but the practical aspect of running these trials is really the major problem. The one outstandingly important practical issue here is how to hang on to your patient population. In certain countries, that is relatively straightforward—in Scandinavia, it is straightforward, and in Britain, it is relatively straightforward—because people are tagged by being part of the national health service. We use a number of other tagging techniques, such as keeping ourselves informed on addresses of relatives and friends, so that if subjects move, we can contact people who would know and care where they have gone to—of course, with their permission. This is just one of a number of different techniques that one might use. You have to look at the population you are studying and decide how feasible it is going to be to achieve reliable follow-up. In Britain, we achieved 98% follow-up of subjects at $7\frac{1}{2}$ to 8 years, who were diffused all over the country. That encouraged us to believe that we could keep tabs on this population. It is slightly more difficult if they move overseas, but still not impossible.

Dr. Hamburger: It's almost impossible in the States.

Dr. Pohlandt: You haven't had time enough to outline all your work, but I think it is important to indicate which variables have been primary ones and which secondary ones, and also what questions you asked after finishing the studies—for example, what about necrotizing enterocolitis?

Dr. Lucas: Anticipating that question, which is a very important one, the three variables I presented to you were absolutely key variables at the outset of our trial: trial size was calculated for differences in neurodevelopmental outcome; growth was obviously a key measurement in the neonatal period to establish that we were looking at differences in nutritional status in the short term, and necrotizing enterocolitis and death were the two most important outcomes in terms of safety. So I haven't fudged the outcomes to provide a story! There are several other outcomes that we have reported that are genuinely secondary outcomes of the study and, therefore, are much more hypothesis-generating than necessarily definitive. I think it is extremely important that investigators in studies like this make it very clear whether a hypothesis is a *post hoc* one or a primary one.

Dr. Uauy: Your studies are multicenter, and I think it is very important to get an idea of how homogeneous the centers are. In our experience with necrotizing enterocolitis, we find some centers with rates as low as in your breast milk group, while others have values of 20% or 30% in babies under 1500 g. So how important is it to have a homogeneous group of centers to test these variables?

Dr. Lucas: What is important, as has been suggested by statisticians here, is that you have a separate randomization in each center. That is absolutely critical because, otherwise, you could have really quite serious bias if you don't have balanced groups from each center. Of course, there are center variations in necrotizing enterocolitis; that is well established. You can't pick up significant differences within individual centers often—that is the whole point of having multicenter studies; but for most of the factors that have shown up as differences in the overall population, we found the expected trends in individual centers when we have done the appropriate analysis. The strength of having many centers is that, provided your nutritional intervention is stereotyped, then the fact that you get an outcome difference despite minor variations in practice between centers gives your answer a robustness and a generalizability for other centers.

Dr. Yolken: I wonder if you could comment more on the feasibility of doing studies in a naturally occurring breast-fed population versus a formula-fed population, where you can't totally randomize the groups. Do you have studies like that?

Dr. Lucas: There have been about 17 studies comparing breast-fed and formula-fed babies, most of them showing an advantage for the breast-fed group. But all of them are potentially confounded, even after adjusting for confounding factors, so what you don't want is repeated verification: more and more studies showing the same thing would be useless. What we need to do is to find circumstances that get around the confounding problems. We have done two studies that avoid the conventional confounders: one used breast milk taken from a donor population, in cases where the mother chose not to provide breast milk herself; the other used premature babies, where there was no breast-feeding, so you get rid of the bonding effect of breast-feeding, and you are just looking at the effect of milk given down a tube. Another way would be to look at populations in which the higher socioeconomic group has chosen to bottle-feed rather than breast-feed and see if you still get the breast-feeding advantage. That may be the way forward; obviously, you can't randomize.

Dr. Lozoff: In relation to your measures for outcome, I would completely agree that those of us who are doing research in clinical nutrition are charged with asking what is important for function. It seems that there are two very different approaches, one looking at very specific mechanisms and parts of the central nervous system, which guided the choice of measures, and the other—as in the work you presented and similar to what I have been doing—taking very crude overall measures. I wonder what your thoughts are about these almost polar opposites.

Dr. Lucas: The choices are probably slightly too stark, in the sense that there have been a huge number of studies on the impact of malnutrition on experimental animals, and also a fair amount of work done on human brain development, which could guide you in this area. For instance, we know that new neurons are being formed in the posterior parts of the brain—in the cerebellum, for instance—during the prenatal period, whereas most neurons are formed earlier in gestation. So we would expect those to be particularly vulnerable in premature babies, and that is why we have put quite a lot of dominance on psychomotor tests in our 9- and 18-month follow-ups, because we felt that we would be most likely to pick up differences in coordinating functions. You appreciate that the Bayley psychomotor test is highly dominated by coordinating and balancing skills. That hypothesis turned out to be true, and we did see our biggest effects on the Bayley psychomotor rather than mental development at that stage. However, because this is an exploratory area, we need to have fairly broad-based tests that are going to pick up differences in function. We are now adopting a much more sophisticated approach, looking at brain imaging and so forth in these populations.

Dr. Uauy: From the information that you provided, and other studies provide, about the effect of human milk versus formula, what do you think are the nutrients involved? Of course, I like the LC-PUFA hypothesis, but have you tested other hypotheses, for example thyroid hormone?

Dr. Lucas: We haven't tested other hypotheses. We are testing the LC-PUFA hypothesis because we consider it to be plausible—it does need to be tested as a possible cause of differences between breast-fed and formula-fed babies, but there are so many other differences, and in particular, the nonnutrient differences as you point out. There is a mass of hormones and growth factors in human milk not present in formula, somewhere between 35 and 50 at the last count, including thyroid hormone, for instance, which you mention, and which has a very potent effect on neurodevelopment. So there are a long list of things to look at, but we are particularly involved with LC-PUFAs at the moment.

Dr. Rey: Can we say that there is no advantage to adding LC-PUFAs to preterm formula according to your data because the IQ at 7 years was exactly the same in banked breast milk and preterm formula without LC-PUFAs?

Dr. Lucas: This is a rather unfair comparison because banked breast milk is nutritionally insufficient for premature babies compared with preterm formulas, so you could be looking at counterbalancing effects. The more realistic comparison is between banked breast milk and term formula, which I showed you, where the nutrient contents are much more similar. There we got a very large difference between groups, and we need to explain it. One possible explanation is LC-PUFAs, but the difference could be related to any number of other factors present in human milk.

Dr. Guesry: I think that to compare own mother's milk with preterm formula is also unfair, because when a mother takes on the burden of coming every day for weeks to provide her own milk for her baby in the neonatal unit, this probably means she will give better care over the rest of the 7 years of observation. We have to be very careful in looking at all these factors.

Dr. Lucas: No one could agree more with that than I. All the studies that compare mother's own milk with formula are confounded, including my own, as I pointed out in my paper. The one bit of confounding that wasn't present in that particular study was that you couldn't say that the advantage was caused by breast-feeding, because the babies received human milk down a tube not from the breast. We did adjust for mother's education, which is a proxy for maternal IQ; we did adjust for social class; but we didn't adjust for positive health behavior, which you have just described, and it could easily be the explanation of our results. That is why it is so important to identify circumstances that get around the confounding, such as the comparison of banked breast milk with term formula, where there is a similar nutrient content and two populations whose mothers have chosen not to provide breast milk. So you have taken out all the positive health behavior. The fact that there is still an advantage to banked breast milk over term formula does at least provide a challenge.

Dr. Rey: I would like your opinion on the long-term effects of malnutrition in infancy. You know about the many papers published by Barker, and the last one was very strange, because he found that the rate of suicide was higher in people with a smaller increment in weight in the first year of life. He found that the group who committed suicide had a weight at 1 year that was 395 g less than the control group (1). I think this is very puzzling. Are you afraid that your children fed with term formula will commit suicide in the future?

Dr. Lucas: From the 1960s onwards, we have had very powerful data from animals suggesting that early diet affects long-term outcome in a variety of species, so the question is whether this is true for humans. There are two approaches that we could adopt to find out. One is the epidemiologic approach, which has been adopted by Barker, that is, to try to find nutritional markers in early life and relate them to long-term health outcomes; the other approach is the experimental intervention approach, which is the one we have adopted. The advantage of Barker's approach is that you can look at the extremes of life very quickly without doing a long-term experiment. The disadvantage is that it doesn't prove cause; we have no idea whether the relationship between birth weight and long-term systolic blood pressure that he has shown, for example, is causally related to maternal and hence fetal nutrition, which is what he hypothesizes. The advantage of the approach we have adopted is that we can get a cause; the disadvantage is that it takes a long time to get the answer. I think in the end Barker's epidemiologic studies are hypothesis-generating. If we want to change public health policy, however, it has got to be on the basis of intervention studies.

Dr. Haschke: Can you also comment on the calcium and phosphorus status in the infants receiving banked breast milk? Did they receive calcium and phosphorus supplements? If yes, what was the outcome? If not, can you also compare the incidence of rickets and abnormal bone structure?

Dr. Lucas: In the early 1980s, we did not give multinutrient fortifiers in breast milk—those products did not exist in Britain. The only supplement that we added to human milk was phosphorus, a small amount bringing the concentration up from 15 to 30 mg/100 ml. Despite doing that, the babies fed on human milk did very badly in terms of short-term bone mineralization; they had a very high incidence of high alkaline phosphatases, and they grew less well in terms of linear growth, not only in the neonatal period, but also for the first 18 months of life. What was fascinating was that when we took a pilot population at 5 years of age and looked at bone mineralization using a rather unsophisticated technique (single-photon absorptiometry), we found that babies who had been randomly assigned to the preterm formula had a lower bone mineral content than babies who had been randomly assigned to banked breast milk after adjustment for body size. That raised the hypothesis that despite the short-term deficits, there might be some value in human milk in long-term bone mineralization. We are currently testing that hypothesis in several hundred children now, and they have reached 12 years of age, but I can't tell you the answer yet. However, we are now doing much more sophisticated studies including bone turnover.

REFERENCE

1. Barker DJ, Osmond C, Rodin I, *et al.* Low weight gain in infancy and suicide in adult life. *Br Med J* 1995;311:1203.

Clinical Trials in Infant Nutrition, edited by
Jay A. Perman and Jean Rey, Nestlé Nutrition
Workshop Series, Vol. 40, Nestec Ltd.,
Vevey/Lippincott-Raven Publishers,
Philadelphia © 1998.

Considering Environmental Factors in Research on Nutrient Deficiencies and Infant Development

Betsy Lozoff

The Center for Human Growth and Development, University of Michigan, Ann Arbor, Michigan, USA

I have become increasingly concerned with the issue of environmental factors over the past 20 years of involvement with clinical trials related to iron deficiency anemia and infant behavior. This concern has been incremental, as each study has taught me lessons about environmental influences. Each study raised new questions, which affected the design of the subsequent study. I review this series of studies to illustrate some of the issues and provide a real-life case study as background for a discussion of environmental factors in clinical trials in infant nutrition. In so doing, however, I want to emphasize that I am approaching this topic as a clinical investigator, not as a statistician or a methodologic expert.

Although a randomized clinical trial is the ideal study design to minimize confounding by environmental influences, the experience with clinical trials related in iron deficiency anemia and infant development illustrates that environmental factors are still of major concern. Before turning to this issue, I briefly summarize the results of the available clinical trials. These studies all used multiple measures to characterize iron status, and most used the Bayley Scales of Infant Development to assess development and behavior. Statistical details are omitted, and only those results at the 0.05 level of statistical significance or better are reported.

All seven of the available studies of iron-deficient anemic infants that included careful definitions of iron status and appropriate comparison groups reported that iron-deficient anemic infants had lower mental test scores than infants with better iron status (1–7), and five showed lower motor scores as well (1,3–6). No association between lower pretreatment test scores and lesser degrees of iron deficiency has been documented (4–6,8). After 1 week, neither intramuscular nor oral iron treatments differed from placebo treatment in effects on scores (4,5,9; M.E.K. Moffatt, *personal communication,* 1987). After 2 to 6 months of treatment, one study reported an overall improvement in mental and motor test scores (6), two studies observed continued lower test scores in the majority of anemic infants, with improved scores in a minority who showed the best response to iron treatment (4,10), and two found no improvement at all, regardless of hematologic response (5,7). Thus, the ability of iron treatment to correct the lower test scores and the conditions under which iron therapy can affect test score improvements remain open questions.

I go over our own studies in more detail to illustrate some issues about environmental influences. The overall lesson is that most of us clinical investigators are naive and simplistic in our approach to environmental factors. Someone tried to teach me this lesson in my initial study in Guatemala years ago, but the issue continues to be challenging in every single subsequent study. In that first study (1), conducted in Guatemala in 1978 in collaboration with the Institute of Nutrition of Central America and Panama (INCAP), the sample was drawn from a socioeconomically homogeneous settlement constructed after the 1976 earthquake. Thus, housing, sanitation, and health care facilities were the same for everyone. In this study, as in all the subsequent ones, babies were candidates for participation only if they had been born at term, were not of low birth weight, and were free of acute or chronic illness. We compared 28 infants with iron deficiency anemia with a nonanemic group of 40 infants and assessed the effects of short-term oral iron and placebo treatment. The mean mental development test score of the infants with iron deficiency anemia (Hb $\leq$ 105 g/liter) was 87, compared to the mean score of 100 among the nonanemic infants (Hb $\geq$ 120 g/liter). A 9-point pretreatment difference in motor scores was also observed. There were no significant differences between anemic and nonanemic groups in birth history, socioeconomic factors, or general nutritional status that might otherwise explain the lower developmental test scores. Mental test score deficits were especially marked in older anemic infants (19- to 24-month-olds), and a substantial correlation between the degree of iron deficiency and mental test scores ($r = 0.73$) was observed in this age group (11). No changes from short-term oral iron treatment were noted. Iron-treated anemic infants did not show significantly greater increases in their Bayley mental or motor test scores than either placebo-treated anemic babies or infants in the iron or placebo-treated nonanemic groups; all groups increased by 4 to 6 points.

When, as a new investigator, I presented these data at the Society for Research and Child Development meetings in 1981, I made a big point of the similarity in all the background factors, arguing this meant that the pretreatment differences really could be attributed to iron deficiency anemia. A member of the audience, neurologist Marcel Kinsbourne, came up to me afterwards and gently pointed out that the usual indicators of socioeconomic status, such as parental education and occupation, might not be nearly as revealing in research in developing countries as in highly industrialized settings. Education might be a good proxy for parental intelligence and socioeconomic status in a country such as the United States but not in a developing country where educational opportunities were limited. At the time, I thought the lesson of the Guatemala study was that ways of assessing environmental influences might need to be different depending on whether the research was conducted in industrialized societies or a developing country. But it really was just the beginning of recognizing that addressing environmental influences adequately is a complicated and sophisticated undertaking.

The next study, started in Costa Rica in 1981 in conjunction with the Hospital Nacional de Niños, was designed to answer some questions posed by the results of studies available at that time. None of the previous studies assessed whether there was a particular degree of iron deficiency at which infant behavior and development was altered. Furthermore, the apparent discrepancies regarding treatment (1,8,9) suggested that oral and intramuscular iron might differ in short-term effects on developmental test scores. We tried to address these issues by enrolling a relatively large number of infants with varied iron status in a single study, including double-blind randomized controlled comparisons of short-term oral iron, intramuscular iron, and placebo treatment, and long-term oral iron or placebo treatment (with placebo only for iron-sufficient children) (4). The sample consisted of 191 12- to 23-month-old infants divided into groups ranging from most to least iron-deficient as follows: (a) iron-deficient anemic (n = 52); (b) intermediate in hemoglobin level and iron-deficient (n = 45); (c) nonanemic iron-deficient (n = 21); (d) nonanemic iron-depleted (n = 38); and (e) nonanemic iron-sufficient (n = 35). The data from the anemic infants were further analyzed with respect to actual Hb level because lower Hb levels indicate more severe iron deficiency once anemia is present. Iron-deficient and iron-depleted conditions were subsequently confirmed by hematologic response to iron treatment.

Infants with moderate iron deficiency anemia (Hb $\leq$ 100 g/liter) were found to have lower mental and motor test scores than appropriate controls; infants with mild anemia (Hb 101 to 105 g/liter) received lower motor scores but not mental scores; and infants with lesser degrees of iron deficiency did not have impairments in developmental test performance (Figs. 1 and 2). The mean mental test score of the moderately anemic infants was 8 points below that of infants with higher Hb levels (>100 g/liter), and the mean motor score of the entire anemic group was 10 points below that of infants with Hb > 105 g/liter. Mental test scores decreased with age in all groups; the differential decrease observed among older anemic infants in the Guatemalan study (11) was not found. However, anemic infants in all age groups seemed to have trouble with particular motor functions involving balance and coordination.

After 1 week of treatment, the increases in Bayley test scores and hematologic variables among iron-deficient infants receiving intramuscular iron did not differ from those of iron-deficient infants receiving oral iron. There was no benefit of iron therapy over placebo on developmental test scores.

More important than short-term outcome, this study was designed to examine the effects of a course of treatment commonly used in practice (3 months of oral iron treatment). All iron-deficient and iron-depleted children were treated with iron, and the iron-sufficient group was randomly assigned to oral iron or placebo treatment. After 3 months, the anemia of all iron-deficient anemic infants was corrected, but the majority (64%) still had biochemical evidence of iron deficiency, suggesting greater severity or chronicity. On average, previously anemic infants continued to have lower test scores in mental and motor development (Figs. 1 and 2). However, in the minority of infants who became completely iron-sufficient after 3 months of treatment, there was some indication that iron treatment benefited test scores. These infants, who probably had less severe or less chronic iron deficiency anemia, showed a 10-point increase in motor test scores and did not show the decline in mental scores observed in the rest of the sample.

Despite the encouraging response in this subset of infants, it was worrying that lower mental and motor test scores persisted among the majority of initially anemic infants. We were again faced with a clinical trial that did not show a test score benefit of iron treatment for most babies. The whole issue of environmental factors becomes crucial in this situation, because establishing a causal relationship between a risk factor and poorer development then depends heavily on eliminating other

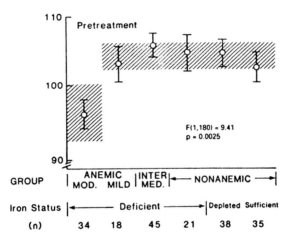

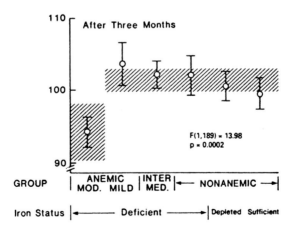

FIG. 1.   Mental development index from the Bayley Scales of Infant Development before and after treatment (4), reproduced with permission.

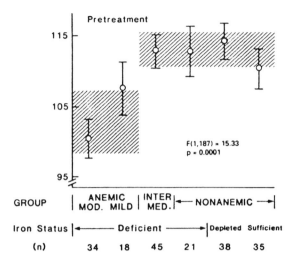

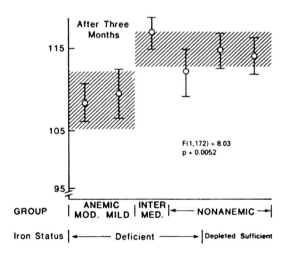

FIG. 2. Psychomotor development index from the Bayley Scales of Infant Development before and after treatment (4), reproduced with permission.

factors that might account for the developmental test score differences. In the Costa Rica study (4), the population was generally lower middle class, highly literate, with excellent health care, and the babies were free of undernutrition, increased blood lead, hemoglobinopathies, and parasitic disease. However, Kinsbourne's comments had led us to include a much more comprehensive assessment of the environment. We administered full-scale IQ tests to the mothers (and to fathers where possible), determined parental weight and height, made home visits to complete the HOME

Inventory (12) (a measure of the stimulation a child receives at home), and collected dietary information. On these more detailed measures, infants with iron deficiency anemia had several environmental disadvantages. They were less likely to have been breast-fed; if breast-fed, they were weaned earlier; they consumed more unmodified cow's milk; their mothers had lower IQ scores; and their home environments were less stimulating (4). Nonetheless, mental and motor test score differences were statistically significant after control for these differences. We also did a stepwise multiple regression entering all of the background variables first and found that iron deficiency anemia contributed significantly to the variance even after control for family background variables.

Initially, I thought that the problem of differences in family background had been handled satisfactorily, and there was reason to conclude that iron deficiency anemia accounted for the lower test scores. Ultimately, however, the lesson from this study was that the coincidence of nutrient deficiencies and other disadvantages must be taken even more seriously (13). As with several other risk conditions, such as low birth weight, raised lead levels, and generalized undernutrition, iron deficiency is associated with environmental disadvantages (14–19). Such disadvantageous conditions might include poverty, limited knowledge of optimal ways to feed and care for infants, lack of stimulation in the home, and so on. These factors are known to have adverse effects on infant development and could account both for nutritional deficiency and for poorer developmental outcome. For instance, parents who are more limited because of restriction of intellectual capacity, stress, or depression might make worse decisions about feeding their children and at the same time provide less stimulating environments, both physically and intellectually. Thus, the association between the nutrient disorder and poorer development might not be a causal one; instead, each might be caused independently by family limitations.

In the clinical trials of iron deficiency anemia and iron treatment, a consistent pattern seemed to be emerging from studies of a routine course of treatment. Not only had the majority of iron-deficient anemic infants continued to receive lower developmental test scores despite 2 to 3 months of treatment and excellent hematologic response to iron in the Costa Rica study, but similar results were obtained in studies in the United Kingdom (10) and Chile (5). However, a recent study by Idjradinata and Pollitt in Indonesia (6) has reopened the question of effective reversal of test score deficits with iron treatment. In a double-blind randomized trial, 12- to 18-month-old infants (50 iron-deficient anemic, 29 nonanemic iron-deficient, and 47 iron-sufficient babies) were assigned within iron status group to oral iron or placebo treatment for 4 months. Before treatment the mean mental and motor scores of the iron-deficient infants were 12 to 15 points lower than those of nonanemic iron-deficient and iron-sufficient groups. Iron-treated anemic infants dramatically improved their mental and motor test scores (+19 points and +23 points, respectively) compared to no change in placebo-treated anemic infants. There was no evidence of lower test scores in nonanemic iron-deficient infants and no effect of iron treatment on test scores in either the nonanemic iron-deficient or iron-sufficient groups. However, the marked improvement in test scores of iron-deficient anemic infants treated with iron provided convincing evidence that iron deficiency anemia in infancy can cause lower developmental test scores.

One possible explanation for improvement in the Indonesia study and lack of clear-cut effects in previous studies was the longer course of iron treatment (4 months). In a new study in Costa Rica in collaboration with the Hospital Nacional de Niños, we assessed the effects of 6 months of oral iron treatment (7). This community study of 12- to 23-month-old infants compared 32 babies with moderate iron deficiency anemia (Hb ≤ 100 g/liter) with 54 nonanemic controls (Hb ≥ 125 g/liter). The iron-deficient anemic group averaged 6 points lower in mental test scores than the nonanemic group. No differences in motor scores were observed. All anemic infants were treated with oral iron for 6 months. Nonanemic infants were randomly assigned to oral iron or placebo treatment, but there was no difference between the two conditions with respect to test score change; all nonanemic infants could therefore constitute a single comparison group. Anemic infants continued to receive lower mental test scores after 3 and 6 months despite an excellent hematologic response with correction of anemia in all infants and iron sufficiency in 71% at both 3 and 6 months.

The seriousness of the challenges presented by the confluence of nutritional and environmental disadvantage is further illustrated by this study. Once again there were differences in family background—in this case lower levels of maternal education, lower HOME scores, and less breast-feeding (7). However, in contrast to the previous study in Costa Rica, developmental test score differences were no longer statistically significant after control for the background factors. In trying to understand the differing results, I became very aware of the issue of power with respect to environmental factors. Power analysis indicated that the sample size was adequate (90% power) to detect a simple main effect but could only have detected a considerably bigger difference (11 points) between anemic and nonanemic groups after control for background variables. Thus, one lesson about environmental factors from this new study is that the sample size necessary to have sufficient power to determine a simple main effect is much smaller than the sample size necessary to be able to identify a main effect after control for a range of environmental factors. I certainly have not considered that problem in the power calculations I have generally used in designing studies.

Given the uncertainty about the reversibility of test score differences with iron treatment, an important related question is whether preventing iron deficiency will prevent poorer developmental test performance. Two preventive trials have been published, and a third large trial is near completion in Chile. The first, by Heywood *et al.* in Papua New Guinea (20), compared 1-year-olds, half of whom received intramuscular iron at 2 months and half a placebo injection. Although the design of the study was strong, the results are difficult to interpret because malaria was endemic, all groups were anemic at 12 months, and iron status measures did not clearly indicate iron deficiency. However, it seemed that iron-treated infants who were malaria-negative showed better attentional abilities. The other preventive trial, recently published by Moffatt *et al.* (21), included 283 Native American infants in

Canada, half of whom received iron-fortified formula and half received unfortified formula from birth, with follow-up until 15 months. The groups were initially compa-rable in iron status, development, and family background but diverged in hemoglo-bin, iron status, and psychomotor test scores at 9 and 12 months, with poorer outcome in the unfortified group. Because of its design, this study also provides convincing evidence that iron deficiency causes lower test scores in infancy. Two findings qualify this conclusion, however: (a) no differences in mental scores were noted, even though they have been consistently found in virtually all case-control studies; (b) the differences in motor scores resolved spontaneously by 15 months. These observations raise the possibility that some other factor explains the differences in mental and motor development in iron-deficient anemic infants.

The third preventive trial, almost completed in Chile, was designed to address the question of a causal relationship between iron deficiency anemia and poorer developmental outcome. It is a double-blind randomized study of preventing iron deficiency through the use of iron supplementation, starting at 6 months of age. There are several reasons for this study design: (a) by the process of random alloca-tion, children at most environmental risk would be equally represented in the supple-mented and unsupplemented groups; (b) by starting the trial at an early age and excluding infants with iron deficiency anemia at the outset, infants would not yet be iron-deficient, and the confounding effects of nutrient deficiency and environmental disadvantage would not yet have occurred. This study has involved 1185 children. (The sample size had to be very large because only 20% to 25% of the unsupple-mented children were expected to develop iron deficiency anemia. Because they are the only ones likely to show lower scores, the overall group difference between supplemented and unsupplemented children would be quite small and hence require a large sample to be detected with confidence.)

What we are finding is surprising (22). The supplemented and unsupplemented children are very different in iron status but do not differ in developmental test scores. These results highlight two issues in particular. Once again, the study raises the possibility that any differences in previous studies are not caused by iron defi-ciency itself but by some other closely associated factor, or by iron deficiency only under certain conditions. For instance, results of a second component of the study, showing evidence of altered neurophysiological variables in 6-month-olds with iron deficiency anemia (23), suggest that factors such as the timing and duration of iron deficiency anemia may be critical. The results of the preventive trial also raise the possibility that when iron status is experimentally manipulated rather than being a product of family decisions, the relationship to developmental test performance is different.

Out of these experiences, I have become increasingly convinced that the issue of environmental disadvantage is a major dilemma for studies of nutritional deficiencies. Figure 3 is a conceptual model of my current thinking about the interrelationship among environmental disadvantage, nutrient deficiency, and poorer developmental outcome in infants (24,25). On the left side of the figure are the more biological explanations that focus on the baby. There is a reduction

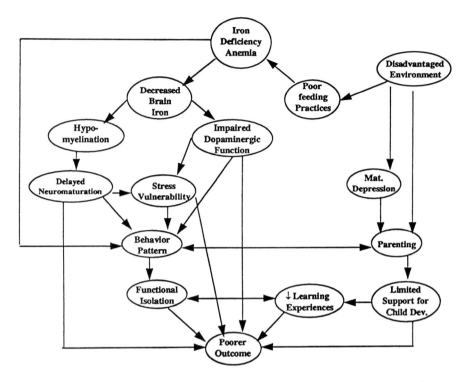

FIG. 3. A conceptual model of the mechanisms accounting for poorer development in iron-deficient anemic infants (25), reproduced with permission.

in brain iron when iron deficiency anemia occurs early in development (26), with concomitant alterations in myelination and neurotransmitter function contributing to stress vulnerability and delayed neuromaturation (23). These combine to produce an altered behavior pattern—increased wariness and proximity seeking and decreased activity (24). On the right side of the figure are the environmental/familial influences. Environmental disadvantage might contribute to poor feeding practices, such as early weaning and use of unmodified cow's milk. Other effects of environmental disadvantage might be mediated through parenting behavior (perhaps through maternal stress and depression). One would expect transactional relationships between the child's behavior pattern and limitations in parenting behavior, such that there would be less support for the child's development, contributing to decreased learning experiences. Again, one would expect transactional relationships between functional isolation as a result of the child's behavior (27,28) and the decreased support of the child's development because of environmental disadvantage. Collectively, these influences would lead to poorer outcome for iron-deficient anemic infants. Such a model provides a useful framework for thinking about how a nutritional deficiency could fit together with environmental disadvantage to produce poorer developmental outcome in affected infants.

I have touched on only a few of the issues of environmental factors in research on nutrient deficiencies and infant development. There are many other concerns. For instance, even though having a model helps guide the choice of factors one should try to assess, measuring the relevant environmental influences is truly challenging. Deciding the right things to measure is also of critical importance in assessing whether differential attrition might affect results, whether the groups in a clinical trial are really comparable, and so on. Furthermore, an intervention might be effective only under certain environmental conditions (for example, the most or the least advantaged environments) or only in infants with certain characteristics (for example, relatively younger or older; at biological risk because of birth weight or health problems; or completely free of health concerns). Finally, there are many methodologic and statistical issues related to confounding and mediating variables. Several recent papers provide thoughtful discussions of these subjects (29–33). In any case, the issues related to environmental factors require expert methodologic advice at all stages, but especially in relation to study design, selection of measures, data analysis, and interpretation.

In sum, researchers in infant nutrition should expect that nutrient deficiencies will go along with environmental disadvantage. Even if we use statistical control for these environmental differences, I am convinced that the families are in fact different in ways that will influence their children's behavioral and developmental outcome. Rather than seeing this as a methodologic annoyance, I have come to think about this concurrence of environmental and nutritional risk as the reality in which children live. The challenge for researchers is to describe this reality in trying to understand what places children at risk and what components are most amenable to intervention.

Acknowledgments

This work was supported in parts by grants from the National Institutes of Health (HD14122 and 31606). I also appreciate the thoughtful ideas of Sandra Jacobson, Ph.D., Department of Psychology, Wayne State University, about the general issues of environmental factors in research on risk factors and infant development.

REFERENCES

1. Lozoff B, Brittenham GM, Viteri FE, Wolf AW, Urrutia JJ. The effects of short-term oral iron therapy on developmental deficits in iron deficient anemic infants. *J Pediatr* 1982;100:351–357.
2. Walter T, Kovalskys J, Stekel A. Effect of mild iron deficiency on infant mental development scores. *J Pediatr* 1983;102:519–522.
3. Grindulis H, Scott PH, Belton NR, Wharton BA. Combined deficiency of iron and vitamin D in Asian toddlers. *Arch Dis Child* 1986;61:843–848.
4. Lozoff B, Brittenham GM, Wolf AW, *et al.* Iron deficiency anemia and iron therapy: effects on infant developmental test performance. *Pediatrics* 1987;79:981–995.
5. Walter T, de Andraca I, Chadud P, Perales CG. Iron deficiency anemia: adverse effects on infant psychomotor development. *Pediatrics* 1989;84:7–17.
6. Idjradinata P, Pollitt E. Reversal of developmental delays in iron-deficient anaemic infants treated with iron. *Lancet* 1993;341:1–4.

7. Lozoff B, Wolf AW, Jimenez E. Effects of extended oral-iron therapy on infant developmental test scores. *J Pediatr* 1996;129:383–389.
8. Oski FA, Honig AS, Helu B, Howanitz P. Effect of iron therapy on behavior performance in nonanemic, iron-deficient infants. *Pediatrics* 1983;71:877–880.
9. Oski FA, Honig AS. The effects of therapy on the developmental scores of iron-deficient infants. *J Pediatr* 1978;92:21–25.
10. Aukett MA, Parks YA, Scott PH, Wharton BA. Treatment with iron increases weight gain and psychomotor development. *Arch Dis Child* 1986;61:849–857.
11. Lozoff B. Developmental deficits in iron deficient infants: effects of age and severity of iron lack. *J Pediatr* 1982;101:948–952.
12. Caldwell BM, Bradley RH. *Home observation for measurement of the environment,* rev ed. Little Rock: University of Arkansas, 1984.
13. Lozoff B. Has iron deficiency been shown to cause altered behavior in infants? In: Dobbing J, ed. *Brain, behavior, and iron in infant diet.* London: Springer-Verlag, 1990:107–131.
14. Lozoff B. Nutrition and behavior. *Am Psychol* 1989;4:231–236.
15. Wachs TD. Environment and the development of disadvantaged children. In: Karp RJ, ed. *Malnourished children in the United States caught in the cycle of poverty.* New York: Springer, 1993:13–30.
16. Czaika-Narins DM, Haddy TB, Kallen DJ. Nutrition and social correlates in iron deficiency anemia. *Am J Clin Nutr* 1978;31:955–960.
17. Owen GM, Lubin AH, Garry PJ. Preschool children in the United States: who has iron deficiency? *J Pediatr* 1971;79:563–568.
18. Zee P, DeLeon M, Roberson P, Chen CH. Nutritional improvement of poor urban preschool children. *JAMA* 1985;253:3269–3272.
19. Life Sciences Research Office. *Assessment of the iron nutrition status of the U.S. population based on data collected in the Second National Health and Nutrition Survey, 1976–1980.* Bethesda, MD: Federation of American Societies for Experimental Biology, 1984.
20. Heywood A, Oppenheimer S, Heywood P, Jolley D. Behavioral effects of iron supplementation in infants in Madang, Papua New Guinea. *Am J Clin Nutr* 1989;50:S630–S640.
21. Moffatt MEK, Longstaffe S, Besant J, Dureski C. Prevention of iron deficiency and psychomotor decline in high risk infants through iron fortified infant formula: a randomized clinical trial. *J Pediatr* 1994;125:527–534.
22. Lozoff B, de Andraca I, Walter T, Pino P. Does preventing iron deficiency anemia (IDA) improve developmental test scores? [abstract]. *Pediatr Res* 1996;39:136A.
23. Roncagliolo M, Garrido M, Williamson A, Lozoff B, Peirano P. Delayed maturation of auditory brainstem responses in iron-deficient anemic infants [abstract]. *Pediatr Res* 1996;39.
24. Lozoff B, Klein NK, Nelson EC, McClish DK, Manuel M, Chacon ME. Behavior of infants with iron deficiency anemia. *Child Dev* (in press).
25. Lozoff B. Explanatory mechanisms for poorer development in iron-deficient anemic infants. In: Grantham McGregor S, ed. *Recent advances in research on the effects of health and nutrition on children's development and school achievement in the Third World.* Pan American Health Organization (in press).
26. Felt BT, Lozoff B. Brain iron and behavior of rats are not normalized by treatment of iron deficiency anemia during early development. *J Nutr* 1996;126:693–701.
27. Levitsky DA. *Malnutrition, environment, and behavior.* Ithaca, NY: Cornell University Press, 1979.
28. Pollitt E, Gorman KS, Engle PL, Martorell R, Rivera J. Early supplementary feeding and cognition. *Monogr Soc Res Child Dev* 1993;58:1–122.
29. Champoux JE, Peters WS. Form, effect size and power in moderated regression analysis. *J Occup Psychol* 1987;60:243–255.
30. Chaplin WF. The next generation of moderator research in personality psychology. *J Pers* 1991;59:143–178.
31. Jacobson JL, Jacobson SW. Methodological issues in human behavioral teratology. In: Rovee-Collier C, Lipsitt LP, eds. *Advances in infancy research,* 6th ed. Norwood, NJ: Ablex, 1990:111–148.
32. Jacobson JL, Jacobson SW. Methodological considerations in behavioral toxicology in infants and children. *Dev Psychol* 1996;32:390–403.
33. McClelland GH, Judd CM. Statistical difficulties of detecting interations and moderator effects. *Psychol Bull* 1993;114:376–390.

DISCUSSION

Dr. Hamburger: Would you go so far as to state that the anemia would make no difference if you really could remove all of the environmental defects?

Dr. Lozoff: I have not reached that conclusion. I would like to make several points about the absence of developmental test score differences in the preventive trial I described (1):

1. Other developmental measures, such as visual attention and motor milestones, have yet to be analyzed;
2. Previous studies in Guatemala and Costa Rica did not find Bayley test score differences at 12 months (the endpoint in the preventive trial) but showed lower scores in older anemic infants;
3. The entrance criteria were different in the preventive trial in Chile: the birth weight cutoff was 3 kg rather than 2.5 kg as in earlier studies, and babies with iron deficiency anemia at 6 months were excluded. Thus, it is possible that the results of previous studies were caused by the inclusion of children whose iron deficiency started earlier and lasted longer. Also, in Chile, all babies were initially breast-fed, whereas cow milk feeding was an important factor contributing to iron deficiency anemia in other samples;
4. Finally, and most importantly, another part of the study in Chile clearly indicates central nervous system effects of early iron deficiency anemia (2). We screened the children at 6 months for anemia and allowed only those with normal hemoglobin levels to enter the trial. The small proportion of children who met criteria for iron deficiency anemia at 6 months and a comparison group who had normal hemoglobin levels went into the neurophysiology part of the study. We found that infants with iron deficiency anemia showed altered nerve conduction in auditory brainstem responses, reduced vagal tone, immature cardiorespiratory control, and so on. So for the very first time in all my years of research, I think we have gotten close to effects on the brain, and the results really do fit with what is coming from the animal model.

Dr. Hamburger: Could it be that the early group were not really severely iron deficient? I noticed you used a 10 g/dl cutoff for hemoglobin. We begin to see problems when they get down around 6 to 8 g/dl, so I wonder if, perhaps, the iron deficiency wasn't severe enough to bring out these differences early on.

Dr. Lozoff: These were community studies in which we decided in advance that any child with a hemoglobin below 6 g/dl would be treated immediately; we wouldn't allow even a week's wait. But we never saw a child with a hemoglobin that low. In fact, the lowest hemoglobin in all of the hundreds of children that we looked at was 7.8 g/dl. However, the average hemoglobin level of anemic infants in the Chile study was very similar to that in our previous studies in Guatemala and Costa Rica, where we did see test score differences.

Dr. Haschke: Is it possible that you found no difference because you eliminated all the severely anemic children from the study?

Dr. Lozoff: In the big NIH study that we are talking about, out of several thousand we screened, only about 2% had iron deficiency anemia at 6 months. Physiologically, it should be uncommon, and it was in fact uncommon. But the problem was still there, and there is still the question whether early iron deficiency could have influenced some of the results in other studies. Chronicity and severity are factors that we haven't had adequate control over in the past. In the preventive trial that I have described here, we know the maximum duration. It can't ever have been more than 6 months because we had hematologic screening at 6-month intervals.

Unidentified participant: The question from the audience is whether the effects are caused by anemia or iron deficiency. Would it be possible to design a matched-pair study comparing thalassemia minor patients with iron-deficient patients based on age, body weight, and hemoglobin? Has anybody done this or has such an approach been considered?

Dr. Lozoff: People have tried to look at this. There are studies looking at children with sickle cell anemia or sickle-C disease (summarized in ref. 3), but they are not particularly good, partly because those who are anemic to the degree we are talking about often have some other problems. The sicklers do have poorer school performance, but no particular cognitive deficits have been identified. I have not seen a study of thalassemia.

Dr. Lucas: We have just started the analysis of a randomized preventive trial on about 450 subjects, which we started at 9 months of age. These were all subjects whose mothers had decided to put them on cow's milk, and we randomly assigned them to stay on cow's milk and to be put on a formula with iron or a formula without iron until 18 months. Iron screening is not routine in Britain, so we were allowed to do this without prior screening because that would have been normal practice. So all the subjects were included regardless of their initial iron status, and presumably there would be quite a few anemic children at 9 months. And again, like Dr. Lozoff, we found absolutely no difference in cognitive scores or in growth between the randomized groups at 18 months. We are at a preliminary stage of analysis, and we haven't got subgroup analyses and so forth, but what is interesting here is that now, we have two randomized studies with 1600 or 1700 children that have gone right in the face of a large amount of existing philosophy on the importance of iron in infant nutrition.

Dr. Hamburger: What level of iron deficiency are you talking about?

Dr. Lucas: We are in the middle of documenting that, but we know from the big national survey that we have done that the incidence of iron deficiency anemia in Britain is about 10% to 15%, and the incidence of low ferritin is around 30% to 40%. So we assume that we are going to be in that range.

Dr. Lozoff: I only learned of this study by coming to this meeting, so this has been very exciting. I thought our study in Chile (1) had produced results that were so at variance with perceived wisdom. The fact that Dr. Lucas has got very similar results in an industrialized society and has also extended the developmental range to 18 months makes the results all the stronger.

Dr. Lucas: Dr. Aggett's department has been looking at the iron status of these children. The preliminary results, and these are very preliminary, suggest—as you've shown—that iron supplementation does make a difference to iron status, so there is an effect on iron status, but it has no corresponding effect on growth and neurodevelopment. This is the power of randomized studies as opposed to epidemiologic ones in confounded research.

Dr. Lozoff: What was the birth weight cutoff in your study?

Dr. Lucas: They were normal term infants.

Dr. Rey: I was always very surprised by the notion of checking mental or motor development after only 8 days of iron supplementation. In your conceptual model, you spoke about the turnover of iron in rat brain being very slow, so if iron deficiency were to have an effect on mental performance, we would expect a long time interval before we saw anything. And in fact, you say now that you observed absolutely no difference. But I recall you published a paper in the *New England Journal of Medicine* a few years ago in which you said that there were some differences between the two groups (4). I am surprised at this. Can you comment?

Dr. Lozoff: First about the short-term studies. Oski argued that if we wanted to detect effects on the brain, we should be looking before there was a change in hemoglobin, at a time when you would be seeing an effect on CNS enzymes. That was the rationale. In addition, he had done two studies showing very rapid changes. Having myself been involved with two studies trying to replicate those results, both of which were negative, I am no longer concerned with that question. Instead, we have focused on the clinical question of what happens if you treat iron deficiency anemia with a full course of iron. With regard to brain iron, it isn't only a question of turnover, it's a question of timing. Barbara Felt looked at this issue in the rat model as part of a behavioral pediatrics fellowship. Her work was published last year in the *Journal of Nutrition* (5). She pointed out that earlier studies showing lower brain iron in iron deficiency anemia in the rat had involved postnatal iron deficiency. Her question was, suppose that the period of iron deficiency and its treatment were earlier in development—might there be a time when brain iron deficit could be reversed? She studied four groups—early gestation, late gestation, early lactation, and late lactation—and there was a deficit in brain iron in all groups, even in the early gestation group, where iron deficiency had been corrected during gestation. We are talking about a 27% to 33% deficit in brain iron here, and the evidence we have so far is that it cannot be corrected by treatment.

With regard to your question about the *New England Journal of Medicine* paper, we are talking about two different studies. The *New England Journal of Medicine* paper was a follow-up of the Costa Rican children, comparing formerly anemic children with the rest of the sample. That was a study where there were several environmental differences, which we controlled statistically. The conclusion to that paper, which I still hold by, was that iron deficiency anemia identifies children at risk for long lasting developmental disadvantage. But did iron deficiency anemia cause the developmental differences? That particular study can never say that the developmental differences were caused solely by iron deficiency anemia. The new study was a preventive trial in which environmental factors were randomly allocated. That could tell us about causality, if differences are found.

Dr. Uauy: In your study, did you identify other home factors or social factors that affected development, and was there interaction with iron status in any way, despite the fact that it was randomized to iron treatment?

Dr. Lozoff: Where we have done the background analyses to the point of satisfaction is in the Costa Rican study. For the Chilean randomized trial, we are awaiting the analyses. For the Costa Rica study, yes, there was a substantial correlation between the HOME score and later development, of the order of 0.3 or 0.4, which is what the home environment typically does, and of course, we have a relation between lower HOME scores and iron deficiency anemia. So this is an interconnected set. I expect to see such relationships in Chile as well.

Dr. Perman: Did you ever look directly at the route of administration? I realize that the iron must be getting absorbed because you were correcting the iron deficiency, but did you study this?

Dr. Lozoff: In this same Costa Rica study, the iron-deficient children with low hemoglobins were randomly allocated to placebo, oral iron, or intramuscular iron in the short term. There was no difference between oral and intramuscular iron. After 1 week, the children on placebo were also treated with oral iron. For the 3-month follow-up, we had children who were just on intramuscular iron and children who were just on oral iron. The only difference was that the iron status of children on oral iron was better than that in those on intramuscular iron. We gave the IM group enough iron to bring the hemoglobin level up to 12.5, while the oral iron group ended the study with hemoglobin levels higher than that.

Dr. Uauy: Very briefly, what is the policy implication of your finding?

Dr. Lozoff: It is hard to argue that having iron deficiency anemia is a good thing for children. On those grounds, I continue to be very comfortable with the idea that prevention is the safest course. But if you are tackling the question of scarce resources and public health priorities, then I would have to say, at present, that I do not think we have the scientific evidence to inform public policy.

Dr. Hamburger: I don't think there is anything radical about the notion that a bad environment contributes to a bad outcome, whether or not you have confounding variables. I think we are looking at this through the narrow vision of people who have to do clinical studies and therefore see poverty, ignorance, filth, and so on. I really don't think that we should be all that surprised that they feed into each other and help to produce that kind of result.

Dr. Lozoff: Nevertheless, around the world, Health Departments are making decisions about iron fortification and iron supplementation. Those decisions are going to affect resources that might go toward relieving some conditions underlying poverty and disadvantage. So, there are real public policy decisions that depend on these trials.

Dr. Sorensen: You mentioned that all these children were healthy, but at 6 to 12 months old, children are rarely entirely healthy, especially in Santiago! They are likely to have had a lot of respiratory infections at the very least, and I wonder if you factored those things in. Such factors are likely to set some children back in their development.

Dr. Lozoff: In both studies, the Costa Rican and the Chilean, we did home monitoring of infections in a prospective fashion. In Costa Rica, we had daily records, and in Chile, we had weekly records. I haven't yet looked at the Chilean data. However, the mean developmental scores of the Chilean children were absolutely average for the standard sample used in the Bayley test. So we do not have any evidence, either for Costa Rica or Chile, that the children were developmentally behind U.S. children.

Dr. Whitehead: This will be the chapter I remember because I think it contains some really salutary results. I would also like to congratulate the organizers of the meeting for deciding to put this paper in at this point. I think there would have been a danger of us going away a bit self-satisfied. We have got to accept that there are a large number of confounding variables, things we don't know anything about, things that perhaps science doesn't yet know anything about, which we clearly can't standardize for. I think that is the main message that you are putting across. I would like to add one more thing that is going to be increasingly important in community studies, and that is gene polymorphism. Once we can really get to terms with that subject, I think it is going to revolutionize our approach, both at national and international level.

Dr. Lucas: I want to explore this message further. What we have discovered today is that environmental factors seriously confound epidemiologic studies in nutrition. We have discussed the number of them—we have discussed the way they confound iron studies, general malnutrition studies, the comparison of breast- and bottle-fed babies, Barker's data, and so forth. The question is whether you feel that your randomized trial, which should equalize out all these factors, actually does take care of the environmental confounders and factors them out. Do you actually feel that the environmental entanglements you showed in your complex diagram have been taken out of the equation to a large extent by randomization, or do you think they are still there?

Dr. Lozoff: I wanted to make the point that all of the studies I showed you were randomized clinical trials. The last one was a preventive trial. In the other ones, they were treatment trials. Had we shown a treatment effect, we could have argued that environmental factors had been taken care of, because children were randomly allocated to treatment or placebo. But there are lots of treatment studies in which, even though they begin out as randomized controlled trials, you don't see a treatment effect, and then, all the environmental issues come up again. In the preventive trial, we certainly saw an effect of iron supplementation on hematologic status, but we didn't see any effect on development. We then went into the data again and looked at just the anemic children compared to the nonanemic children in the no-iron group—that would have been the equivalent of the eight earlier studies that made such comparisons. Children with iron deficiency anemia from the no-iron arm of the preventive trial did not have lower developmental test scores than the nonanemic children. So there is something different about this study. I am not satisfied that we can simply say that environmental factors are irrelevant; within this trial, the environmental factors were randomly allocated, but that doesn't mean environmental influences are unimportant.

REFERENCES

1. Lozoff B, de Andraca I, Walter T, Pino P. Does preventing iron-deficiency anemia (IDA) improve developmental test scores? *Pediatr Res* 1996;39:136A.
2. Roncagliolo M, Garrido M, Williamson A, *et al.* Delayed maturation of auditory brainstem responses in iron-deficient anemic infants. *Pediatr Res* 1996;39:20A.
3. Nettles AL. Scholastic performance of children with sickle cell disease. *J Health Soc Policy* 1994;5: 123–140.
4. Lozoff B, Jimenez E, Wolf AW. Long-term developmental outcome of infants with iron deficiency. *N Engl J Med* 1991;325:687–694.
5. Felt BT, Lozoff B. Brain iron and behavior of rats are not normalized by treatment of iron deficiency anemia during early development. *J Nutr* 1996;126:693–701.

Clinical Trials in Infant Nutrition, edited by
Jay A. Perman and Jean Rey, Nestlé Nutrition
Workshop Series, Vol. 40, Nestec Ltd.,
Vevey/Lippincott-Raven Publishers,
Philadelphia © 1998.

Health Claims for Infant Formulas and Foods: U.S. Regulations

Elisabeth A. Yetley

*Center for Food Safety and Applied Nutrition, U.S. Food and Drug Administration,
Washington DC, USA*

Food label claims are statements on a product label or in accompanying materials such as consumer brochures or information manuals for health care professionals. Health claims, one type of food label claim, describe the relationship between a food substance and a disease or health-related condition. Their use must be consistent with FDA regulations. Sound science is an essential component in making decisions to permit health claims. In this chapter, I highlight some of the issues that commonly arise in the decision-making process whereby sound scientific principles and evidence are integrated into the general regulatory requirements for health claims. I also discuss some of the specific and unique challenges in applying general health claim principles to infant formulas and foods.

LABEL CLAIMS: GENERAL REGULATORY FRAMEWORK

There are two regulatory categories for infant formulas in the United States. One category is "regular" infant formula—products intended for use by the general population of healthy infants. These formulas must be nutritionally complete and be capable of supporting healthy growth in infants when consumed as the sole source of nutriture during the first year of life. The other regulatory category is "exempt" infant formula. Exempt formulas are intended for use by infants with inborn errors of metabolism, low birth weight, or with other unusual medical or dietary problems. An example would be products specifically formulated to be low in or free of the amino acid phenylalanine for use by infants with phenylketonuria (PKU). These types of formulas may need to be exempted from some of the nutritional requirements for the general population of healthy infants because of special nutritional or dietary management needs of infants with medical and health conditions. Additionally, because these formulas may not meet the nutritional needs of healthy infants, they could pose a safety concern if not used under close medical supervision.

For the purposes of this discussion, "infant foods" include foods intended for use by infants and toddlers less than 2 years of age. Infant foods may be intended for use by the general population of healthy infants (e.g., infant cereals and juices). Additionally, some infant foods may be specifically designed to be used in the dietary management of a disease or health-related condition that has distinctive nutritional requirements. These latter types of infant foods are regulated as "medical foods" and must be used under close medical supervision.

Label claims for infant formulas and foods come under general food law requirements that label information be "truthful and not misleading." This means that not only must a label statement be truthful, but the statement may also need to include "material" information that is necessary to prevent a truthful statement from being misunderstood by consumers. For example, a statement on a regular infant formula that the formula meets 100% of the calcium requirement of an infant, or that it has more calcium than other infant formula products, although factual, would be misleading without a clear indication that all infant formulas have adequate calcium to meet the nutritional needs of infants and that calcium intakes significantly in excess of the requirements do not provide any added benefit and may, under certain conditions, cause harm.

Several types of label claims on infant formulas and foods also come under the Nutrition Labeling and Education Act (NLEA). This is the 1990 amendment to the Food, Drug and Cosmetic Act (hereinafter, the act) that governs, among other things, nutrient content claims (e.g., "high protein" or "low fat") and health claims (e.g., "diets low in sodium may reduce your risk of hypertension") on foods for the general population. Health claims can be made only when the FDA has promulgated regulations and the claim meets specified criteria, such as: use of defined terms, prescribed message components, and the conditions that a food must meet before it is eligible to bear a claim. There is a petition process by which an interested person can request that the FDA amend existing or authorize new health or nutrient content claim regulations.

Infant formulas and foods, to bear nutrient content and health claims, must follow the same general principles as foods for the general population. However, NLEA-type health claims for foods for the general population cannot be used on infant formulas and foods unless they have been specifically authorized for these foods. For example, the authorized health claim for sodium and hypertension cannot be used on infant formulas and foods because there is no specific provision in the authorizing regulation for its use on products marketed for infants.

In this chapter, I limit my discussion to NLEA-type health claims for "regular" infant formulas intended for use by healthy, full-term infants and to those infant foods marketed for the general population of healthy infants. To date, there are no authorizing regulations for health claims for infant formulas and foods under the NLEA provisions of the act. Claims on exempt infant formulas and medical foods are outside the scope of this chapter, because they are exempted from NLEA requirements. Additionally, claims that a product is useful in the diagnosis, cure, treatment, mitigation, or prevention of a disease could cause a product to be regulated as a drug and are also outside the scope of this chapter.

HEALTH CLAIMS: GENERAL ISSUES

What is a health claim under NLEA? A health claim has two components: the food substance that is the subject of the claim and the disease or health-related condition that is affected by consumption of the food substance. Reference to the disease or health-related condition may be explicitly stated or implied through use of symbols or other means. Examples of implicit claims include "third party" endorsements (e.g., the American Heart Association recommends . . .), written statements (e.g., a brand name including a term such as "heart healthy"), symbols (e.g., a picture of a heart), or vignettes that would likely be understood to assert a claimed benefit for the product.

The scientific standard that a food substance/disease relationship must meet to be authorized for use as a health claim is defined as "significant scientific agreement, among experts qualified by scientific training and experience to evaluate such claims, that the claim is supported by such evidence." This agreement must be based on the totality of the available scientific evidence. Any data that are used to develop this regulation must be publicly available. The underlying scientific evidence does not have to be in peer-reviewed journals, but it must be in the public domain and available through the FDA's public docket when a regulation is proposed or finalized. Review of a potential health claim topic can be initiated through action of the Food and Drug Administration or, more commonly, by a petition from an interested person.

To understand health claims for infant formulas and foods, it is necessary to understand health claims as applied to foods for the general U.S. population. Health claims on foods differ in several ways from the dietary management/special nutritional needs claims of medical foods/exempt infant formulas and disease-related drug claims. Food health claims usually describe risk-reduction benefits for the general population of healthy people. With health claims, the food substance/disease relationship must be described within the context of a total daily diet (e.g., diets low in fat may reduce the risk of some types of cancer). Intakes needed to achieve the expected benefit do not need to be provided by a single serving of a food or single product but can be achieved by selecting multiple servings from "good sources" of the targeted substance (i.e., more than 10% of the RDI per reference serving) if that substance is a "positive nutrient" (e.g., calcium) or "low" sources of a "negative nutrient" (e.g., fat).

For food health claims, the expected benefit is often a future benefit, delayed in its effect (e.g., high calcium intakes in adolescent years may reduce the risk of osteoporosis in later years). The expected benefit often applies to some but not all persons. For example, with the fat and cancer health claim, not all persons are at equal risk of cancer, and not all cancer risks are responsive to lowered intakes of fat. Thus, the number of persons benefiting from a low-fat diet with respect to development of cancer is likely smaller than the number of persons following the general dietary guidance to consume low-fat diets for this purpose. Indeed, without practical ways for consumers to identify their risks and individual responsiveness to dietary guidelines, most health claims are broad-brushed, encouraging dietary modifications for the general population. Conversely, for medical foods/exempt infant formulas and drugs, use is generally targeted to those persons who exhibit the signs and symptoms associated with a disease or health condition. Persons unlikely to benefit are not likely to be exposed to the substance of interest.

HEALTH CLAIMS: INFANT FORMULAS AND FOODS

There are unique characteristics of regular infant formulas that raise questions about how best to apply the NLEA health claims provisions to these formulas. In the United States, we have requirements that all regular infant formulas meet certain nutrient composition and bioavailability criteria. All of these formulas are required by regulation to meet the nutritional needs of rapidly growing infants when consumed as the sole source of nutrition. Therefore, the question arises: If health claims would give some infant formulas "specialness" over other marketed formulas because of a contained substance that is claimed to have advantages relative to an infant's risk of a disease or health condition, what should the substances be? If all marketed formulas are nutritionally adequate, does that mean that health claims should be used only for substances other than essential nutrients? If health claims are focused primarily on reduction in risk of future health problems or disease conditions, what role do they serve in infant formulas? At this time, one can only speculate as to the kinds of conditions that might be forwarded as possible topics for health claims on infant formulas and foods because, to date, the FDA has not received any petitions for these claims. Would it be appropriate to allow health claims on infant formulas containing substances that will reduce the risk (i.e., incidence, severity, or duration) of common infant illnesses (e.g., childhood viruses, ear infections, or diarrhea) or decrease the likelihood of developing or delay the onset or severity of food intolerances and sensitivities (e.g., protein allergies)? Are health claims appropriate for other common conditions of young infants (e.g., colic, spitting-up, and regurgitation)? These issues will undoubtedly provoke considerable debate in the next few years.

One question in reviewing health claims for infant formulas and foods will be an identification of who will benefit? If there is convincing substantiation that the food substance/disease relationship is valid and there are no unresolved safety concerns, there are at least four possible scenarios as to who benefits. The first is the case where all infants would benefit. In this case, the health claim needs to be authorized expeditiously because failure to do so would deny provision of an optimum formula. However, this scenario also suggests that the regulatory nutrient requirements for all infant formulas be revised to require mandatory addition of the documented beneficial substance to all marketed formulas. Moreover, if the result is that all infant formulas must contain the substance of interest, this quickly becomes a situation where a health claim is inappropriate because it implies differences among formulas that are no longer the case.

The second possible scenario is that there is no demonstrable benefit under the conditions in which the formula would be used, but there are data from quite different conditions of use (e.g., higher-risk subgroup or larger intakes). To implement a heath claim under these conditions requires extrapolation of results from one condition to a quite different, more general condition of use. Extrapolations of this type, although requiring a great deal of judgment, are commonly encountered challenges, particularly where it may be impractical or costly to substantiate a benefit under conditions that more closely mimic actual use. The key need is to define what principles and criteria should be followed for making data extrapolations from one context to another when evaluating the validity of a food substance/disease relationship for infant formulas and foods. This is currently, and is likely to remain, a very controversial issue.

The third possible scenario is the case where a subgroup of healthy infants would benefit, and health care providers or parents can accurately indentify those children. In this case, label information may be useful for targeting the groups that will benefit and those that will not benefit. To date, this scenario has been rarely encountered.

Finally, a common scenario is a subgroup of infants that is likely to benefit, but the health care providers or parents in that subgroup cannot reliably identify their infants as responders or nonresponders. In this case, safety of exposure to the test substance must be documented for all infants, regardless of expected benefit, because all could be exposed.

SAFETY

A single formula product frequently serves as the sole source of nutrition for several months or more in young infants who are undergoing a very rapid and crucial period of growth and development. Additionally, the intake of infants and, consequently, the exposure of infants to substances in that formula, is higher on a per-kilogram body weight basis than at any other stage of the life cycle. With these high exposures and developmental vulnerabilities, there is simply no room for error. We can't allow a claim that would cause a manufacturer to be motivated to make an unsafe product. We also cannot allow a claim that would motivate parents to use a product in an unsafe way. Unlike foods consumed as part of a mixed diet by adults, infant formulas and foods have a much narrower tolerance for mistakes. Consequently, safety evaluations done for ingredients for the general food supply may need to be reexamined for infant use because of the higher exposures and more immature physiological systems of young infants.

Potential safety concerns should be resolved before health claim topics are evaluated. Often, people tend to address the possible benefits and give relatively little attention to safety questions. However, it cannot be assumed that a study designed to show benefit is an adequate basis to establish safety. For example, a larger sample size is often needed to document safety than to document a benefit. Moreover, safety problems may be undetected or undocumented if the study design and conduct fail to identify and systematically monitor endpoints related to safety.

Safety concerns are of two types: (a) the ingredient source that provides the substance of interest and (b) the substance that is being added for a particular benefit.

Nutrients and beneficial food substances are rarely added solely as nutrients or isolated substances. Rather, they are added as food ingredients that contain other substances. Sometimes, a nutrient is the major component of the source material (e.g., vitamin B_6 from pyridoxine hydrochloride). Sometimes, it is a minor component of the source material (e.g., linoleic acid in an oil ingredient). For ingredients' sources, a key question is what else comes with the targeted nutrient/substance? Many ingredients have a long history of use in infant formulas and raise no concerns. However, increasingly, manufacturers are interested in adding ingredients without a history of use. These ingredients may be produced by novel means or from novel sources (e.g., fungal/algal sources of LC-PUFAs) or may be added in fairly large amounts (e.g., oils, sources of fatty acids).

Ingredient additions rarely result in unidirectional change, i.e., in increasing the food substance of interest without changing anything else. The new ingredient frequently dilutes or replaces other ingredients and, as noted above, brings other substances with it. The new ingredient may change ratios among nutrients (e.g., among fatty acids or amino acids), may result in interactions that alter the bioavailability of the food substance or other nutrients/desired substances in the formula, or may displace another substance with an unrecognized benefit. Thus, to minimize the likelihood of unintended and unexpected adverse effects, adequate evaluation of safety is an essential prerequisite to health claim evaluations for infants.

The safety of the food substance *per se* may also need to be addressed. These are presumably biologically active substances, and, as such, they can produce benefit and/or risk. A frequent assumption is that adding a food substance to formula at the same level as is found in human milk is adequate assurance of safety. However, similar chemical composition does not necessarily equal biological equivalence in terms of both benefit and risk. For example, if infant formula is designed to contain the same level of iron as human milk, the infant would receive inadequate iron nutriture. If ratios among fatty acids are significantly modified, they may alter eicosanoid production, resulting in adverse effects on immune function. Thus, chemical equivalence of a food substance in a formula to human milk is a necessary part of the safety evaluation but may be an insufficient basis for evaluating safety. Biological effects in the consuming infant will also need to be evaluated.

SCIENTIFIC EVIDENCE

The nature of health claims (e.g., risk reduction or future benefit in currently healthy infants) presents scientific challenges that must be resolved with sound evidence. A current controversy relative to health claims on food products in the United States is what kind of research is needed, how many studies are needed, and how best to integrate information from different types of studies. These knotty questions will likely be debated for some time.

Science generally follows a continuum from hypothesis to consensus. The legal concept of "significant scientific agreement" occurs somewhere between these two poles. If we authorize health claims with very preliminary data, we will have many claims, but there will be little motivation for manufacturers to do more research. Thus, the state-of-the-art knowledge base likely will not progress beyond a very preliminary level. If health claims are prematurely authorized, the expected benefits may not be real, and parents will be misled. Moreover, if the data are preliminary, unexpected safety concerns may arise under conditions of widespread use. Conversely, if scientific standards are too high, it will be too costly to carry out the research, and this will discourage funding of research needed to substantiate new claims.

Regardless of the philosophical and legal arguments as to what types and numbers of studies are needed, available evidence relied on to make health claims decisions must be consistent with sound scientific principles of study design and conduct. In evaluating evidence from studies, including clinical trials, documentation of such elements as the randomization scheme, attrition rates and causes, adherence to study protocol, and long-term follow-up is essential for evaluating the quality of the science. Asking questions about these types of study issues doesn't mean that a drug standard is being imposed for food health claims. Good science is good science. It is not unique to drugs. The difference between foods and drugs should not be that food claims are allowed to be based on bad science while drug decisions must rely on good science. Rather, the differences between the underlying science for foods and drugs evolve from differences in the nature of the hypotheses posed, the test substances used, the target population and conditions of use, and the nature of the endpoints examined. Being able to describe elements of good study design and conduct is good science for health claims for foods as well as for drugs.

SUMMARY

Health claims are food label claims, authorized by regulation, that describe a relationship between a food substance and a disease or health-related condition. To date, no health claims have been considered for infant formulas and foods. In this chapter, the regulatory frameworks and some likely scientific challenges underlying the making of such future decisions are discussed.

REFERENCES

From the 21 Code of Federal Regulations

Part 101: Food Labeling
  Subpart A: General Provisions
    §101.14 Health claims: General Requirements.
Part 107: Infant Formula
  Subpart A: General Provisions
    §107.3 Definitions
  Subpart B: Labeling
    §107.10 Nutrient information

Subpart C: Exempt Infant Formulas
  §107.50 Terms and conditions
Subpart D: Nutrient Requirements
  §107.100 Nutrient specifications

From the *Federal Register*

Food labeling: general requirements for health claims for food. *FR* 58(3) 1993 (Jan 6):2478–2536.

DISCUSSION

Dr. Perman: To what extent is the process collaborative, and to what extent is it judgmental? And does it have to be judgmental and adversarial, even legalistic, by its rules and regulations?

Dr. Yetley: We have an open-door policy for persons who want to come in and talk with us. We also have very limited staff resources, so there is always a limitation on how much time we can spend with individuals. The process does have to occur by rule making, however. Once the petitioner has sent in a petition, the FDA has 100 days to decide whether or not to file the petition in the public docket. During this first 100 days, the petition remains confidential. Within this period of confidentiality, the FDA may inform the petitioner if the agency has particularly serious concerns about the quality or completeness of the petition. The petitioner then has the opportunity to withdraw the petition and consider resubmitting at a later date. By 100 days, however, a decision must be made by the FDA as to whether the petition is complete enough to be filed or whether it should be denied. If it is filed, then the petition becomes public. Ninety days later, the FDA has to either deny the petition or publish a proposed regulation. Once it is proposed, a regulation is open for public comment. The final regulation must address the issues raised in the comments received.

Dr. Uauy: The standards that are being applied now may be different from those that have been applied over the last decade or so. Do you undertake review of existing approvals, or is something that got in 10 years ago no longer subjected to review?

Dr. Yetley: Once the FDA has promulgated an authorizing regulation, it is published in the *Code of Federal Regulations.* Rule making is required to amend or delete it. The FDA would normally go back and review an existing health claim regulation only if there were significant new data. At this point, either the FDA or a petitioner could decide to reexamine the original decision and evaluate the need for revision. If the new data were compelling enough to determine that the original decision needed updating, the FDA would revise the existing regulation through rule making. I also note, however, that the legal authority and implementing regulations for health claims only came into place in January 1993. To date, there are no regulations for health claims for infant formulas and foods.

Dr. Iber: Could you speak of the use of outside consultants and the resources that you have in house to do these reviews if they are complex?

Dr. Yetley: We work very closely with other members of the Public Health Service, for example, with the National Institutes of Health, the Centers for Disease Control, and other Centers within the Food and Drug Administration. We also can go to the FDA Food Advisory Committee (or an *ad hoc* working group of that Committee) or contract with an external authoritative group (e.g., the Food and Nutrition Board of the Institute of Medicine). The use of individual outside consultants can also be done on an *ad hoc* basis but requires that they be brought on as special goverment employees. This means, among other things, that they must be free of conflicts of interest. It may also trigger requirements for open public meetings.

Dr. Whitehead: I wonder if you could just clarify for me how you decide whether or not something is going to be dealt with as a food or as a drug. For example, melatonin is an anomaly: it is sold in a small capsule but dealt with as a dietary supplement when it is quite clearly a drug. Also, how do you differentiate between a health claim and what one might call a medicinal claim? In other words, what happens if a product is added to a food that is supposed to either prevent a disease or indeed cure it? It seems to me there is quite a big difference between the American way of looking at this and that of the European Union.

Dr. Yetley: Under certain circumstances, melatonin is currently being marketed in the United States as a dietary supplement. As such, it is covered under the Dietary Supplement Health and Education Act, which allows dietary supplements to be marketed without any premarket approval or review by the agency, and which exempts ingredients in these products from FDA's food additive provisions, providing the supplement product is properly labeled and meets all applicable legal requirements. The legal requirements for dietary supplements differ significantly from requirements for infant formulas and foods. As for differentiating between a drug versus a food claim, if you have a product that is labeled "For the dietary management of diarrhea in infants," that product may be an exempt formula or a medical food because it is marketed for the dietary management of a disease and is to be used under close medical supervision because you are dealing with a sick child. If the claim is for "reducing the risk of diarrhea," the product is presumably for consumption by a healthy child, and there is the expectation that, at some time in the future, use of this product will be protective against getting the disease or will reduce the severity of the disease if it is contracted, then this product may be regulated as a food, perhaps as a regular infant formula for which a health claim must be authorized through rule making. Label information suggesting usefulness in the treatment, mitigation, cure, or prevention of a disease renders the product a drug, and it would be regulated under drug provisions of the law. Thus, it is the "intended use" of a product, as defined by accompanying label/labeling information from the manufacturer or retailer, that primarily determines the regulatory status of a product.

Dr. Rey: The FDA is in a very difficult situation with the law because it cannot oppose a claim for a dietary supplement unless it can prove that it causes harm. The burden of proof lies with the administration, not the producer. Have you authorized any health claims for regular infant formula?

Dr. Yetley: We have not received a petition for a health claim for an infant formula, and we have not authorized any such claims for infant products. Again, however, infant formulas are not under the same regulatory provisions as dietary supplements.

Dr. Lucas: The current interest in infant nutrition is no longer nutritional, in a sense. That is a slight exaggeration, but by and large, we know how to meet infant nutritional needs, and we have guidelines for ranges of nutrient intakes. The current excitement in the field is the impact of nutrition on health, that is, within that range of acceptable nutrients, we may in fact be altering long-term health outcomes in children. That type of research is expanding rapidly. It is highly likely that, in the future, a number of medical claims, which you have defined under FDA regulations as drug-type claims, will be made for infant food. I would reckon that for normal infant formulas, that is likely to happen in the next 5 years; it is already happening for specialized formulas. How equipped is the FDA to deal with that as it arises—for instance, modulation of the energy content of formulas could produce significant effects on later body composition that might have implications for obesity? How well are you going to be able to deal with proper randomized intervention research that meets all your criteria but that actually makes a drug-type claim for healthy infant foods in terms of disease prevention.

Dr. Yetley: I think this comes back to my earlier answer—that we will very quickly search out the necessary expertise from other sources; we have extensive expertise in the National Institutes of Health, in other branches of the Public Health Service, and in other FDA Centers. Experts from these agencies have been very helpful. We also have statutory deadlines to meet, so we have to get health claim petitions and infant formula notifications reviewed and done within the statutory time lines. It is the notifier's or petitioner's responsibility to collate and document the scientific evidence to facilitate FDA's review of new or modified infant formulas and health claim petitions. Moreover, all authorizations of heath claims are finalized through a public rule-making process in which FDA proposes an action and describes the basis for each of the proposed provisions. The proposal is then open for public comment. After the comment period, FDA finalizes the regulation based on acceptance or justified rejection of the public comments. This public notice and comment process, itself, can provide considerable input from scientists if they choose to participate.

Dr. Yolken: Formulas have additions and modifications that are based on the composition of breast milk. Does the FDA have any regulations or guidelines on the eventual advertising of claims concerning a formula's resemblance to breast milk?

Dr. Yetley: Advertising is controlled by the Federal Trade Commission rather than the FDA. There are really two issues here. One issue is the claim that says the formula is more like breast milk. This is really outside the health claim purview and falls into the "truthful and not misleading" criteria. The second issue is a scientific one, where the claim is that a formula product is improved over other similar products, and the improvement takes it nearer to breast milk in quality. This is a difficult scientific question in terms of what you use for a control group and how you evaluate the evidence. If you wanted to make a claim of this type, you would likely need to compare infants consuming your formula both to infants consuming the formula that is being replaced and to breast-fed infants.

Dr. Yolken: If advertising is dealt with by a different agency, is there any way in which you can try to make sure that health claims made in advertising balance the ones you have approved?

Dr. Yetley: The Federal Trade Commission regulates advertising, but FDA and FTC do coordinate on a number of issues. We have a memorandum of understanding to try to be as consistent as possible and as harmonious as possible in terms of how we deal with health claims and other nutrition labeling issues.

Dr. Clarke: To my mind, the ultimate health claim is that "breast-feeding provides the best nutrition for your baby," and, in compliance with the WHO code, we are required to claim this in Europe on every product label for infant formulas. I think that is a health claim, but philosophically, it is rather strange to have a health claim for a product which has no label attached to it. In Europe, we are required to have a very densely packed label stating the social and economic disadvantages of changing to infant formula feeding and so on. My question is, is soy formula considered to be exempt or not?

Dr. Yetley: Generally, soy formulas are considered to be regular formulas.

Dr. Rey: The directive that regulates infant formula in Europe was published in 1991, and we have accepted only six claims so far. These are all descriptive claims: "lactose-free," "sucrose-free," "lactose-only," "low-sodium," "iron-enriched," and "protein-adapted" (if the whey protein:casein ratio is not less than 1 and if the total amount of protein is less than 2.5 g/100 kcal). According to the directive 96/4/EC amending the directive 91/321/EEC, reference to ''reduced allergen or antigen'' properties is now allowed, but several conditions warranting the claim are required. For us, the major one is that the scientific evidence behind the claim should be available to the authorities. So if a company has made a large number of studies to demonstrate or try to demonstrate that the incidence of eczema is reduced with hypoallergenic formula, they can write on the label that the formula is adapted to decrease the incidence of allergy, but if the company has never made any studies to prove such an advantage, it should be under obligation to prove it.

Dr. Fairchild: Dr. Yetley, you talked about three different categories of infant formula claims—the exempt, the health claims, and regular formulas not making health claims—that would be judged on whether the claims were truthful and not misleading. In the area of health claims, we have a name for the standard of substantiation, we call it ''significant scientific agreement.'' In the other two areas, there is no name for the level of substantiation. I wonder if you could say something about the nature of the difference in the data you would expect to see in those three categories.

Dr. Yetley: There are no formal definitions or guidelines. Currently, these other claims are evaluated on a case-by-case basis.

Dr. Lucas: It seems to me that legislation is potentially out of key with what is about to happen or is happening in research in the field. Let us suppose, for instance, that two studies involving over 2000 babies had shown that iron improves neurodevelopment. A formula company involved in both studies could claim legitimately in scientific terms that a formula with iron improves neurodevelopment. As I understand it, legislation prevents that claim from being made in the United States. Why is that?

Dr. Yetley: That is not necessarily true. I don't know exactly how the agency would deal with a claim for neurodevelopment—whether we would call it a health-related condition, in which case it would be covered in the health claim rules, or whether we would deal with it under the ''truthful and not misleading'' provisions. In either case, the agency would look at the totality of the evidence and would ask what conclusions the qualified world experts would make with the same questions and the same available evidence.

Dr. Glinsmann: Because the infant formula may be the sole source of nutrition for the infant for a period of time, there should not be any formulas that are not supplemented with iron because iron is necessary for neural development. I think eventually the agency must rethink the composition of infant formulas and perhaps have that as a requirement.

Dr. Yetley: The information on the label has to be not only truthful, but not misleading, and it could be that if you simply said it was useful for neural development, it could be very misleading.

Dr. Rey: Dr. Glinsmann already has given a good answer to Dr. Lucas's question. If a nutrient improves the neurodevelopment of a child, it is mandatory to add this to the formula. But in the case of iron, there are two possibilities: the producer can add iron or not add iron in the formula, and if iron is added, he can say that iron is added to the formula. So I think the situation is very clear.

Dr. Przyrembel: There seems to be a major difference between claims on infant formulas in Europe and the United States. In Europe, it is sufficient to say there is iron in a formula, not that it is required for neurodevelopmental function and so on. We expect the people who want to buy it or the doctors who want to prescribe it to know the reasons for doing so. The same is true for LC-PUFAs. Nobody is allowed to say that LC-PUFAs are good for your brain or for your visual acuity.

Clinical Trials in Infant Nutrition, edited by
Jay A. Perman and Jean Rey, Nestlé Nutrition
Workshop Series, Vol. 40, Nestec Ltd.,
Vevey/Lippincott-Raven Publishers,
Philadelphia © 1998.

Regulation of Claims on Infant Foods in Canada

Margaret C. Cheney and Christina M. Zehaluk

Food Directorate, Health Protection Branch, Ottawa, Ontario, Canada

Because the only infant foods for which claims are made in Canada are infant formulas, I am going to discuss the different types of claims that we are encountering at present, our current regulatory system, and our thoughts on what changes need to be made to this system in the light of new developments in claims. In Canada, manufacturers are now more than ever competing for market share by means of claims. Claims for formulas are directed both to the health worker and to the consumer through a variety of advertising means. The fact that claims are being targeted to consumers indicates that the choice of formula is no longer dictated by the health worker. It is therefore essential that these claims be meaningful to the consumer as well as accurate. The health worker also relies on claims and indications for use when advising mothers on which formulas to use.

It is our experience in Canada that both consumers and health workers assume that the claims made for infant formulas have been validated and approved by the government. Claims for formulas may be divided into four categories.

The first type of claim is a description of the composition of the product, e.g., protein base, absence of lactose, which is useful in guiding health professionals in recommending formulas to mothers and for mothers in choosing formulas; these claims are obviously easy to substantiate and to regulate.

The second type of claim is the statement or claim made for a specific formula but that is applicable to all standard infant formulas by virtue of the basic compositional requirements necessary to sell a formula. We take objection to claims such as "this formula is closest to breast milk" because it is not possible to duplicate the composition of breast milk; instead, it is acceptable to indicate that formulas are modeled after breast milk. When a claim is stated in a manner suggesting that a particular brand of formula is easily digested, and by implication that all other brands are not easy to digest, the claim is considered misleading. These claims can be couched in a manner that is not misleading by making it clear that this brand, like all other infant formulas, is easy to digest. Manufacturers have traditionally not made claims that their formulas contain higher levels of nutrients than other formulas, and we hope that this practice will continue.

The third type of claim is the statement or claim related to dietary management of a disease or condition. These claims have been used for decades for specialized formulas such as those for inborn errors of metabolism and other conditions and for allergies to milk and soy proteins. The data required to substantiate these claims vary depending on the condition. If the principles of dietary management of a condition are well defined, only growth, development, and tolerance studies may be required for the formula. Hypoallergenic claims are acceptable for formulas meeting criteria set up by the Canadian Paediatric Society. Claims for prophylaxis, however, are not as well accepted. In more recent years, we have seen claims related to such conditions as diarrhea or colic, where the data required to substantiate the claims have not been defined either by experience or by expert advice.

The fourth type of claim that is beginning to appear is the claim that the formula will result in superior mental or physical performance or enhanced immune function based on the presence of ingredients that are normally present in breast milk but that have not been traditional ingredients of infant formulas. This is a new dimension of claim that raises a host of issues with respect to substantiation such as the appropriateness of endpoints, meaningfulness, the length of follow-up, and so on.

In 1990, regulations were introduced in Canada requiring manufacturers to notify the Health Protection Branch 90 days before the sale or the advertising for sale of any new infant formula or of an infant formula that had undergone a major change. At that time claims were not an issue. The types of formula on the market were few, and the only claims were those describing the composition of the formula and the well-established indications for the use of special formulas. As a result, the requirements for premarket notification concentrated on the provision of information on the specifications, manufacturing process, quality control procedures, and the other matters considered necessary for safety. When filing a premarket notification, the manufacturer or importer must provide details of the evidence relied on to establish that the new infant formula is nutritionally adequate to promote acceptable growth and development in infants when consumed in accordance with the directions for use. The manufacturer or importer must also provide the written text of all labels, including package inserts.

The definition of ''major change'' is confined to a change of ingredient or in the amount of an ingredient or in the processing or packaging of the human milk substitute, where experience or theory would predict an adverse effect on the levels or availability of nutrients in, or the microbiological or chemical safety of, the formula. Thus, the regulatory requirements for clinical data are confined to the nutritional adequacy or safety of the formula and do not extend to data to substantiate any claims for indications for use. Furthermore, the definition of ''major change'' does not include changes in labels for new claims or indications for use.

The Health Protection Branch must therefore rely on the general provisions of the Canadian Food and Drugs Act respecting misleading and deceptive labeling practices, which are found in section 5 of the Act, to control claims for infant formulas. At the moment, the onus is on the Health Protection Branch to prove that the claims are misleading or likely to create an erroneous impression as to the value of the food. In our view, this method of operating is not providing optimal protection to either the mother or the infant.

There has been a proliferation of different types of formula since premarket notification was introduced, competition is becoming fiercer, and with it there is an expansion of claims. We are increasingly being called on to investigate claims after a product is on the market. We feel that infant formulas are too important a class of foods to be treated like ordinary foods when it comes to claims.

Consumers and health workers should have confidence that the claims on an infant formula are justified by appropriate studies in much the same way as they rely on the indications for the use of drugs in Canada. In Canada, the Food and Drugs Act permits the making of regulations respecting the conditions of sale of any food, to prevent a consumer from being misled as to the composition, merit, safety, etc. of the product. Under the authority of this section, it would be possible for us to include in the premarket notification requirements for evidence to substantiate any claims that are made for the benefits of the formula related to health, or for the dietary management of any disease or disorder or condition. It would also be possible to include in the definition of ''major change'' any change to the label regarding claims for health benefits or dietary management of diseases, and so on. These changes would have the effect of shifting the onus to the manufacturer to justify claims before marketing. Given the increasing sophistication of the claims and their proliferation, we believe that this approach would offer a greater protection to the Canadian public and is worthy of consideration.

In 1992, the Health Protection Branch established an *ad hoc* expert consultation to advise on the composition and testing of formulas for preterm infants. Their report was published in 1995 and provides valuable guidance to us in the evaluation of preterm formulas. In the future our branch and other regulatory bodies will need advice and guidance from experts on the types and designs of clinical studies required to support the various types of claims.

DISCUSSION

Dr. Uauy: What claims have there been in Canada recently that you are concerned may be misleading?

Dr. Cheney: We have seen claims for colic and claims for dietary management of diarrhea in particular.

Dr. Yolken: I understand from your presentation that you would not accept the claim that formula X is closer to breast milk than formula Y. But I have seen advertising along those lines from Canada. Do you not have the ability to control this, or is some other mechanism involved?

Dr. Cheney: In Canada, if those claims are deemed misleading, action is taken after the fact.

Dr. Aggett: I understand that people can make claims, and then, only if somebody raises an objection can you actually examine the claim and its veracity?

Dr. Cheney: No. In Canada, claims are brought to our attention either through trade complaints or by our finding them.

Dr. Aggett: So people don't come to you before making a claim; they make the claim and may get away with it. Is that the situation?

Dr. Cheney: This is why we are proposing a change.

Dr. Aggett: So if you do catch up with them, can you actually stop them continuing with the claims?

Dr. Cheney: Yes, but you then get into the "is it false, misleading, or deceptive" situation, and if you end up arguing under those conditions, it becomes extremely time-consuming, involves a lot of expert testimony, and is ultimately dependent on a judge's decision. This is not a good way to resolve these issues.

Dr. Clarke: To stand in solidarity with my two colleagues, because I do a very similar job in the United Kingdom, I should say that not only is the whole issue a gray area, but it also becomes highly emotive because the primary objective is benefit, and the safety issue is often forgotten or swept to one side. I am sure that the three of us have been in a similar position where it has been said that we are denying infants the benefits of having particular products in infant formulas. It is a thankless task to withhold permission on the basis of safety, but I would remind everyone that regulations are designed not to hinder progress but to protect and benefit the population.

Dr. Przyrembel: This is, in fact, why in Germany—in addition to the seven claims that European regulations allow—manufacturers may also list what they have added to a formula, but not why. Thus, they may add LC-PUFAs and state so on the label but not say why they have added them. It is for informed people to make their choice.

Dr. Uauy: If you start putting things on the label that the public cannot clearly interpret, it is potentially misleading. The regulatory agencies should be concerned with what the public reaction will be. I would like to know what the public reaction is in Canada or in Germany to this sort of claim. Are people calling up and asking the regulatory agency about it? Who is orienting the public?

Dr. Cheney: I would admit that claims on the label, such as "contains added nucleotides," may not mean very much to consumers, and this is why there is a temptation to go beyond that and to start explaining what the benefits are of those particular added ingredients. In Canada, the only issue that periodically comes up in the media is "Why don't Canadian formulas contain DHA?"

Dr. Przyrembel: So far as the German situation is concerned, I think the motivation of the government in passing this law was to encourage manufacturers to do more research, not to stop with the composition regulations that the European Commission had set up. It is up to the physician, to the pediatrician, to read about the subject and to form his own opinion.

Dr. Steenhout: I agree with your comment that the pediatrician must offer an intellectual reflection on what is on the label. However, I had a lot of experience in private practice before joining Nestlé, and I can tell you that when mothers see this sort of advertising on the label, they are attracted by it, and if you prescribe a formula from another company without any advertising, you get asked why. I think we must be very careful with this sort of legislation; good science must come before pure marketing.

Dr. Lucas: In the past, proper efficacy and safety studies have been very rare, and when they have been done, they have not been done well, and many of the claims that have been made have been misleading and unacceptable. It is becoming clear now that we are moving into a new area of research, where claims will be supported by the medical profession as a whole in a proper way, that is, after properly randomized long-term efficacy studies with proper safety and numbers, more than one study, and so on, and if we have all those things, then it seems to me extremely important that regulatory bodies are able to respond by allowing legitimate and medically supported claims to be made. I believe this for two reasons: one is that it is informative for the public; the other is that because a large amount of funding for research comes from industry, there is very little incentive for industry to support really important outcome research if they are unable to make any kind of claim for the health benefits at the end, even if they have been legitimately proven. So my concern is that the foundations are laid down by regulatory bodies so that they can respond to what is going to be a new wave of research in the next few years.

Dr. Cheney: I think that is a very good point: it would be most unfortunate if a regulatory structure were set up that discouraged developments. That would be an extremely negative outcome. There is a need for consumer protection and also for the protection of companies that do the research, so that they themselves get the benefits of it as well.

Dr. Guesry: Do you think that the interpretation of the rules has changed recently? I see differences between the situation 10 years ago and that now. Ten years ago, the addition of taurine was accepted purely on the basis that it was present in human milk, even though no effect whatsoever on the health of the baby had been proven. Now, we have the nucleotide issue, which is comparable: no effect has been demonstrated in infants, but nucleotides are present in human milk. However, the addition of nucleotides is banned by most of the regulatory bodies. So do you think there has been an evolution of the rules, so that the fact that a compound is present in human milk is now insufficient to support a claim for its inclusion in an infant formula?

Dr. Cheney: Yes. There are now safety issues involving not only the novel ingredient but also its source. Safety has to be established for both.

Clinical Trials in Infant Nutrition, edited by
Jay A. Perman and Jean Rey, Nestlé Nutrition
Workshop Series, Vol. 40, Nestec Ltd.,
Vevey/Lippincott-Raven Publishers,
Philadelphia © 1998.

Health and Functional Claims in the European Union

Jean Rey

Department of Pediatrics, Hôpital des Enfants Malades, Paris, France

Consumers are becoming increasingly interested in their diet and its relation to health. The recent crisis over mad cow disease (1) and the fear that the bovine spongiform encephalopathy (BSE) agent could be transmitted to man (2,3) is the most recent illustration. Interest in these questions is not, however, a new phenomenon. To convince yourself of this, just go and see Alan Parker's film *The Road to Wellville* (4) or read the *Ladies guide in health and disease* (Battle Creek, MI: Modern Medicine Publishing Co., 1893), one of the 50 books of the 19th century food reform advocate who believed that a high protein diet stimulated sexual drive, which he regarded as an undesirable effect, leading in practice to dissipation and exhaustion (5).

The present extent of the phenomenon can be judged by the size of the audience for television programs on these subjects, the place devoted to them in women's magazines (*Elle, Marie-Claire, Cosmopolitan, Votre Santé, Vital,* etc.), and the success of numerous books such as *La diététique du cerveau* (6) or *Comment maigrir en faisant des repas d'affaires* (7). The myth wins out, doubtless because men and women have never been so healthy, and because their life expectancy, at least in the industrialized countries, has attained a level that threatens both the balance of social expenditure (pensions, medical costs) and the organization of society itself (8).

It is in this context of almost limitless food supplies and ferocious competition between suppliers that consumers' associations and the public in general are demanding more and more information on food labels, even if most are incapable of understanding their significance. The manufacturers, on their side, are lobbying the public bodies—that is, the Food and Drug Administration (FDA) and the Congress in the United States, the Brussels Commission and the Parliament in the European Union—to seek authorization for a growing number of claims to be included in the labeling and advertising of foodstuffs. However, they are well aware of the dangers and know that such a policy could boomerang. Too much information kills information. In addition, everyone realizes the difficulty of finding the happy medium between rules that are too strict and limit the message and unbridled liberty that would give the competitor a free rein. Nothing would be gained if everyone were free to say what he or she wanted or, on the other hand, constrained to adopt the same wording.

This is the present position of the Brussels Commission, the French authorities, and particularly of the *Codex Alimentarius* Committee and our own view on the question, which is presented in this chapter.

NUTRITION LABELING

Scope of the Council Directive of 24 September 1990 (90/496/CEE)

> This Directive concerns nutrition labelling of foodstuffs to be delivered as such to the ultimate consumer. It [also applies] to foodstuffs intended for supply to restaurants, hospitals, canteens and other similar mass caterers [. . . but not] to natural mineral waters or other waters intended for human consumption and to diet integrators/food supplements. [Article 1; 1,2]

However,

> in the case of non-prepackaged foodstuffs put up for sale to the ultimate consumer or to mass caterers, and foodstuffs packed at the point of sale at the request of the purchaser or prepackaged with a view to immediate sale, the extent of the information [requested] and the manner of its communication may be determined by national provisions until the eventual adoption of Community measures. [Article 8] (9).

Thus, European regulations apply for the moment only to prepacked foodstuffs, in contrast to the American regulations that result from the adoption by the United States Congress of the Nutrition Labeling and Education Act (NLEA) of 1990, which adds major food labeling amendments to the Federal Food, Drug and Cosmetic Act (FD&C Act) (10). Major intentions of Congress in this legislation were to clarify and strengthen the federal authority to require the majority of food products to carry nutrition labeling and to establish the conditions under which health and nutrient content claims could be made for specific foods (10,11).

The U.S. FDA's Proposal

Before the passage of the 1990 amendments, the FD&C Act did not specifically mention nutrition labeling. Section 403[q] of the NLEA states that a food shall be deemed to be misbranded if, with certain exceptions, it fails to bear nutrition labeling. Moreover, section 201[n] of the FD&C Act states that the labeling of a food is misleading if it fails to reveal factual material about the possible consequences of using the food. For this reason, the agency stated that:

> Given the history of use of nutrition labeling, the advances in nutrition science [. . .] and the public interest in healthful diets, FDA concludes that the nutritional content of a food is a material fact, and that a food label is misleading if it fails to bear nutrition information[. . . .] (12)

The Final Rule on Nutrition Labeling from the U.S. FDA and USDA

Nutrition labeling is required for all retail food products intended for human consumption and offered for sale unless an exemption is provided for the product listed in paragraph 101.9(j) of Title 21 of the Code of Federal Regulation (13). Foods exempt from *mandatory* nutrition labeling requirements include: (a) food offered for sale by manufacturers with annual gross sales below US $500,000 per year; (b) food sold in restaurants or other establishments in which food is served for immediate human consumption (for example, schools, hospitals, cafeterias, trains, and airplanes); (c) foods that contain insignificant amounts of all of the nutrients and food components subject to this rule, for example, coffee and tea; (d) dietary supplements, except those in conventional food form, for example, a breakfast cereal; (e) medical foods; (f) custom-processed fish or game meats; (g) foods shipped in bulk form or sold from bulk containers; and (h) infant formulas, subject to special regulation. Otherwise exempted foods that bear nutrition claims or other nutrition information in any context on the label or in labeling or advertising forfeit the exemption (13,14). Fresh produce, fish, seafood, meat, and poultry must also be labeled by a certain percentage of retail stores, subject to continuing review of implementation.

Mandatory Versus Optional Nutrition Labeling

Article 2(2) of the Directive 90/496/EEC actually specifies that ''where a nutrition claim appears on labelling, in presentation or in advertising, with the exclusion of generic advertising, nutrition labelling shall be compulsory.'' Therefore, in this respect, the European legislation is not different from the American one. Nevertheless, its philosophy is just the opposite of that of the new FDA final regulation in that article 2(1) of the Directive states that (subject to paragraph 2), ''nutrition labelling shall be optional.'' Indeed, the idea of the Commission is that ''to avoid any possible technical barriers to trade, the nutrition labelling should be presented in a standardized form throughout the Community'' (recital no. 6 of the Directive) and that ''foodstuffs bearing nutrition labelling should conform to the rules laid down [, . . . and] all other forms of nutrition labelling should be prohibited'' (recitals nos. 7 and 8). But, ''to appeal to the average consumer and to serve the purpose for which it is introduced, and given the current low level of knowledge on the subject of nutrition, the information provided should be simple and easily understood'' (recital no. 9). Moreover, ''to encourage interested parties, especially small and medium-sized undertakings, to provide nutrition labelling for as many products as possible, measures to make information more complete and more balanced should be introduced gradually'' (recital no. 11). Finally, ''application of [the] Directive for a certain length of time will enable valuable experience [. . .] to be gained and consumer reaction [. . .] to be evaluated, thus enabling the Commission to review the rules and propose any appropriate amendments'' (recital no. 10). This explains why, until further notice, "foodstuffs bearing no nutrition labelling should be able to circulate freely [throughout the Community]" (recital no. 8), provided "[no] nutrition claim appears on labelling in presentation or in advertising" [Article 2(2)] (9).

Despite their differences, Directive 90/496/EEC and the FDA's final rules (21 CFR Ch.1 §101.9) are thus in fact in agreement with the provisions of the *Codex* draft guidelines for use of nutrition claims (at step 8 of the Procedure, Ottawa, 14–17 May 1996), which specifies that "any food for which a nutrition claim is made should be labelled with a nutrient declaration in accordance with section 3 of the *Codex* guidelines on nutrition labelling" (15).

CLAIMS CONCERNING FOODSTUFFS

Two main categories of claims concerning foodstuffs can generally be distinguished: (a) *nutrition claims,* strictly speaking, which concern the content in nutrients, energy, ingredients, and other substances; and (b) *health claims,* which, in the broad sense, are defined to encompass explicit as well as implied messages that state or suggest any relationship between a food or a food ingredient and a disease or health-related condition.

Nutrition Claims

The Codex *Guidelines for Nutrition Claims*

The definition adopted by the FAO/WHO *Codex* Committee on Food Labelling (CCFL) in its above-mentioned proposed draft guidelines for use of nutrition claims is identical to the definition in the *Codex* guidelines on nutrition labeling (CAC/GL 2-1985, Rev. 1-1993). For the *Codex* committee, "nutrition claim" means "any representation which states, suggests or implies that a food has particular nutritional properties including but not limited to the energy value and to the content of protein, fat and carbohydrates, as well as the content of vitamins and minerals."

The *Codex* distinguishes three types of nutrition claims: (a) *nutrient contents claims,* which declare that a foodstuff is "source" or "free," "low," "very low," or "high"; (b) the *comparative claims* "reduced" or "increased" and "less" or "more," which concern different versions of the same food or similar foods, provided that there is a relative difference of at least 25% in the energy value or nutrient content (except for micronutrients, where a 10% difference in the nutritional reference value, NRV, is acceptable) between the compared foods, and a minimum absolute difference equivalent to the figure defined as "low" or "source"; and (c) *nutrient function claims,* which describe the physiological role of certain nutrients in growth, development, and normal functions of the body and should not imply or include any statement to the effect that the nutrient or nutrients would offer a cure or treatment for or protection from disease (15).

The Community Legislation

The Community legislation has adopted almost word for word the *Codex* definition of nutrition claim in its previously mentioned 90/496/EEC Directive on nutrition labeling for foodstuffs. Indeed, article 1(4)(b) of the Directive states: *"nutrition claim* means any representation and any advertising message which states, suggests or implies that a foodstuff has particular nutrition properties due to the energy (caloric value) it provides, provides at a reduced or increased rate, or does not provide, and/or due to the nutrients it contains, contains in reduced or increased proportions, or does not contain." As in the *Codex* draft guidelines for use of nutrition claims (15), Directive 90/496/EEC adds that "a reference to qualities or quantities of a nutrient does not constitute a nutrition claim in so far as it is required by legislation." Thus, quantitative and qualitative claims are covered by the Directive without it being necessary to add anything further because, insofar as it concerns claims, Council Directive 90/496/EEC is limited to defining the concept of "nutrition labeling" and restricting the use of such claims to specific nutrients for which recommended daily allowances (RDAs) have been defined (9). This last measure differs very little from that contained in section 7.1 of the *Codex* draft guidelines for use of nutrition claims, which stipulates that "only those essential nutrients for which an NRV has been established in the *Codex* guidelines on nutrition labelling or those nutrients which are mentioned in officially recognized dietary guidelines of the national authority having jurisdiction, should be the subject of a nutrient function claim" (15).

Community legislation has not included until now any criteria for use of *comparative claims* ("reduced" or "increased" levels) or of *quantitative claims* ("low" or "high" levels) that may be used in labeling of foodstuffs. The Commission services indeed submitted a proposal in 1992 for a Council Directive on the use of claims concerning foodstuffs (Doc-SPC/62/ORIG-Fr/Rev.2). Article 4(4) of this document stipulated in detail the conditions under which a claim may refer to the content in energy or nutrients of a foodstuff; the types of claim ("low," "weak," or "poor"; "high" or "rich"; "source of," "does not contain," "no addition of"; "reduced" or "increased"), the general conditions, as well as the specific requirements to be complied with, were also mentioned in items I to VIII of the annex of this proposal. However, subsequent versions of this document no longer mention the list of descriptors authorized, nor, as a result, the conditions under which they may be used.

Regulations on Claims in the EU Member States

Independently of the general principles concerning the labeling and advertising of foodstuffs, most member states of the European Union have adopted or intend to adopt specific provisions to regulate the use of claims referring in particular to the nutritional content of foodstuffs. The most important of these provisions are the Warenwetbesluit Voedingswaarde-informatie levensmiddelen (Nutrition Labeling

Order of 7 September 1993) in The Netherlands; the ''Nährwert-Kennzeichnungsverordnung'' (Nutrition Labeling Decree) of 25 November 1994 in Germany; the ''Arrêté royal sur la publicité des denrées alimentaires'' (Royal Decree on the advertising of foodstuffs) of 17 April 1988, which does not cover nutrition claims, in Belgium; the Food Labelling Regulation of 1984 and the recommendations issued by the Food Advisory Committee in 1989 in the United Kingdom, and, in France, the four decrees of 30 December 1988 defining the terms ''allégé'' (reduced) and ''frais'' (fresh) as used for certain specific products.

French regulations include a whole series of decrees and opinions of consultative bodies that may or may not have been published in the *Official Journal of the French Republic* that fix, under the general provisions concerning nonmisleading advertising (art. L.121.1 of the Code de la Consommation, Consumer Protection Act) the conditions of use for claims (for example, ''enriched'' in fiber, proteins, or fat; ''reduced'' in proteins or in cholesterol; ''free'' of cholesterol) authorized for ordinary foods and for foods for special dietary uses. These national regulations cause difficulties in interpretation and are obstacles to the free circulation of merchandise in the European Union. In consequence, a European agreement on these matters is urgent, if possible based on the *Codex Alimentarius*.

The Descriptor Terms of the U.S. Final Rule

The Final Rule implementing the U.S. NLEA, issued in the *Federal Register* on 6 January 1993, establishes nutrient reference values for use in nutrition labeling of food and defines very precisely the descriptor terms for the nutrient content claims ''free,'' ''low,'' ''light'' or ''lite,'' ''reduced,'' ''less,'' and ''high'' as well as selected synonyms. The FDA also defines ''good source,'' ''very low'' (for sodium only), ''lean,'' ''extra lean,'' ''fewer,'' and ''more'' (or ''added,'' ''fortified,'' ''enriched,'' or ''extra''). The Agency is also providing for circumstances under which various implied claims may be used. The term ''healthy'' is also defined.

The FDA requirements concerning *quantitative claims* (''free,'' ''low,'' ''high,'' or ''source'') are very similar to the *Codex* draft guidelines on nutrition claims (Table 1). In the FDA regulation, however, the criteria for ''low,'' ''very low,'' or ''free'' are based on reference serving sizes and, for products having reference amounts less than 30 g or 2 tablespoons, per 50 g (14).

In the previous version of the *Codex* guidelines for nutrition (and health claims) on food product labeling (CX/NFSDU 92/7, May 1992), quantitative claims were also based on reference servings and/or were expressed per 100 g (solids) or 100 ml (liquids). At the 18th meeting (Bonn-Bad Godesberg, Germany, 28 September to 2 October 1992) of the *Codex* Committee on Nutrition and Foods for Special Dietary Uses (CCNFSDU), it was nevertheless agreed to suppress all reference to ''per serving'' despite the reservations of the United States and the United Kingdom (ALINORM 93/26 §61). This point was recently discussed again in Ottawa, Canada, at the 24th meeting of the CCFL (14 to 17 May 1996), and the Committee agreed to ask the CCNFSDU to reconsider this question at its next meeting (7 to 11 October 1996).

TABLE 1. *Specific requirements to be complied with for nutrition claims*

	FDA (14) (per serving)[a]	*Codex* (15) (per 100 g)
Energy (kcal)		
Low	<40	<40 (20)[b]
Free	<5	—
Fat (g)		
Low	<3	<3 (1.5)
Free	<0.5	<0.15 (0.15)
Saturated fat (g)		
Low	<1 g and not more than 15% of energy	<1.5 (0.75) and not more than 10% of energy
Free	<0.5[c]	—
Cholesterol (mg)		
Low	<20[d]	<20 (10) and less than 1.5 g of saturated fat/100 g
Free	<2[d]	—
Sodium (mg)		
Low	<140	<120
Very low	<35	<40
Free	<5	<5

[a] Per 50 g for products having reference amounts of less than 30 g or 2 tablespoons.
[b] Per 100 ml.
[c] Less than 0.5 g saturated fat and *trans* fatty acids not exceeding 1% of grams of total fat.
[d] Only on foods that contain 2 g or less of saturated fat per reference serving.

The FDA specifications for *qualitative claims* are also much more precise than those of the *Codex* draft guidelines for use of nutrition claims. In contrast to the *Codex* guidelines, the FDA Final Rule stipulates in particular that for "light," "reduced," and "added," the reference food must be similar to the product bearing the claim (for example, potato chips for potato chips); for "less," "fewer," and "more," however, the reference food may also be a dissimilar food within a product category that can generally be substituted in the diet for the labeled food (for example, pretzels for potato chips). Moreover, the criteria for "reduced" and its synonyms are different (at least 25% less of the nutrient than the reference food) from those for "more" or "added" (at least 10% more of the daily value per reference serving than the reference food). The figures themselves can be questioned, but this approach is more coherent than that finally adopted by the CCFL, which combines criteria of relative variation (difference of at least 25%) and absolute difference, which has to be at least equal to a quantity defined as "low" (energy, fat, saturated fat, cholesterol, sugar, sodium) or "source" (fiber, proteins, vitamins, and minerals).

Before the Ottawa meeting, France had drawn the attention of the CCFL to certain inconsistencies in connection with this, but the drafting of the paragraph in question (point 6.3) was not appreciably improved. The French *Codex* committee had also made known its opposition to the proposition of the CCFL secretariat to subject the use of the term "light" to the same criteria as those for the term "reduced." These terms are not equivalent under either the 1988 decrees or the FDA Final Rule (14), and their apparent correspondence could confuse the consumer.

HEALTH CLAIMS

Modern distribution facilities and the increasingly wide variety of foodstuffs supplied to purchasers and consumers are leading to the growing use of diverse claims, including explicit or implicit references to the prevention of certain health risks (16).

The Legal Status for Medical Claims in the European Union

The overall principles concerning *medical claims*[1] relating to foodstuffs are contained in two Council Directives dealing with the subject in general terms: (a) Council Directive 79/112/EEC of 18 December 1978 on the approximation of the laws of the member states relating to the labeling, presentation, and advertising of foodstuffs (17); and (b) Council Directive 89/398/EEC of 3 May 1989 on the approximation of the laws of the member states relating to foodstuffs intended for particular nutritional uses (18).

Article 2 of Directive 79/112/EEC states that labeling and advertising must not be such as could mislead the purchaser as to the characteristics of the product or attribute to it the property of preventing or curing human disease. The relevant excerpts of this article 2 are cited hereafter: ''The labelling and methods used must not . . . attribute to any foodstuff the property of preventing, treating or curing a human disease or refer to such properties'' (17).

These general measures apply equally to foods for special dietary uses, despite the fact that article 1 of the Framework Directive 89/398/EEC defines these foodstuffs as ''suitable for their claimed nutritional purposes and . . . marketed in such a way as to indicate such suitability.'' In fact, article 6 states: ''The labelling and the labelling methods used, the presentation and the advertising of the products referred to in Article 1 must not attribute properties for the prevention, treatment or cure of human disease to such products or imply such properties.'' Nevertheless, this provision ''shall not prevent the dissemination of any useful information or recommendations exclusively intended for persons having qualifications in medicine, nutrition or pharmacy,'' and in addition, there is a procedure to authorize certain derogations (18).

Medical claims are therefore prohibited in the European Union, as indeed they were in the first drafts of the *Codex* General Guidelines on nutrition and health claims for food labeling (CX/FL 91/9 Appendix I).

The FDA's Final Regulations on Health Claims for Foods

As mentioned earlier, The Nutrition Labeling and Education Act of 1990 has authorized and regulated health claims. Health claims are defined by the Act to

---

[1] What are called ''health claims'' in the United States are considered ''medical claims'' under Community law.

encompass explicit as well as implied claims, such as symbols (for example, the symbol of a heart) or other forms of communication, that characterize the relationship between a nutrient and a disease or health-related condition. Under this law, health claims are in fact prohibited unless they conform to specific FDA regulations. The legislation requires that specific health claims for foods be allowed only where the FDA finds that such a claim is based on the "totality of publicly available scientific evidence . . . that there is significant scientific agreement among experts qualified by scientific training and experience." Allowable claims are required to be stated in a way that accurately represents the nutrient/disease relationship *in the context of a total daily diet.*

According to the FDA's Final Rule issued on 6 January 1993, a food bearing a health claim (except for dietary supplements not in conventional food form) must be a good source for at least one of the following nutrients: vitamin A, vitamin C, iron, calcium, protein, or fiber, before the addition of any nutrient to the food. On the other hand, health claims may not be made if the food contains "disqualifying nutrient levels," that is, specified levels of total fat, saturated fat, cholesterol, and sodium above which a food will be disqualified from making a health claim because it contains one or more of these nutrients in an amount that would make it difficult for a consumer to construct a daily diet that conforms with widely accepted guidelines for reducing the risk of diet-related diseases. Brief summaries of the regulations on the seven authorized claims are published in *Nutrition Reviews* (19) and in France in *Médecine et Nutrition* (20). More recently, the FDA has approved two new health claims for folate in the prevention of certain birth defects and the lack of a relationship between sugar alcohols and dental caries.

The *Codex* Guidelines on Nutrition Claims

The last version of the *Codex* draft guidelines for use of nutrition claims, at step 8 of the procedure (see above), and subject to confirmation by the CCNFSDU of the information contained in the annex, no longer mentions *health claims.* The Committee had an extensive discussion on the extent to which health-related claims should be permitted and included in the guidelines. Some delegations were of the view that reference to the reduction in risk of a disease could be allowed under certain conditions, but other delegations did not accept any reference to disease. There was a consensus to exclude claims relating to the prevention, cure, and treatment of disease and adverse health-related conditions, but the Committee could not come to an agreement on other health claims. It was therefore agreed that health claims would not be included in the guidelines at this stage; all references to health claims throughout the text were therefore deleted, including the definitions. The Committee agreed that further consideration could be given to this issue in the future in the light of additional information; in consequence, the term "health claims" was eliminated from the guidelines title. It should, however, be noted that section 8 of the document (which is at step 8 and could be definitively adopted shortly) allows *claims related to dietary guidelines or healthy diets* but specifies: "Foods should not be described as *healthy* or be represented in a manner that implies that a food in and of itself will impact health" (15). One can only agree with this stipulation, which is common to the FDA (10,19) and the European Community (16). We will see later that other provisions of this section, particularly paragraph 8.6, are very questionable.

Community Approach to Regulating Healthy Diet Claims

The EC Commission Services Proposal

In their draft proposal for a Council Directive on the use of claims concerning foodstuffs, the EC Commission services have taken into account the banning of medical claims in the European Union (see above). Consequently, they addressed only the issues involved in two particular types of health claims: (a) *healthy diet claims* that describe the relationship between a foodstuff, including its characteristics, and a healthy diet as recommended by the competent authorities [Article 4(2)]; and (b) the *physiological role* of nutrient claims [Article 4(3)] (see below, section on Functional Claims). The idea was to authorize healthy diet claims "provided that the following conditions are complied with: (a) the claim refers to official dietary recommendations issued or recognized by the authorities of the member states; and (b) although a certain flexibility is allowed, the wording used remained faithful to the eating patterns included in these recommendations or to an essential part thereof" [Article 4(2)] (16).

The Opinion of the Scientific Committee for Food

This proposal was the subject of much criticism at the consultation of the Scientific Committee for Food (SCF). In an explanatory note prepared on this occasion by the Secretariat of the SCF, it was pointed out that the dividing line between an implied medical/medicinal claim (which is forbidden) and a health claim (as defined above by the Commission services) is far from clear. This point of view was taken up again by the SCF in an opinion given 4 to 5 March 1993, in which it affirmed that this distinction was "conceptually impossible" (21).

One of the provisions of the EC Commission services proposal was: "Claims are regarded as false, misleading or likely to be misleading [if they] state, imply or suggest that a balanced diet based on products of everyday consumption cannot supply all nutritional elements in quantities sufficient for the need of the population in general" [Article 3(1)(d)]. This excellent principle would, however, indisputably be contradicted by the possibility of calling a particular foodstuff healthy (22). Any constituent of a balanced diet is, by definition, healthy provided it is not consumed in excess or in insufficient quantities and is not combined with other substances that are known or considered to be harmful. Green vegetables and fruit are "healthy," but too many nitrates could be harmful. Water is "healthy," but all epidemiologic studies show a negative relationship between the consumption of alcohol and the incidence of ischemic heart disease (23). Milk is an excellent source of proteins and calcium, but milk fats are not universally recommended for preventing atheroma. Dissenting voices are beginning to be heard even in the chorus of support for food-stuffs that are low in cholesterol and saturated fats and are reputed to be "good for the heart." The ultraconservative American Heart Association, for example, wonders whether screening for and systematic treatment of hypercholesterolemia is justified; in their report entitled "Health policy and blood cholesterol—time to change directions," Hulley *et al.* state that a cholesterol-lowering diet may not be prudent for those adults whose cholesterol levels place them on the left hand limb of the total mortality U (24).

Even if it is possible to claim a link between a particular foodstuff and health, which the SCF has questioned, such health claims can surely not be allowed to refer implicitly or explicitly to "official recommendations" issued or recognized by the authorities of the Member States. Complete chaos is likely to arise from the application of such a system, and the proposed means of dealing with the foreseeable difficulties appear inadequate. The Member States should, at least, be required to inform the EC Commission of their administrative practice and legal precedents, but this was not provided for in the proposed Directive. Above all, the SCF, consulted under Article 9 of the proposal, would be likely to find its agenda cluttered with trivial questions (22).

The only reasonable position in this respect is that of the FDA, which results from the implementation of the Nutrition Labeling and Education Act (10) (see above). Health claims, if they should one day be authorized in the European Union, could only be so under conditions strictly defined in advance (that is, in a positive list), and only for those that are supported by valid and substantial scientific evidence (14). However, it would still be necessary that the contribution that a food makes to the intake of a specific nutrient (for example, soluble fiber) not be ignored. Potatoes are not normally labeled. Let us imagine they were. Claims such as "source of fiber" would not be possible simply because their content in soluble fiber, expressed per 100 g or per serving, is too low. On the other hand, most breakfast cereals do qualify. However, potatoes, by virtue of their high consumption in some member states (for example, Ireland), are as important a source of fiber as breakfast cereals (25).

Consider now a claim that a particular brand of breakfast cereal is high in soluble fiber, which can contribute as part of a low-fat diet to a reduction in blood cholesterol. Such a claim could be permitted only if the following elements were each shown to be true: (a) an average serving of the breakfast cereal contains enough soluble fiber to be effective in lowering blood cholesterol; (b) the effect applies to all levels of blood cholesterol and is not confined to the mildly hypercholesterolemic; and (c) the effects are not dependent on the level of fat in the diet. What needs to be established is that, if a consumer chooses this breakfast cereal on the basis of the claim, the dose of the active ingredient is sufficient to exert an effect on blood cholesterol independent of the initial blood cholesterol level or the level of fat in the diet. Otherwise it is misleading (25).

The SCF considered, therefore, that health claims expose more problems than they solve. Any health claim about an ingredient (if they should one day be formally authorized) ought to take into account the minimum inclusion of the ingredient in the food, average exposure to the ingredient, and a threshold intake for efficacy of the ingredient (21).

The French Authorities' Opinion

In application of the above-mentioned Directive 79/112/EEC, the French authorities have constantly made known their opposition to claims based on the concept of disease and to claims relating to prevention, treatment, and curing of disease. In addition, they have always had reservations concerning health claims as defined by the EC Commission services: the distinction between these claims and the nutrient function claims (see below) has not seemed to them either clear or really necessary. The fact that the CCFL has finally deleted all references to health claims throughout the draft of the *Codex* guidelines on nutrition claims seems wise, even if all the provisions of section 8 concerning "claims related to dietary guidelines or healthy diets" have been retained in the text (15). One can only regret the ambiguity of such provisions, in particular those of paragraph 8.6, which states: "Foods may be described as part of a healthy diet provided that the label carries a statement relating the food to the pattern of eating described in the dietary guidelines (officially recognized by the appropriate national authority)."

FUNCTIONAL CLAIMS

As mentioned earlier, *nutrient function claims,* so-called *functional claims,* refer to the physiological role of a nutrient.

The *Codex* Guidelines

The *Codex* draft guidelines for use of nutrient claims are not very explicit on *nutrient function claims.* Some examples are nevertheless given, such as "calcium aids in the development of strong bones and teeth" or "iron is a factor in red blood cell formation" or "folic acid contributes to the normal growth of the fetus." According to the *Codex* document, only those essential nutrients for which an NRV has been established or those that are mentioned in officially recognized dietary guidelines of the national authority having juridiction should be the subject of such claims. The food for which the claim is made should be a significant source of the nutrient in the diet. The nutrient function should be based on the scientific consensus, which is supported by the competent authority (ALINORM 97/22) (15).

The EC Approach

In their initial proposal for a Council Directive on the use of claims concerning foodstuffs, the EC Commission services have defined the claims that refer to the physiological role of the nutrients as claims that relate to actions or effects recognized as having been corroborated by generally accepted scientific evidence and that indicate that the nutrient is a factor or aid in maintaining the structure and functions of the body that are vital to sustaining good health and normal growth and development (16).

The SCF Opinion

The opinion of the SCF was that all nutrients have a physiological role and that their effects have been recognized on "generally accepted scientific evidence." Only a few ultratrace elements remain controversial, but the essentiality of most of them (nickel, silicon, arsenic, lithium, boron, etc.) has been demonstrated, although there are wide differences of opinion (26,27). If claims referring to the physiological role of nutrients were allowed, there would therefore be no reason to restrict such claims to certain nutrients only, insofar as a particular foodstuff is a significant source of an essential nutrient (22). It would still be necessary, it is true, to be able to define this foodstuff as the "source" of a nutrient for which no NRV has been established. In any case, the SCF felt that functional claims should relate solely to the main physiological function of the nutrient (for example, calcium for bone growth, iron for oxygen transport) and not to an effect that could be related to health issues, for example, the cholesterol-lowering effect of unsaturated fatty acids (21).

The French Authorities' Opinion

The French authorities support the idea that functional claims should be authorized only for nutrients that are present in significant amounts in a foodstuff, that is, those that can be considered a "source" according to Council Directive 90/496/EC of 24 September 1990 on nutrition labeling for foodstuffs (9), which implies that they are authorized only for nutrients for which NRV have been established. We have seen earlier that this restriction was the subject of a commentary of the SCF Nutrition Working Group (22).

In view of their concern regarding improper use of this type of claim and the confusion that could result for consumers, the French authorities have continually insisted that the regulatory framework for health claims in general should be reinforced. At the last meeting of the CCFL (Ottawa, May 1996), France had in particular expressed the wish that certain provisions of the *Codex* draft guidelines for use of nutrition claims be maintained and that, furthermore, a clause should be added stating that claims should not be permitted to use the word "health" or any other word evoking health to be associated with the brand or the name of the food. The French delegation also wished that the principle of "disqualifying nutrient levels," which is present in the FDA final regulations on health claims for foods (19) (see above), should be introduced into the *Codex* guidelines. Unfortunately, no consensus could be reached on these suggestions at the Ottawa meeting; thus, these principles do not figure in the final version (15).

The present position of the French authorities is that it would be wise to make provision for these functional claims, even if the manufacturer could be allowed a certain flexibility within the framework of a specific list. This approach is inspired by the Swiss example. Since 1957 they have maintained a positive list of nutrient function claims (for example, "folate plays a role in the metabolism of cell division and in the regeneration of blood and nerve cells, particularly erythrocytes"). The French Committee on foods for special dietary use (CEDAP) has been given the task of preparing a similar list. Its first step has been to define the essential metabolic functions of nutrients for which NRV exist for labeling. To take the authorized Swiss example given above, one could say that the folates "function as coenzymes (*or* are implicated) in the metabolism of certain amino acids and the synthesis of nucleic acids (*or* of purine and pyrimidine bases)." The claims could make use of all or part of the message or even resort to less scientific terms such as "necessary for (*or* essential to, *or* promoting) the synthesis of nucleic acids" or such as "necessary for (*or* essential to, *or* promoting) cell division (*and* cell multiplication)." The idea is that substitutions (indicated by *or*) are possible and that the message can be elaborated to a greater or less extent (possible additions indicated by *and*).

The French Conseil National de l'Alimentation (CNA), established by the decree of 27 November 1985, which is consulted on French food policy, considered that the message to give consumers was first and foremost the importance of a varied and balanced diet. The CNA has recently stressed that there is an urgent need to define acceptable claims. They consider that there is no reason to authorize the use of partial messages unless these are systematically accompanied by a general message, and they are pressing the authorities to make it obligatory for all nutritional claims to be accompanied by the following message: "Only a diversified diet can ensure a good well-balanced diet" (28).

History will decide which decisions are finally taken in this case. The disadvantage of leaving national authorities to decide what claims they will authorize is that they create technical barriers to the free circulation of goods. It is not entirely certain that the Brussels authorities will not oppose the French propositions. France is well aware of this. Thus, the only hope is that these propositions, which we personally support, will be taken up again one day at the community level.

THE POINT OF VIEW OF EUROPEAN INDUSTRY

The fact that industry is in favor of health claims will surprise no one. Indeed, the development of new food products with improved health-promoting properties is a costly undertaking. Therefore, manufacturers will be reluctant to invest in such developments if claims concerning these health benefits are not allowed. On the other hand, regulators have the responsibility of assuring that the foodstuffs are safe and that the claims are not false or misleading. Consequently, according to the Confederation of Food and Drink Industries of the EU (Confédération des Industries Agro-Alimentaires de l'UE, CIAA), regulations should leave sufficient room for innovation but be strict enough to prevent false and misleading claims (29).

European industry today accepts that claims attributing to a foodstuff the property of treating or curing a human disease should not be allowed. These claims must be reserved for drugs. All other claims should be allowed, provided they are based on scientific evidence. The demarcation should be between claims on treatment and cure, which should be forbidden, and the other health claims, which should be allowed. Claims for the dietary management of diseases and disorders, however, should continue to be allowed for foods for special medical purposes (29).

In fact, much of the difficulty in regulating "health claims" comes from the fact that the differents types of health claim need to be clearly distinguished. The International Special Dietary Foods Industries (ISDI) and the CIAA have both proposed that four subsections should be distinguished under the general definition of health claim: (a) *nutrient function claims* (that is, functional claims), which promote the role of a nutrient in the normal physiological functions of the body (for example, calcium is necessary for strong and healthy[2] bones and teeth); (b) *claims related to healthy eating patterns,* which refer to official recommendations (for example, ". . . contains x mg of calcium; a daily intake of y mg of calcium is recommended by . . ."); (c) *claims related to health effects,* which refer to a specific . . . effect of a food or any of its constituents on the body, on a physiological function, or on a biological variable (for example, "calcium improves bone density," or "product x reduces cholesterolemia"); and (d) *claims related to the reduction of a disease risk,* which means that the consumption of a food or any of its constituents, or the reduced consumption of a food constituent, may help reduce the risk of a disease (for example, "adequate calcium intake will help reduce the risk of osteoporosis in later life," or "x is low in saturated fat, which reduces risk of heart disease" (29,30).

Of course, the CIAA is aware that the European Labelling Directive (79/112/EEC) does not allow disease-risk-related claims but is of the opinion that an amendment to the Directive is justified and in the interest of public health (29). On the other hand, in its proposal for draft *Codex* guidelines for use of (health and) nutrition claims, ISDI made the suggestion that section 8.5, which states that "foods should not be described as 'healthy' or be represented in a manner that implies that a food in and of itself will impact health" is unnecessary and should be deleted (30). We have already pointed out above (see sections on Health Claims and Functional Claims: The SCF opinion) that we do not share this point of view (21,22,25).

---

[2] Note the addition of "healthy" in the CIAA proposition (29), which crops up again in a draft working document of IDACE (Association of the Food Industries for Particular Nutritional Uses of the European Union) (31).

THE FINAL PROPOSAL FOR EUROPEAN LEGISLATION

The EC Commission services have revised their proposal several times for a Council Directive on the use of claims concerning foodstuffs. Having taken into account the observations of consumer organizations, the food and drink industry, and the opinion of the SCF, the Consumer Policy Service (now DG XXIV) has finally removed all reference to health claims and functional claims from its project. Document SPC/4/62/Orig.FR/Rev.5 establishes a very broad definition of claims, quite close to that of the *Codex,* and specifies that the dispositions of the Directive should apply to all types of claims. The general principle, which goes in the same direction as that desired by the European industry (see above), is simple: "Any claim shall be authorized that is not false or misleading." Three essential provisions are added: (a) the banning of "medical claims"; (b) the banning of claims that state, imply, or suggest that a balanced diet of everyday foodstuffs cannot provide all the nutritive substances in a sufficient quantity for the needs of the population in general; (c) the obligation of the manufacturer to be able to prove the truthfulness and accuracy of the objective characteristics stated or suggested when requested to do so by the competent authority (Article 3) (32).

Thus, the burden of proof would switch from the competent authorities to the manufacturers, which is exactly the opposite of that recently decided for dietary supplements in the United States by the Dietary Supplement Health and Education Act of 1994 (PL 103-417). Because supplement ingredients are now exempt from the definition of a food additive under the provisions of this Act, the agency will have to use the general food safety provision, which requires it to show that an ingredient is "ordinarily injurious to health," meaning that it would be expected to harm most people who consume it. This standard is obviously much harder to meet and enforce. Moreover, because the Act excludes supplement ingredients from regulation as a food additive or drug, products marketed as supplements do not need to undergo premarket regulation. There is therefore some concern that manufacturers may choose to market their products as supplements rather than as drugs to avoid going through the drug approval process (33).

It is not certain, however, that the project of the Directive on the use of claims will ever be published, because most of its provisions are already incorporated in the European legislation, in particular in Council Directive 84/450/EEC of 10 September 1984 concerning misleading advertising. It can only be regretted that this text has not at least been released as a Commission Communication, because the rules of the game would today be much clearer for everyone.

REFERENCES

1. *Le Monde,* Wednesday 27 March, Thursday 28 March, Saturday 8 June, Thursday 13 June, Friday 14 June, Sunday 16 June, Monday 17 June, Saturday 6 July, Saturday 3 August 1996.
2. Will RG, Ironside JW, Zeidler M, *et al.* A new variant of Creutzfeldt–Jakob disease in the UK. *Lancet* 1996;347:921–925.

3. Brown P. Bovine spongiform encephalopathy and Creutzfeldt–Jakob disease. *Br Med J* 1996;312: 790–791.
4. Fowler R. Road to Battle Creek: movie worries cereal capital. *International Herald Tribune,* Thursday, 27 October 1994.
5. Carpenter KJ. Protein requirements of adults from an evolutionary perspective. *Am J Clin Nutr* 1992; 55:913–917.
6. Bourre JM. *La diététique du cerveau, de l'intelligence et du plaisir.* Paris: Editions Odile Jacob, 1990.
7. Montignac M. *Comment maigrir en faisant des repas d'affaires.* Paris: Editions Flammarion, 1986.
8. Meyer P. *Le mythe de jouvence.* Paris: Editions Odile Jacob, 1987.
9. Council Directive of 24 September 1990 on nutrition labeling for foodstuffs (90/496/EEC). *Off J Eur Commun* L 276/40–44, 6 Oct. 1990.
10. Tillotson JE. United States Nutrition Labeling and Education Act of 1990. *Nutr Rev* 1991;49:273–276.
11. *House of Representatives Report* No. 538, 101st Congress, 2nd Session, 1990.
12. Department of Health and Human Services. Food and Drug Administration. Food labeling—proposed rules. *Fed Register* 1991(Nov 27) vol 56(229):60367.
13. Department of Health and Human Services, Food and Drug Administration. *Code of Federal Regulation 21 CFR 101.9.* Washington, DC: DHHS, 4 Jan 1994.
14. Anonymous. Mandatory nutrition labeling—FDA's final rule. *Nutr Rev* 1993;51:101–105.
15. *Codex Alimentarius* Commission—Codex Committee on Food Labelling. *Draft guidelines for use of nutrition claims.* Rome: FAO/WHO, ALINORM 97/22 Appendix II.
16. Commission of the European Communities. *Draft proposal for a Council Directive on the use of claims concerning foodstuffs.* Doc. SPC/62/Orig. Fr/Rev. 2.
17. Council Directive of 18 December 1978 on the approximation of the laws of the Member States relating to the labelling, presentation and advertising of foodstuffs (79/112/EEC). *Off J Eur Commun* L 33/1–11, 8 Feb 1979.
18. Council Directive of 3 May 1989 on the approximation of laws of the Member States relating to foodstuffs intended for particular nutritional uses (89/398/EEC). *Off J Eur Commun* L 186/27–32, 30 June 1989.
19. Anonymous. The FDA's final regulations on health claims for foods. *Nutr Rev* 1993;51:90–93.
20. Astier-Dumas M. Position de la Food and Drug Administration sur les allégations concernant la santé. *Med Nutr* 1993;24:182–184,241–245.
21. Scientific Committee for Food. *Opinion on Claims Directive expressed on 4–5 March 1993.* Minutes of the 88th Meeting of the Scientific Committee for Food.
22. Rey J. *Comments on the draft proposal for a Council Directive on the use of claims concerning foodstuffs.* Unpublished Working Document, SCF code CS/NUT/9.
23. Rimm EB, Giovanucci EL, Willett WC, *et al.* Prospective study of alcohol consumption and risk of coronary disease in men. *Lancet* 1991;338:464–468.
24. Hulley SB, Walsh JMB, Newman TB. Health policy on blood cholesterol. Time to change directions. *Circulation* 1992;86:1026–1029.
25. Gibney MJ. *Comments on the draft proposal for a Council Directive on the use of claims concerning foodstuffs.* Unpublished Working Document, SCF code CS/NUT/8.
26. Nielsen FH. Nutritional significance of the ultratrace elements. *Nutr Rev* 1988;46:337–341.
27. Mertz W. Essential trace metals: new definitions based on new paradigms. *Nutr Rev* 1993;51: 287–295.
28. Institut Français pour la Nutrition. *L'alimentation: ses allégations santé. Dossier scientifique de l'IFN-N° 6.* Paris: Institut Français pour la Nutrition, 1995.
29. CIAA. *Claims on nutrition and health. Draft position paper on the regulatory aspects.* Unpublished document.
30. ISDI. *ISDI proposal for Draft Codex Guidelines for use of health and nutrition claims.* Unpublished document.
31. IDACE. *Food supplements. Draft working document 94/670.* Unpublished document.
32. Commission of the European Communities. *Proposition de Directive du Parlement Européen et du Conseil relative à l'utilisation d'allégations concernant les denrées alimentaires.* Doc. SPC/4/62/ Orig.FR/Rév.5.
33. Anonymous. Dietary supplements: recent chronology. *Nutr Rev* 1995;53:31–36.

DISCUSSION

Dr. Haschke: I accept what you say that one should not use medical claims for alcohol when one presents only part of the story; it is clear that alcohol has beneficial effects and adverse effects, so if one takes a balanced view, one cannot make a health claim for alcohol. But in an infant product where research can demonstrate a health benefit, and where there is no evidence of adverse effects, and where this is based on scientific opinion and not on the view of one researcher, why are you against making health claims in that situation?

Dr. Rey: In such a situation, I am not against it. If you are able to prove something, I will accept it. I have proved this in the past by supporting the modification to the EC directive allowing reduced-antigen-content infant formulas. If the producer is able to prove that the antigen content is really reduced, and if he can prove there is benefit for the child, it is acceptable. If we are convinced that there is a benefit for infants in general, we are in favor of changing the regulation. The main problem is that it may take many years to change a directive. There is presently some discussion in Brussels to try to find a procedure to accelerate this and to permit a manufacturer to use a nutrient for a 2-year period if he has a good enough argument to convince at least the Scientific Committee for Food.

Dr. Pohlandt: If you accept that proven findings justify claims, how do you decide that something is proven?

Dr. Rey: It is a crucial point. In Canada, Dr. Cheney said that she has no right to exert *a priori* control and that it is practically impossible to exert *a posteriori* control because it takes too much time and too many experts, and sometimes it is too late to change the opinion of the consumer. In the United States, health claims are decided by the FDA, so it is an *a priori* decision of the FDA to accept a health claim. I think this is a difficult route to follow. In Europe, I believe we should try to organize a system in which the member states have full control of the claims made by industry *a posteriori*. But industry should have proof of any claims they propose. It is not the task of the administration to prove that a claim is misleading. But somebody has to be in control, and I don't believe the Scientific Committee for Food can spare the time to do this kind of job.

Dr. Lucas: We have an interesting paradox. As I was saying yesterday, the vast majority of nutritional research in pediatrics is based on short-term physiological studies, so that all the directives and indeed all the recommendations made by official bodies on nutrient intakes are not in fact largely made on a long-term health basis. By and large, the recommendations are made simply on the basis of what is actually required to prevent deficiency. So we have a paradox in the sense that in the future, as we become more and more interested in the impact of nutrition on health, the directives will be based less and less on the principles that pediatricians would like them to be based on. I think this is an argument in favor of health claims, because we need an intervening period of being able to make specific points about particular patterns of nutrients until we get to the point where a whole new directive could be produced that designs nutrient intake on the basis of functional rather than physiological outcomes. That is going to take a very long time to do in a comprehensive way. In the meantime, it seems that one will need some kind of intermediate way of flagging those particular patterns of nutrient intake that are important for health, as opposed to just meeting nutrient needs.

Dr. Rey: The role of the health authorities is mainly to protect the consumer from false or irrelevant information, and nutrition labeling could be considered a type of irrelevant information. How can you manage your shopping if you have to read on the label that this rice provides 12% of your RDA for vitamin B_{12}, for example? Indeed, you need a computer! The main criticism against it is that it is only intended for prepacked food and not for fresh food, and most food consumed in Europe is not prepacked.

Dr. Przyrembel: The situation in Europe is different for infant foods because these are the only foods that are regulated according to their composition. The idea behind this is that these foods should be optimal according to our present knowledge, so it should be totally unnecessary to allow a health claim for such an almost completely regulated food. I think the only thing missing at the moment is the possibility for someone who has really found out something new and interesting and helpful to promote his product, but I don't think a health claim is the solution to that.

Dr. Lucas: I am still not completely happy that I have got an answer to my question. Let us suppose that we take any nutrient you like—protein, calcium, anything—and we look at a directive and see that there is 100% range of what is acceptable in an infant formula, it could be 400 to 800 mg a day, and that entire intake range is compatible with the short-term prevention of nutritional deficiencies; that is, it is what you need to put into your body to maintain yourself in a normal physiological state, and if you have too much, you pour out the rest in your urine. That is the basis we have for the current recommendations on intake. But supposing that two or three reputable groups of scientists do outcome studies and show that if you are very narrowly at the lower end of that range, you improve long-term neurodevelopment, probably permanently. Now what do you do with that information, given current legislation? Clearly the public has a right to know that a formula that is at one end of that range rather than the other might be better for neurodevelopment.

Dr. Rey: We would change the regulation.

Dr. Lucas: If you could do that, I would agree that would be good, but regulations need to be conservative because somebody may discover a downside later on, and it takes a long time—a decade or more—to get multiple nations to change a directive. So what do you do about the public in the meantime with that information?

Dr. Rey: I think it is the responsibility of industry. If there is information, for example, that 60 kcal per 100 ml is too low, they should increase the energy density of their product and give the information to the public. Industry has a great responsibility; it is not only the competent authorities that have a responsibility. We should let the industry make their own product as they want and try to regulate it afterwards, not before.

Dr. Aggett: I don't think you have answered Dr. Lucas's point. I think he is actually asking whether industry would be allowed to do just what you are saying industry should do in such circumstances, and I think he is saying that if they do, they should in some way be rewarded for doing so. Is that what you are asking?

Dr. Lucas: I am much more obviously in the child's position here, if new knowledge shows that a more narrowed intake than the one that is necessary for supporting nutrition is better for health. That information needs to be disseminated. One way of it being disseminated is in the form of a claim. I am not thinking of this in terms of industry, although obviously there is the important side effect that if industry is allowed to make such a claim legitimately, and it is supported by medical evidence, that would be an incentive for industry to put more money into improving the health of children, which would be good.

Dr. Aggett: The other suggestion is that people should be able to make statements—not a claim, but if there is a widely acknowledged, peer-reviewed and approved study, then a statement could be made without actually making a claim—in other words, a specific statement for the product based on the specific studies done with that product.

Dr. Hamburger: As you know, industry often makes claims by selective presentation of data. However, in one of your figures, you showed France as having the lowest coronary artery disease of many countries, but you did not include in that slide the incidence of liver disease and cirrhosis, which places France very near the top!

Dr. Rey: Yes, it is true that the incidence of cirrhosis is very high. The number of deaths from alcohol in France is approximately 60,000 per year, and the same for smoking; annual deaths in France now total 500,000, so I would agree that at 12% of total deaths, morbidity and mortality from alcohol are excessively high. But you cannot survive indefinitely, and if you decrease the incidence of ischemic heart disease, for example, you will probably increase the incidence of cancer, because these are the main causes of death in industrialized countries. When you ask Canadian medical doctors how they would prefer to die when the time has arrived, 90% put sudden death and ischemic heart disease as first choice (1). So, what is your choice?

Dr. Uauy: The consumer responds to claims and also to the amount of scientific information disseminated in the media. Industry responds to the latter by saying ''we may have a product.'' I think we are all responsible for this push for claims when we publish our science before we have definitive proof of something. This is opening the door to industry to come forward with claims. If we are to defuse this issue, we should probably start with the way scientific information is presented to the public and the level of certainty attached to this information. Then, we probably need to do more to counteract the need for claims by educating the public about healthy diets and promoting dietary guidelines in an organized manner. Until we do that, it won't be any surprise to me that industry wants to put forward claims. There is only one reason they do it: consumers are willing to buy products that have claims associated with them.

Dr. Rey: I agree completely with you. It is difficult for the industry to promote a really healthy diet because a healthy diet is to eat less. If you decrease your energy intake, you probably increase your life expectancy, and you decrease your morbidity. Divide everything by 2 and you will be in good health. This is not a good message for industry.

Dr. Guesry: I completely disagree with what you say. The challenge of the modern food industry is specially to make foods that contain less fat, less energy, less sodium, more fiber—more good things, less bad things—and to sell these products. To put your finger on the vested interests of industry is wrong. There are many examples: you have now butter and margarine with 40% of the energy of normal margarine; you have low-fat milk; there are thousands of examples. Industry wants to make new products because people are interested in novelty. So contrary to what you say, it is in the interests of the industry to make healthy foods.

Dr. Rey: I am not sure, for example, that reduced-fat butter has any advantage. If you reduce your butter consumption by one half, you will obtain the same result. The main problem of society is that people are unable to regulate their food intake. If you give them food with reduced energy, they will eat more and keep the same energy intake as before.

Dr. Guesry: No, I am sorry, but it has been proven that when you increase the energy density of the food, you eat less, but your total energy intake is increased, and when you reduce energy density, you eat more, but your total energy intake is less (2–4).

Dr. Rey: The country where people use the most aspartame is the United States, and that is the country where the incidence of obesity is highest.

Dr. Przyrembel: But I think we know already that a reduction in sugar intake does not have much influence—the sugar we eat is not the main part of our diet.

Dr. Walter: I wanted to comment on your international data on the relationship between mortality and alcohol intake. There is a phenomenon known to epidemiologists as the ecologic fallacy, which occurs when you take aggregated data in population groups, particularly large population groups such as nations, and find associations that don't apply at the individual level. So you could see an apparent association between exposure and risk in the nation as a whole, but when you look at particular individuals within the population, who of course vary enormously in their intake patterns, that same association may or may not be present. If you look at the fertility rates in German towns and measure the number of storks on the chimneys, there is indeed an association, but few of us believe that it is a causal association. In this particular instance, you may be able to document by other studies that the same relationship with alcohol intake still applies at the individual level, but you do have to be very careful in the way you present the information, because it is known scientifically to be rather weak. Another specific point on the graph you showed was that the ecologic fallacy is much more likely to occur when you have an asymmetric distribution of the data points, and it seemed to me that France was quite a long way out on the right-hand side relative to most of the other countries, so France was very influential in determining the relationship. I won't comment on whether that is or is not appropriate.

Dr. Haschke: During this meeting, we have had a lot of discussion on the safety of LC-PUFAs, and from Dr. Lucas's data at least, there is a suggestion that the addition of those substances in certain concentrations may not be safe for premature infants, though more research is needed, of course. Now two different agencies, one in Europe and one in the United States, have taken completely different points of view. Europe has allowed LC-PUFAs and has even made it a requirement that they should be in feeds for premature infants. In the United States, on the other hand, the addition of LC-PUFAs to infant formula was recently turned down because of the lack of safety data. How do you see the responsibility of a committee such as the Scientific Committee for Food when you are aware as a Committee member that something could go wrong? We cannot leave it to the industry or the researchers to demonstrate that these things are safe or not safe. The committee *per se* has to act if safety issues come up. How do you see your role in the future?

Dr. Rey: Indeed, if there is a health problem, a decision will be taken by the European Commission after consulting the Scientific Committee for Food.

REFERENCES

1. Reeves RA, Chen E. Who wants to eliminate heart disease?. *J Clin Epidemiol* 1994;47:667–670.
2. Duncan KH, Bacon JA, Weinsier RL. The effect of high and low energy density diets on satiety, energy intake, and eating time of obese and nonobese subjects. *Am J Clin Nutr* 1983;37:763–767.
3. Sanchez-Grinan MI, Peerson JM, Brown KH. Effect of dietary energy density on total *ad-libitum* energy consumption by recovering malnourished children. *Eur J Clin Nutr* 1992;46:197–204.
4. Stephenson DM, Gardner JM, Walker SP, Ashworth A. Weaning-food viscosity and energy density: their effect on *ad libitum* consumption and energy intakes in Jamaican children. *Am J Clin Nutr* 1994; 60:465–469.

Clinical Trials in Infant Nutrition, edited by
Jay A. Perman and Jean Rey, Nestlé Nutrition
Workshop Series, Vol. 40, Nestec Ltd.,
Vevey/Lippincott-Raven Publishers,
Philadelphia © 1998.

Clinical Trials in Infant Nutrition: The Role of the American Academy of Pediatrics and the Committee on Nutrition

John N. Udall, Jr., and Robert M. Suskind

Department of Pediatrics, Gastroenterology and Nutrition Division, Louisiana State University Medical Center, New Orleans, Louisiana, USA

The American Academy of Pediatrics (AAP) is committed to the attainment of optimal physical, mental, and social health for all infants, children, adolescents, and young adults (1). To this end, the members of the Academy dedicate their efforts and resources. The Academy has established approximately 30 committees that help in developing guidelines to assist health care professionals, governmental agencies, and industry in the care of infants, children, and adolescents. The Committee on Nutrition (CON) is the group appointed to help in the development of AAP policy concerning nutrition.

RECENT COMMITTEE ON NUTRITION STATEMENTS

Statements from the CON are reviewed by individuals with expertise in the subject matter of the statement, circulated to the individual Committee members, amended and modified, and finally reviewed and approved by the board of directors of the AAP. This can be a lengthy process. The time interval from when it is realized that there is a need for a statement on a given subject to when the statement is finally published in *Pediatrics* can be up to 2 to 3 years. In some instances, a subcommittee of CON or a special work group will be established to accelerate the process for a given subject. The following are brief summaries of the seven statements published by the CON or work groups of the CON since 1990 (Table 1).

Statement 1: Practical Significance of Lactose Intolerance in Children

This statement was prompted in part by a major comprehensive report that concluded that it is unwise to discourage the use of milk in children from a population with a high rate of lactose malabsorption unless these children are suffering from

259

TABLE 1. *Committee on Nutrition statements since 1990 (with references)*

Practical Significance of Lactose Intolerance in Children (2)
Statement on Cholesterol (3)
The Use of Whole Cow's Milk in Infancy (4)
Infant Feeding Practices and Possible Relationship to the Etiology of Diabetes Mellitus (5)
Reimbursement for Medical Foods for Inborn Errors of Metabolism (10)
Fluoride Supplementation for Children: Interim Policy Recommendation (11)
Aluminum Toxicity in Infants and Children (12)

severe diarrhea or show a definite intolerance to milk or milk products. This clinical conclusion is similar to the one reported by the AAP/CON in 1978. In general, evidence for malabsorption of lactose as a clinical problem is not manifest until after 5 to 7 years of age, although this age can be variable. Nondigesters (adults) who continue to drink milk might tolerate as much as 240 ml of whole milk. This adaptation is presumed to be a result of a change in the intestinal flora.

The CON concluded in this statement that individuals can increase their tolerance to dairy products by ingesting fermented products such as yogurt, hard cheeses, cottage cheese, and acidophilus milk. The Committee noted that there are also enzyme preparations on the market that predigest the lactose in the milk and render it almost lactose-free (2).

Statement 2: Statement on Cholesterol

The AAP and the National Cholesterol Education Program both endorse the principle that the diet of children and adolescents should be adequate to support normal growth and development. A varied diet including foods from each of the major food groups provides the best assurance of nutritional adequacy. Dietary guidelines that restrict fat and cholesterol should not apply to infants from birth to age 2 years. This CON statement gives recommendations for screening children 2 years of age and older for hypercholesterolemia (3).

Statement 3: The Use of Whole Cow's Milk in Infancy

Optimal nutrition of infants involves selecting the appropriate milk source and eventually introducing infant solid foods. To achieve this goal, in this statement, the AAP recommends that infants be fed breast milk for the first 6 to 12 months. The only acceptable alternative to breast milk is iron-fortified infant formula. Appropriate solid foods should be added between the ages of 4 and 6 months. Consumption of breast milk or iron-fortified formula, along with age-appropriate solid foods and juices, during the first 12 months of life allows for more balanced nutrition. The AAP recommends that whole cow's milk and low-iron formulas not be used during the first year of life (4).

Statement 4: Infant Feeding Practices and Their Possible Relation to the Etiology of Diabetes Mellitus

This statement was written by a Work Group and then cleared by the CON and approved by the board of directors of the AAP (5). The Work Group's recommendations are as follows:

1. Breast-feeding is strongly endorsed as the primary source of nutrition during the first year of life for all infants.
2. In families with a strong history of insulin-dependent diabetes mellitus (IDDM), particularly if a sibling has diabetes, breast-feeding and avoidance of commercially available cow's milk and products containing intact cow's milk protein during the first year of life are strongly encouraged.
3. Because the antigenicity of infant formulas and cow's milk may be different, and there is no evidence against the use of formula for infants whose mothers do not breast-feed, commercial infant formulas utilizing cow's milk protein remain the approved alternate.
4. The substitution of soy-based formulas for milk-based formulas is not advised for either general or high-risk infant feeding practices because of animal studies linking the ingestion of soybean protein intake to the development of diabetes.
5. The substitution of elemental formulas for milk-based formulas has intellectual appeal, as potential antigenically harmful large proteins have been replaced by dipeptides, tripeptides, and oligopeptides. However, because no scientific studies in humans confirming their benefit are yet available, this feeding option cannot be endorsed.
6. A prospective randomized trial in which genetically susceptible infants avoid the ingestion of cow's milk should be developed through collaborative national and international arrangements.

Following publication of the statement, a letter was submitted to the editor of *Pediatrics* (6). The letter noted that

in the statement by the American Academy of Pediatrics (AAP) Work Group on Cow's Milk Protein and Diabetes Mellitus, it was concluded that "The substitution of soy-based formulas for milk-based formulas is not advised for either general or high-risk infant feeding practices because of animal studies linking the ingestion of soy protein intake to the development of diabetes." This AAP statement leaves the impression that there is evidence that soy protein causes insulin-dependent diabetes mellitus (IDDM) and that it is sufficient to conclude that soy formulas should no longer be fed to human infants. Based on our reading of literature cited in the statement and additional studies that do not appear to have been considered, we do not believe this to be the case. . . . We believe this statement should be clarified to recommend that given our current state of knowledge, no changes in feeding practices during infancy are warranted to avoid IDDM. (6)

The response of the chairman of the Work Group to the above letter was:

The American Academy of Pediatrics appointed and directed the Work Group on Cow's Milk Protein and Diabetes Mellitus to undertake a review of the available research and

TABLE 2. *Fluoride supplementation[a] for children:*
Interim policy recommendations

Age	Water fluoride content (ppm)		
	<0.3	0.3–0.6	>0.6
Birth–6 mo	0	0	0
6 mo–3 yr	0.25	0	0
3–6 yr	0.50	0.25	0
6–16 yr	1.0	0.50	0

[a] Fluoride daily doses are given in milligrams (11).

publications on possible connections between childhood nutrition and the development of IDDM. The purpose of this activity was to bring to the pediatric community a position paper that would provide interim conclusions while providing direction for future research into the important area. This has been accomplished. After a period of approximately 18 months of review, deliberation, and multiple reediting, the position paper was finally published in *Pediatrics* in November 1994. Our final conclusion and recommendation deserves reemphasis. Research directed toward further defining the possible relationship between infant feeding practices and the development of IDDM is needed. A prospective randomized trial in which genetically susceptible infants avoid the ingestion of cow's milk should be developed through collaborative national and international arrangements. (7)

It should be noted that two other letters were written in response to the statement (8,9).

Statement 5: Reimbursement for Medical Foods for Inborn Errors of Metabolism

It is the position of the AAP that special medical foods that are used in the treatment of amino acid and urea cycle disorders are medical expenses that should be reimbursed (10).

Statement 6: Fluoride Supplementation for Children: Interim Policy

Fluoride supplementation is no longer recommended from birth, and doses have been decreased during the first 6 years of life because of an increased incidence of dental fluorosis in children living in the United States (11; Table 2).

Statement 7: Aluminum Toxicity in Infants and Children

The recommendations of the CON in this statement are as follows:

1. Aluminum-containing phosphate binders should not be given to infants and children with renal failure.

2. Continued efforts should be made to reduce the levels of aluminum in products that are added to intravenous solutions used for premature infants and infants and children with renal failure.
3. Continued efforts should be made to reduce the aluminum content of all formulas used for infants, but especially soy formulas and formulas tailored specifically for premature infants.
4. In infants at risk for aluminum toxicity (renal failure and prematurity), attention should be paid to the aluminum content of the water used in reconstitution of infant formulas (12).

OTHER STATEMENTS AND/OR REPORTS

Reports prepared under FDA contracts do not necessarily constitute AAP policy. A recent report concerning cow and soy milk allergy was prepared for the FDA. It did not undergo Board of Directors review. This technical advisory report was prepared by Dr. Ronald E. Kleinman, Chairman of the CON, and a subcommittee on nutrition/allergic disease. The report was not published in a peer-reviewed journal. It is summarized as follows (13):

Allergic, immune-complex, and cell-mediated immune reactions to cow milk and other dietary proteins encountered during infancy are responsible for some of the adverse symptoms and syndromes observed in infants intolerant to cow milk, infant formulas, and occasionally human milk. Iron deficiency anemia associated with gastrointestinal blood loss, protein-losing enteropathy, enterocolitis, colitis, and malabsorption syndrome are examples of nonallergic (i.e., non-IgE-mediated), putative immune-mediated reactions to dietary antigens that occur in infancy. However, the immunopathogenesis of these syndromes remains to be elucidated and confirmed. A number of symptoms referable to the gastrointestinal tract, such as vomiting, colic, and chronic nonspecific diarrhea, occur in infants both with and without immune-mediated reactions to dietary antigens. None of these gastrointestinal symptoms are pathognomonic for food allergy or immune-mediated reactions to dietary antigens in infancy.

Verification of adverse reactions to dietary antigens, including allergic reactions, should be accomplished through the use of double-blind, placebo-controlled food challenge, with the dietary antigen to be tested presented in a liquid vehicle or, in older children, in capsule form. Most of the symptoms and adverse effects of offending dietary antigens are reversed within days after removal of the offending antigen from the diet. For the most part, except for those infants and young children with malabsorption syndrome (an increasingly rare consequence of milk allergy), nutritional support remains the same as for an otherwise healthy infant.

Dietary proteins that retain their antigenicity when tested by *in vitro* methods or *in vivo* cannot be considered hypoallergenic. Approximately 8% to 25% of children with immediate hypersensitivity to cow milk have been found to be allergic to soy products. Soy and other intact protein substitutes for cow milk, such as beef- and lamb-based formulas, have produced anaphylactic reactions both in human infants and in animal models. Few scientifically valid studies have been published evaluating the sole use of alternative formulas in *the prevention* of cow milk allergy or allergic disease.

Preclinical testing of infant formulas is necessary to characterize the molecular properties of the protein or peptide to be used in the hypoallergenic formula. This includes physicochemical tests, such as gel permeation chromatography and sodium dodecylsufate polyacrylamide gel electrophoresis (SDS-PAGE), and immunochemical tests conducted both *in vivo*, e.g., guinea pigs, mouse, or rat, and *in vitro*, e.g., ELISA and RIA. The *sine qua non*, however, for defining and declaring an infant formula as hypoallergenic requires clinical testing of the formula in human infants and children. This should be performed as a double-blind placebo-controlled challenge followed by open challenge in an appropriate number of infants or young children with milk allergy proven by oral challenge within 2 months of the new formula challenge. The number of infants or children should be sufficient to project with 95% confidence that 90% of milk-allergic infants will not react to the product. The studies should be conducted on at least 24 subjects at a minimum of two centers, and each center should contribute at least six subjects. Open challenge should follow the successful completion of the double-blind, placebo-controlled challenge, and in this open challenge the test formula should be fed for at least 24 hr to subjects who are under the direct supervision of the investigator. Further observation should occur for 6 days at home, and the subjects should be assessed by a clinical scoring system for allergic responses.

Finally, it is theoretically possible that formulas might prevent or delay allergy. Clinical testing to support a claim for delay or prevention of atopic disease should include infants from families with a strong history of allergy who are fed the product for at least 6 months under the conditions of a blinded controlled and randomized study. These infants should be followed for at least 1 year after the blinded study and must demonstrate a statistically significantly lower prevalence of allergy than infants fed a standard milk-based control formula over the same 6-month period of time. Formulas that successfully produce these clinical results with 1-year follow-up may be claimed by manufacturers to delay food allergy, and with 2- to 3-year follow-up to prevent food allergy, *but cannot be termed hypoallergenic* (13).

IMPACT OF STATEMENTS

Several points should be considered when assessing the impact of CON statements. First, the tragic error that resulted in some infants suffering when the infants were fed formulas low in chloride could have been averted by closer regulation and more open lines of communication among the AAP, industry, and the FDA. This error occurred during 1978 and 1979, when two infant formulas deficient in chloride were marketed in the United States by Syntex, Inc. Some of the children who ingested these formulas developed a variety of problems including failure to thrive, lethargy, anorexia, and weakness. In addition, severe metabolic derangements including hypochloremia, alkalosis, hypokalemia, hyponatremia, hyperaldosteronism, and increased plasma renin activity were present in some of these children. The aggregation of these signs, symptoms, and laboratory findings has been termed the chloride depletion syndrome or the dietary chloride deficiency syndrome. Although resolution of these acute problems occurred following the restoration of a diet adequate in chloride, the question of whether these children would experience long-term effects has been raised. In one study, 21 of these exposed children were developmentally evaluated at 2 years of age, and 18 of these returned for reexamination at 4 years of age (14). When other known predictors of developmental outcome were taken into account by means of multiple linear regression analyses, exclusive formula use emerged as an important predictor of the children's cognitive functioning at 2 years and of quantitative, perceptual, and fine motor ability at 4 years of age. These data raise concern about the developmental outcome of the children exposed to the chloride-deficient formula (14).

In another study of infants who ingested one of these chloride-deficient formulas, a representative sample of such children was identified in a southern county in the Southeastern United States through a mailing to the homes of 3639 first- and second-grade children in the public schools (15). Of the 2329 (64%) who responded, 56 reported use of deficient formula and were invited to have developmental testing by one of four study psychologists at their school. Of the 310 users of other soy formulas, 112 were selected for testing as matched controls on the basis of their sex, feeding history, age, birth weight, and socioeconomic status (as indicated by school attended). Children who used chloride-deficient formula were found to average 4.9 IQ points less than the controls. The largest difference was in the quantitative subscale. The data showed a statistically significant although small effect of chloride-deficient formula on the long-term developmental outcome of exposed children; however, further study of the results is needed for full confirmation (15).

A second point to address concerns whether statements are accepted and whether they have any impact on how physicians or industry performs. In 1985, the AAP published a policy statement on the treatment of infants with acute diarrhea complicated by mild to moderate dehydration (16). To determine how closely physicians in the United States followed this statement, a questionnaire was sent to 457 pediatricians and 360 family practitioners (17). The questionnaire presented a hypothetical infant with acute diarrhea complicated by mild to moderate dehydration and included questions regarding the number of such patients seen yearly, length of time used to rehydrate the infant, and how formula or solids are introduced following rehydration. Overall, the findings suggest that very few pediatricians and family practitioners follow all aspects of the AAP's treatment guidelines for infants with acute diarrhea complicated by mild to moderate dehydration (17).

These examples point out first that the CON, industry, and the FDA should cooperate to better regulate formulas and foods for infants and children. Second, more should be done to disseminate recommendations to physicians and interested parties so they may be better utilized.

COMMITTEE ON NUTRITION AND INDUSTRY INTERACTIONS

There are a various ways the CON and industry may work together to improve the health of infants, children, adolescents, and young adults according to whether a topic of interest is CON or industry driven (Table 3).

Committee-Driven Interests

The CON should keep industry updated in areas that they feel need research. When the CON is developing policy statements, it should also confer with appropriate qualified representatives of industry. These individuals may have information

TABLE 3. *Suggestions for CON and industry*

CON-driven interests
The CON should keep industry appraised of areas of nutrition that need research.
The CON, when developing policy statements related to nutrition, should confer with appropriate qualified representatives of industry for expertise otherwise not available to the CON.
Industry-driven interests
Industry should work with the CON to help set guidelines for formulas.
Industry should advise the CON when introducing new formulas, components of formulas, or alternatives to currently commercially available food products for infants, children, adolescents, and young adults.
Industry should confer with the CON concerning the marketing of potentially controversial products.

concerning the production, storage, and/or use of formulas and foods for children that the CON would not otherwise be able to gain access to.

Industry-Driven Interests

Industry should work with the CON to set guidelines for formulas and advise the CON when they introduce new formulas, components of formulas, or new food products for infants, children, adolescents, and young adults. Industry should confer with the CON when they market potentially controversial products, for example, bovine somatostatin or fat and sugar substitutes.

It is hoped that with better cooperation and lines of communication among the CON, industry, and the FDA, improved nutritional products for infants, children, adolescents, and young adults will be made available. In addition, it is hoped that errors in formula and food composition will be eliminated, and tragedies such as the dietary chloride deficiency syndrome resulting from formulas inadequate in chloride content will be averted. Because young infants are totally dependent on breast and/or bottle formulas, there is little leeway for human error.

REFERENCES

1. American Academy of Pediatrics. *Policy reference guide: a comprehensive guide to AAP policy statements published through June 1988,* 2nd ed. Elk Grove Village, IL: AAP, 1988.
2. Committee on Nutrition. Practical significance of lactose intolerance in children: supplement. *Pediatrics* 1990;86:643–644.
3. Committee on Nutrition. Statement on cholesterol. *Pediatrics* 1992;90:469–473.
4. Committee on Nutrition. The use of whole cow's milk in infancy. *Pediatrics* 1992;89:1105–1109.
5. American Academy of Pediatrics. Infant feeding practices and their possible relationship to the etiology of diabetes mellitus: work group on cow's milk protein and diabetes mellitus. *Pediatrics* 1994;94:752–754.
6. MacLean WC. Cow's milk and diabetes debate [letter]. *Pediatrics* 1995;96:541–542.
7. Drash AL. Cow's milk and diabetes debate [letter]. *Pediatrics* 1995;96:542.
8. Elliott RB. Cow's milk and the diabetes debate [letter]. *Pediatrics* 1995;96:541.

9. Scott FW. AAP recommendations on cow milk, soy, and early infant feeding. Commentaries. *Pediatrics* 1995;96:515–517.
10. Committee on Nutrition. Reimbursement for medical foods for inborn errors of metabolism. *Pediatrics* 1994;93:860.
11. Committee on Nutrition. Fluoride supplementation for children: interim policy recommendation. *Pediatrics* 1995;95:777
12. Committee on Nutrition. Aluminum toxicity in infants and children. *Pediatrics* 1996;97:413–416.
13. Subcommittee on Nutrition and Allergic Disease. *Infant formulas and allergic disease.* Manuscript prepared under FDA contract No. 223-86117, 1990 (unpublished).
14. Willoughby A, Moss HA, Hubbard VS, *et al.* Developmental outcome in children exposed to chloride-deficient formula. *Pediatrics* 1987;79:851–857.
15. Willoughby A, Graubard BI, Hocker A, *et al.* Population-based study of the developmental outcome of children exposed to chloride-deficient infant formula. *Pediatrics* 1990;85:485–490.
16. Committee on Nutrition. Use of oral fluid therapy and posttreatment feeding following enteritis in children in a developed country. *Pediatrics* 1985;75:358–361.
17. Bezerra JA, Stathos TH, Duncan B, *et al.* Treatment of infants with acute diarrhea: what's recommended and what's practiced. *Pediatrics* 1992;90:1–4.

DISCUSSION

Dr. Iber: The failure of the majority of your members to undertake your recommendations on diarrhea suggests that, perhaps, the committee is a specialized or elite fraction of the society that may not be representative. I would be interested in your comments on that.

Dr. Udall: Classically, the treatment of acute diarrhea in the otherwise normal child was to fast the child for 12 to 24 hr and then keep the child on clear liquids for 2 to 3 days or longer. Gradually, dilute formulas and later solid foods were reintroduced. What the Committee did in 1985, when they made the recommendations for the treatment of acute diarrhea, was to condense this sequence and suggest that the rehydration take not 24 hr but 4 to 6 hr, with the child being reintroduced to foods within 24 hr of seeing the physician. It wasn't a case of dramatically altering the recommendation but of having the infant progress through the sequence much more rapidly. I think that one of the problems we had was breaking down the barriers of the traditional approach. It takes time to do that.

Dr. Perman: You have shown us in reviewing the statements over the past 5 years that at least some of them, or components of the statements, are open to challenge. Has the entire production of statements from the Committee on Nutrition over the years been scrutinized to see how these statements have withstood the test of time? By and large, do you find that the Committee's work has been supported by subsequent scientific evidence?

Dr. Udall: To my knowledge, there is no mechanism to evaluate the success of each of the statements in terms of their acceptability, or how they are used in the field. I think one of the disappointments to the members of the Committee on Nutrition is that the Technical Advisory Group from industry has been abolished from the Committee. Is that correct, Dr. Klish?

Dr. Klish: It has not been totally abolished, but it has been more difficult to request the interaction with industry over the past year or so.

Dr. Udall: Your point about tracking the statements to see how successful they are is something that we might consider. It has not been done.

Dr. Klish: Can I address that question. I think there is a misconception about what the Committee on Nutrition of the American Academy of Pediatrics is really supposed to be doing. Primarily, the Academy of Pediatrics is a professional organization that is intended to educate its own membership, so these policy statements are not national policy statements, they are recommendations given to the membership of the Academy about how they should deal with particular issues that happen to have public relevance. We do get asked at times to become involved in policy issues, and I think sometimes the Committee recommendations are used in that way. But that is not always the intent for these particular statements. The Committee on Nutrition is made up of people from all over the United States—they are selected not only for their scientific expertise but also for the region of the country that they come from. There is a selection process that allows the Academy to select certain individuals who we think are going to be able to respond to issues that we know are coming along. We have no mechanism to force anybody to follow our statements because they are in essence educational statements rather than policy statements.

Dr. Udall: These statements go through many layers of review, and people come at them from different points of view. That is one of the reasons it can take so long to get them out, but as Dr. Klish mentioned, they are really to help the practitioner in the field more than anything else.

Dr. Klish: We do review every statement every 3 years though, and we retire those that are no longer relevant. Unfortunately, they are all published, and not everybody recognizes the fact that some of them may be retired statements.

Dr. Hamburger: You probably could avoid some of the problems that you create by floating the statements as drafts first in the publications of the Academy to allow a response from the general membership, because that is how you discover whether you were either premature or taking too strong a position one way or another. It would be sensible to put them out as a draft, wait about 3 months, and then come back with a definitive statement after you have allowed for much wider criticism than the multiple layers that you are using now.

Dr. Udall: That is a very good comment. However, I would be a little concerned because some individuals have their own very strong opinions and their own agenda—that is one of the problems with developing these statements. My concern would be that you are going to get many diverse comments, and it will be very difficult to respond to them all without alienating some people.

Dr. Klish: There actually is now a mechanism for publicizing the issues in advance of a statement, and that is the use of *AAP News.* We are publishing articles there about issues that we know are somewhat controversial, to test the waters with the membership and try to see what kind of response we got. We did that with fluoride, and we are doing it in the next issue with the long-chain polyunsaturated fatty acids. I agree there wasn't a mechanism in the past, but we are now in the process of developing that mechanism.

Dr. Rey: I have a comment about fluoride. It seems paradoxical to recommend not adding fluoride between birth and 6 months and then adding it after 6 months, because after 6 months is the time when the child starts to absorb toothpaste with a high fluoride content. I would like to know the basis of this recommendation.

Dr. Udall: The fluoride statement evolved over a number of months. The American Dental Association convened a group to discuss this. Dr. Susan Baker from the Committee on Nutrition of the AAP attended those meetings. There was considerable discussion pro and con for fluoride supplementation in the first 6 months of life. Water is not fluoridated to a uniform level throughout the United States, and young children ingest significant but variable amounts of fluoride while brushing their teeth with fluoride-containing toothpaste. Because both these sources of fluoride are difficult to control, attention has been directed at the dosage of fluoride supplements to prevent dental fluorosis.

Dr. Rey: I have two other comments. The first is that, in France at least, and probably in Europe as a whole, we very much appreciate the publications from the Committee on Nutrition.

They are an excellent source of information for everyone, are very well presented and discussed, and it is a real pleasure to read them. I am not absolutely sure whether you read the recommendations of ESPGAN (European Society for Gastroenterology and Nutrition), but we read yours and we try to quote them. My last comment is about relations with industry. I think your proposal is very wise. For the past 2 or 3 years, we have had a Committee on Nutrition in France, not as important as yours, of course, but we meet the Association of Infant Food Producers twice a year and discuss our problems with them. They reveal their own difficulties, and we give them our papers before they are published to obtain their comment. We also have representatives of industry in the Subcommittee on Foods for Special Dietary Use, and they are consulted before any decision is taken. When they don't agree with a decision, they can come and explain to the Subcommittee why they disagree. It is very important to have this type of exchange among nutritionists, pediatricians, and industry. It is a source of profit for everybody.

Dr. Udall: In regard to the Committee on Nutrition and the American Academy of Pediatrics cooperating with industry, I agree wholeheartedly with your thoughts. Personally, I feel that this is a matter of communication. When I was asked to come here and address this particular topic, I sent a copy of the paper to Dr. Klish, the current chair of the Committee on Nutrition, to Dr. Ron Kleinman, the previous chair of the Committee on Nutrition, and also to the American Academy of Pediatrics. I wanted them to review it and did not want to publish a manuscript that they were not in agreement with. They had an opportunity to make changes in the manuscript and suggested some alterations that were incorporated. So when we talk about industry and the Committee on Nutrition and the American Academy of Pediatrics working together, we need to stress communication and make sure that the lines of communication remain open.

Clinical Trials in Infant Nutrition, edited by
Jay A. Perman and Jean Rey, Nestlé Nutrition
Workshop Series, Vol. 40, Nestec Ltd.,
Vevey/Lippincott-Raven Publishers,
Philadelphia © 1998.

Conclusions

Dr. Perman: In this conclusion to the workshop, I want to look back at what we have done with a view to discussing how we provide the general community with the results of our 3 days of discussion and of the work that is represented in the chapters. I want to have an open discussion about these issues. But before I do, I want, on behalf of Jean Rey and me, to acknowledge the work of Dr. Steenhout, who was so instrumental in organizing this workshop. Thank you very much for all your efforts.

I don't intend to summarize the meeting as part of this conclusion. There have been so many points that to try to highlight important points would do many a disservice. The title of this workshop was "Clinical Trials in Infant Nutrition." As a first point of discussion, it seems to me that if we were to give this title to the monograph, it would not really reflect the work that we have done. That title suggests to me a compendium of clinical trials in infant nutrition. To be sure, we have heard original research during the 3 days of this meeting, but much of that was presented as illustration. It seems to me that what we have really done here is to have a vigorous discussion of the conduct of clinical trials in infant nutrition. I don't know that we need to settle what we should call the ensuing volume right now, but I think that Dr. Steenhout, Jean Rey, and I would be very happy to hear your comments on this matter. It seems to me that what we want is a publication that serves not only the medical community interested in nutrition but also clinical investigators, ethics committees, aspiring clinical investigators, members of staff of regulatory bodies, and editorial staff of journals that publish in clinical nutrition.

Dr. Glinsmann: Certainly a large portion of this was not really didactic in terms of how you do a clinical trial. A lot of it dealt with the claims issue and the purposes of clinical trials and their sponsorship, so I think the claims context should be reflected in the workshop.

Dr. Hamburger: I agree that the title as listed in the cover of the workshop announcement is misleading and does need changing. Perhaps a title of "Clinical Trials in Infant Nutrition" with a subtitle using some of the section heads such as methodology, ethics, statistics, and claims should be considered.

Dr. Walter: I had the reaction that I think you did, that referring to this workshop as being entirely on clinical trials is inappropriate. Many people, when they see the words "clinical trials," think of randomized clinical trials almost automatically, but in fact, much of the evidence that we have seen here was related to observational studies, and so the title might be construed as misleading. I wonder whether it should be something like "Research in Nutrition" or "Recent Results in Clinical Nutrition" to make it much broader.

Dr. Uauy: I don't think we should put "clinical trials" as a sole purpose of the meeting because we have been very selective, mainly concentrating on methodology, ethics, and statistics.

Dr. Perman: I agree that we ought to say in the title what is inside the covers, without making it unwieldy. Are there any other thoughts about promulgating some of the points that we have covered? We are not organized as any kind of an official body, but I would like to give everybody the opportunity to comment. There were some very important points made over these 3 days that deserve the attention of members of ethics committees and regulatory bodies. So there should be a broader audience than the medical and scientific community only.

Dr. Hamburger: After publication of the first book in the Nestlé Nutrition Workshop Series, Nestlé decided to produce a more readable version for the average physician in the form of a small monograph for wider distribution to pediatricians. I think that was a very effective vehicle for getting the message to where much clinical research is being done these days—not by experts but by practitioners in the field. They need to see the results of a meeting such as this.

Dr. Steenhout: We publish 40,000 booklets of each workshop and distribute them all around the world, and in different languages: English, French, German, and Spanish, and this booklet will be also published in Chinese.

Dr. Perman: On behalf of Jean Rey, the organizers from Nestlé, and myself, I want to express our deep gratitude for the time and effort that you have put into making this workshop a success. Thank you all very much.

Subject Index